INVENTING
THE CALIFORNIA
LOOK

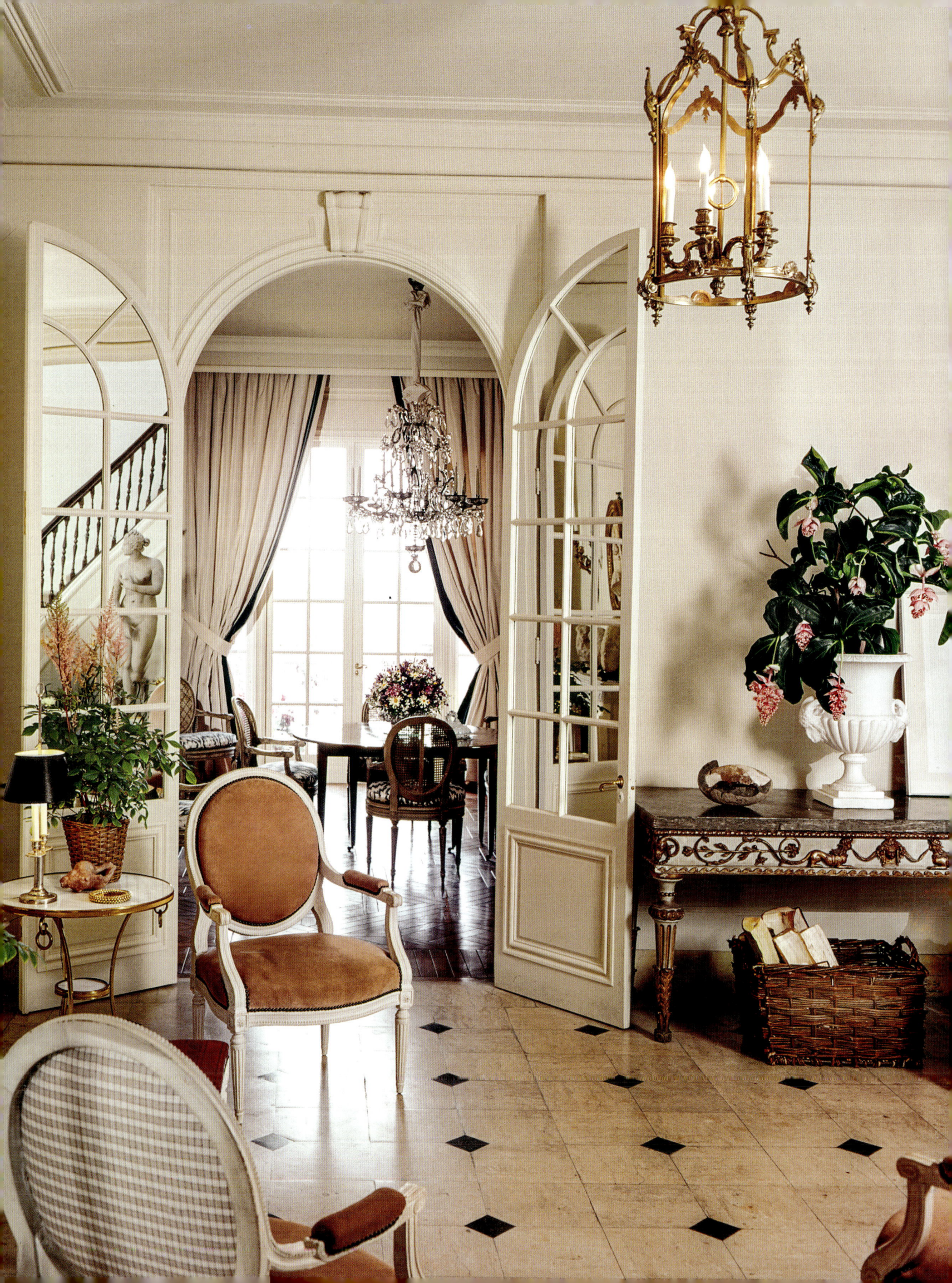

INVENTING
THE CALIFORNIA
LOOK

Interiors of Frances Elkins, Michael Taylor,
John Dickinson, and Other Design Innovators

Through the Lens of
FRED LYON

PHILIP E. MEZA
FOREWORD BY JARED GOSS

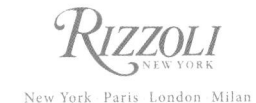
RIZZOLI
NEW YORK

New York Paris London Milan

To Penny Rozis and Marjorie Qualey

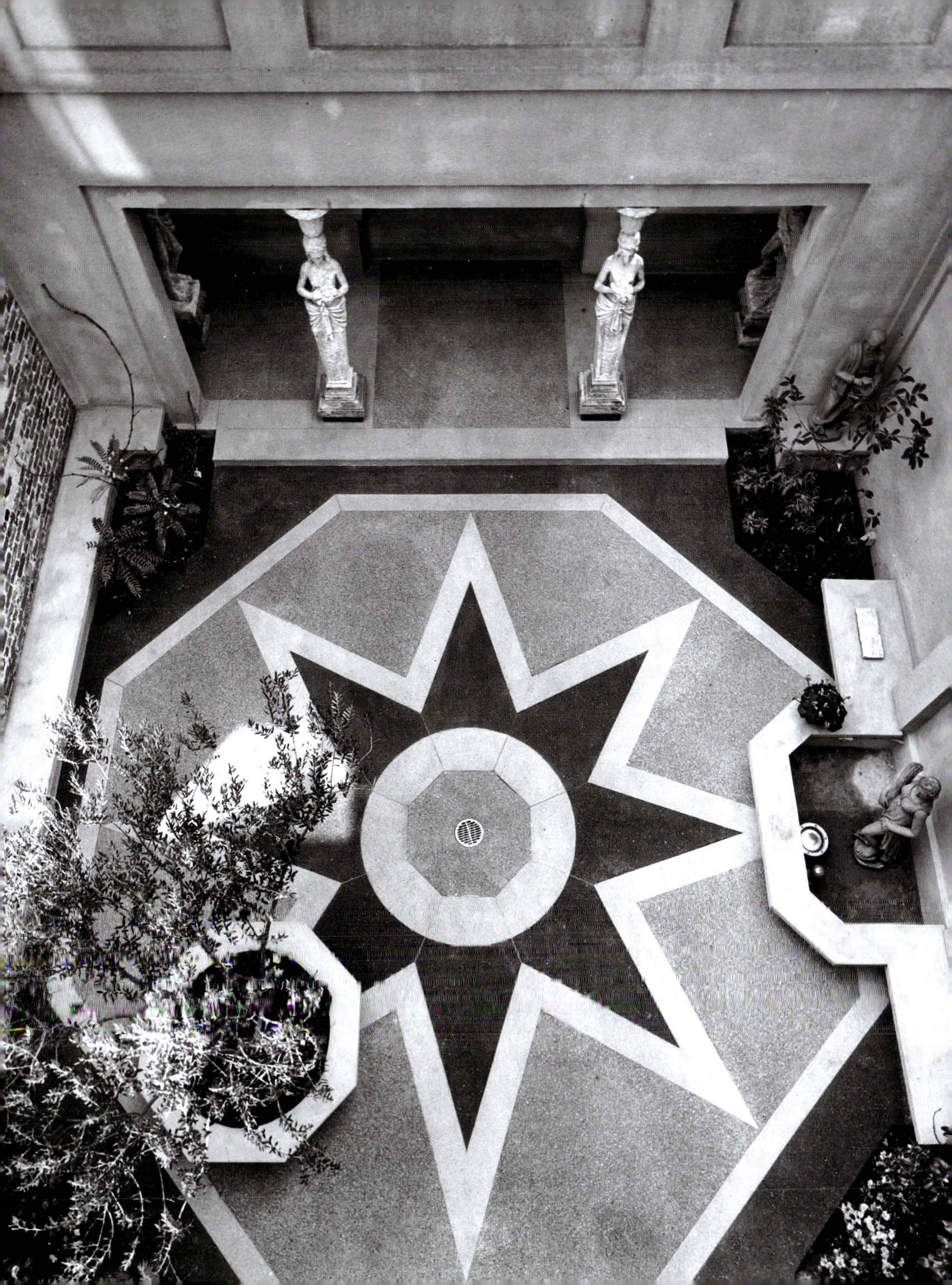

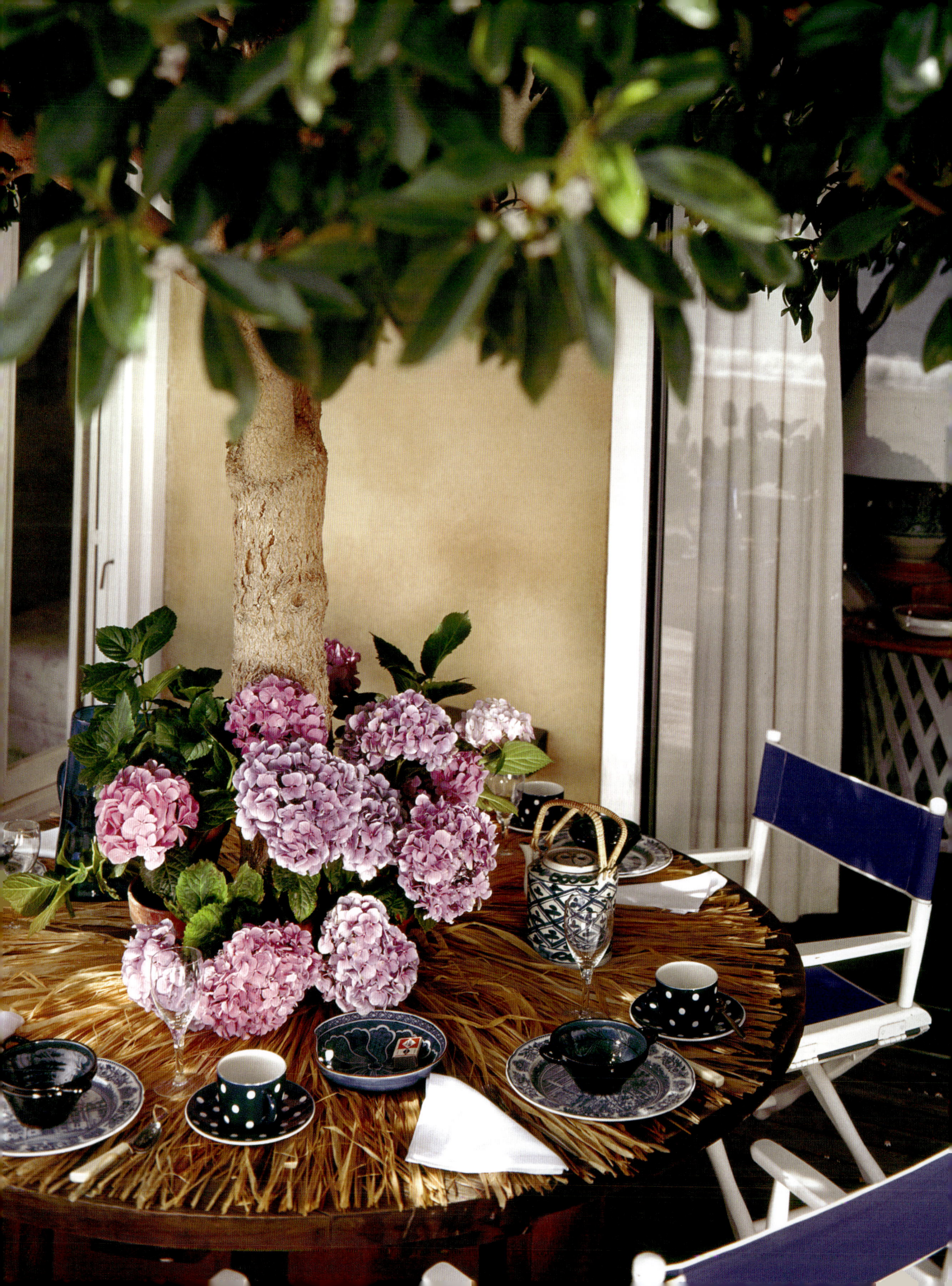

CONTENTS

FOREWORD BY JARED GOSS
Fred Lyon and the California Look: An Assessment 9

INTRODUCTION 20

I. LEARNING HIS ART 24

II. A WORKING PHOTOGRAPHER 32

III. A LUCKY BREAK ON TELEGRAPH HILL 38

Bear River Ranch, Sacramento Valley, 1948 46

Whitney Warren Jr. House, San Francisco, 1947 50

Whitney Warren Jr. House, San Francisco, 1974 56

Jerome Hill Ski House, Sugar Bowl, Norden, 1947 62

V. C. Morris Gift Shop, San Francisco, 1949 68

IV. DOROTHEA WALKER AND
A HOST OF COLLABORATORS 72

V. THE WILD TALENT OF
MICHAEL TAYLOR 82

Michael Taylor Showrooms, San Francisco, 1957–1960 92

Irma and Albert Schlesinger House, Atherton, 1958 101

Gerry and William Roberts House, Woodside, 1965 106

Maryon Davies Lewis House, San Francisco, 1966 114

Pat and Sandy Walker House, San Francisco, 1970 119

Auberge du Soleil, Rutherford, circa 1984 124

VI. ELEGANT ANTHONY HAIL AND
INVENTIVE JOHN DICKINSON 132

Anthony Hail Residences, San Francisco, circa 1969 and 1972 136

Guignécourt, Hillsborough, 1961 and 1964 140

John Dickinson House, San Francisco, 1970 and 1973 149

Sonoma Mission Inn, Sonoma, 1980 162

VII. SKIDMORE, OWINGS & MERRILL:
FROM WILD BIRD TO THE
BANK OF AMERICA BUILDING 166

Wild Bird, Big Sur, 1959 172

VIII. HOLIDAY AND HIGH SOCIETY 180

Fred Lyon House, Oakville, 1997 186

Penelope Rozis House, Napa, 2010 192

IX. UNDIMINISHED BY TIME: LOOKING
BACK AT DESIGN LUMINARIES 202

La Cuesta Encantada, San Simeon, 1958 206

Casa Amesti, Monterey, 1983 211

Hester and Allen Griffin House, Pebble Beach, 1983 218

Ruth and Paul Winslow House, Pebble Beach, 1983 222

Hana and James Zellerbach House, San Francisco, 1983 226

Elizabeth and Leon Roos House, San Francisco, 1983 230

Edwin C. Young House, San Francisco, 1983 237

Private Residence, Pebble Beach, 1999 241

X. CODA: NEW LOVE AND A RETURN TO
INTERIOR PHOTOGRAPHY 245

AFTERWORD BY FRED LYON
The Craft beneath the Art 250

Acknowledgments 252

Endnotes 254

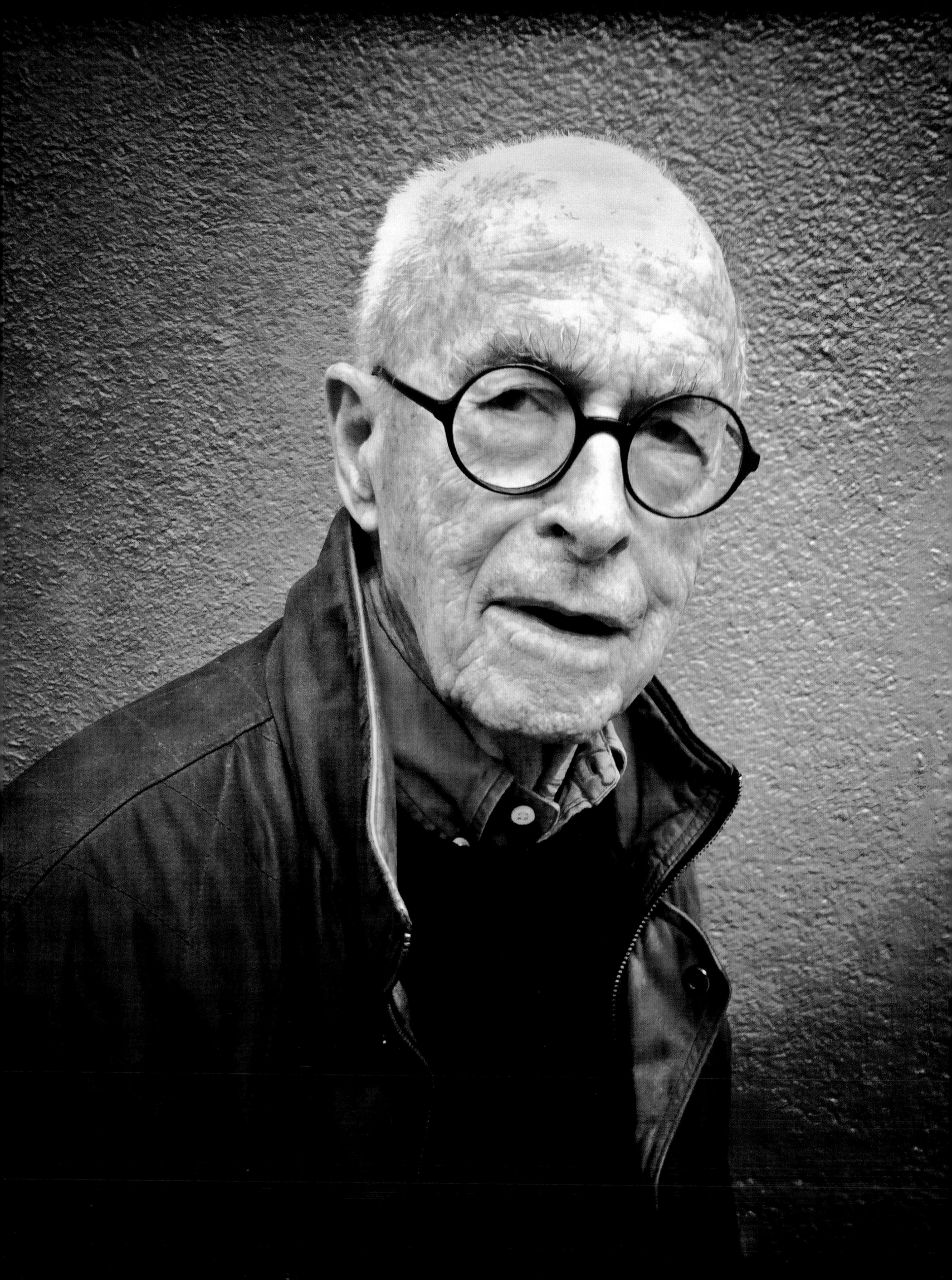

FOREWORD BY JARED GOSS
Fred Lyon and the California Look: An Assessment

Although its title is not explicit, this is a book focused on Fred Lyon and his work. But why a book on Fred Lyon? Why *this* book on Fred Lyon?

Lyon is well known, both as a versatile photographer, comfortable with creating a range of widely published imagery from cityscapes to fashion shots, and as a personality active within the cultural and social life of his native San Francisco from the 1940s until the present day. This book, however, focuses on Lyon's lesser-known work as a documenter of interiors: rooms—mainly in Northern California—designed by a roster of American architects and interior designers whose work has come to define the California Look, among them Frances Elkins, Anthony Hail, Michael Taylor, John Dickinson, and Charles Pfister. Although Lyon was not the only photographer to document the work of these creators, he was perhaps the most prolific; accordingly, his important role documenting their work makes him an integral contributor to the California Look.

Interior design is among the most ephemeral of the creative arts. Because taste in furnishings and usage change often, rooms seldom exist in an unaltered state for even one full generation. With every shift, owners adjust, change, and redecorate their spaces. Fully realized rooms—precisely as imagined by their designers—rarely survive intact, except as captured in documentation: written records, drawings, paintings, and photographs. Indeed, without documentation, a vanished room might never have existed. . . . Although countless books have been written about interior decorators and the rooms they design, curiously few address those who, like Fred Lyon, document that work and explore how they do it.

Historically, the documentation of interiors has encompassed both the written and the visual: from dry, detailed inventories to flowery literary descriptions; from precise architectural drawings to atmospheric painterly impressions. But the old saw "a picture is worth a thousand words"—hackneyed though it may be—is based on a fundamental truth and provides the very raison d'être for someone like Fred Lyon and a book like this one. Before the modern era, it was mainly architects and painters who provided visual records of interiors;

now, that role is filled instead by photographers in both still and moving images.

Fred Lyon is certainly not the only notable photographer of interiors. Among those working in California have been Morley Baer, Russell McMasters, Gabriel Moulin, Maynard Parker, and Julius Shulman. Farther afield have been Thérèse Bonney, Samuel Gottscho, Horst P. Horst, Wallace Nutting, and Ezra Stoller. A later generation includes Miguel Flores-Vianna, Oberto Gili, François Halard, Tim Street-Porter, Simon Watson, and numerous talented others. Each photographer has made important contributions to the way in which interiors are recorded; Fred Lyon takes his place alongside them.

A camera can only produce an image of what it sees; "how" a camera sees its subject is where the skill of the photographer comes into play. During its early days in the first half of the nineteenth century, photography was considered primarily a documentary medium, its mechanically produced images regarded as little more than objective representations of their subjects. Because lengthy exposure times required whatever was being captured to remain still, interiors were deemed ideal subjects for photographers from the earliest days of the medium (exemplified by the images of Lacock Abbey as photographed by William Fox Talbot in 1835). But over time, as photography evolved into a creative art and the photographer's role transformed from mere registrar to fine artist, the practice of photographing interiors followed in kind. Straightforward "record" images (documenting an architectural space, an arrangement of furnishings, or other physical particulars) were joined by more creative "artistic" ones (using mood and nuance—rather than specific details—to evoke a room).

Photographers employ a variety of perspectives—from objective to subjective—in "seeing" rooms. A purely documentary viewpoint records an interior precisely as it exists, with little or no intervention from the photographer, and ranges from informal, warts-and-all snapshots to controlled, composed portraits (Bonney, Gottscho, and Stoller used the latter approach when documenting rooms). A "styled" image involves editing, embellishing, or otherwise manipulating an extant decor to suggest a particular lifestyle: for example, using dramatic flower arrangements, sumptuous bowls of fruit, or an elegantly set dining table to create a gala mood (Horst was a master of this approach). An imagined interior is fabricated entirely by the

OPPOSITE: Four approaches to photographing interiors (CLOCKWISE FROM TOP LEFT): Ezra Stoller, stair hall, Lester Armour residence (Lake Bluff, Illinois) by architect David Adler, 1931; Horst P. Horst, winter garden, residence of interior designers Robert Denning and Vincent Fourcade (Long Island, New York), 1975; Wallace Nutting, entrance hall, Wentworth-Gardner House (Portsmouth, New Hampshire), ca. 1915; Simon Watson, bedroom, Schloss Hollenegg (Austria), 2017.

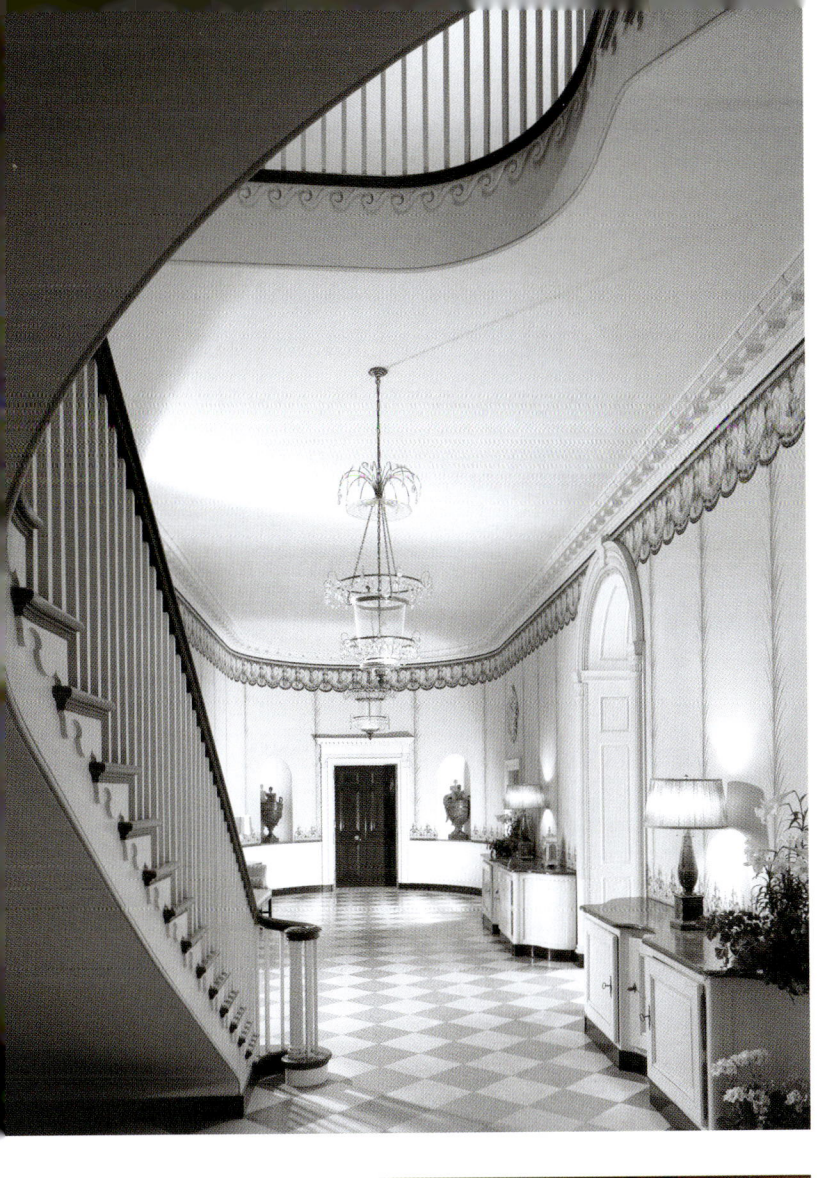
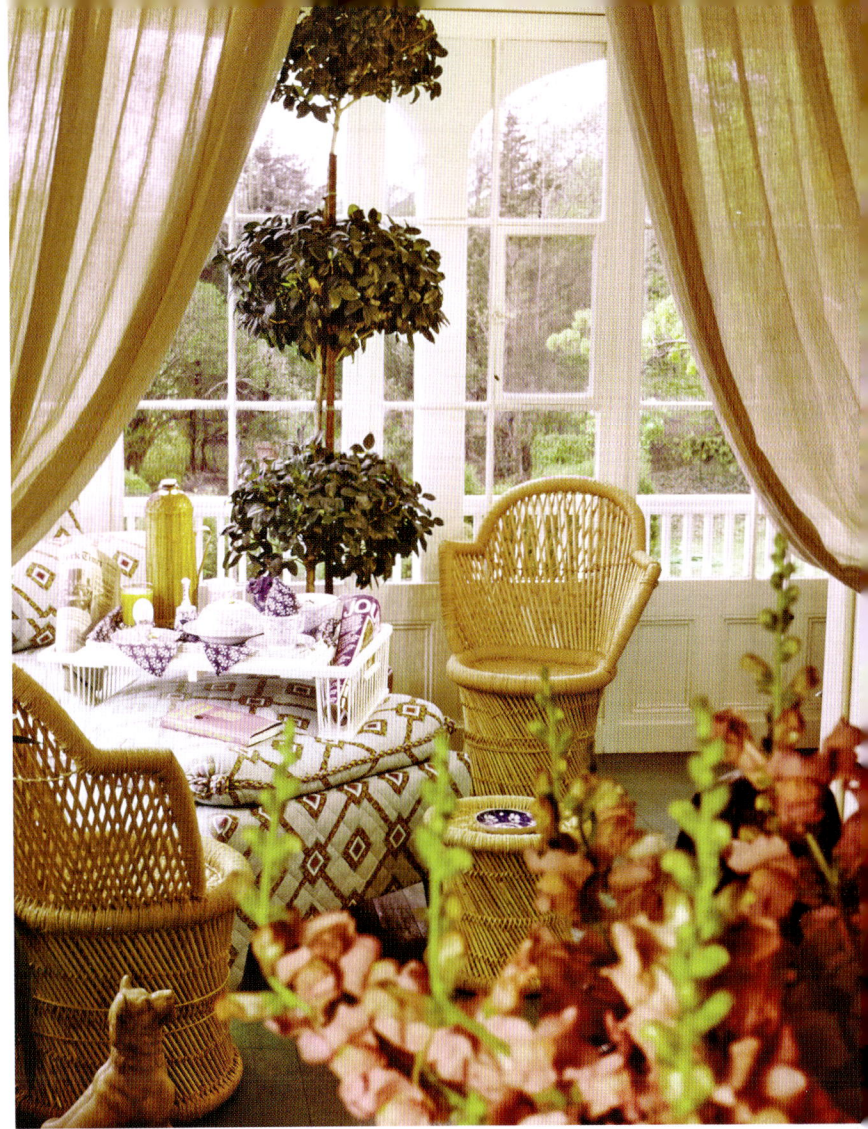
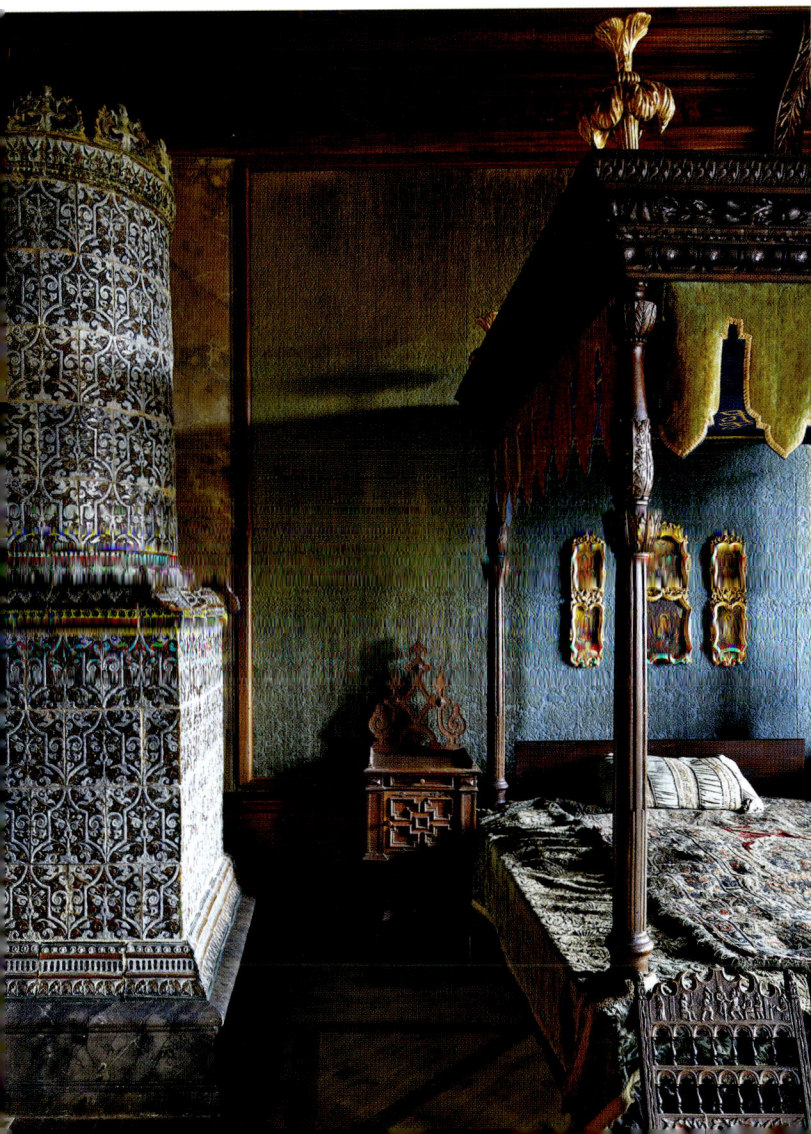
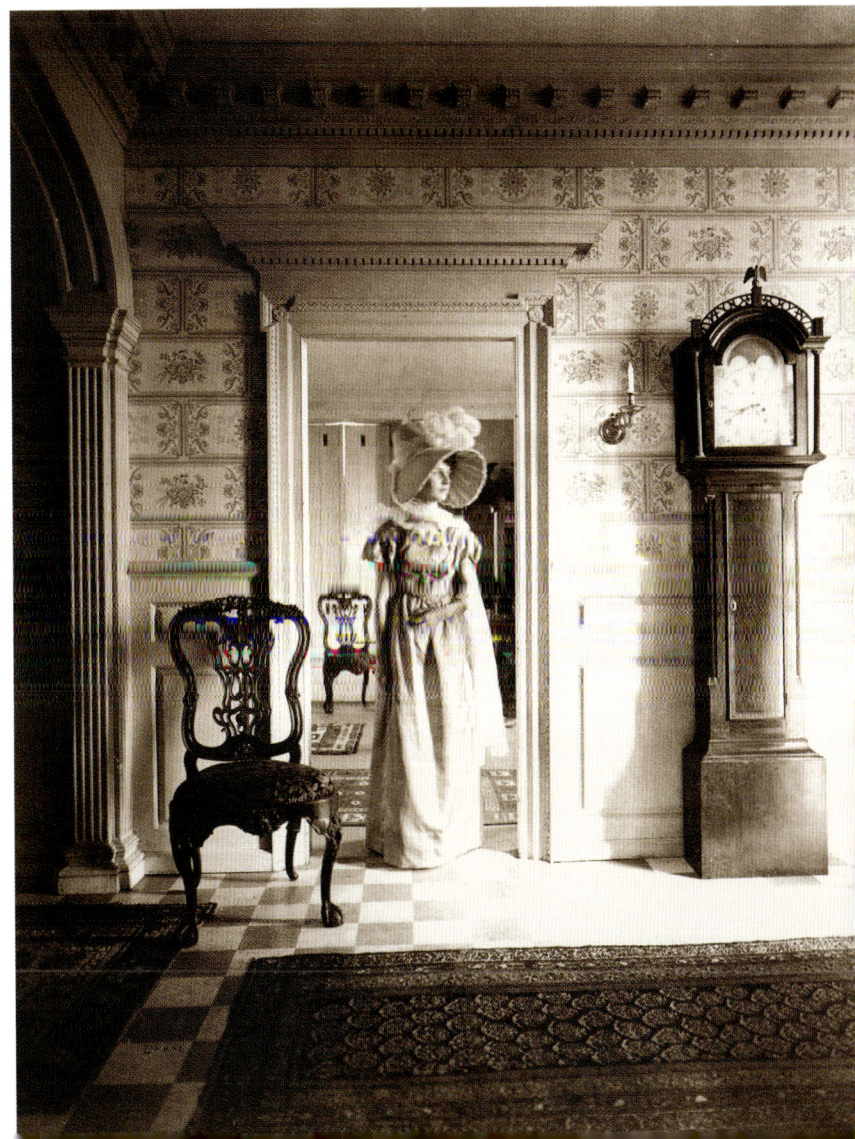

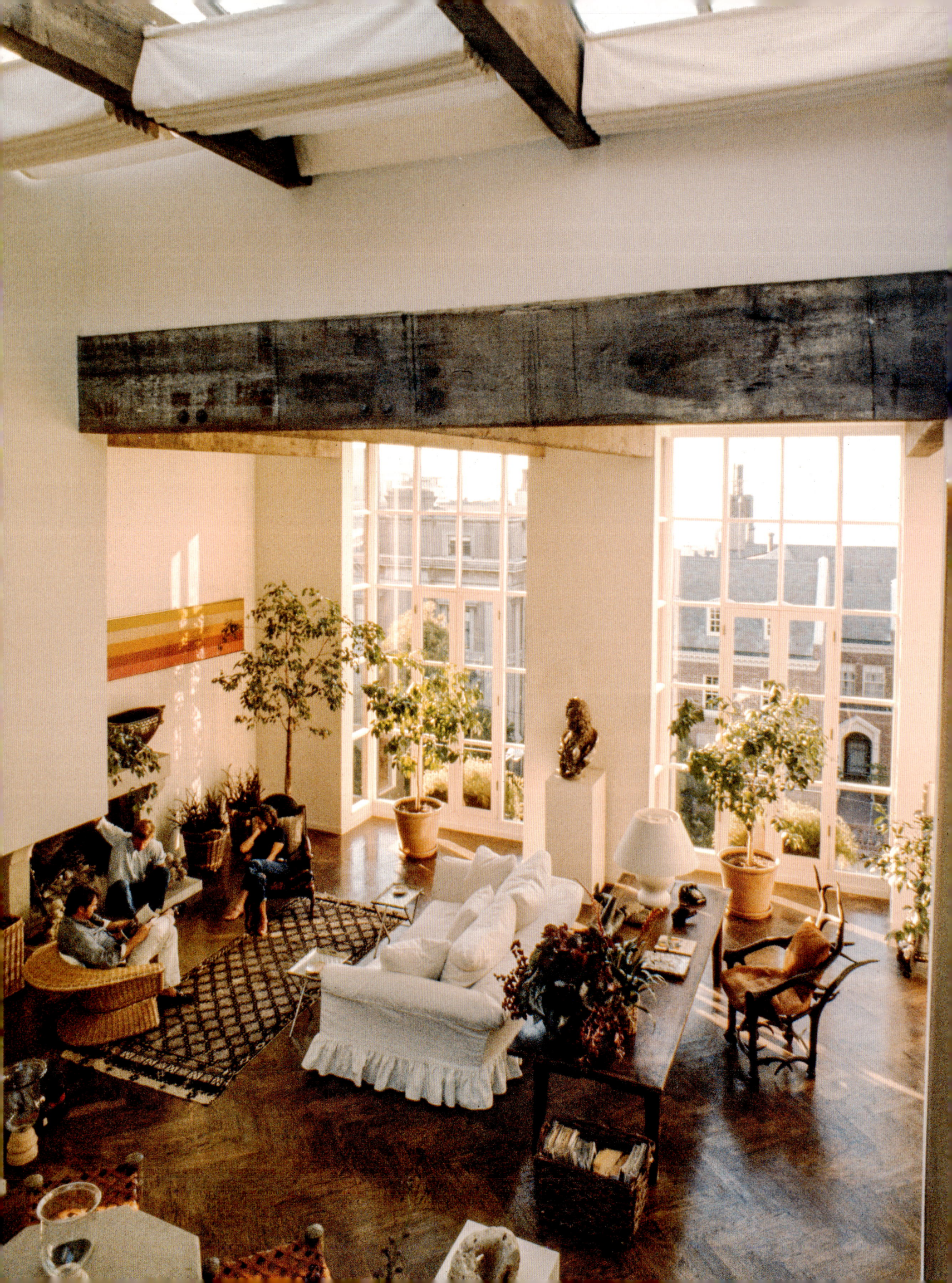

photographer, much like the pseudo–Early American environments staged by Wallace Nutting for his popular prints and postcards. And an atmospheric approach might explore the ephemeral and sensory effects of light, color, and texture (in the manner of Simon Watson).

Fred Lyon's extensive technical and compositional knowledge—acquired first during his youthful apprenticeship with Gabriel Moulin in San Francisco and again later when he studied under the famous California photographer Ansel Adams at the Art Center School in Los Angeles—has given him many of the skills found in all these approaches to interior photography. He is fully able to express the divergent qualities of both "living" interiors (in active use when he photographed them, such as those at the Nathaniel Owings house in Big Sur) and historic ones (no longer in domestic use, such as Hearst Castle by architect Julia Morgan and Casa Amesti, the former residence of Frances Elkins). In his own words: "I have always taken a journalist's approach to photography, trying to make my work descriptive and graphic."[1]

With his first House & Garden commissions in the late 1940s, Fred Lyon began photographing interiors at an ideal time, during the heyday of popular illustrated magazines. In the late nine-

teenth century—thanks to technical advances in photomechanical reproduction—numerous titles (many aimed at female readers) began featuring photographs of interiors. Among these were the Ladies' Home Journal and Life (both founded in 1883), Vogue (1892), and House Beautiful (1896). They were joined in the early twentieth century by House & Garden (1901), Architectural Digest (1920), Better Homes & Gardens (1922), and Interior Design (1932). Throughout his career, Lyon has regularly contributed to many of these, including House & Garden, Architectural Digest, and Life.

Concurrently, influential books focused on interior decoration—most notably Edith Wharton and Ogden Codman Jr.'s The Decoration of Houses (1897) and Elsie de Wolfe's The House in Good Taste (1913)—increasingly used photographs of both historic and living interiors to educate readers. Since then, such illustrated books have remained an important staple of the publishing industry, many, of course, including Fred Lyon images.

In spite of this Golden Age, throughout much of the twentieth century illustrative photographers were not always identified by name. If and when done, it generally involved little more than a discreet credit adjacent to an image. Only over the past few decades have interior photographers begun to receive more prominent recognition

OPPOSITE: Fred Lyon, living room, Pat and Sandy Walker residence (San Francisco, California), 1970. This interior was furnished by Michael Taylor specifically for the photo shoot. The image shows Taylor sitting with the Walkers on the day of the shoot.

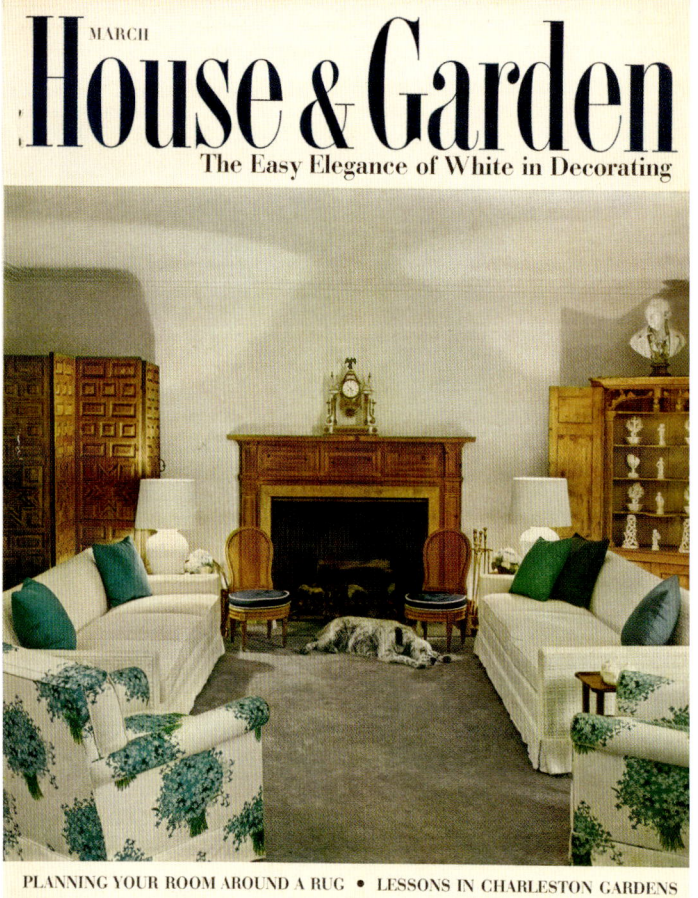

House & Garden
The Easy Elegance of White in Decorating

PLANNING YOUR ROOM AROUND A RUG • LESSONS IN CHARLESTON GARDENS

COPYRIGHT 1957, THE CONDÉ NAST PUBLICATIONS INC. 50 CENTS

LEFT: Fred Lyon, cover for *House & Garden* (March 1957) showing the living room of a residence (Burlingame, California) as designed by Michael Taylor. OPPOSITE: Page from Lyon's job log, listing projects undertaken for magazines and other clients, 1948.

for their contributions to books and magazines, with their names appearing on bylines and title pages alongside those of writers and other creatives. And some, like Lyon, are now even the subjects of monographs.

In retrospect, an especially fortuitous moment in Lyon's career came when, as a young professional in New York, he returned to his native San Francisco (rather than moving to Paris, where—he was told—there were ample photographers at work, unlike in his hometown).[2] There, he would focus his camera on the output of a number of interior designers who were living and practicing in Northern California, including Elkins, Hail, Dickinson, Taylor, and Pfister. In doing so, he not only associated his own name

with theirs, but also with the budding notion of the California Look.

What exactly is meant by the "California Look"? This unscientific term—of unclear origin, but in wide use since the 1970s, most often in reference to the San Francisco decorator Michael Taylor—is ambiguous. In 1980, it was loosely defined by writer Suzanne Slesin (who specified it as Taylor's "famous California look") in a *New York Times* article. She characterized the look as "light and airy," and embodied by Taylor's "tasteful monochromatic rooms with stripped floors, curtainless windows, natural wood furniture, over-scale wicker pieces, fat pillows, an oversize plant in its oversize pot and often an early Roman stone fragment or a rare Egyptian, Greek or Chinese piece."[3]

27

Mar.	48	Woman's Home Companion - Stanley Pollard
31 Mar.	48	Chas. B. Henderson - Portrait
Apr.	48	Woman's Home Comp. - Olivia De Havilland
Apr.	48	Woman's Home Comp. - Dinah Shore
Apr.	48	House & Garden - Arthur Vincent
Apr.	48	House & Garden - Brandeis House
Apr.	48	House & Garden - Piersoll House
Apr.	48	House & Garden - Richardson House
Apr.	48	House & Garden - Inn Rancho Santa Fe
May	48	Rapho. Guillumette - Tourists N.Y.C.
20 May	48	House & Garden - Brunschwig House
June	48	House & Garden - Cancelled
June	48	Rapho - Guillumette - S.F. Waterfront
12 June	48	Mademoiselle's Living - Nan White House
20 June	48	Lyon & Hoag - Broadway Bldg.
24 June	48	True Experiences - Cover Girl - Seattle
June	48	Dorothy Liebes - Color interiors Cancelled
10 June	48	Gardner Dailey - Red Cross Bldg. S.F.
June	48	House & Garden - Frances Elkins
May	48	Woman's Home Comp. - Vincent Mullen Apt.
28 June	48	Benjamin Sonnenberg - Luckman Ranch
1 July	48	House & Garden - Fred Sullivan Ho.
2 July	48	James B. Mills - Editorial Portrait
2 July	48	House - Line copy New Yorker
9 July	48	Life - Holy City
July	48	Rapho - Guillumette - Cajon Pass Fire
4 Aug.	48	Audubon Society - Sugar Bowl
17 Aug.	48	Life - Chickens of Tomorrow

Taylor's taste proved to be broader and more nuanced than Slesin's formula might suggest (for example, he enthusiastically incorporated formal antique furnishings into many of his commissions), and indeed the term has come to refer more generally to the aesthetic sensibility shared by those Northern California decorators. But if Taylor epitomized the California Look, then others in his milieu must be recognized for giving it shape and for refining its sensibility both before and after his name became synonymous with it.

Lyon's initial commission from *House & Garden* (in 1947) was to photograph the interiors of the first Whitney Warren Jr. residence in San Francisco. The professional significance of this project was especially important for him as it marked his literal introduction to the California Look. Frances Elkins was present at the shoot,[4] and the quality of the images he produced with her that day would lead him to magazine editor Dorothea Walker, the perennial champion of those—including Elkins—whose design work defines the California Look. (Walker discovered their disparate talents and brought them to Lyon's attention.) But the project also marked his introduction to the California Look itself, as embodied in Warren's interior.

While perhaps at first glance the opposite of Michael Taylor's "light and airy" approach,

Warren's interior in fact conjures an early iteration of the California Look *avant la lettre*. Managing to look backward and forward at once, the antique Continental furnishings (including the elaborately carved doorframe, the giltwood furniture, and the crystal chandelier) speak to the fashions of an earlier generation (specifically that of his famous Beaux-Arts architect father, Whitney Warren Sr.). But their effect, which could have been grand and imposing, is instead offset and softened by four details that would soon become signatures of the California Look: the unadorned, modernist white space (designed by architect Gardner Dailey); the incorporation of "found" objects (Warren repurposed numerous architectural fragments); the use of oversize upholstered furniture (especially corner sofas, which inherently thwart formality in the furniture arrangement); and the inclusion of nature (an abundance of exotic potted plants is visible). Lyon's photographs of Warren's house beautifully capture the sophisticated yet relaxed atmosphere, the home of an informed—but not reverential—connoisseur. These exact details and qualities were carefully replicated in Warren's second home in San Francisco, which Lyon photographed in 1963 and again in 1974.

Although Warren's first interior was conceived largely by the man himself, it seems he accepted

OPPOSITE: Fred Lyon, living room, Whitney Warren Jr.'s second residence (San Francisco, California), 1974. Detail view showing corner seating area.

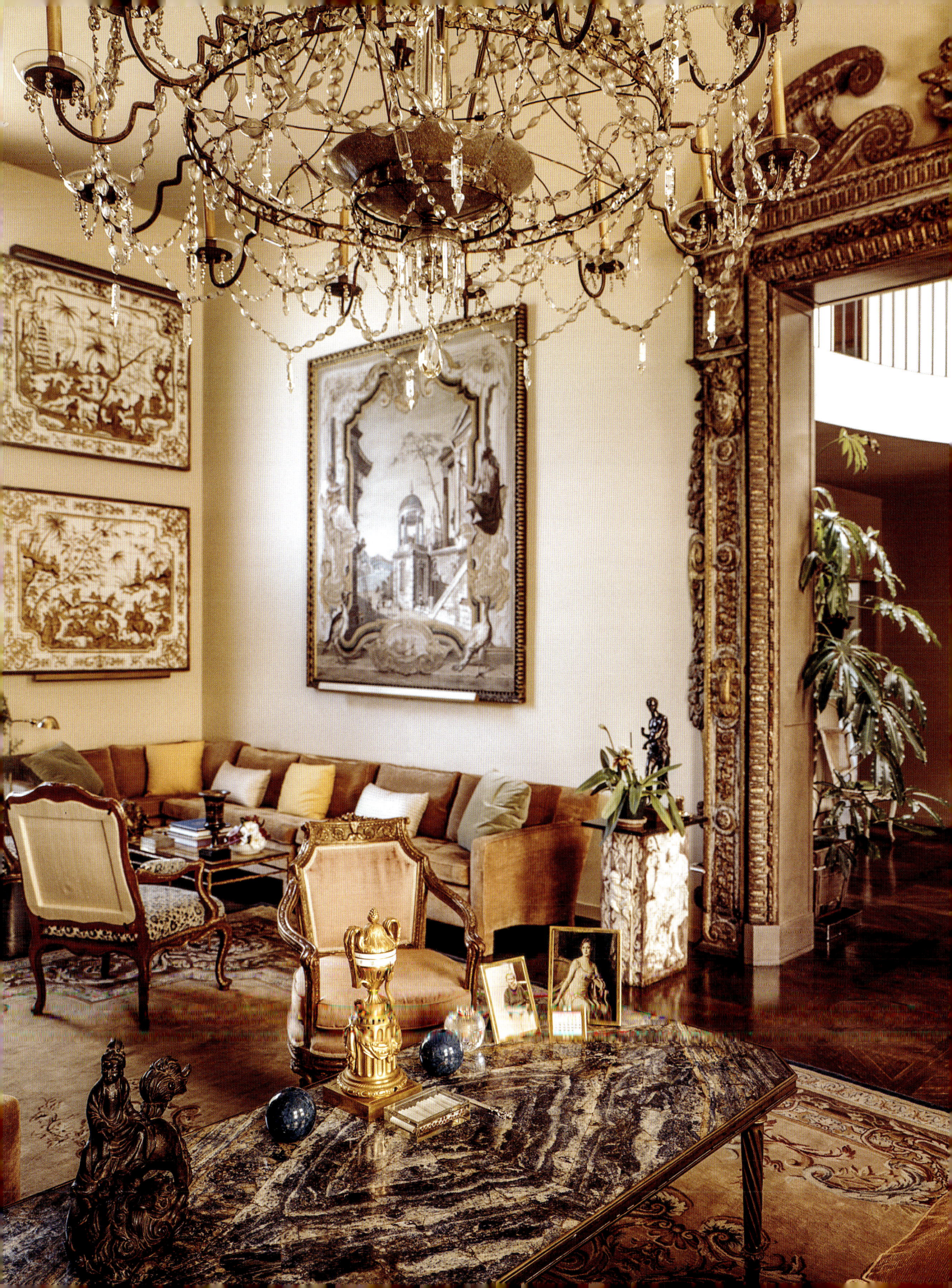

some involvement from his friends Elkins and Van Day Truex (another influential American designer and educator, who lived much of his life in France). Although their precise roles are unknown, their contributions are noteworthy because they mark a link with the influential French interior designer Jean-Michel Frank. Both Elkins and Truex were friends with—and, to an extent, professional disciples of—Frank, who perhaps can be credited with creating the very first California Look interior in San Francisco when he decorated the penthouse apartment of railroad and banking heir Templeton Crocker in 1927. Crocker's spare, unornamented interiors had walls and ceilings covered with squares of parchment or patterns of straw marquetry, and they were filled with blocky white-upholstered furniture, lamps hewn from raw chunks of rock crystal, and the owner's collection of ethnographic materials and natural specimens. Both Elkins and Truex appreciated and adopted Frank's reductive ethos and taste for natural materials. Elkins often incorporated furniture and decorative objects by Frank into her own interiors (the Griffin, Winslow, and Zellerbach residences, for example) and also served as his representative in the United States—producing for the American market many of his designs (notably plaster lighting fixtures that he originally commissioned from the famed sculptor Alberto Giacometti). Truex befriended Frank while teaching interior decoration in Paris during the 1920s, and in later years he

drew on Frank's aesthetic influence for the series of vacation houses that he designed for himself in the South of France.

If Frank planted the seeds for the California Look, Warren's embryonic first residence provided—by way of Elkins—an important model for a younger generation of Northern California decorators including Anthony Hail (who in 1960 helped Warren install his second residence in San Francisco), John Dickinson, Michael Taylor, and Charles Pfister. Hail's interiors—rooted in tradition and filled with exquisite Continental and Asian furnishings, but edited with a spare modern sensibility—appear perhaps most similar to Warren's. By contrast, Dickinson's spaces—particularly suggestive of those by Frank and Truex—are filled with his own primitive, fetishistic designs (many made with found objects); like Warren's, they strive to break free of the past but are also heavily indebted to it. Taylor's approach, with mixes of old and new, falls somewhere in between. And although Pfister is best known as a modernist, he too was also able to mix old and new adeptly. But in one way or another, all four clearly drew on the lessons learned from their predecessors.

The notion of a "look" inherently implies the act of seeing; it is precisely through seeing that a "look" is identified, codified, and recorded. Given that, it is clear that the California Look owes as much to Lyon and his lens as to the decorators and rooms behind it. Indeed, so closely are his photo-

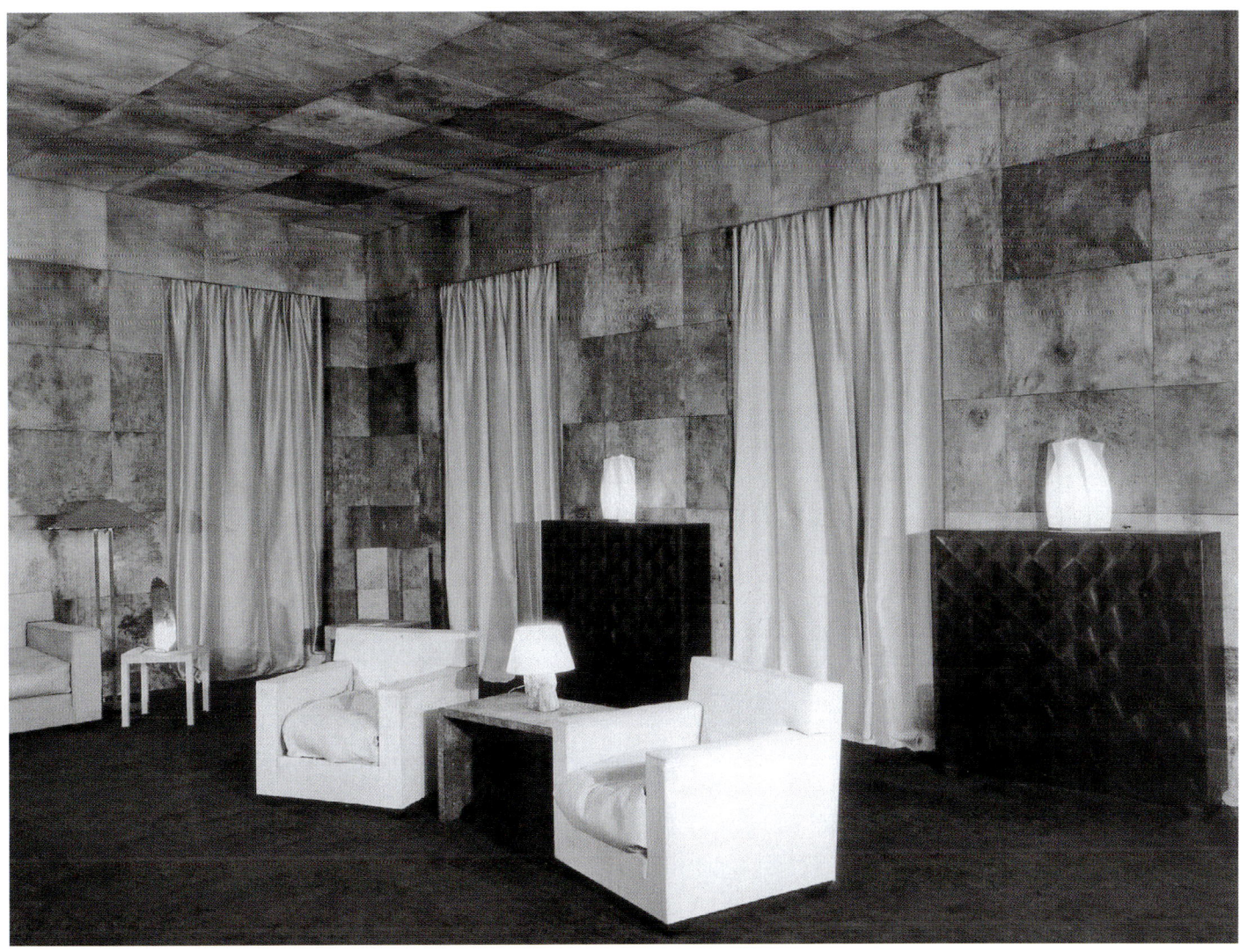

graphs associated with the California Look that today its decorators and rooms are known primarily through them: Elkins's Casa Amesti, Hail's de Guigné pool house, Dickinson's firehouse, Taylor's Auberge du Soleil, Pfister's penthouse at the Mark Hopkins Hotel; and so on. Without Lyon's photographs, there might never have been a California Look in the first place, and without Lyon's photographs, we might already have forgotten about it.

In the introduction to this book, Stephen M. Salny accurately states that Fred Lyon "captured an era that will never exist again . . . the lifestyle is gone." So too, the California Look designers themselves are gone, as are most of the rooms they created. What remains, however, are Fred Lyon's photographs, which vividly remind us why the California Look remains relevant. Happily, Lyon's photographs captured more than just lifestyle; they also provide important documentary records of the rooms that no longer exist and will define the California Look for generations to come.

ABOVE: Sonia, living room, Templeton Crocker residence (San Francisco, California) as designed by Jean-Michel Frank, 1927.

INTRODUCTION

San Francisco society once was more modestly and, some say, tastefully wealthy. Small in number and interlinked, the city's elite contented themselves with living luxuriously in only a few residences, usually a mansion or penthouse atop one of the hills, a vineyard in nearby Sonoma or Napa, perhaps a hacienda on the coast in Monterey or a ski lodge near Lake Tahoe.

From the 1940s through the 1990s, some of the best of these interiors were decorated by a coterie of designers whose names were recognized only by the cognoscenti of interior design in Northern California. Beginning with the doyenne of California interior decor, Frances Elkins, followed by the best of the generation after her—unique talents including the marvelously inventive John Dickinson; the decorator's decorator Anthony Hail; Charles Pfister, whose unfussy opulence became his trademark; and the incorrigible and wildly talented Michael Taylor—these artists created fresh, wonderful, and revolutionary settings that were idiomatic of their place and time. In the decades since the last of these giants died, several taken at the pinnacles of their careers by the AIDS epidemic, most of the rooms they created have vanished or vastly changed, overwritten like palimpsests to reflect different tastes and new styles. These projects are reappreciated today for their innovation and splendor, but all that remains, apart from a few surviving, highly coveted pieces of furniture, is the wonderful interior design photography of Fred Lyon.

Fred Lyon is a man of outstanding talent and longevity. He is perhaps the only artist who personally knew and photographed the work of every one of the aforementioned great decorators. Lyon worked closely with these decorators as well as with the seminal landscape architect Thomas Church and influential architect Gardner Dailey, all of whom sought out Lyon to capture their best designs. Lyon and his photographs in this book link decades of artistry that shaped Northern California interior design. They are glimpses into an especially stylish past.

OPPOSITE: Fred Lyon with a camera he devised for panoramic photography, 1966.

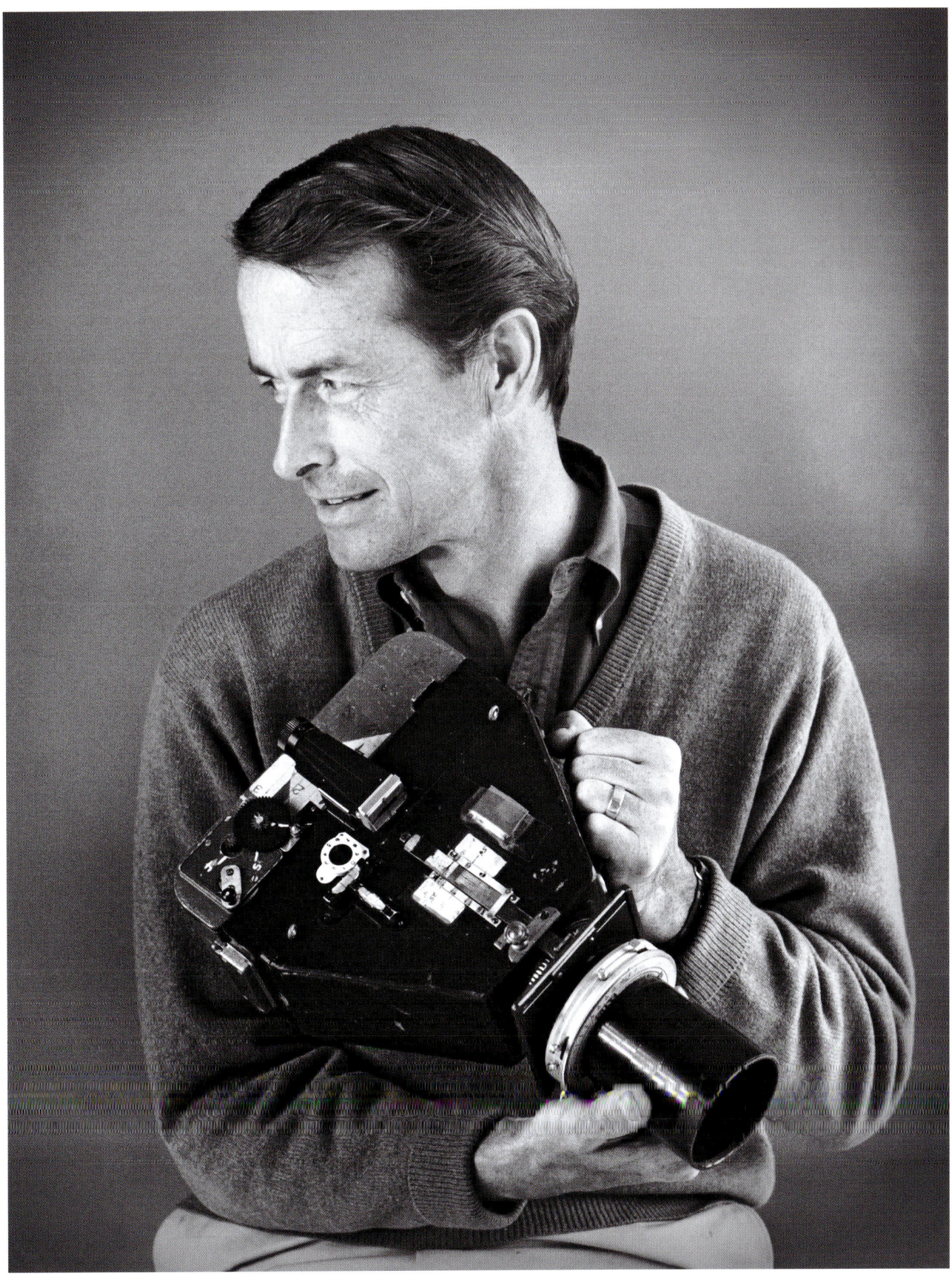

Today known as a fine art photographer—whose best work, according to noted gallerist Peter Fetterman, is the equivalent of Brassaï or Cartier-Bresson—Lyon began his career in New York photographing fashion and rubbing elbows with Richard Avedon, another young man also just out of the service in the Second World War and, like Lyon, starting a career in photography. For Lyon, however, fashion was a brief way station. His first big break came while still in his early twenties when he was selected by *House & Garden* to work with Frances Elkins, considered one of the "twentieth century's most remarkable and avant-garde decorators,"[5] to photograph one of her most significant projects: a residence of prominent socialite Whitney Warren Jr., a tour-de-force town house designed by Gardner Dailey. Lyon also had the good fortune to be mentored early in his career by the legendary *Vogue* West Coast editor Dorothea Walker, who instructed him in the social norms of Northern California society. Because of Lyon's intimacy with the designers and often their clients, the stories and photographs in this book are revealing portraits of the artists and their work.

By the late 1940s, Lyon was becoming known for the versatility of his interior design photography, working in black and white and color at a time when most architectural and design photography was rendered in black and white. Over seven decades, Lyon developed his career as a photojournalist, working for iconic magazines including *House & Garden*, *Vogue*, *Life*, and *Holiday* and as an editorial photographer during the *Mad Men* era of advertising. Noted design author Stephen M. Salny, who has researched and written about some of the greatest American designers and architects of the twentieth century, says, "Fred captured an era that will never exist again. There is greater wealth today, but the lifestyle is gone."[6] Fred Lyon's photographs and stories create a singular window into a special place and time in Northern California interior design.

OPPOSITE: Publicity materials for an exhibition of Lyon's early work at the San Francisco Museum of Art (now San Francisco Museum of Modern Art) in 1949. The show was a personal and critical success for Lyon.

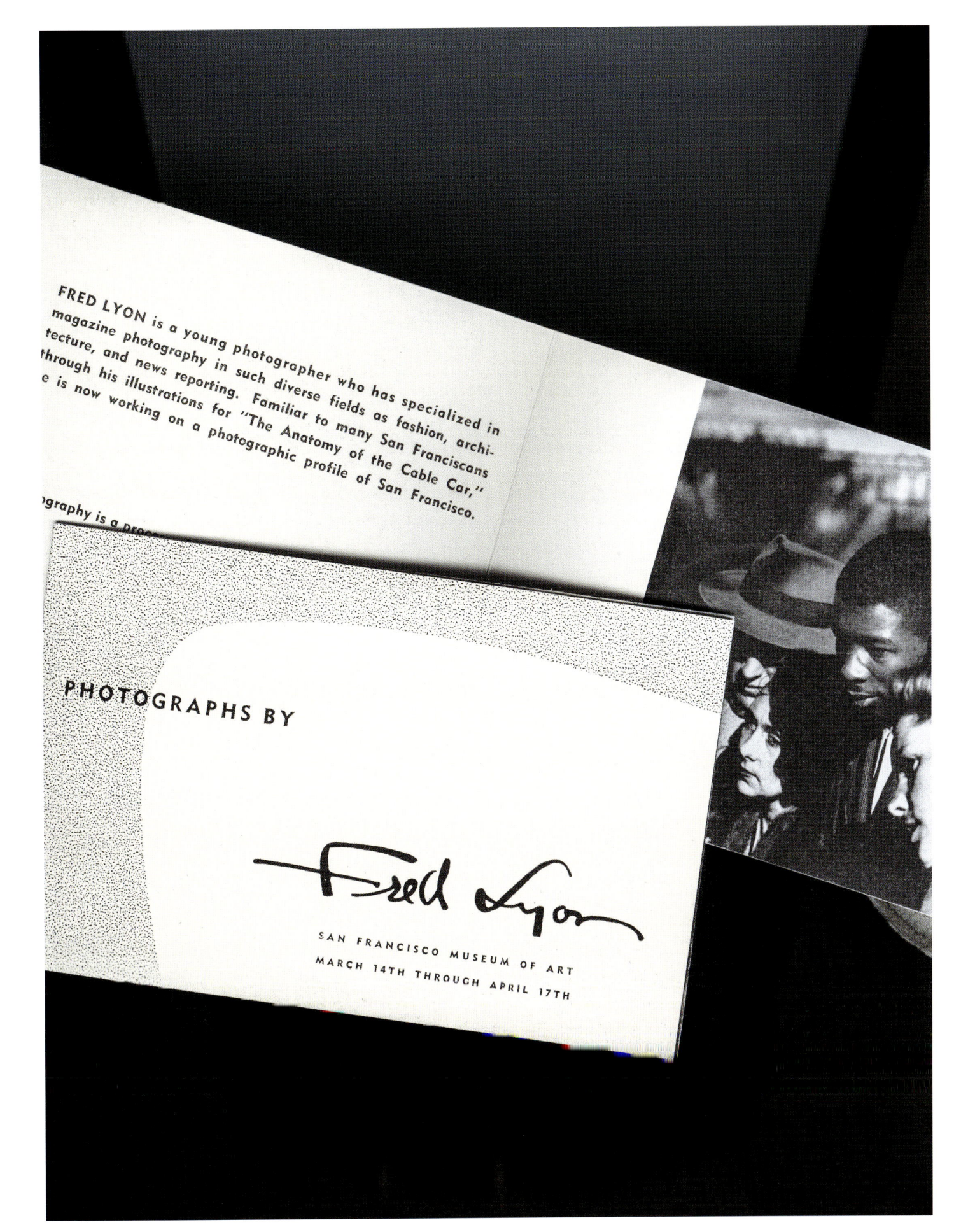

FRED LYON is a young photographer who has specialized in magazine photography in such diverse fields as fashion, architecture, and news reporting. Familiar to many San Franciscans through his illustrations for "The Anatomy of the Cable Car," e is now working on a photographic profile of San Francisco.

ography is a proc

PHOTOGRAPHS BY

Fred Lyon

SAN FRANCISCO MUSEUM OF ART
MARCH 14TH THROUGH APRIL 17TH

23

I.

LEARNING HIS ART

Fred Lyon was born in San Francisco in 1924. By the time he started high school, his family had moved to Burlingame, which was often the country home of the social elite of San Francisco, drawn there by its bucolic spaces and weather that is reliably more pleasant than the often foggy city. Those seeking even more exclusivity built larger country estates in the neighboring town of Hillsborough. If in Boston the Lowells talk to the Cabots and the Cabots talk only to God, Hillsborough played Cabots to Burlingame's Lowells.[7]

Lyon's interest in photography started when he was twelve and begged his parents to buy him a camera. They indulged him with a pretty good one that Lyon still remembers, all these years later, cost $36. Lyon contributed his nascent photography skills to the Burlingame High School 1941 senior class yearbook. In his published candid photos, the students look Ivy League prep, girls in cashmere sweater sets and pleated skirts, boys in trousers and sweaters or sports coats.[8] There are scenes of classmates driving in convertibles and lounging next to swimming pools. Fred's life in high school revolved around photography, music, and dancing. After school, Fred and his friends cruised the town's main street. "One corner had a pharmacy and soda shop; diagonally across a little beyond the corner was the music store where they sold sheet music, which was still happening then, and records. They had one or two listening booths. That was heaven."[9] Lyon remembers. Heaven especially if he and a pretty classmate could share the booth. If things went well, there was the possibility of making a date for the movies at the theater that was steps away. The frisson of these moments is still palpable across eight decades.

The Second World War was already raging across Asia and Europe, but America was still at peace. The photos Fred took of his classmates poolside, at the beach, or playing tennis hold their subjects in a kind of amber that captures a Northern California idyll. When Lyon entered high school in the late 1930s, California in general and San Francisco in particular were special places to be. The historian Kevin Starr, who dedicated much of his life to studying the impact California has had on the United States and the world, wrote, "Like so much else in the 1930s, California . . . expressed elite values that would become mainstream after the war."[10] Much of the ethos, values, and tastes that formed Lyon and San Francisco and California, and later the country, were happening around him as he was growing up.

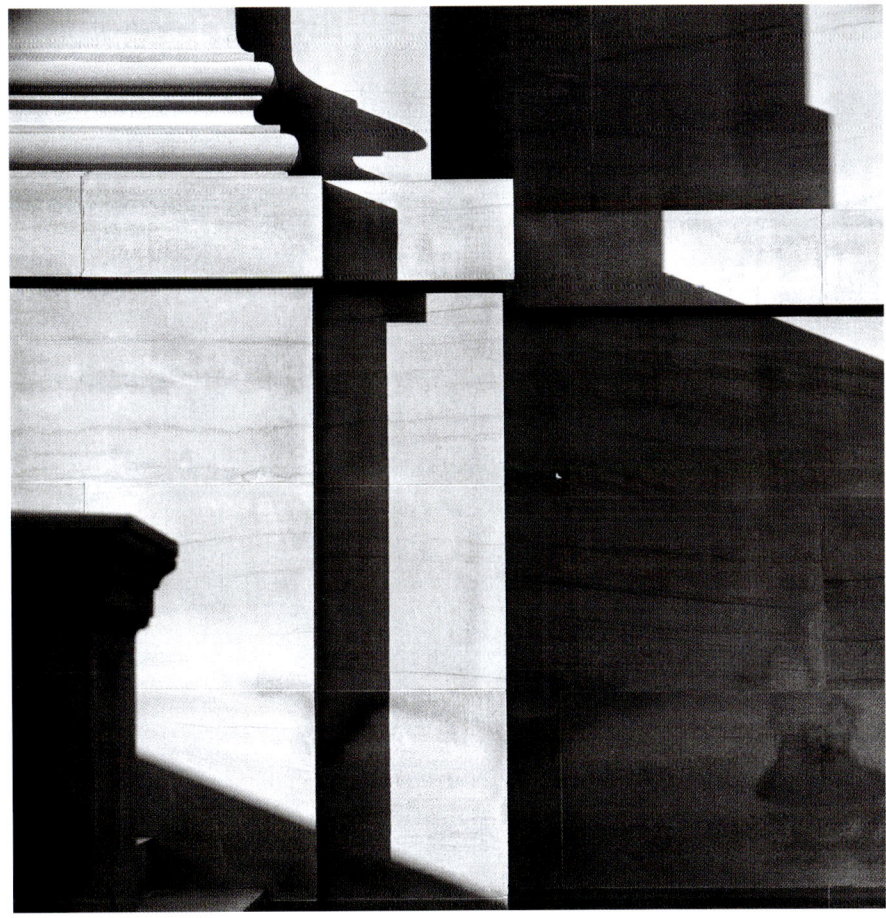

Before he went off to college, Lyon got a job with the premier photography studio in San Francisco, Moulin Studios. This outfit described itself as "the major force on the West Coast in commercial and portrait photography."[11] Working as a family, Gabriel Moulin and his two sons operated a portrait studio and a large commercial photography studio. This is where Lyon first learned the nuts and bolts of the professional photographer's trade. Moulin was noted for well-composed, sharp photographs that created "a perfection of balance, of framing, of vanishing point, and depth of field."[12] At the studio, Lyon did whatever needed doing: moving heavy equipment, setting lights, and taking the occasional photograph. The Moulins were also adept at working outside the studio, and they rode cranes and even a steel beam as it was lifted into place on a high-rise under construction to get their photographs. Lyon absorbed the Moulins' can-do attitude and appreciation for technical skill.

After high school, Lyon moved to Los Angeles to attend the Art Center School (now ArtCenter College of Design). It was then a relatively new art college located near downtown Los Angeles. Lyon was barely seventeen years old at the time he enrolled, but he already had a sense of the kind of artist he wanted to become. The fastest route to that destination ran through Los Angeles. The city "was supporting a strong art community, centered around Westlake Park, where many artists

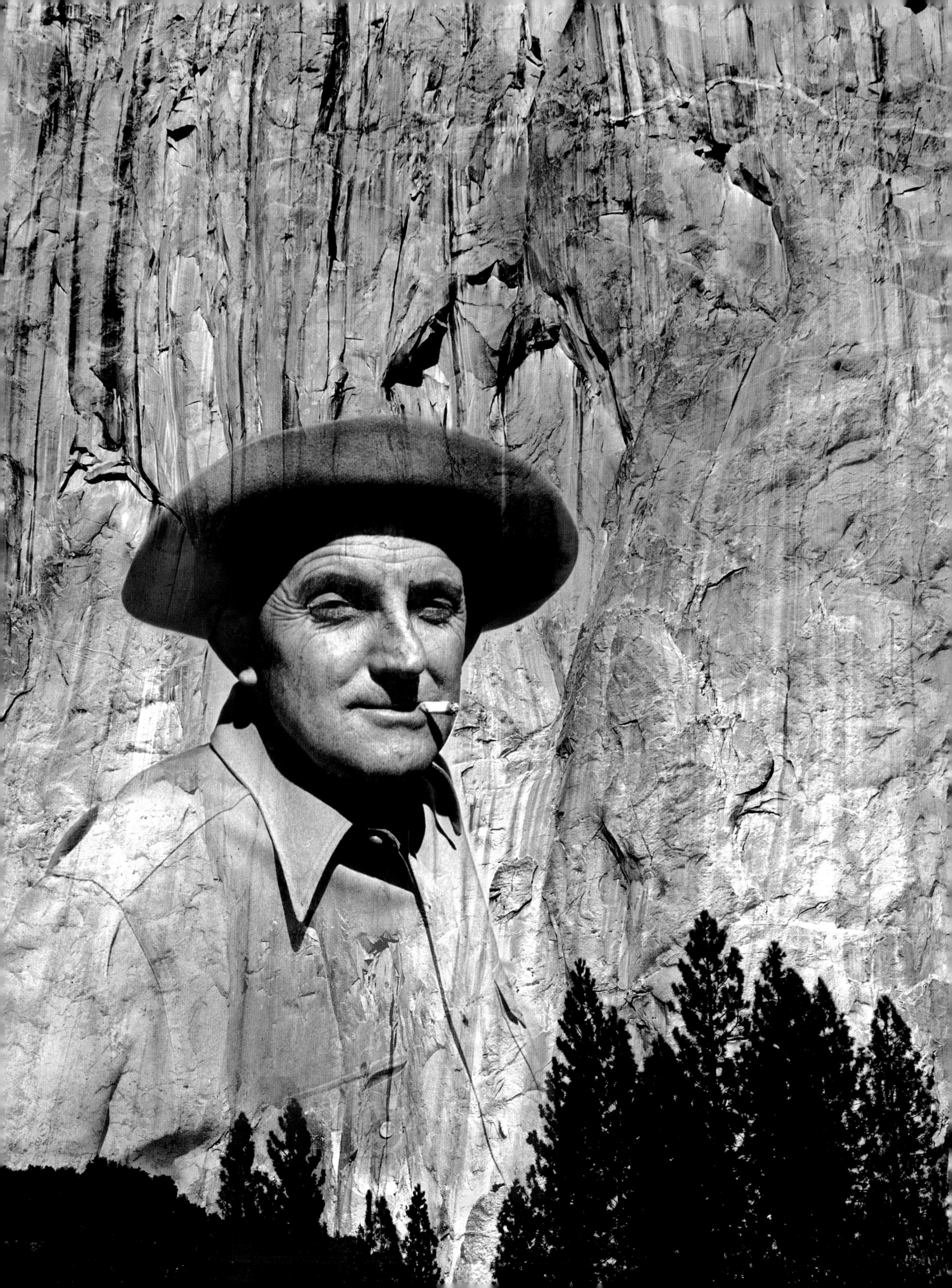

lived,"[13] and was home to three good art schools: Otis Art Institute, Chouinard Art Institute, and the newest addition, Art Center School, all of which opened in the years since the movie business moved to Los Angeles.

Founded in 1930 with only twelve teachers and fewer students, the Art Center School boasted in its first brochure that its initial faculty offered students a sum total of "104 years of experience."[14] This brochure, a gem of composition that stands up today, turned Lyon's head. "It really got to me," he recalls. "It had such excellent design."[15] Students closely interacted with all members of the small faculty, and they were expected to work hard at their art and make progress toward becoming skilled professional artists. At the end of every month, all the work produced that month by each student was critiqued by the entire faculty. The curriculum was intended to produce well-trained, working artists and "to make art pay" for the practitioners the school produced.[16] This professional approach to art instruction proved popular. When Lyon arrived there in the fall of 1941, the institution had matured to offer specialization in several types of art, including advertising design, industrial design, painting and illustration, and photography. Lyon, of course, chose photography, which, the college reassured its students, "as a new medium . . .

offers the greatest field for future expansion."[17]

Lyon learned to become adept at working in color as well as black and white, a versatility that many photographers at that time did not possess. Looking back after almost eighty years, Lyon says, "A lot of photographers these days, who are accustomed to working only in color, can't see in black and white. I see in masses of tone. One should study good poster art to see this done well, using masses of tone to achieve excellent graphic design. This is especially useful for working in black and white, and if you can't achieve your vision in shades of black and white, color is only going to confuse you."[18] The first page of the Art Center School brochure that captured Lyon's attention all those years ago bears a banner reading "Fundamentals First!" in all caps. Lyon went there to learn and refine the fundamentals of his art.

When Lyon enrolled, the Art Center School's faculty already boasted notable photographers and had recently attracted an especially prominent one, the soon-to-be-legendary Ansel Adams, who was a guest instructor. The way Adams taught was to find out what his students wanted to express with a photo and help them accomplish it their way. This approach to teaching suited Lyon. He took classes from Adams and experienced monthly critiques of his work by Adams and other faculty.

OPPOSITE: Fred Lyon, portrait of Ansel Adams superimposed on an image of a rock face at Yosemite National Park, 1942. This was a project for the Art Center School.

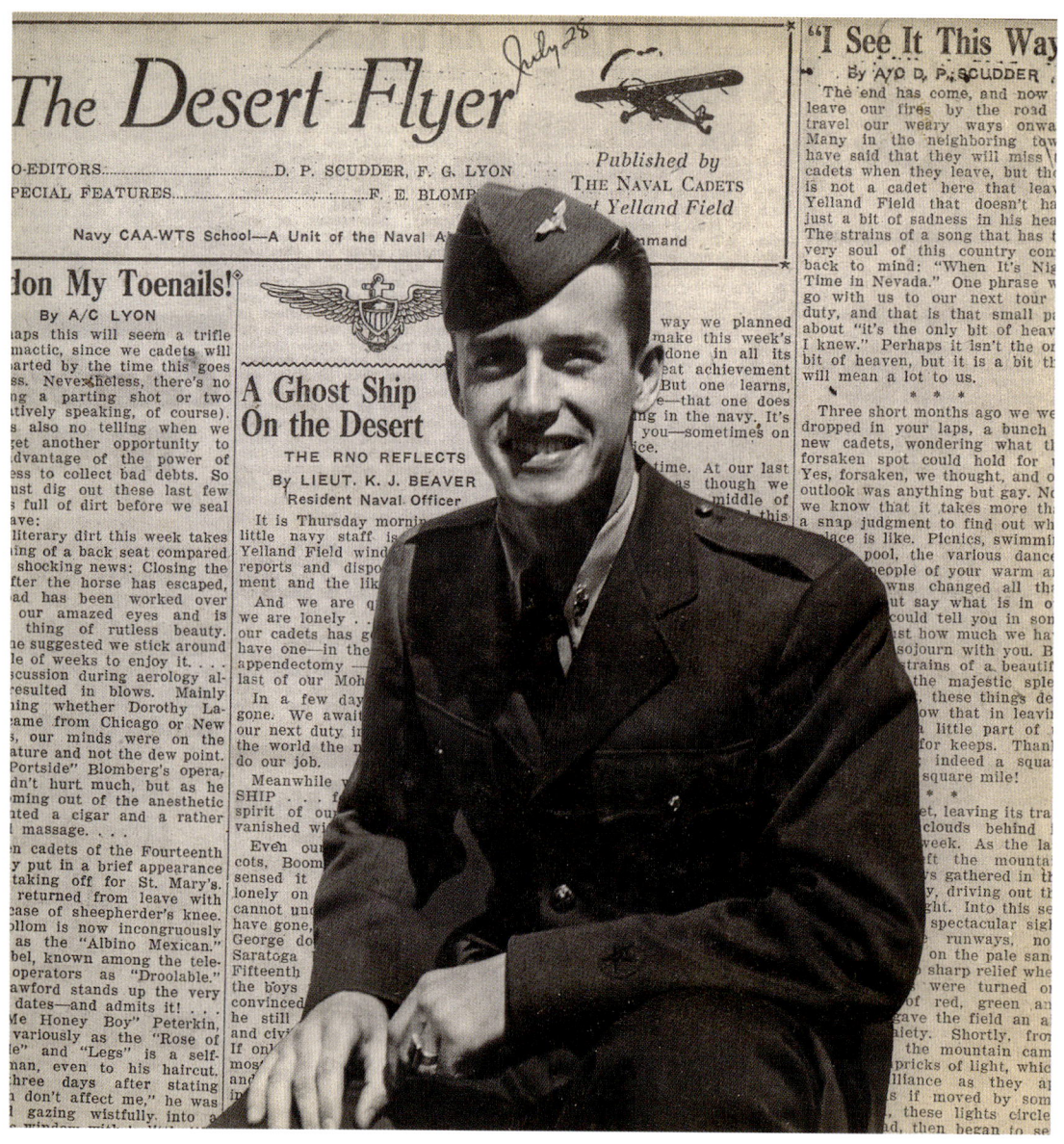

ABOVE: Fred Lyon as a Navy aviation cadet, 1943.

For Adams, "Yosemite was like a siren enticing you back,"[19] and some years while he was teaching at the Art Center School, Adams took a small group of students with him to photograph Yosemite. In the fall of 1942, Lyon was among that select group of students. He says, "A small group from my class went with Adams to Tenaya Lake and other places in Yosemite. Ansel knew the whole park like the back of his hand."[20] Their first night in the park, Adams entertained the students in his fami-

ly's Yosemite home. Lyon says, "There was constant laughter. He mixed us wonderful Old Fashioneds. I've never had one since that tasted better. Ansel had a wonderful and impish sense of humor. He was like a little bouncy ball of energy. He had a bowl of oranges. He picked up two oranges and ran over to the grand piano in his living room. Ansel played piano to an extraordinarily high standard. He sat down and rolled the oranges up and down the keyboard and somehow made lovely music. He was laughing the whole time. Ansel was a wonderful host."[21]

The group spent their days tramping over Yosemite, solving the technical problems of how best to capture the splendor that surrounded them, while exploring the artistic question of what the photographer wished to achieve. Lyon took from Adams certain artistic tenets, such as Adams's famous admonition, "There's nothing worse than a very sharp image of a very fuzzy concept."[22] But even then, Lyon knew he needed to become his own photographer. "My feeling was that I could never learn all Ansel knew. I could never be more than a miniature Ansel Adams if I tried to be like him, and I knew I was never going to become a landscape photographer. I always seem to need to include some of the works of man in my work. Ansel was terrific and inspirational, but I didn't want to emulate what he was doing."[23] Adams later wrote, "My world has been . . . one of peace and beauty. I believe in beauty."[24] Adams shared some of his beautiful world to his students in their time at Yosemite.

But Lyon would soon face a very different world. The year after the Japanese attack at Pearl Harbor, when Lyon turned eighteen, he signed up for the US Navy's elite Aviation Cadet program. "I wanted to become a pilot because that seemed like the best way to get into the fight and make sure I didn't get put into some corner somewhere," Lyon remembers.[25] In the summer of 1943, he was called to report for training to become a pilot—in Navy parlance, an aviator. Prior to the war, military aviation training had been extremely selective and elite. With the war raging around the globe, military aviation training had to be greatly expanded while remaining elite. A big change from the prewar years was that candidates for training did not need to be college graduates or enrolled in an accredited college. Lyon had completed four years of high school and one year of college at the Art Center School when he joined the Navy. In prewar times, that résumé would not have qualified for aviation training. But when Lyon enlisted, the Navy desperately needed pilots. There were thousands of young men like Lyon who were smart enough, fit enough, gung-ho enough, and willing to undertake the nearly year-and-a-half-long rigorous training to learn to fly the Navy way.[26] Still, when Lyon left college to become an officer and a gentleman, in his kit bag taking up precious space with his socks and underwear was his Rolleiflex camera.

Lyon's Navy records show excellent academic and physical performance throughout preflight and into primary training. US successes in the Pacific by late 1943, however, meant the Navy needed fewer pilots than expected in the darkest days early in the war. Pilot training was slowed and turned dog eat dog as cadets competed for the diminishing number of slots for advanced training. Lyon dropped out of the program to get into the war sooner. As his Navy records put it, "Separated from flight training while in good standing . . . as a result of quota restrictions. Is fully qualified and recommended for reassignment to flight training at a later time. Recommended by his commanding officer under any service quotas which may be established in the future."[27] In other words, if he survived what came next, and if the war was still being fought, the Navy would be willing for him to resume aviation training.

After going through boot camp at the Great Lakes Naval Training Station, in Illinois, Lyon was not assigned to the fighting war but instead to Washington, DC, to become the Navy Press Office's newest photographer. The operation ran much like a big-city newspaper. There were rows of desks for Navy journalists and film labs for Navy photographers. In the office next door, accredited civilian reporters and photographers had their own desks surrounding a teletype. Lyon got to know the journalists and press photographers and learn their business.

There is a cardinal rule in the military: never volunteer for anything. Lyon took the opposite approach: he volunteered for everything. Within Lyon's first few days in Washington, his commanding officer came into the pressroom and asked who would be willing to go to the White House to take the Christmas portrait of President Franklin Roosevelt and his family. The hard-bitten experienced photographers who had

temporarily found themselves in uniform looked down on this kind of assignment. Lyon didn't. He raised his hand, and off he went. Lyon says, "I was always conscious of my appearance. My uniform was pressed and my shoes were shined so I was ready to go."[28] Lyon packed his 4 x 5 Speed Graphic, which weighed nine pounds, and heavy lights that weighed far more and set off for the White House. It was a tough shoot. Corralling the Roosevelt family, including babies and Fala, the president's Scottish terrier, around the seated FDR turned out to be sweaty work, to say nothing of coming face-to-face with the man who had been president since Lyon was eight years old. The shoot was nerve-racking and hard physical labor. "I got back to the office looking like I had slept in a cement mixer," Lyon remembers.[29]

This was to be the first of many times Lyon met FDR, and he enjoyed them all. "Roosevelt had such good props on his desk in the Oval Office, and he handled the press well," he remembers. "FDR knew reporters had to come back with a story and photographers had to come back with a picture. He always made sure reporters left with something they could write and that photographers got their shots."[30] Roosevelt's desk obscured his wheelchair even from tall photographers like Lyon. There was a tacit agreement among photographers not to photograph FDR getting in or out of his wheelchair or in any other way seeming to be infirm. "All such pictures . . . were to be voluntarily

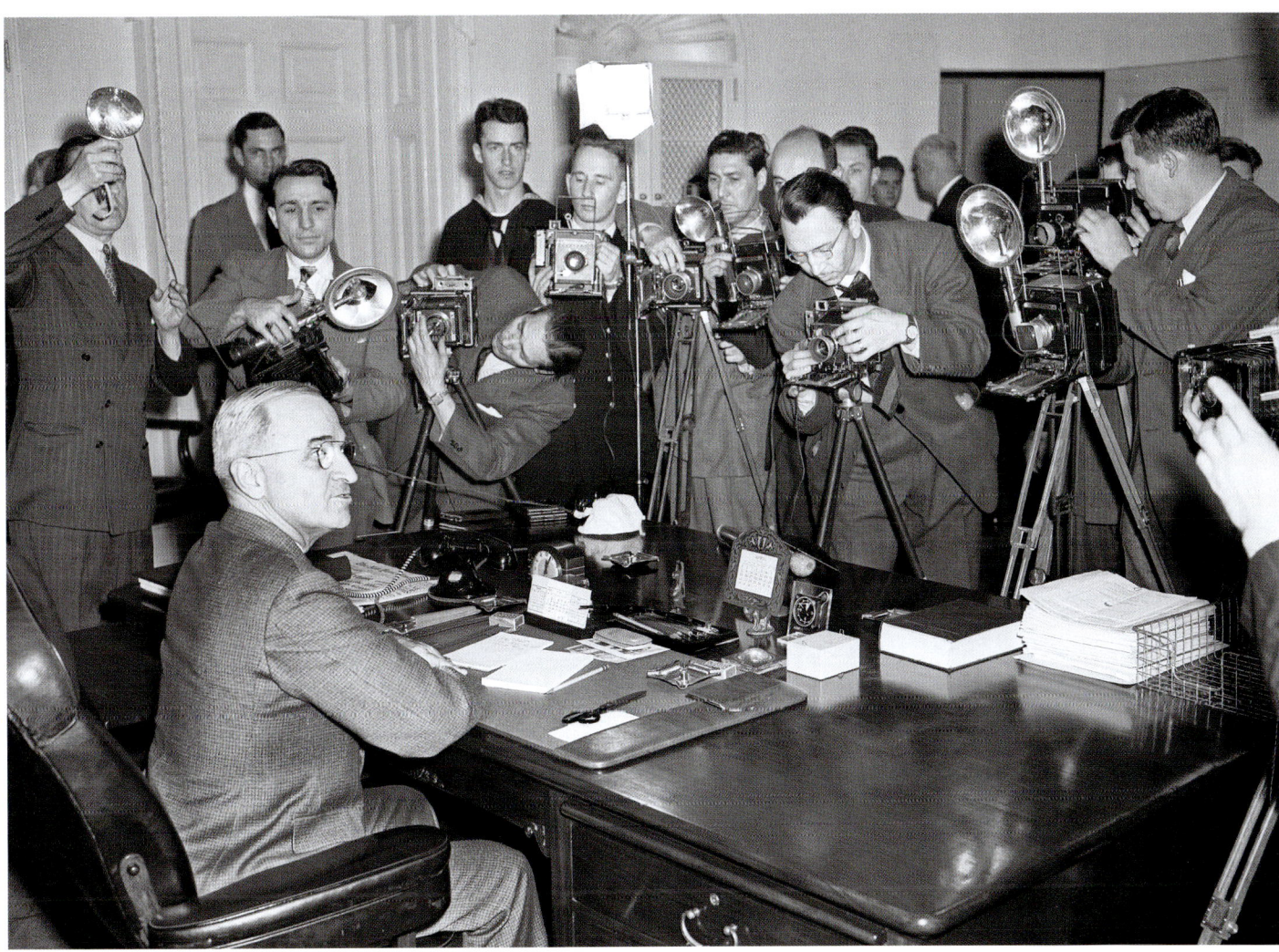

withheld and destroyed."[31] It wouldn't have mattered to Lyon anyway. Just twenty years old, he had already decided he didn't want to partake in what he calls "armpit" photography. Lyon was never going to become a paparazzo.

Two weeks after Roosevelt's death on April 12, 1945, Lyon returned to the White House to photograph the new president, Harry S. Truman, who had been vice president for less than three months and was largely unknown to the public. Lyon and perhaps a dozen other photographers were ushered into the Oval Office to meet and photograph the new president. Watching Truman speak from behind his desk, Lyon worried about the glare that reflected off the new president's spectacles. When the time for photos was at hand, Truman casually removed his glasses and replaced them with frames without lenses and smiled for the photographers. Lyon got his shots. In a few months, the war ended and Fred Lyon, like millions of others serving for the duration, was again a civilian

ABOVE: President Harry S. Truman poses at his desk for a group of White House photographers, 1945. Fred Lyon, in Navy uniform, stands to the right of the closed door in rear.

II.
A WORKING PHOTOGRAPHER

The great essayist of city and country life E. B. White wrote, "No one should come to New York to live unless he is willing to be lucky."[32] Lyon was willing to be lucky when he left the Navy and headed to Manhattan in 1946. "I got my Navy mustering-out pay," Lyon says. "Temporarily flush, I decided to go there and look for photography opportunities."[33] He had met many well-established photographers during his hitch in the Navy, and they gave him leads to their friends in the business. One of these leads took Lyon to a photography agent named Charles Rado, cofounder of the Rapho Guillumette photo agency in New York.

Although Lyon did not know it when he first met Rado, the agent was one of the hottest in the business. "I came to New York with a spiral-bound book of my original prints, some from college courses and some from the Navy, in my sea bag. I took that book with me to see Charles. That's all I had to show him," he recalls.[34] Rado had no need to take on unproven photographers, but he took on Lyon. This was a great coup for Lyon, even if he did not realize it at the time. When Lyon signed with Rapho Guillumette,

Charles Rado was already a fixture in the New York picture agency business and had relationships with the art directors who purchased photographs for magazines, books, advertising, and corporate reports. Rado represented a group of handpicked star photographers Lyon admired, including Brassaï, Robert Doisneau, Yousuf Karsh, André Kertész, Sabine Weiss, Ylla, and Lyon's personal favorite photographer, Bill Brandt.

Having secured an agent, Lyon needed to find a regular photography job in order to build his portfolio of work, to give Rado something to show the art directors at magazines and advertising agencies, the main buyers of photography at that time. Following another lead from a friend, Lyon visited a small fashion photography operation called Wilcox Studio. Wilcox operated out of an elegant Park Avenue brownstone. Lyon opened the studio's front door and was greeted by the receptionist. "A snappy lady sat behind a Louis desk positioned across from a large marble fireplace," he remembers.[35] Moments after Lyon arrived, "out came a caricature of an advertising account executive in a three-piece Brooks Brothers gray flannel suit. I told him I had been referred

OPPOSITE: For Russeks department store in Manhattan, fashion model Rosemary Lutz poses under a DC-3 airplane propeller, 1946.

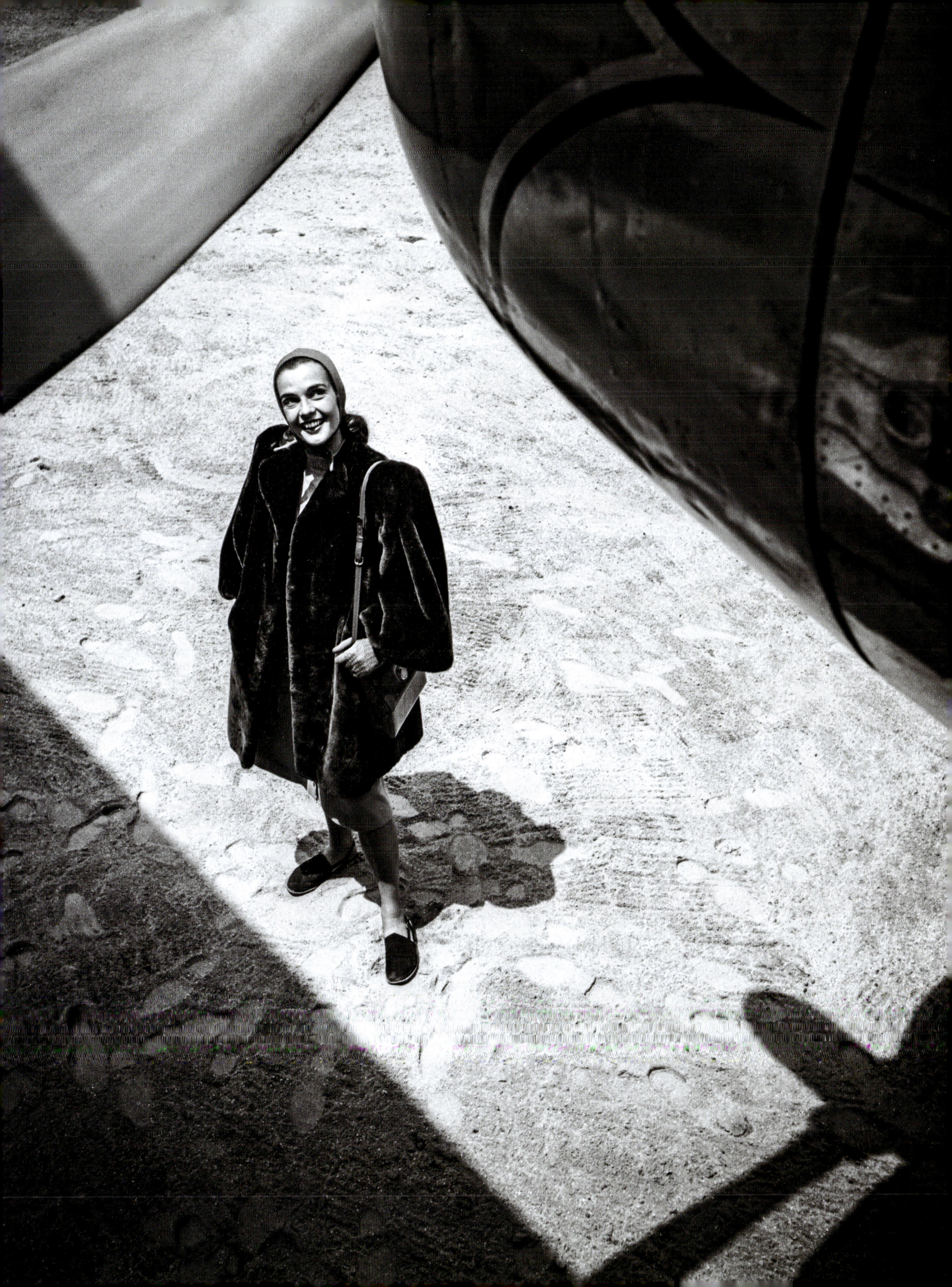

to him and showed him my book. He said, 'I don't see any fashion in here.' I responded, 'The same principles apply to fashion.'"[36] Somehow, Lyon got the job.

This was the beginning of a new age for fashion photography, and New York was the epicenter of the art and commerce surrounding photography and fashion. Established photographers such as Irving Penn and rising talents like the soon-to-be-famous Richard Avedon and William Helburn, the latter two contemporaries of Lyon, were building on the work pioneered by Martin Munkácsi to introduce "dynamism, speed, and energy"[37] to the previously static world of fashion photography. Models who could move well and look good doing so, and the photographers who directed them, were breathing new life into fashion photography, sometimes producing images that rose to the level of fine art photography and that remain vibrant and exciting after more than seventy years.

The practice of fashion photography was far simpler in the 1940s than today. For Lyon, a fashion shoot usually included just the model, who did her own hair and makeup, and him. New York was alive with talent on both sides of the lens. Lyon quickly learned to respect the role fashion models played in the success of his work. After his first few weeks on the job, Lyon was selecting and booking his models as well as photographing them. "I always tried to book the best models, and was exceedingly nice and respectful to them. If they liked you, they really helped you out," he says.[38]

"We only had one photo studio at Wilcox; it was the dining room of the town house. If the studio was being used by the head photographer, I took the model, my Rolleiflex, some rolls of film, and shot on location. Models were booked by the hour, and they sometimes scheduled several jobs during a day," Lyon recalls.[39] He did not have the time to linger over fashion shoots. Lyon was still learning his way around New York, so he often relied on his models to suggest nearby locations. The distance they could travel from Midtown was limited by time and "the budget for cab fare. That decided how far afield you could go."[40] Listening to Lyon recall his fashion shoots, you can feel the bustle of the city and the excitement as he, carrying his equipment, and his model, carrying her makeup kit, rushed to the location, maybe an empty lot, a street corner, a park, or an Automat.

Lyon developed an appreciation for two models in particular. One was Dorian Leigh, "who combined pristine blue eyes, curling eyelashes, an arresting intelligence, and intoxicating sexuality to become one of history's most photographed models, perhaps the first to truly merit the adjective super."[41] The year Lyon worked with her, Leigh appeared on seven *Vogue* covers. She famously was "as demanding as the

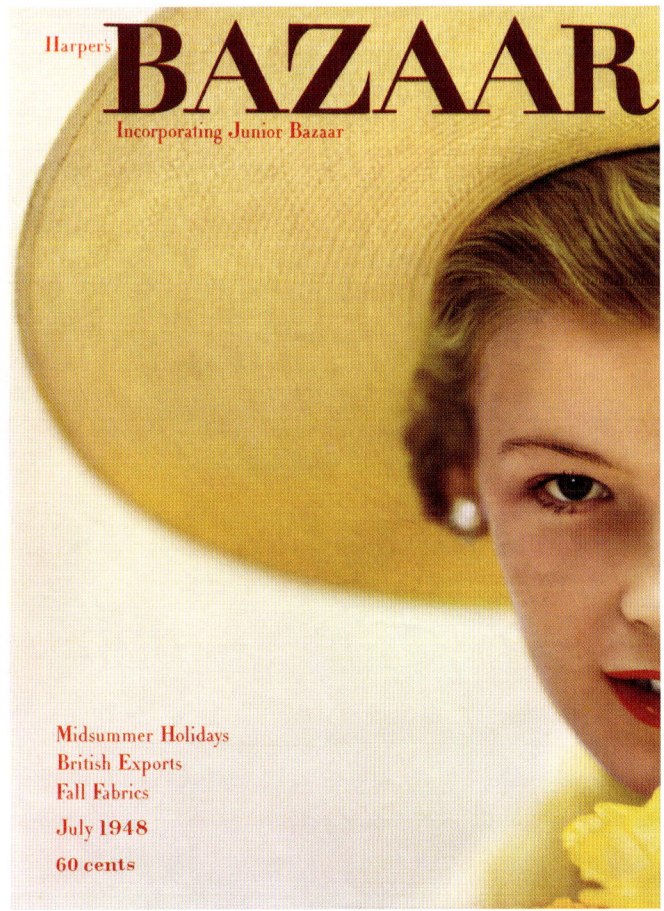

eminent photographers who shot her, including Louise Dahl-Wolfe and Irving Penn."[42] Lyon says, "Dorian was a great model; she was very experienced and a pleasure to work with."[43] Leigh had her pick of assignments in 1946 when she agreed to work with Lyon, so she must have seen something she liked in him.

The other model was a "skinny blonde kid" named Anne Murray. Lyon says, "I loved working with Anne. She really moved well, which was important because I hated static fashion photography."[44] Lyon and Anne also got along personally. "We would be playful with each other during our shoots."[45] It seems that Anne, who was booked solid during this time, was not in a hurry to get to her next job when she was modeling for Lyon. Their relationship then was platonic: "I knew she went out with millionaires, so I never asked her out."[46] Instead, they circulated in the same groups and grew to confide in each other. Lyon was just starting out in the business, but Anne was already well established and in demand. Models often found themselves teamed by photographers. Richard Avedon sometimes teamed blonde Anne Murray with her brunette friend Theo Graham. "Dick Avedon liked their contrast," says Lyon.[47]

By the time he was twenty-three years old, Lyon had gone from high school directly to college for a year and then straight into the Navy.

Approximately two-thirds of the Americans who served in the Second World War were posted overseas; Lyon had not been among them. He wanted to see the world. At a country-house party, Lyon met Naomi Barry, a writer who was a few years older. Sitting by a stream, Lyon took a photo of her while they talked. Barry had a wonderful idea. "'Air France is going to start service from New York to Paris. I'm a writer; you're a photographer. We can sell some magazine stories and get a free flight to France.' She had already sold two or three magazines on this idea," Lyon recalls.[48]

Excited at the prospect of living in Paris, Lyon quit his job at Wilcox Studio and got ready to leave. There was one hitch: in those days, for a military-age male to get a passport, he had to obtain a release from his local draft board even if, as Lyon had, he already had been discharged from service. Passport releases were a low priority for Lyon's hometown draft board, and it became clear that a release would not be forthcoming in time to make the trip to Paris. He decided instead to go home to San Francisco to spend time with his family. Lyon says, "I went with Naomi to the Condé Nast office to tell the editor I couldn't make the trip to Paris. We were talking to an editor at *House & Garden*. She asked what I was going to do instead of going to Paris. I told her I was going back to San Francisco. She said, 'San Francisco, that's much better. We have lots of photographers in Paris; we don't have anybody in San Francisco.' She told me she would be in touch."[49]

Grand schemes made in one's twenties almost never unfold as planned. Naomi Barry's did. She went to France and became a resident correspondent for *Gourmet* magazine for forty years. She had a charmed life, developing a specialty reviewing restaurants. Barry "savored life" and, into her nineties, "liked to describe herself and her friends as 'great broads'—charming, sassy, intelligent women of un-certain age."[50] Food writer, editor, and restaurant critic Ruth Reichl, who was Barry's editor for several years at *Gourmet*, wrote this about her: "It takes a writer of extraordinary abilities to make you care about meals that you will never be able to eat. . . . Barry offers up such a rich slice of life that you feel you are sitting at the next table eavesdropping on your neighbors chatting with the chef. Her reviews are like little time machines that not only allow you to taste the food she is eating, but somehow transport you back to a city that no longer exists."[51] Imagine what she and Lyon could have accomplished together in France. C'est la vie.

OPPOSITE: Writer Naomi Barry, photographed by Fred Lyon, 1946.

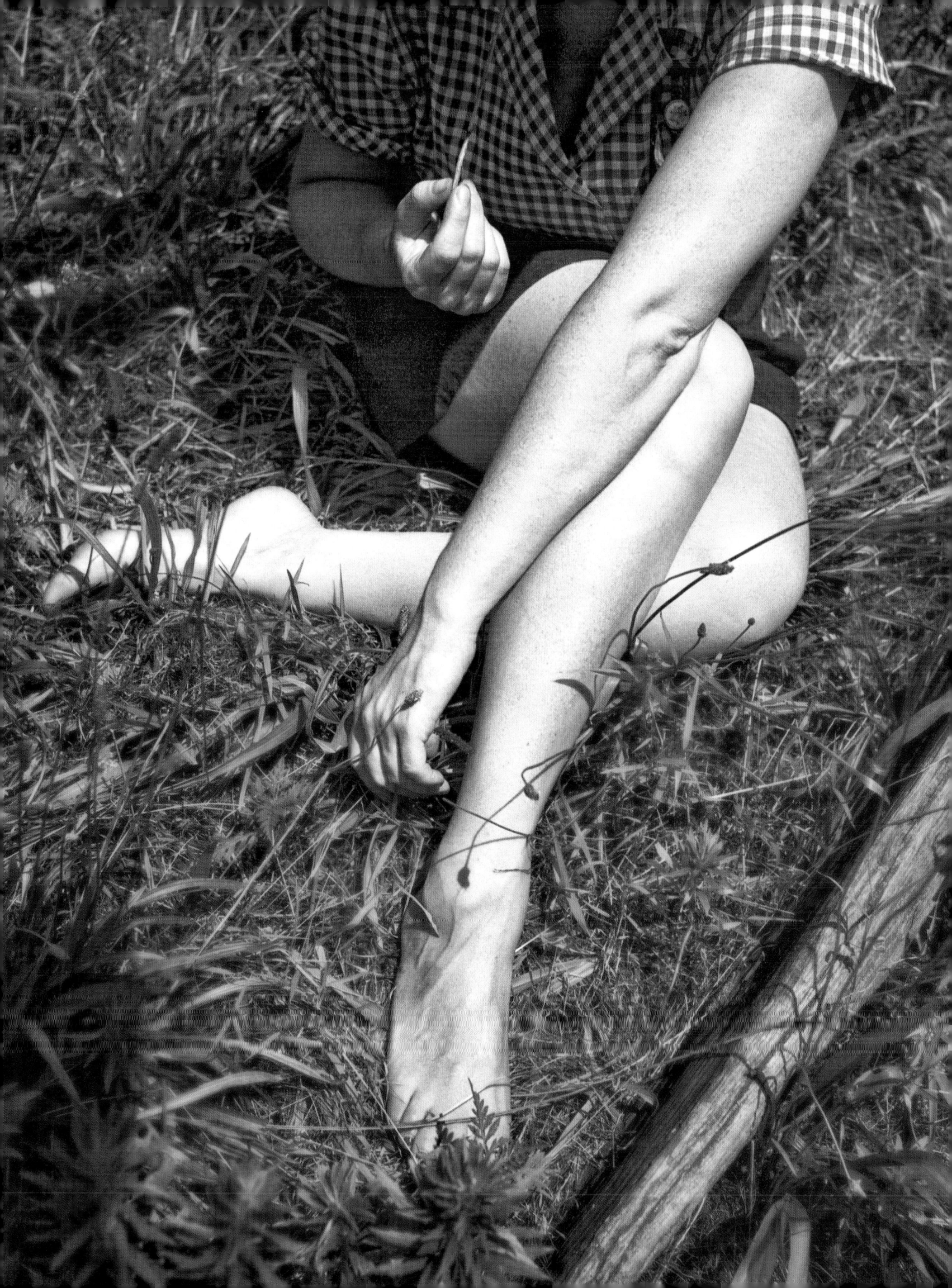

III.
A LUCKY BREAK ON TELEGRAPH HILL

Fred Lyon was willing to be lucky in San Francisco, too. After spending a year in Manhattan as a fashion photographer, he returned to his native Bay Area at the beginning of 1947. For the first time since he reported for Navy aviation training, Lyon was back living with his parents.

With no job and no leads for one, but on the strength of his meeting in New York with that editor from *House & Garden*, Lyon called himself a magazine photographer. He installed a darkroom in the attic of his family's house to complete the effect. "My parents' friends would ask what I was

doing for work, and I told them I was a magazine photographer. I had no idea what that entailed."[52] This soon changed. "I was working on my suntan," Lyon remembers. "One day, my mother came out and said there was a long-distance phone call for me. She had a stricken look on her face, because in those days long distance meant somebody had died. The caller said, 'We have an assignment for you.'"[53]

It was *House & Garden* calling. They hired Lyon to photograph the storied residence of San Francisco socialite Whitney Warren Jr. atop Telegraph Hill, at the base of Coit Tower. It had been

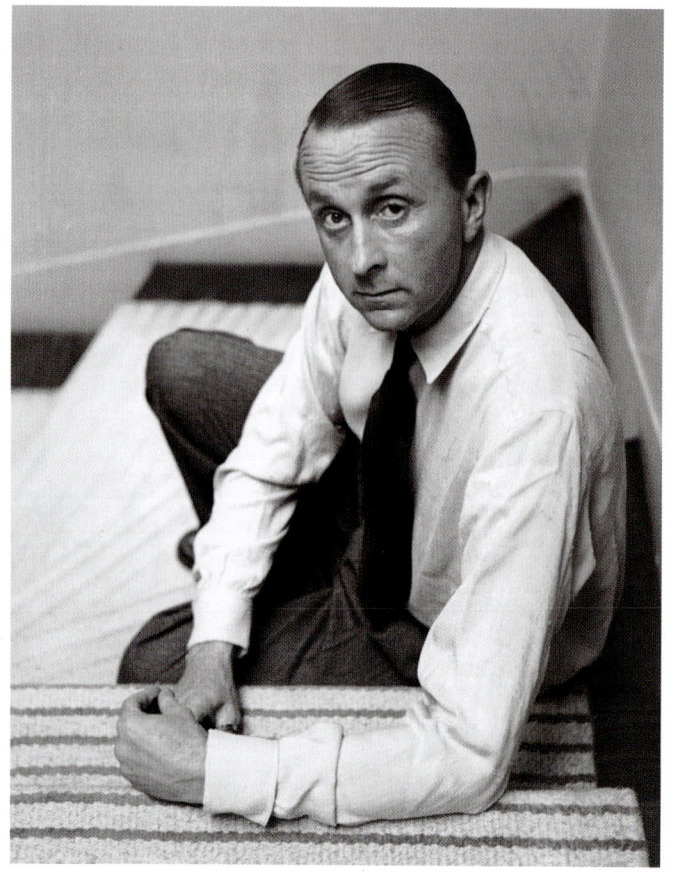

LEFT: Whitney Warren Jr. in his first house on Telegraph Hill, San Francisco, 1947. OPPOSITE: Lyon's photograph of Warren's library appeared as a rare—for the period—full-page color image in the October 1947 issue of *House & Garden*. The distinguished mix of traditional sculpture, paintings, and tapestries was juxtaposed with modern furnishings including tables and a corner sofa.

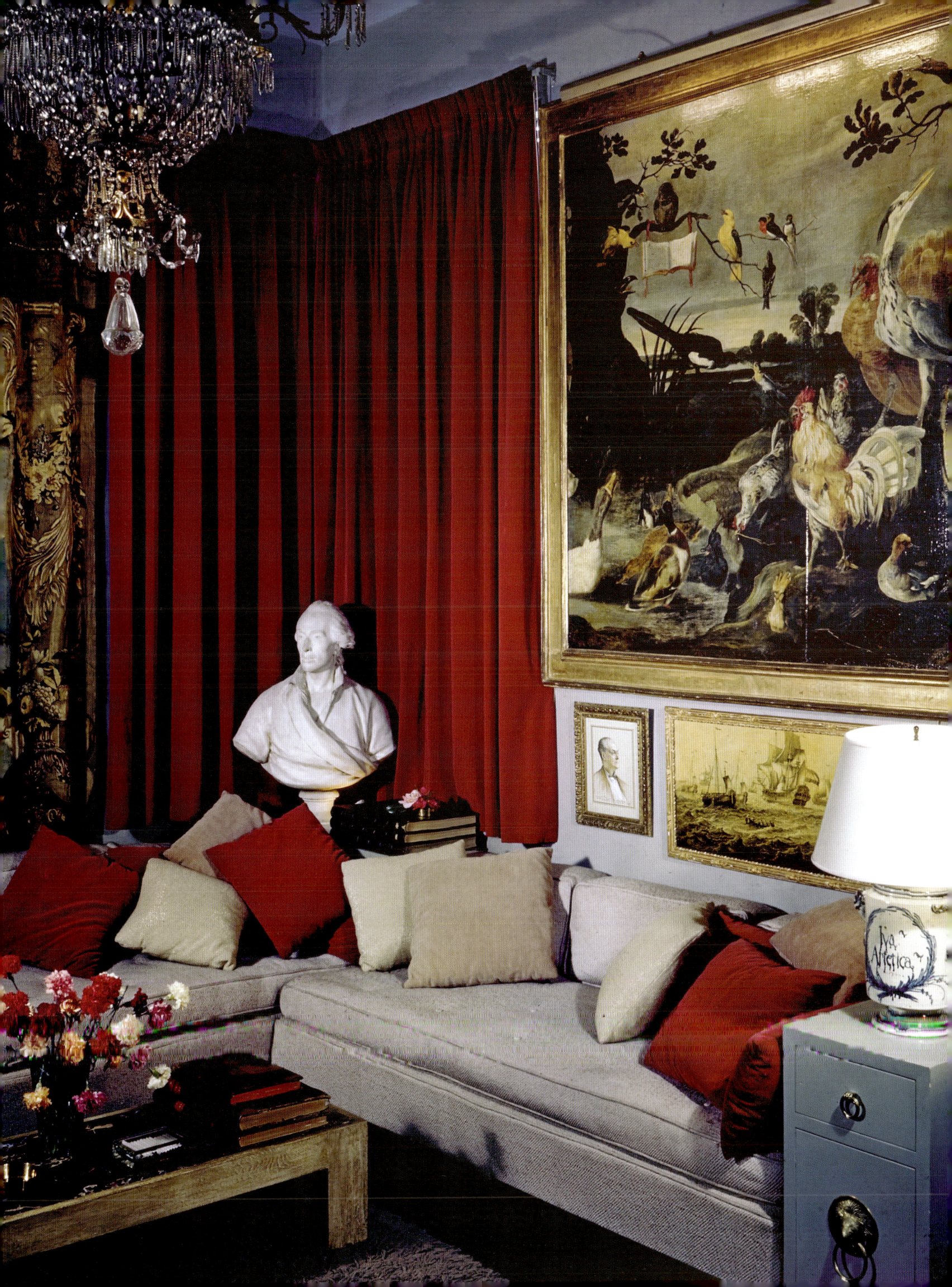

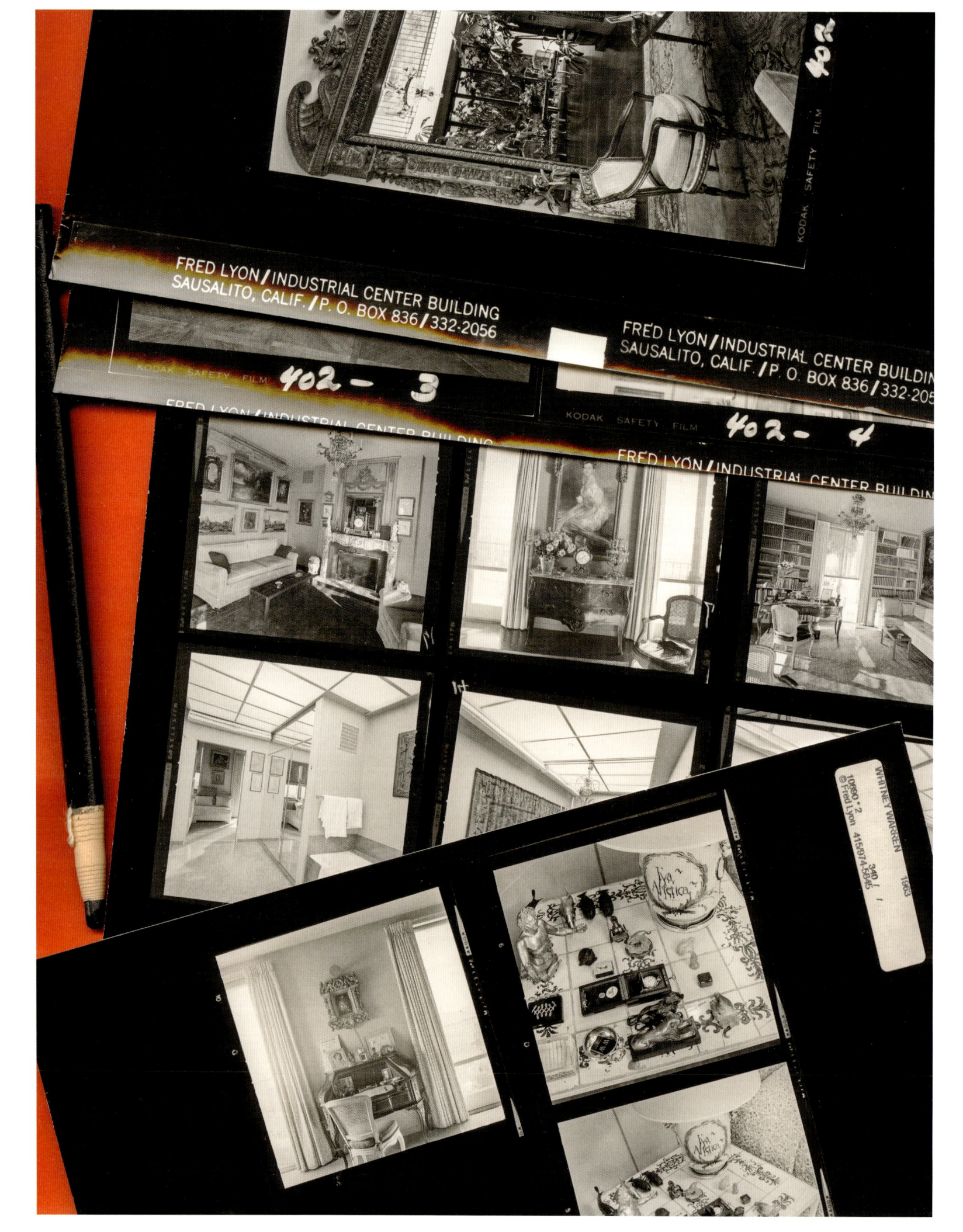

FRED LYON/INDUSTRIAL CENTER BUILDING
SAUSALITO, CALIF./P. O. BOX 836/332-2056

FRED LYON/INDUSTRIAL CENTER BUILDING
SAUSALITO, CALIF./P. O. BOX 836/332-205

KODAK SAFETY FILM   402 - 3

KODAK SAFETY FILM   402 - 4

FRED LYON/INDUSTRIAL CENTER BUILDING

WHITNEY WARREN
10890 · 2   340 /
© Fred Lyon   415/974-5645   1963

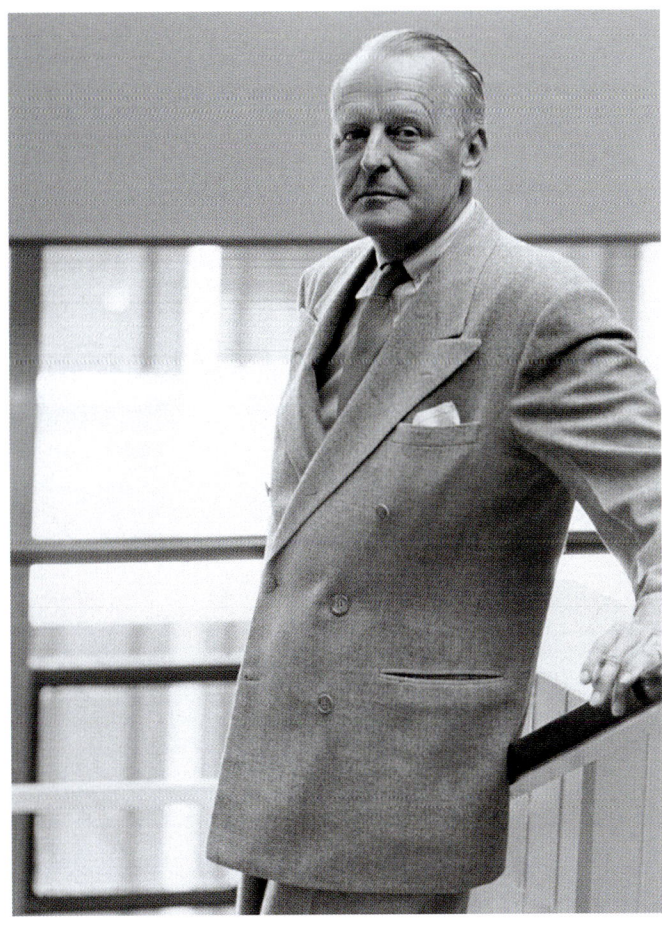

OPPOSITE: Fred Lyon photographed Whitney Warren Jr.'s second house on Telegraph Hill multiple times. These contact sheets are from a shoot in 1963. RIGHT: Architect Gardner Dailey, who helped introduce modernism to Northern California, 1948.

designed by master architect Gardner Dailey (1895–1967), who was well known for his elegant, modern designs.[54] The interior, as Lyon remembers it, was designed by a team only Warren could have assembled: "Frances Elkins and I think maybe Van Day Truex each had a hand in decorating it."[55] The assignment called for black-and-white and color pictures. Most interior photography up to that time had been in black and white, and many photographers were not yet adept at using color. Lyon was. He says, "I had shot a little color at Art Center, and I used Kodachrome in the Navy whenever I could: indoors, outdoors, on transport aircraft in flight, with all kinds of lighting. I wasn't afraid of working in color."[56]

Warren was the son of Whitney Warren Sr., the prizewinning architect of Grand Central Terminal in New York and other landmarks, and a bon vivant "active in New York Society, most notably in Stanford White's inner circle."[57] The Warren family was part of the old elite of New York. The younger Warren, who relocated west to attend Berkeley, was later known as the most civilized man in San Francisco. He became famous enough to attract the venom of a waspish Cecil Beaton, who wrote in his diary, "He knows his mind even if it is a small one."[58] Despite Beaton's claim, Whitney Warren Jr. seems like a very interesting man. He settled in San Francisco after leaving a colorful trail from New York. He fought in the First World War, going to France in 1916 at the age of eighteen, a year before the United States entered the war. He served

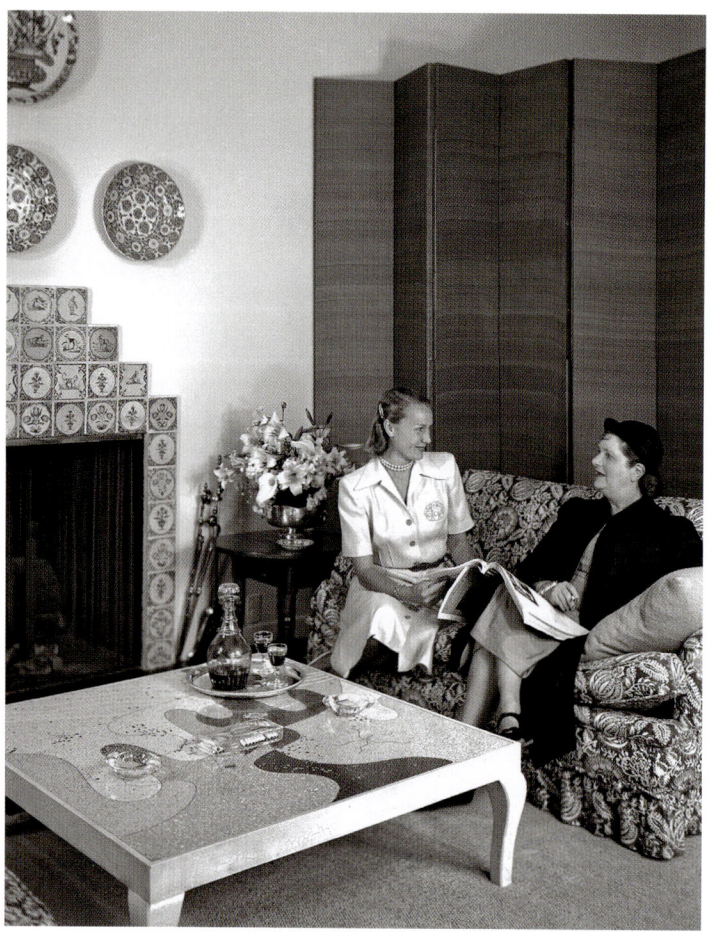

bravely, receiving the Croix de Guerre and the Médaille Militaire.[59] He was wounded in the autumn of 1918 and returned home. Back in New York, Warren attracted headlines for a series of romances with an heiress and a starlet. In the years since, Warren was thought to have been discreetly gay. Or perhaps not so discreetly. The *San Francisco Chronicle* reported that Warren "was known to be flamboyant and decadent, and during World War II, [his] house was off limits to the military because of its notorious reputation."[60]

When Lyon met Warren in 1947, he was a pillar of San Francisco society and his house was definitely on limits. Lyon says, "Photographing his house was a coup for me. On the day of the assignment, I took every bit of gear I owned to that house."[61] The

House & Garden editor had told Lyon a woman would meet him at Warren's place. The editor did not tell him who the woman was or her role in the shoot, probably assuming Lyon would figure it out. When he arrived at Warren's house, Lyon says, "I was met by this lady who had spit curls and was flat-footed, so she waddled walking around. She kept tweaking furniture. I didn't know who she was."[62]

The woman was Frances Elkins (1888–1953), the interior decorator whom the *New York Times* has described as a "creator of rooms that in fact deserved the description 'timeless.'"[63] Lyon says, "When I started in interior photography, I just did it my way."[64] He adds, "Because I had experience in photography, but no experience in interior design or decor, I was impatient with the stuff I saw in the

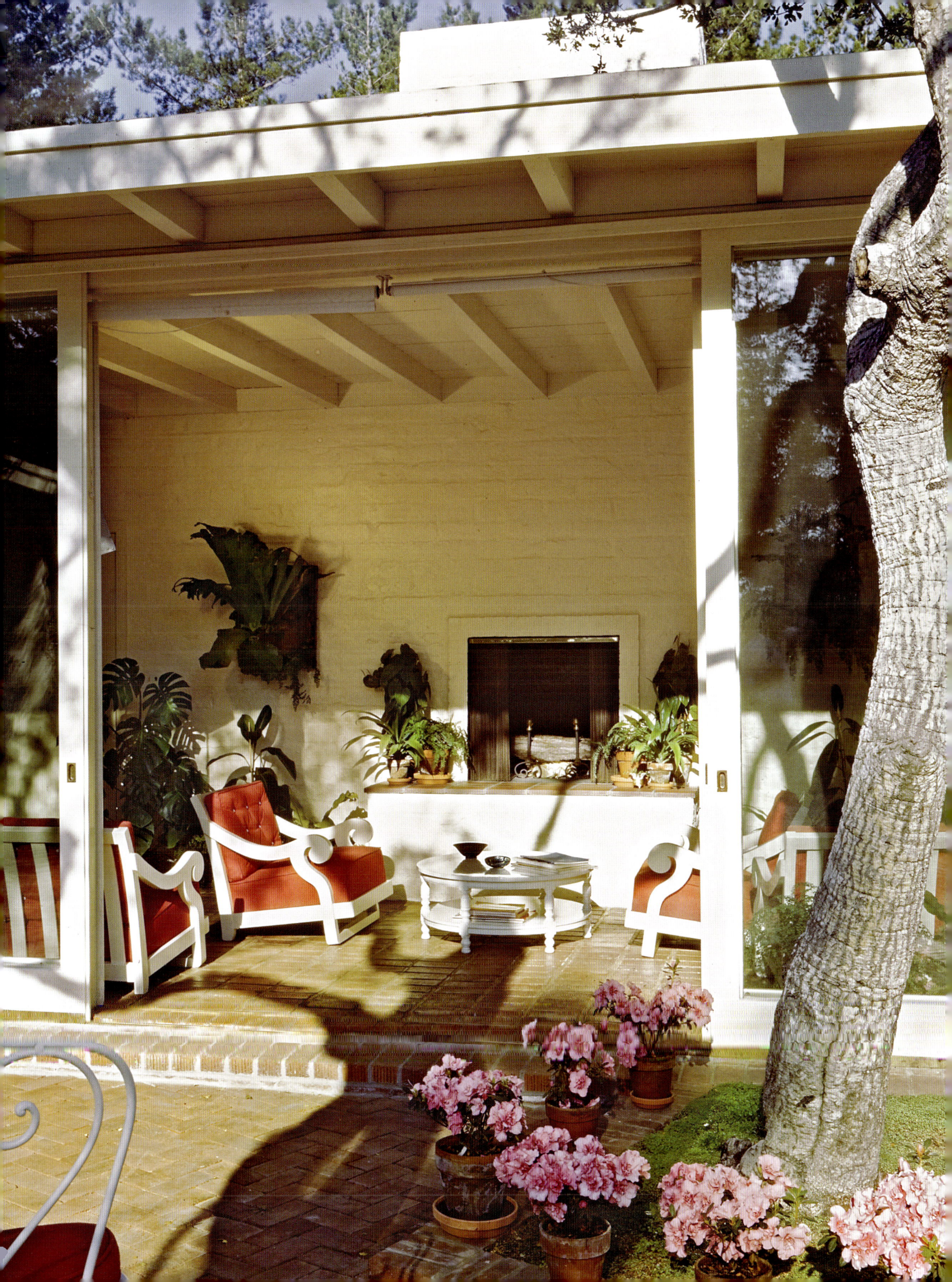

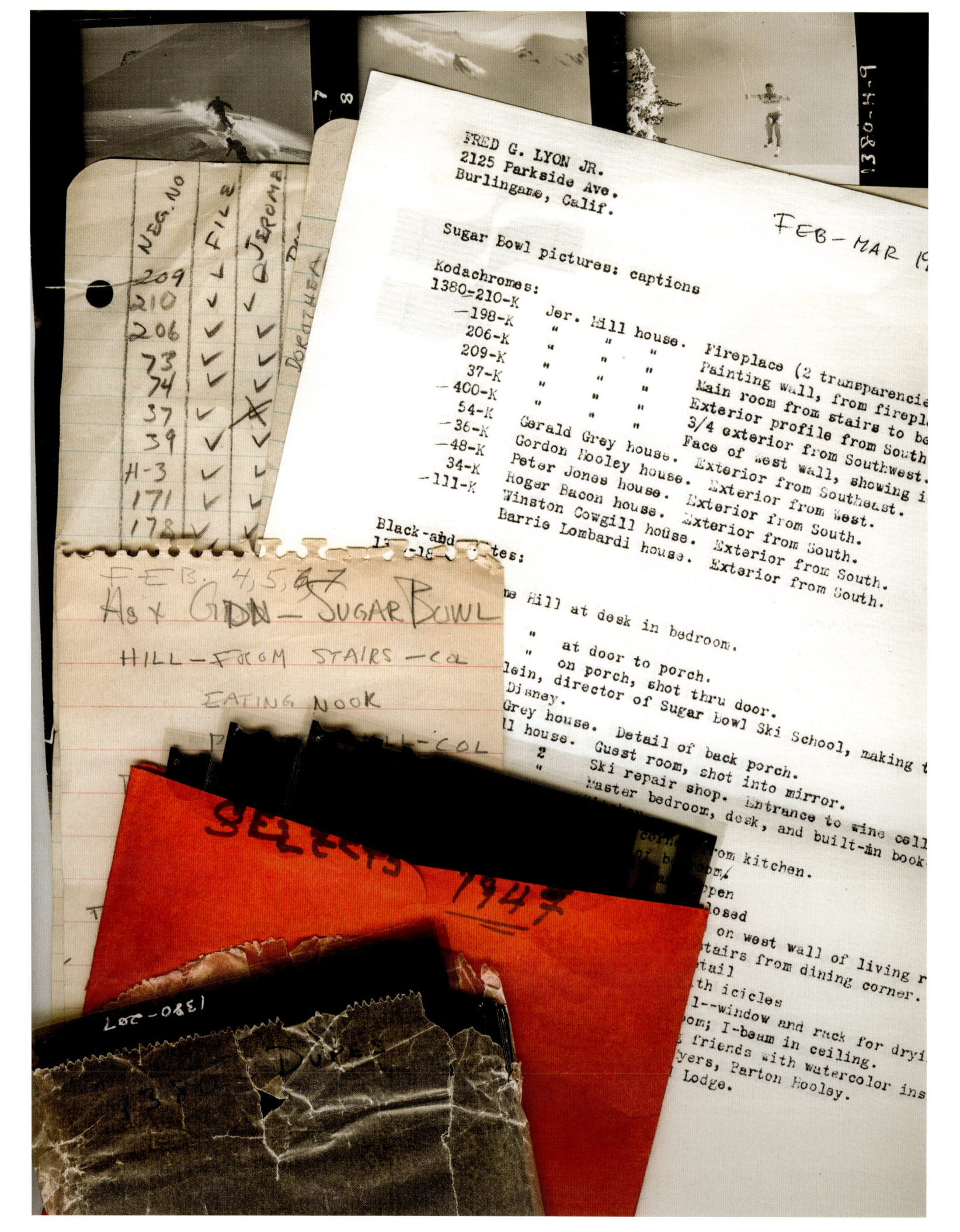

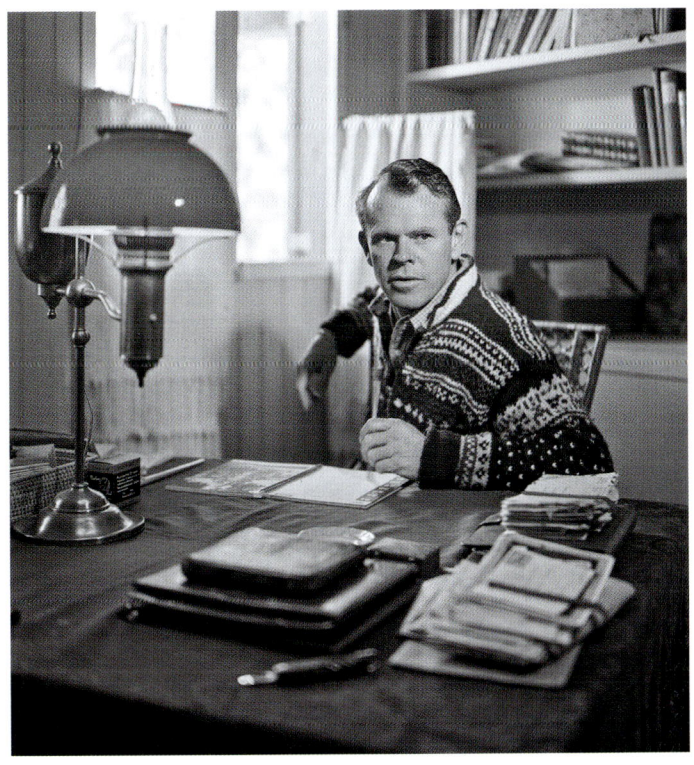

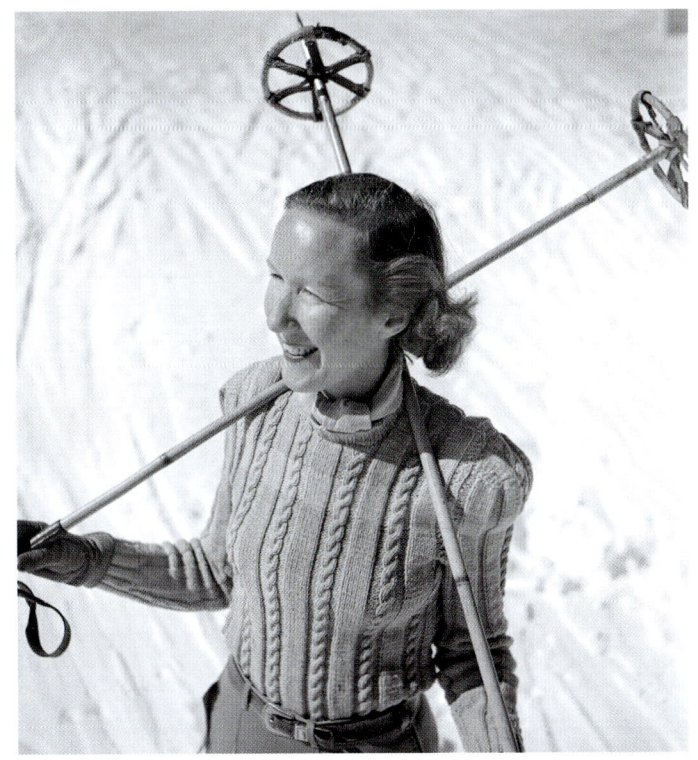

magazines and paid no attention to it."[65] When the story appeared in *House & Garden* twenty months later, in November 1948, it was a success and had a major impact on Lyon's career.[66] "They were damn good pictures. We scored very heavily," Lyon says.[67] "I had no idea how important this would be for me. Frances Elkins called me on the telephone and said, 'I thought we did very well. I have a number of jobs I am working on. I would like you to look at them because I would like you to photograph them.' I was desperate for money, so I jumped at it."[68]

As for the magazine, they liked Lyon's work enough to send him out again in March 1947, a few weeks after the photo shoot, to the tony Sugar Bowl ski resort along the Donner Pass in the

Sierra Nevada, to photograph the mountain retreat of Jerome Hill, the grandson of J. J. Hill, the head of the Great Northern Railway. Lyon says, "Jerome Hill was a young man with great charm and talent. He was gay and lived very well. He built the house because he was a great skier. I think he might have designed it himself."[69] Lyon's shoot coincided with a party Hill was giving. When an unexpected storm snowed in the group for a few days, the guests got to know each other during what was a much happier version of the Donner party. Lyon says, "Among the guests was a petite lady, Dorothea Walker, the West Coast editor of *Vogue*. She knew everybody in California society."[70] Dorothea and Fred had time to get acquainted.

OPPOSITE: Negatives, contact sheets, and notes from Lyon's shoot of Jerome Hill's ski house at Sugar Bowl in Norden, during the first week of February 1947. ABOVE LEFT: Jerome Hill at his ski house, 1947. ABOVE RIGHT: Dorothea Walker, *Vogue*'s West Coast editor, was a guest at Hill's house when Lyon photographed it for *House & Garden* in 1947. Walker and Lyon would collaborate on magazine stories for many years.

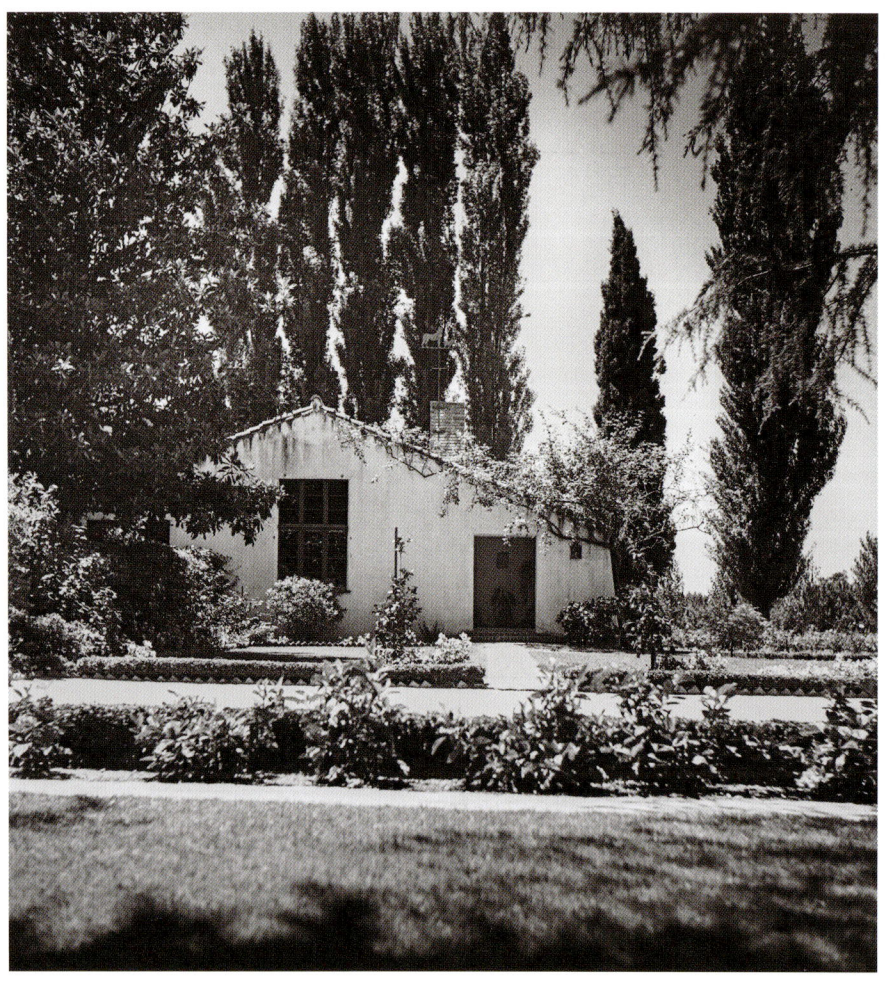

BEAR RIVER RANCH
Sacramento Valley, 1948

The great San Francisco socialite Whitney Warren Jr.'s Bear River Ranch was a working ranch, with many acres of orchards growing peaches, pears, almonds, and walnuts. Whitney spent most of his weekdays there overseeing the work. I know from my family's ranch in the Sacramento Delta area that in ranching, there are two seasons: mud and dust. But Whitney being Whitney, his ranch house was decorated and equipped to entertain marvelously. There were poured-concrete floors, polished and stained black, and white furniture. The decoration worked very well, even if it wasn't practical for ranching.

It gets very hot in the Sacramento Valley, and I took these photographs on a steamy summer day, so the ranch's wonderful

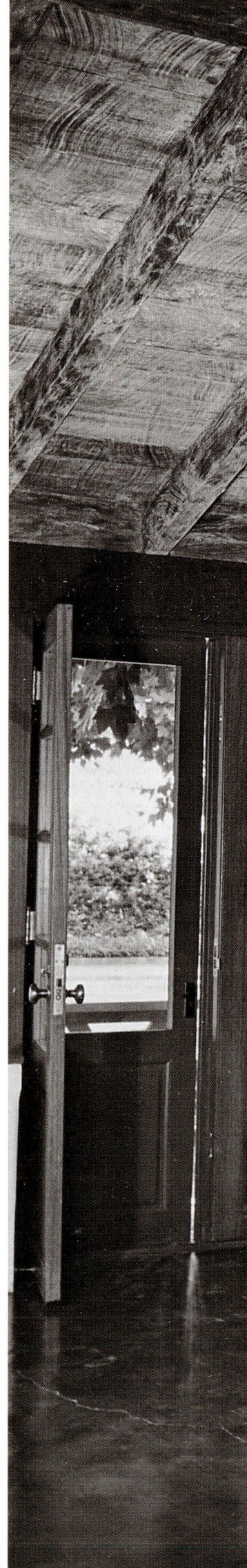

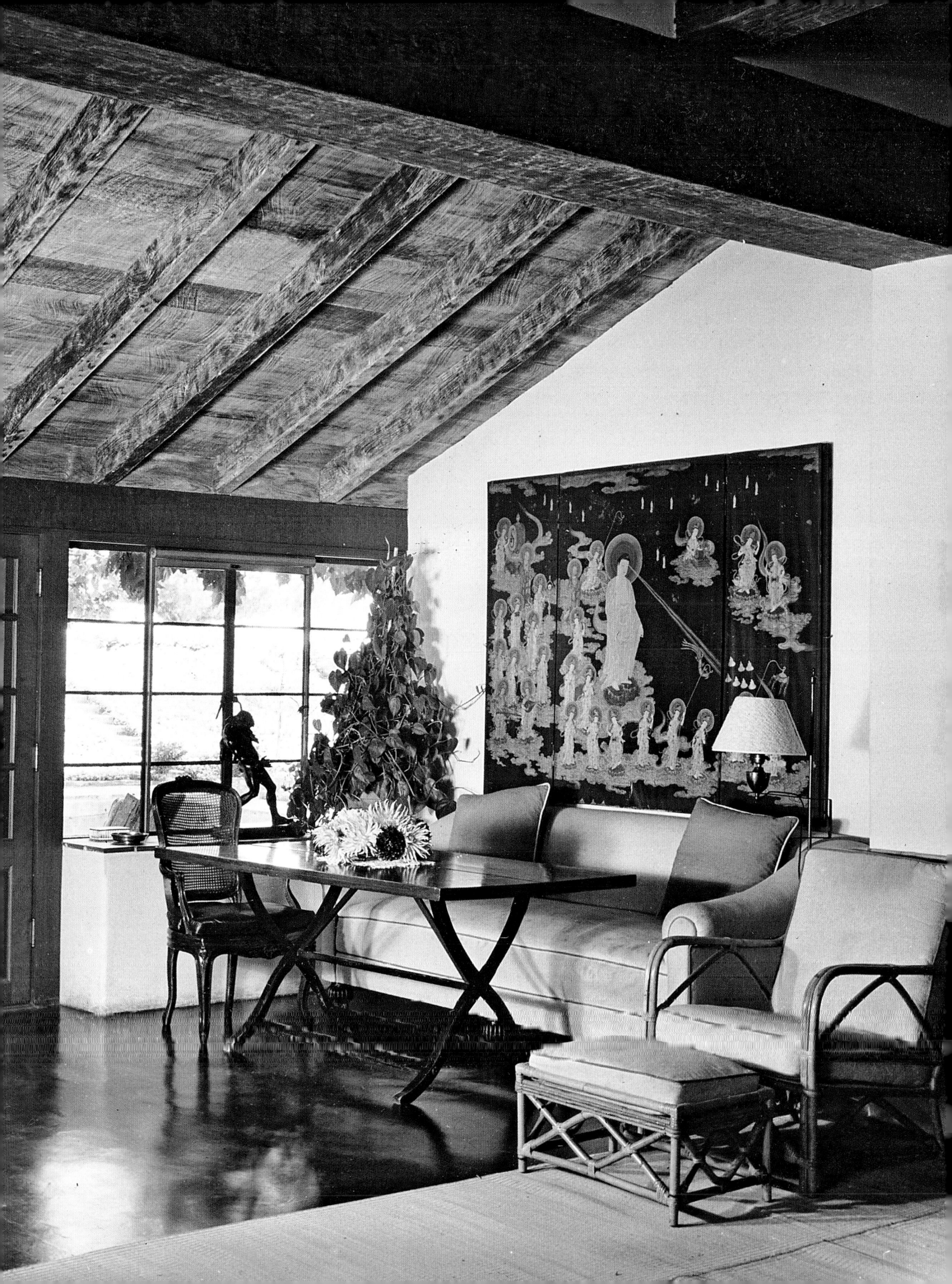

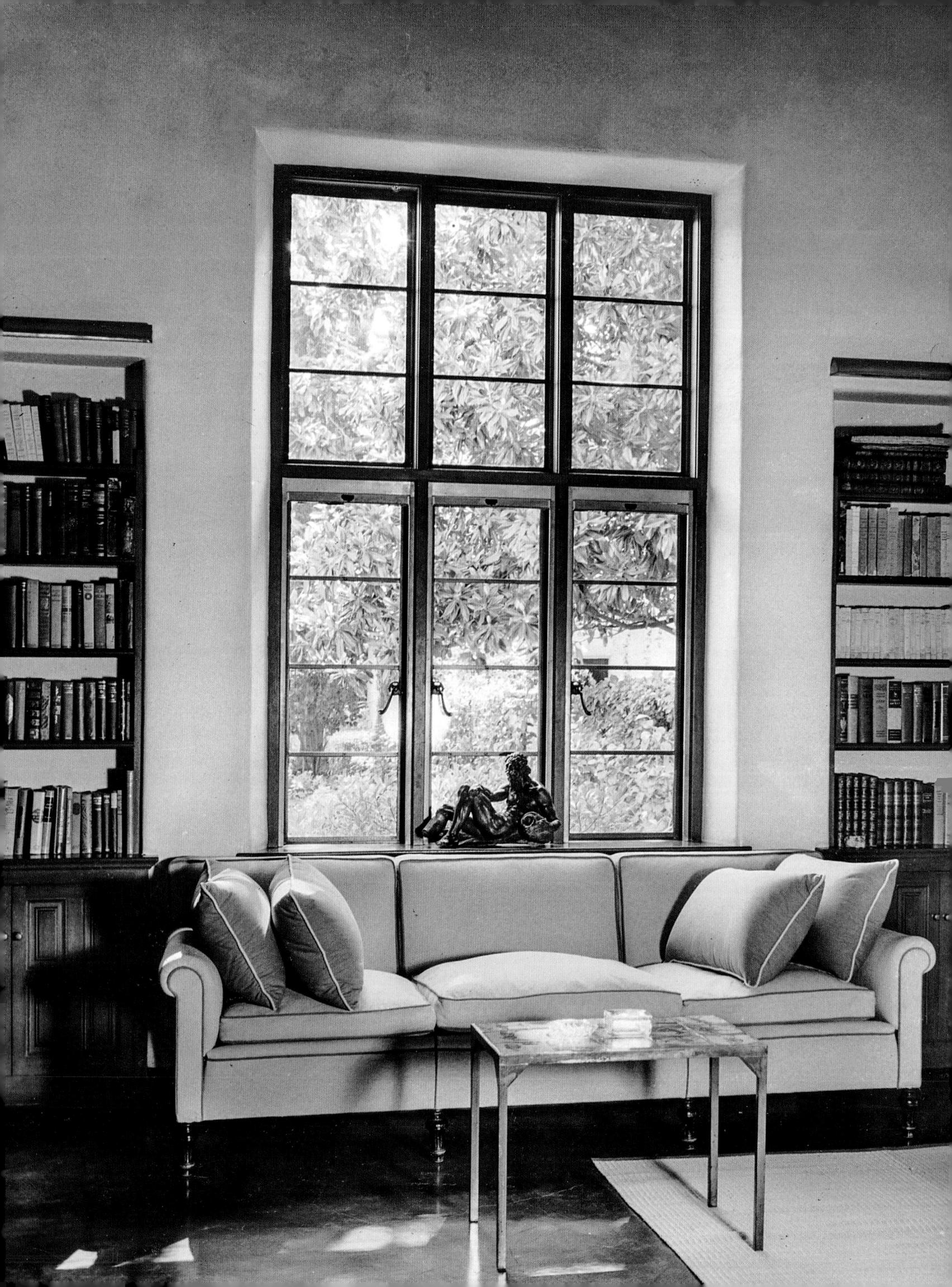

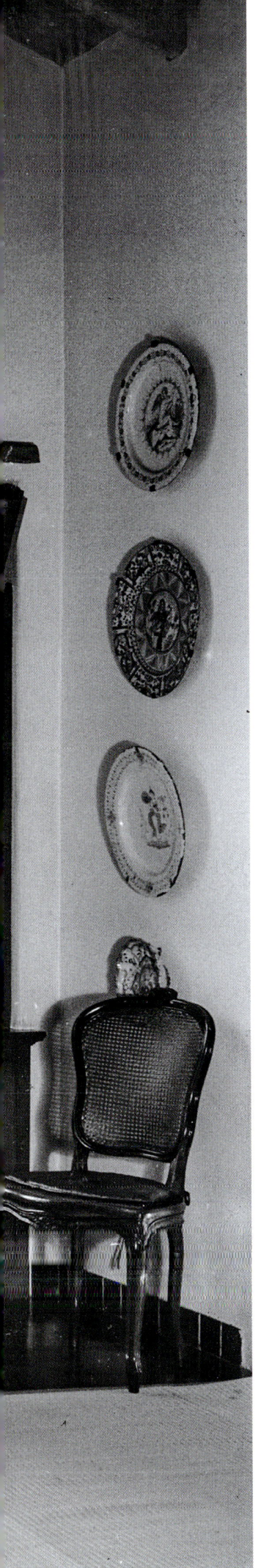

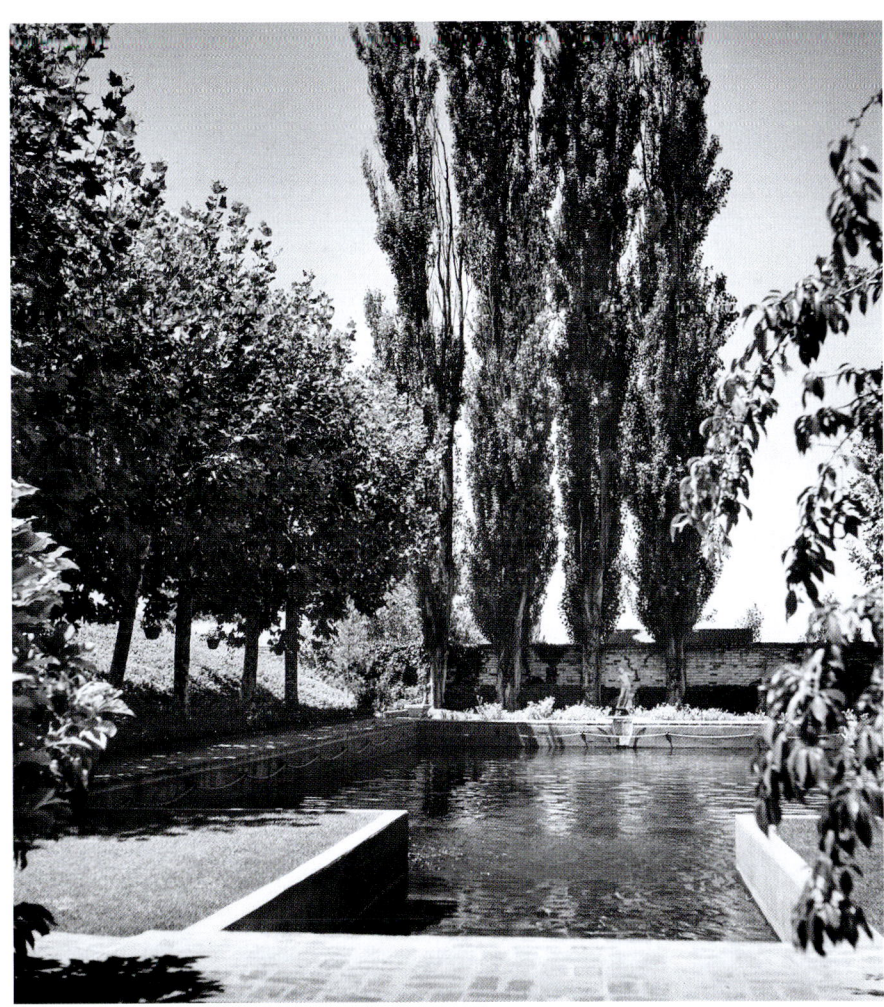

swimming pool was central to my shoot. It was an isle of cool respite amid a peach orchard. Dorothea Walker, whom I had met only a few months earlier at Jerome Hill's ski house, and I worked together on this shoot. The photographs appeared in the November 1948 issue of *House & Garden*, along with images from Warren's San Francisco house, in an article titled "Week End in Reverse," alluding to the fact that Warren spent weekdays in the country and weekends in the city. Whitney was not present for this shoot, but he made sure everything was ready for us.   —*F.L.*

The exterior of Whitney Warren Jr.'s Sacramento Valley ranch house (PAGE 46) had white plaster walls and a tile roof. The interior spaces had rough-hewn redwood beams stippled in whitewash, and the furnishings reflected the owner's refined taste: a Japanese screen, oyster-white upholstered seating, books, and majolica. Pleached plane trees, beds of petunias, tall Lombardy poplars, and a marble sculpture surrounded the pool (ABOVE). Lyon photographed the house in 1948.

WHITNEY WARREN JR. HOUSE
San Francisco, 1947

During his life, Whitney Warren Jr. owned, in succession, two residences on Telegraph Hill, each designed by Gardner Dailey. I photographed both places. Taken in February 1947, these photographs are from my first assignment for *House & Garden*—and mark the first time I met Frances Elkins. I look at this shoot as the start of my career in interior photography.

I arrived at Whitney's house and was greeted by a short lady with spit curls. This, of course, was Frances Elkins, but I had no idea who she was or that she had decorated the place. I set about photographing the house, and Frances watched me work and made small adjustments to the furniture. I was planning a shot through an ornate doorway. There was a framed picture hanging on a wall that I thought was not good for the photograph I wanted to make, so I took it down. Frances put it back up. When she left the room, I took it back down and made the exposures. I wasn't going to argue with her, but I was going to get the photograph I wanted. Frances and I were there all day for this shoot. Whitney was not present.

Frances Elkins was excited by the photographs—the story, with Warren's ranch and city house, in the November 1948 issue of *House & Garden*, and especially a photograph from the Telegraph Hill shoot that was previously printed in the magazine's October 1947 issue (see page 39). She called me to say how much she liked the pictures and that she had various projects she would like me to photograph. We worked together for the rest of her life.　　　—F.L.

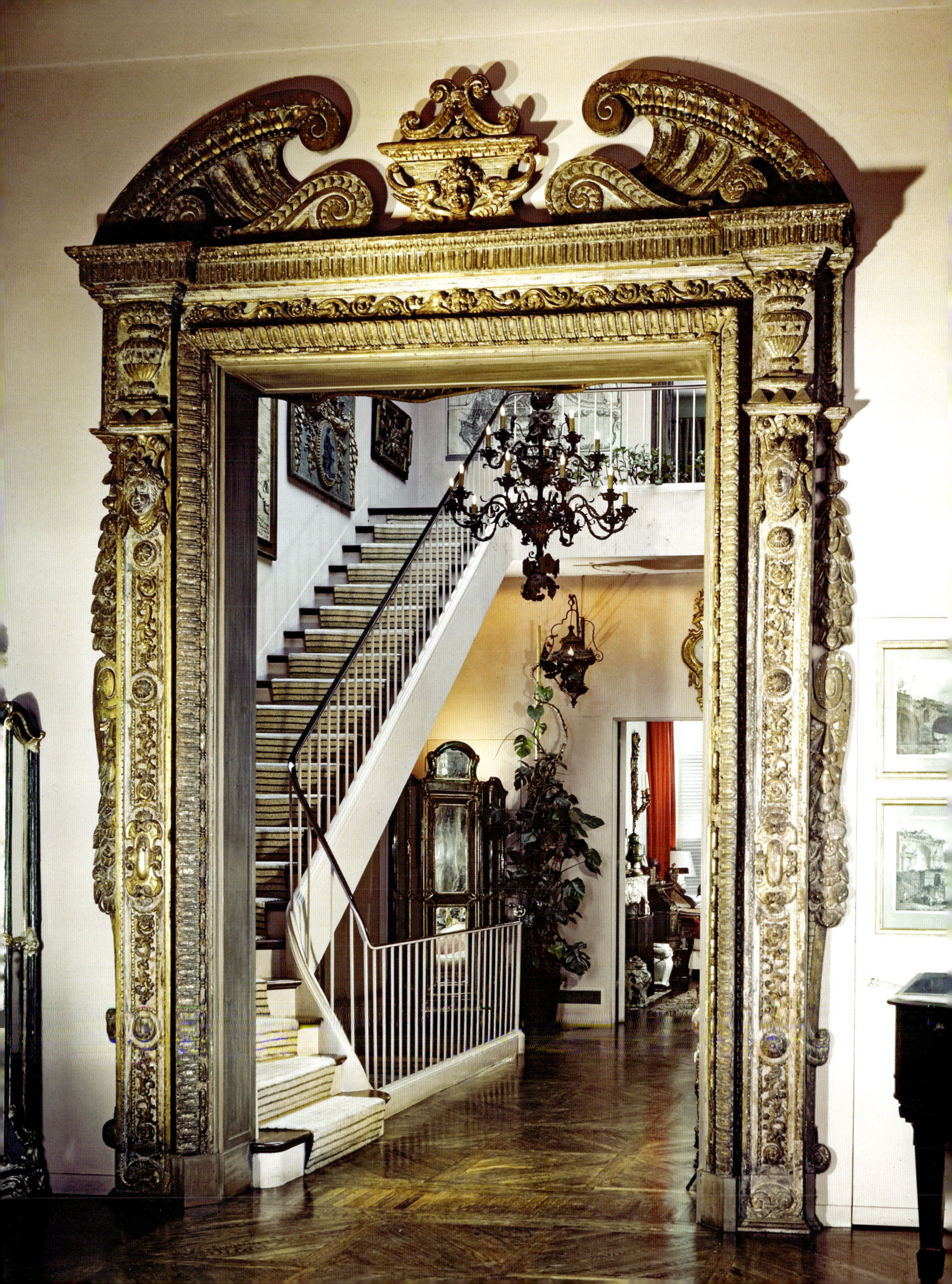

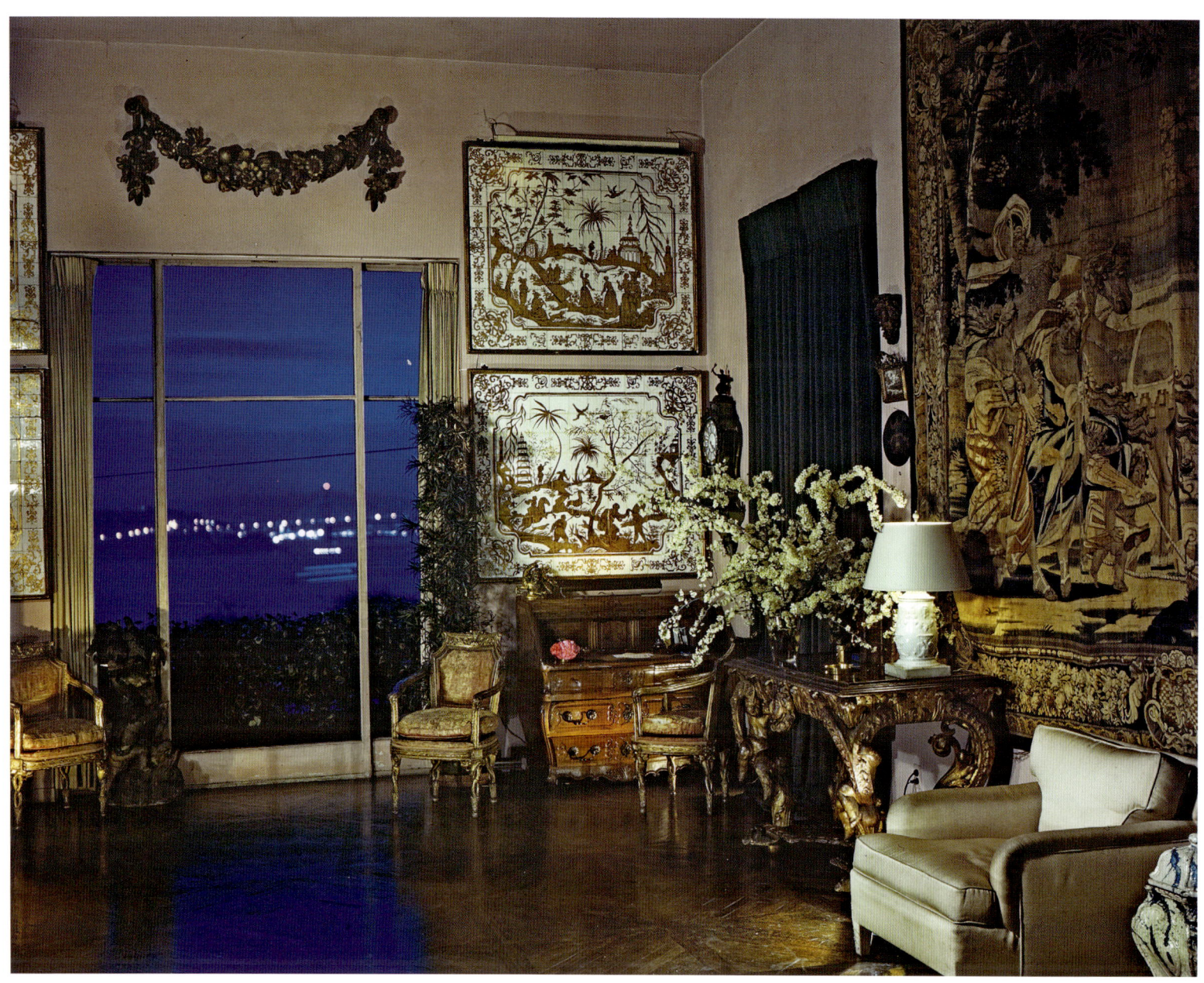

PAGE 51: Whitney Warren Jr.'s first house on Telegraph Hill, San Francisco, 1947. Lyon's view of the stair hall, as seen from the living room, is framed by the Florentine Renaissance door surround. ABOVE: The living room, with a nighttime view of San Francisco Bay and the Bay Bridge, revealed the owner's eclectic taste for antique and modern furnishings, including Baroque tapestries and decorative tile panels. OPPOSITE, CLOCKWISE FROM TOP LEFT: Warren's library, with its French eighteenth-century mantelpiece and overmantel; view from Warren's bedroom to the stair hall, with a carved door originally made for an Italian confessional; a portrait of Warren's mother by Giovanni Boldini hangs above a French commode; a corner of the intimate library, with Warren's writing desk and red velvet curtains.

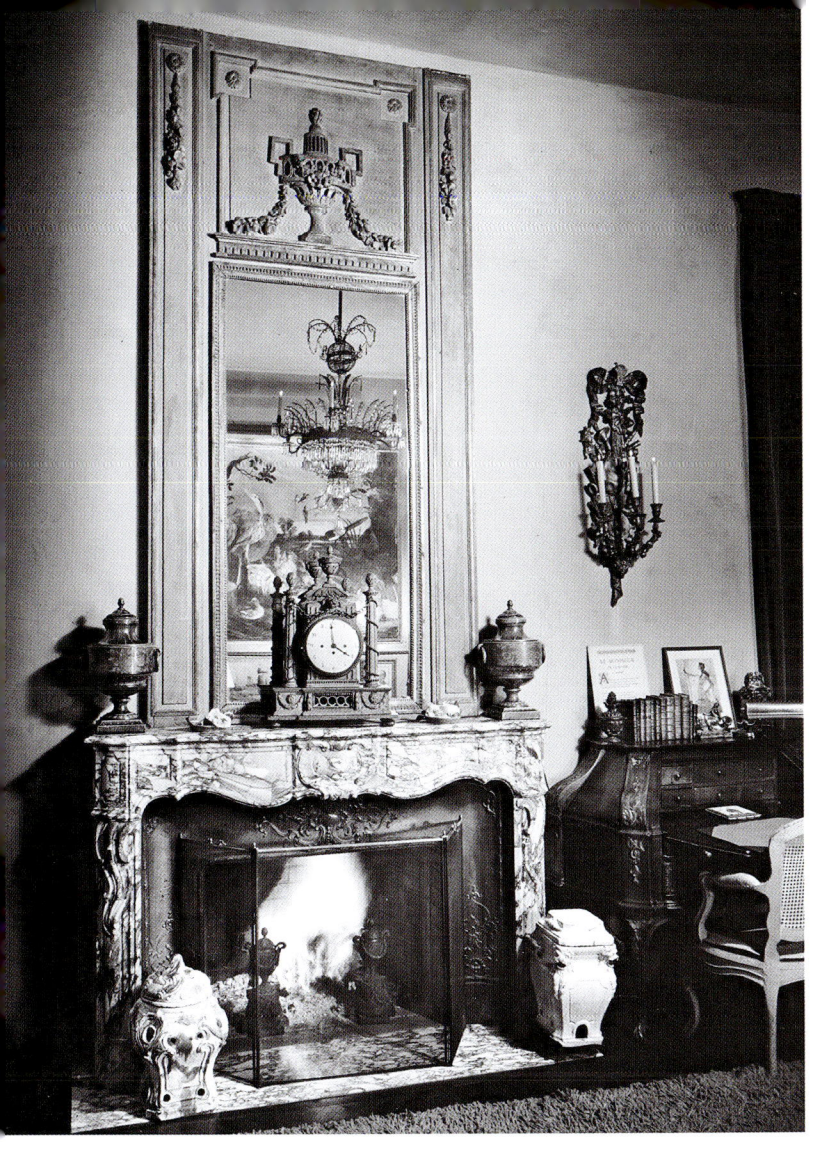

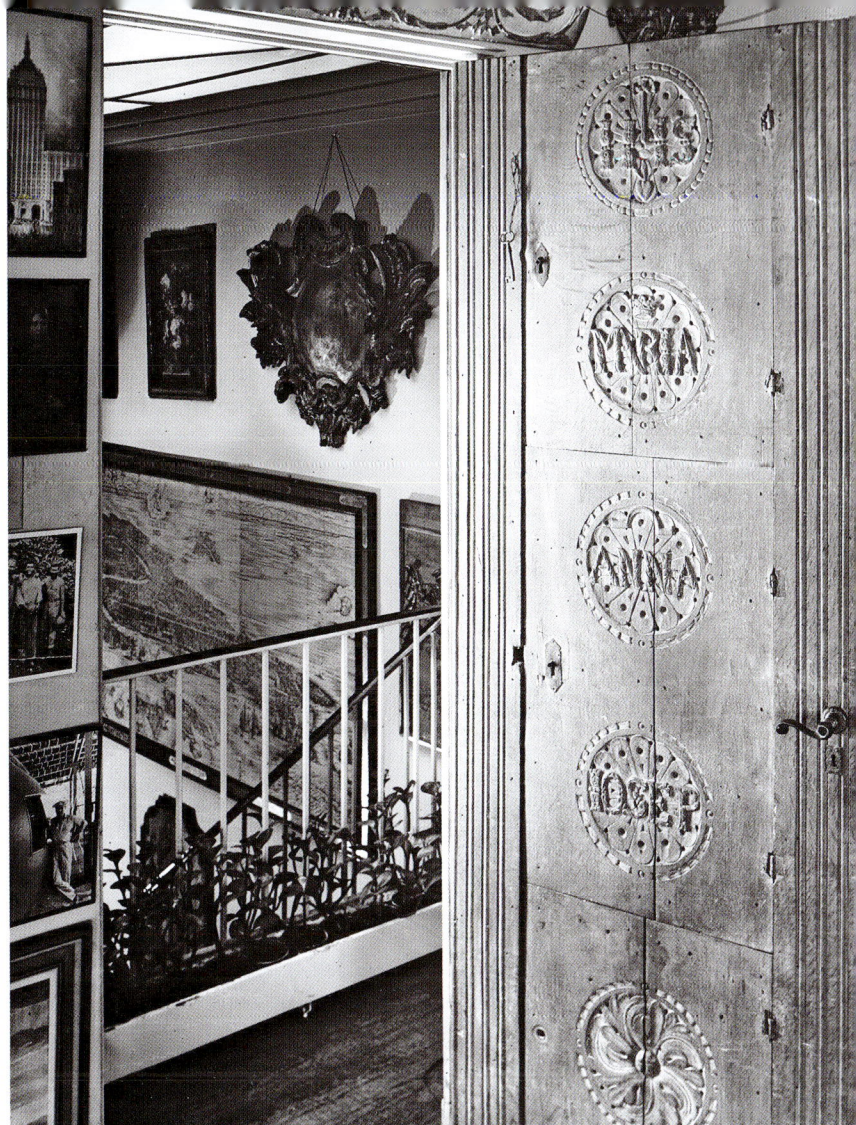

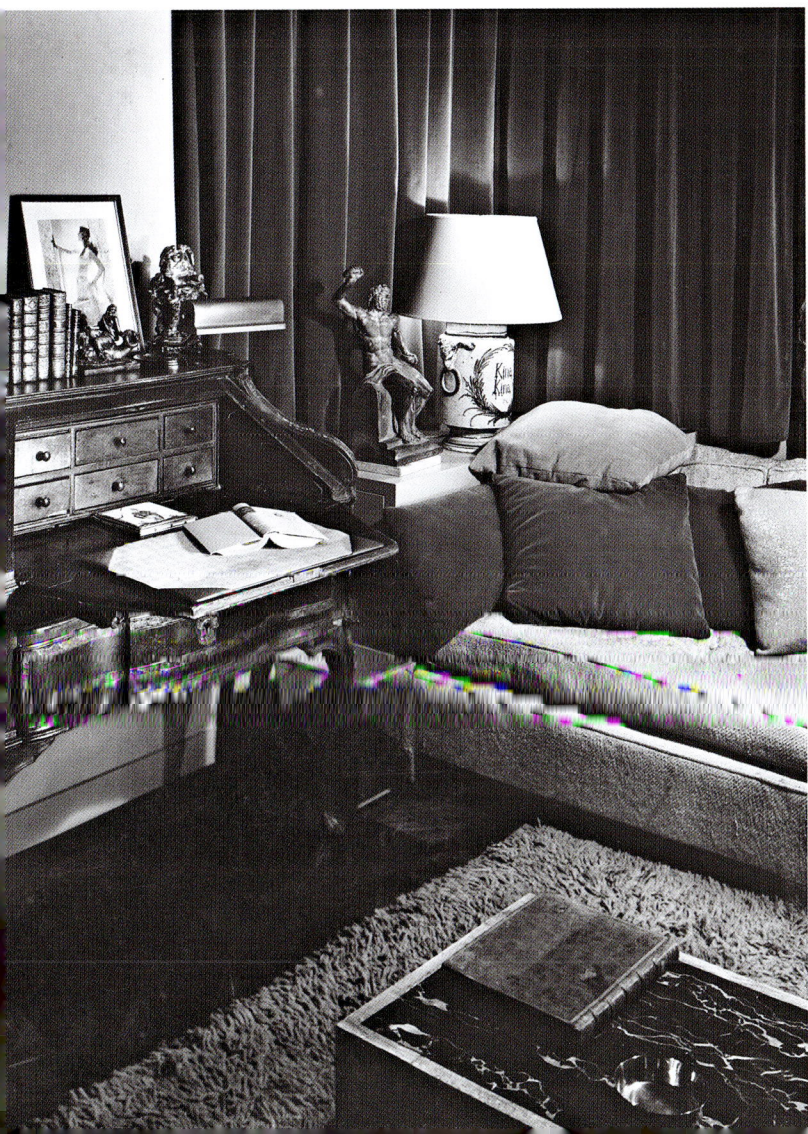

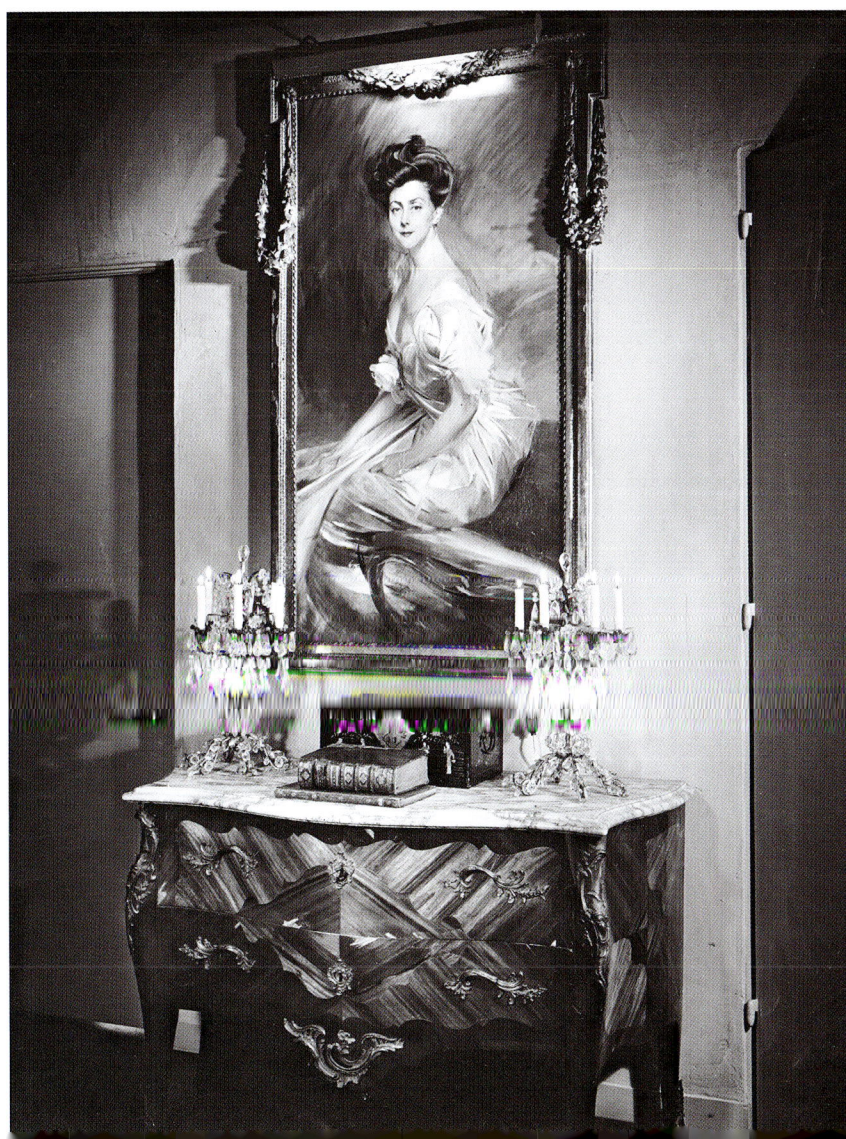

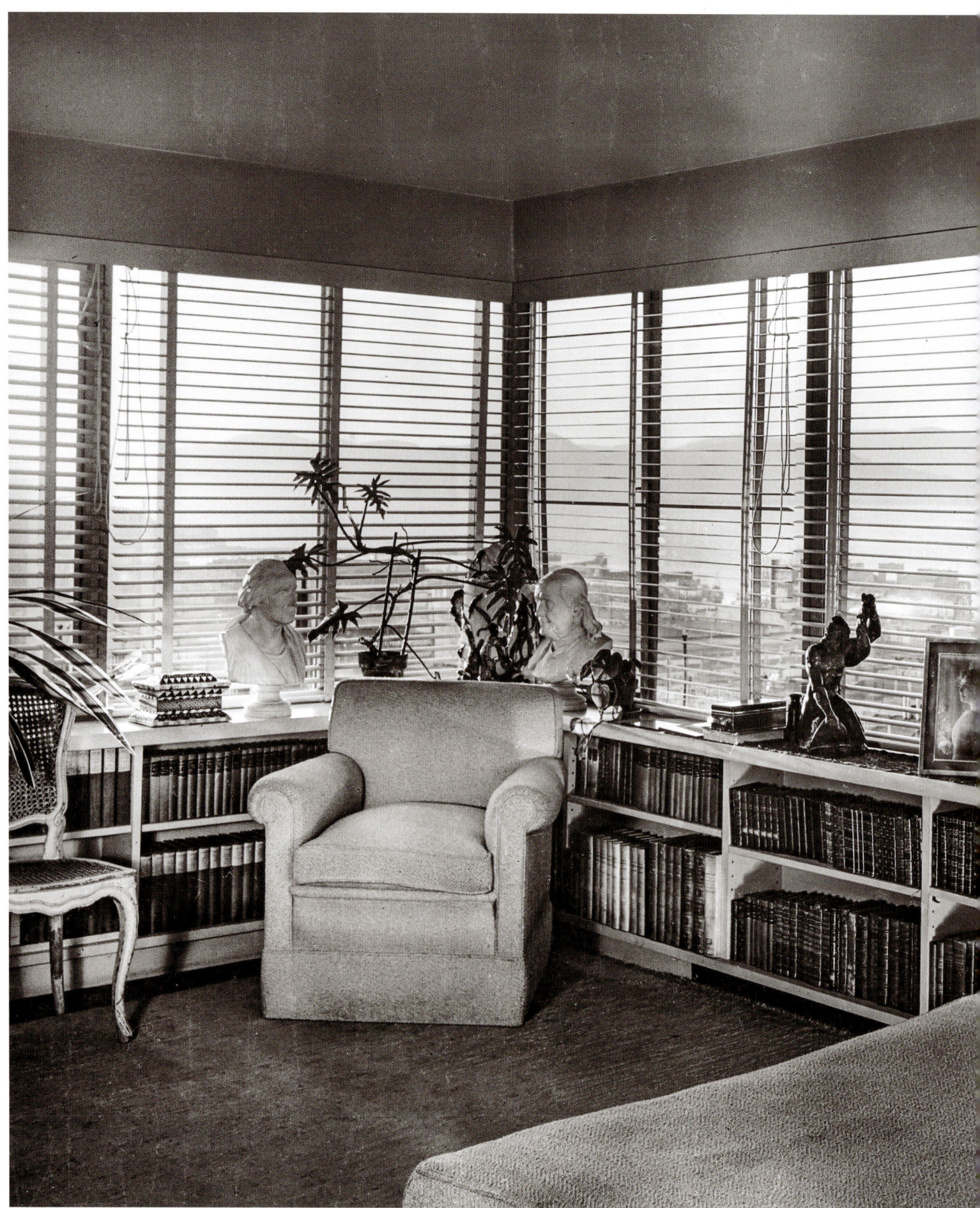

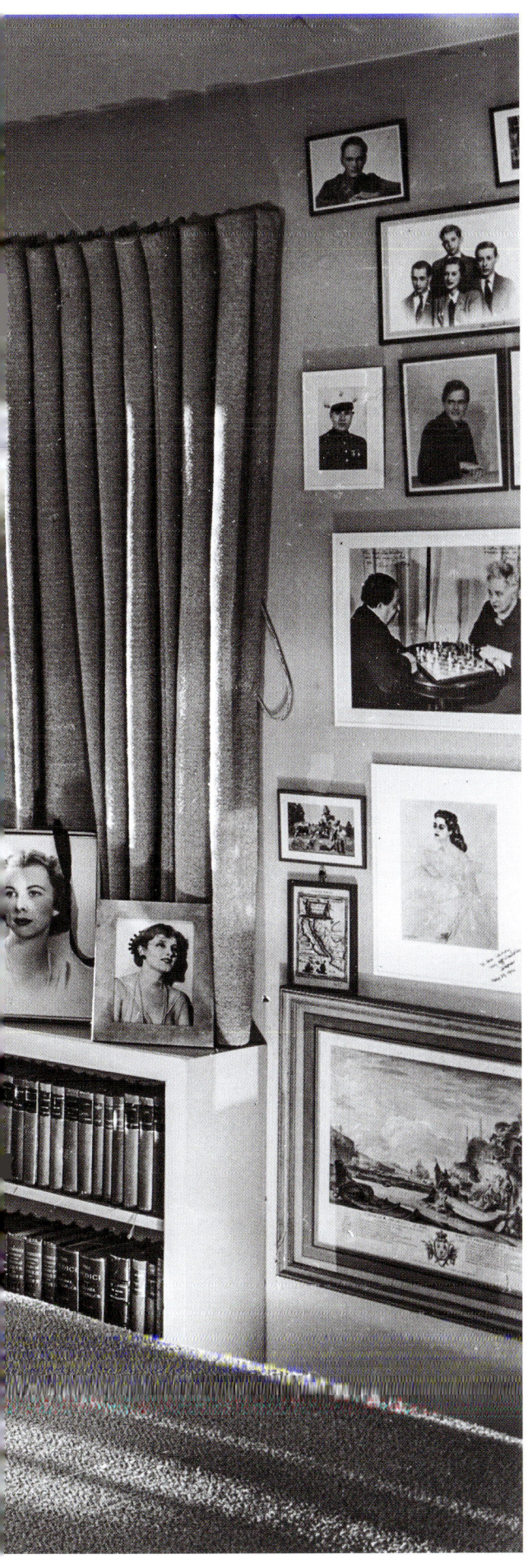

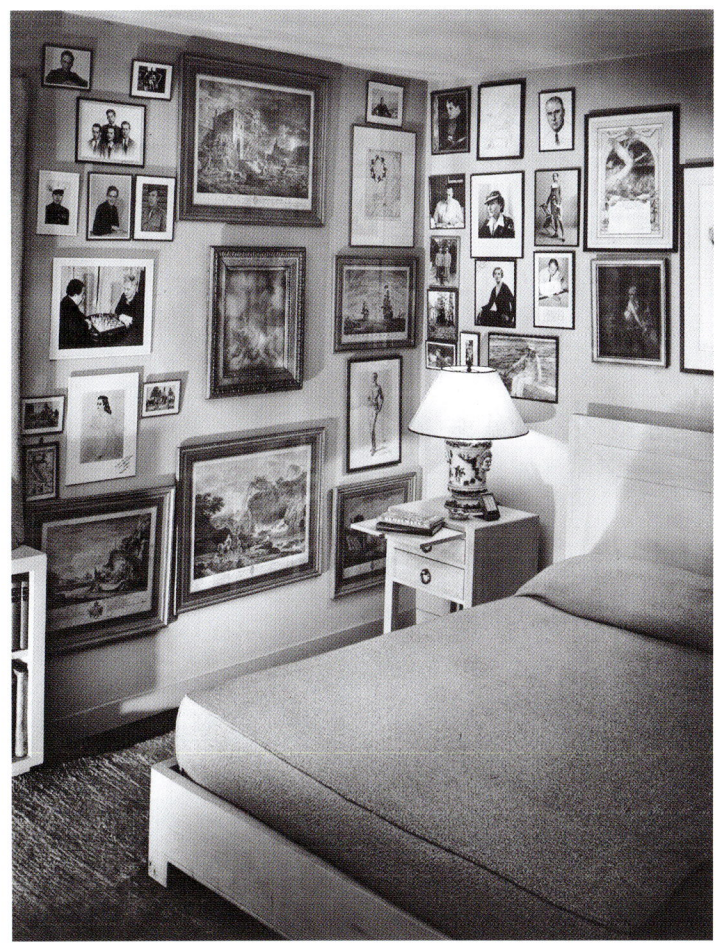

LEFT AND ABOVE: Gardner Dailey designed Warren's bedroom with an open corner view of San Francisco Bay. Frances Elkins used a Dorothy Liebes sea-green textile for the chair upholstery and bed covering. Family photographs and prints cover celadon-painted walls.

WHITNEY WARREN JR. HOUSE
San Francisco, 1974

In 1960, Whitney moved to a different Gardner Dailey house, located about sixty degrees clockwise around Telegraph Hill from his earlier residence. It was situated a little lower down the hill, but it had much better views, facing downtown San Francisco, and received more sunlight.

These photographs of Whitney's second home on Telegraph Hill were taken for the May/June 1974 issue of *Architectural Digest*. That magazine was unique among the notable magazines of the day in its editorial practice. Its powerful editor, Paige Rense, insisted that photographers (or the designers themselves) bear the cost of providing the photography. Because the magazine was such an important venue for architects, interior designers, and photographers, she usually got her way. Rense wanted Whitney's interiors and asked him to allow access. Whitney told her, "Well, you can send Mr. Horst or Fred Lyon." It's doubtful that Rense ever approached Horst P. Horst, and I refused to work for free. Because of Whitney's demand, Rense was stuck having to use, and pay for, me.

The decor of Whitney's second Telegraph Hill house is often credited to Billy Baldwin and Tony Hail. I think they may have been involved in decorating it, but I remember the decoration of the main spaces being faithful reproductions of Frances Elkins's work in Whitney's earlier Telegraph Hill house. In fact, I think he had Gardner Dailey design the new house to reproduce the spaces and accommodate the decor Whitney liked from his former residence. I attended parties at this second Telegraph Hill house. They were very social and fun. The second house has notoriety in San Francisco because it was to have been the scene of the wedding between the wealthy hotelier Newton Cope, a good friend of Whitney's, and Lee Radziwill, the sister of Jacqueline Kennedy Onassis. It was going to be a big social event of the city. The wedding had been long planned, but it was canceled at the last minute.   —F.L.

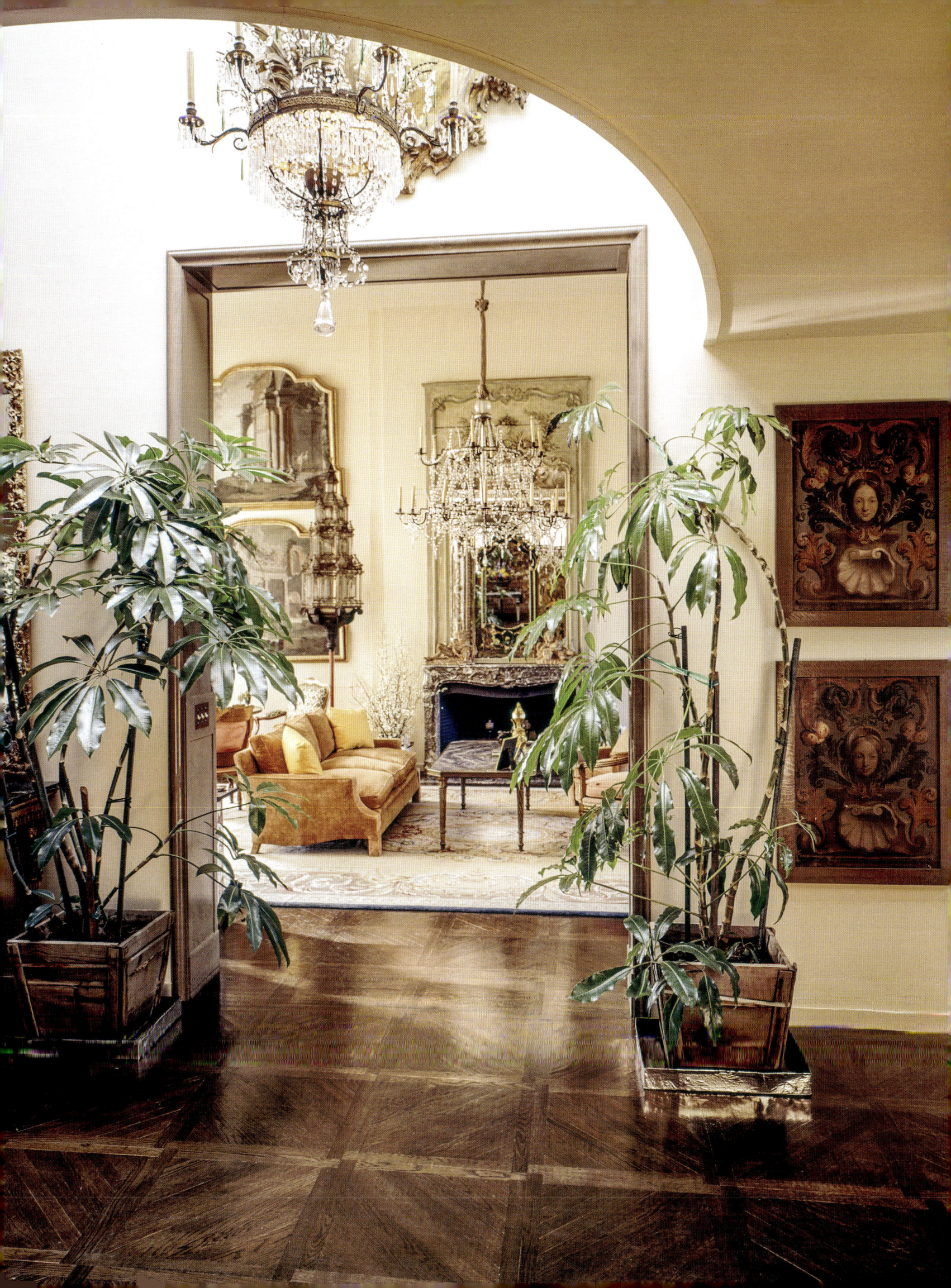

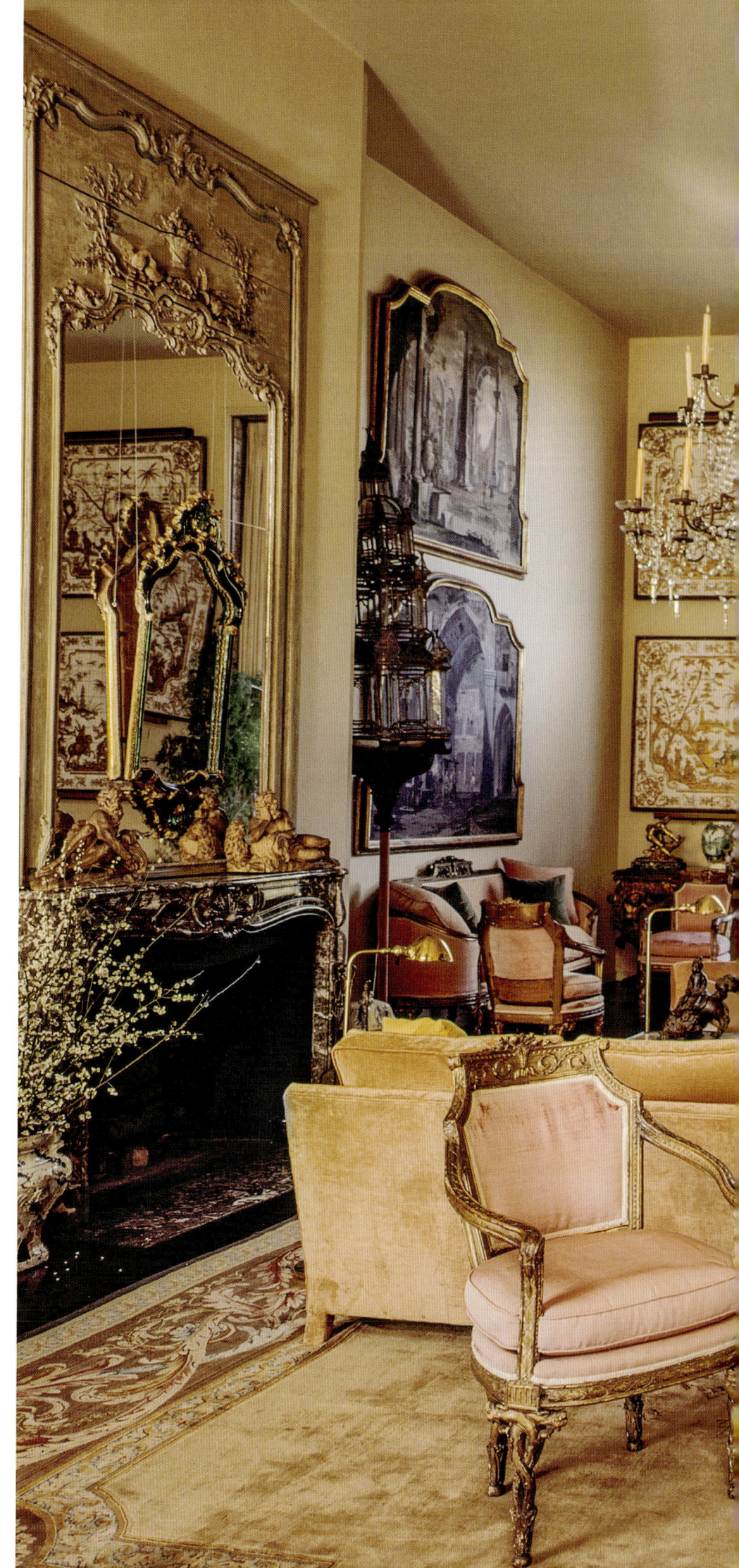

PAGE 57: The skylit entrance hall of Whitney Warren Jr.'s second house on Telegraph Hill, designed by Gardner Dailey and photographed by Lyon in 1974. RIGHT AND PAGE 60: Living room with Louis XV mantelpiece and trumeau mirror. The window is flanked by four Italian gilt-decorated white-tile panels after designs by Giovanni Battista Tiepolo. An eighteenth-century chandelier hangs from the nineteen-foot ceiling. PAGE 61: A marble bust of the Marquis de Méjanes by Jean-Antoine Houdon surveys the room. Two eighteenth-century Piedmontese chairs flank a hard-stone-topped table with a lapis lazuli amphora.

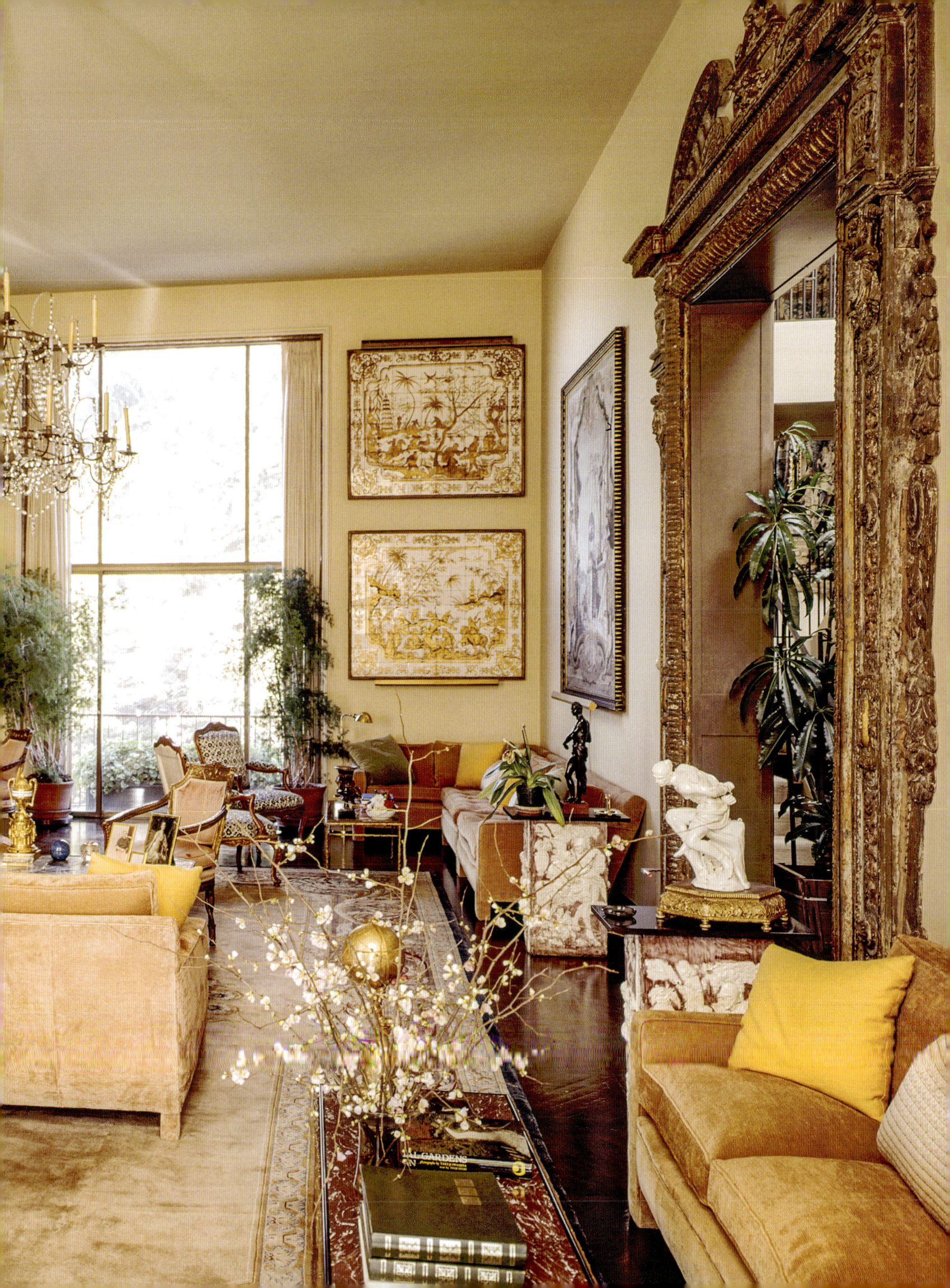

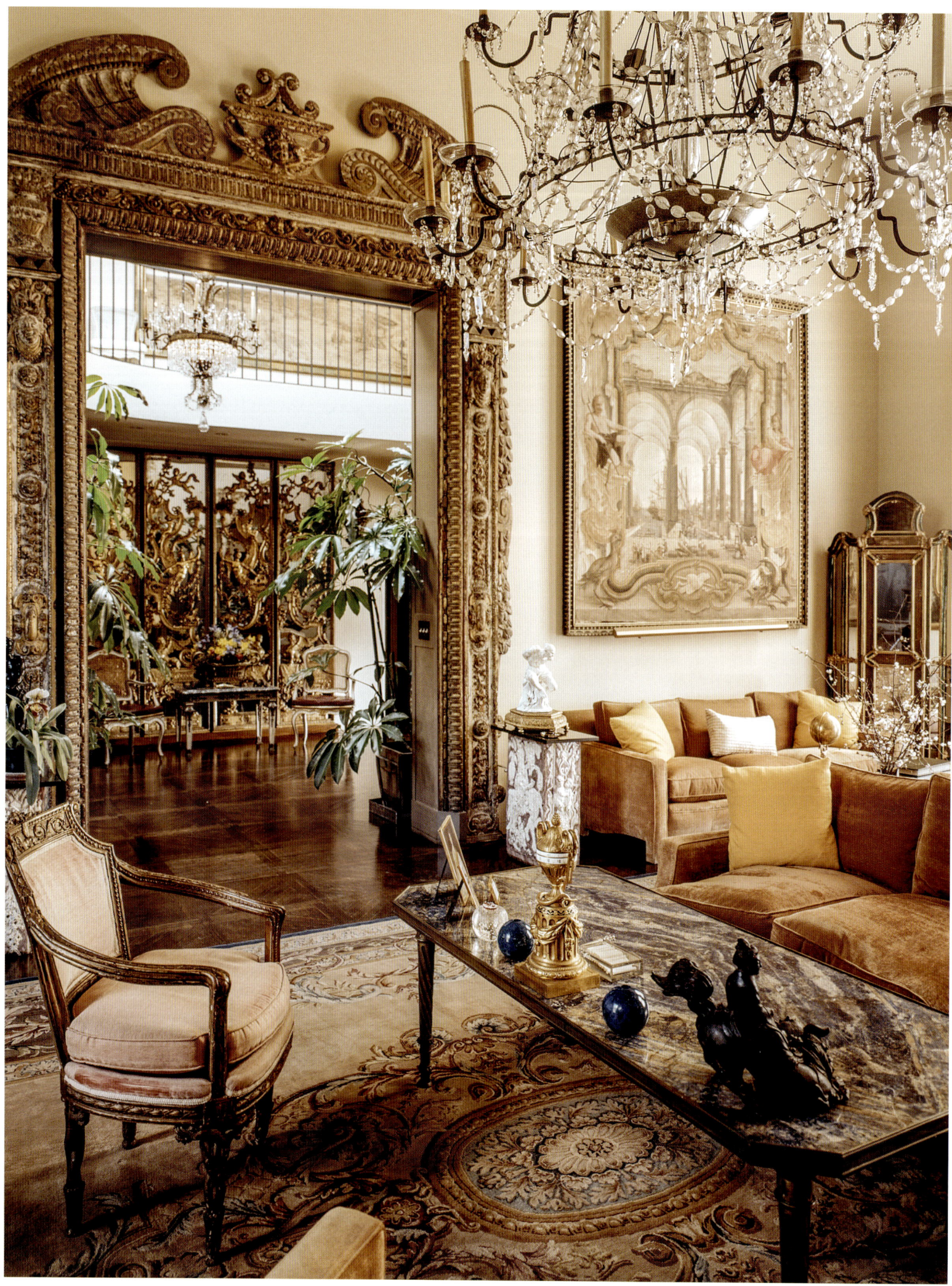

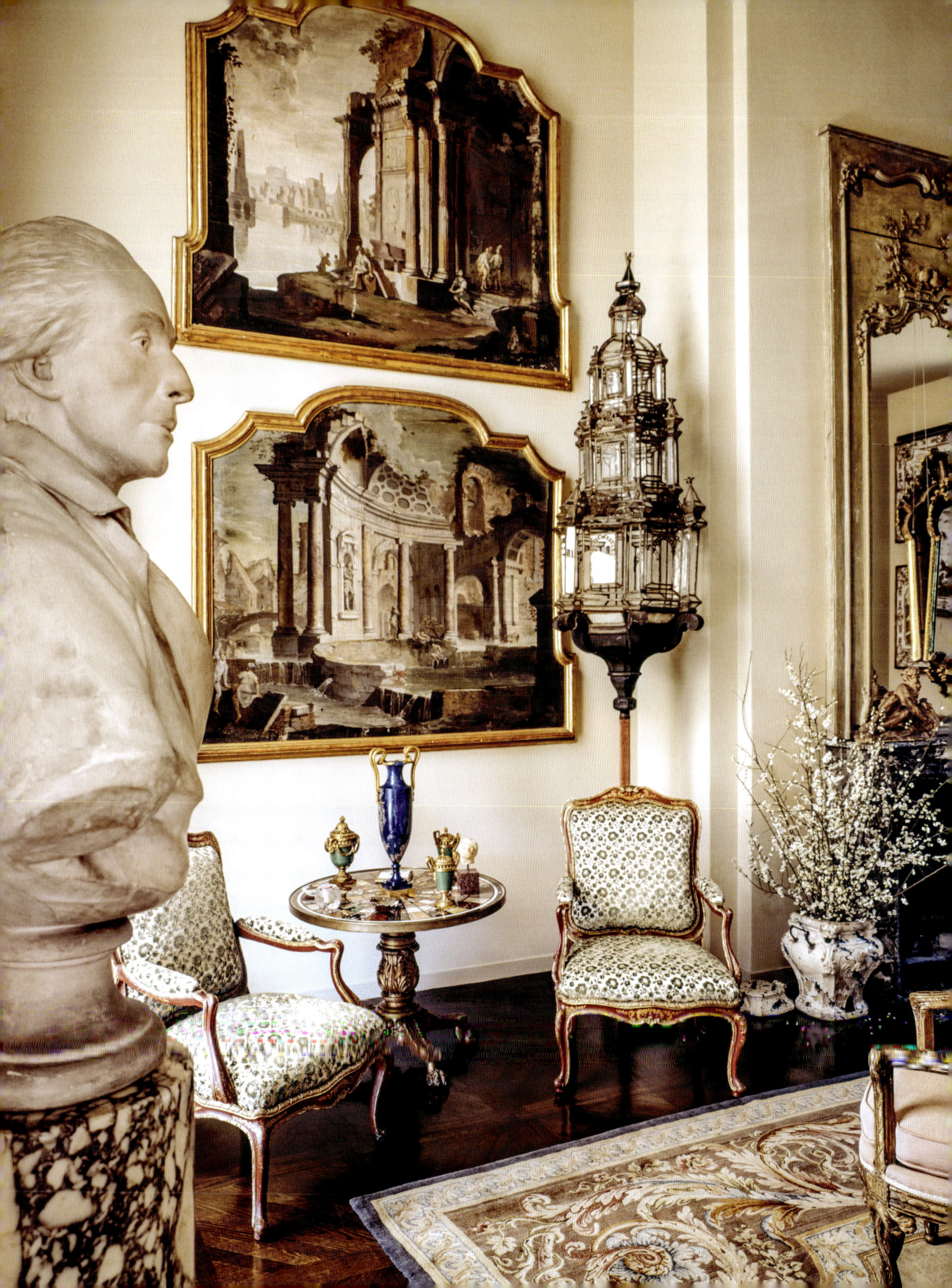

JEROME HILL SKI HOUSE

Sugar Bowl, Norden, 1947

Jerome Hill, the grandson of railroad magnate J. J. Hill, was a philanthropist and documentary filmmaker. I remember him as being
charming, multitalented, and possessing exquisite taste in his large
collection of French paintings. Hill was later nominated for two
Academy Awards, winning an Oscar in 1957 for Best Documentary
Feature. I took these photographs of his residence at Sugar Bowl ski
resort in March 1947 for the December issue of *House & Garden*.

Hill's house was the highest one on the hill at that time. I think
he did much of the architecture himself—he really understood ski
houses. Depending on the depth of snow, one gained access to the
house on skis or by tractor, which would pick one up by the highway.
The house was designed to support a lot of weight, with stone walls
and substantial beams. The footprint of the building was a square,
and the beams stretched from wall to wall. The paintings looked
wonderfully dramatic against the rough walls. In the lower level of
the house, Hill had a series of bins that contained additional paintings. He had a lot of works by Pierre Bonnard.

Hill told me he got the couches and chairs from Montgomery
Ward department store. He just added slipcovers. There was an alcove with a banquette and a circular table—this was where meals
were taken and games played. It was the main gathering spot. Hill
spent a lot of time at his desk in the upstairs suite. The upper floor
was also a source of egress if the snow blocked the main entrance of
the house. When we were snowed in during this shoot, we exited
the house from upstairs. I don't know if he ever had to use the third
level as a way to get out.

Hill divided his time between this house, one in New York, and a
place in Cassis in the South of France. This was a joyous place.   —*F.L.*

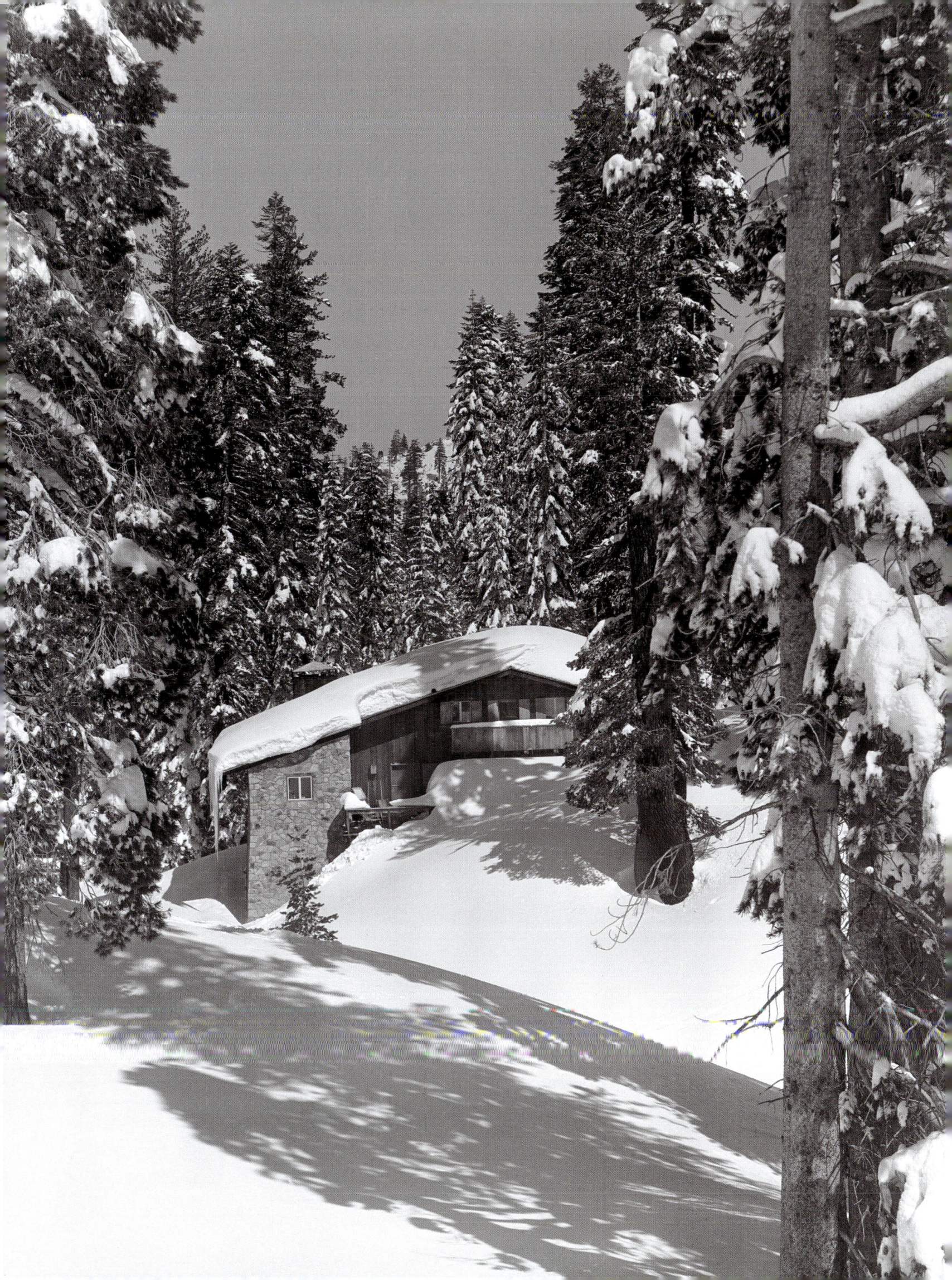

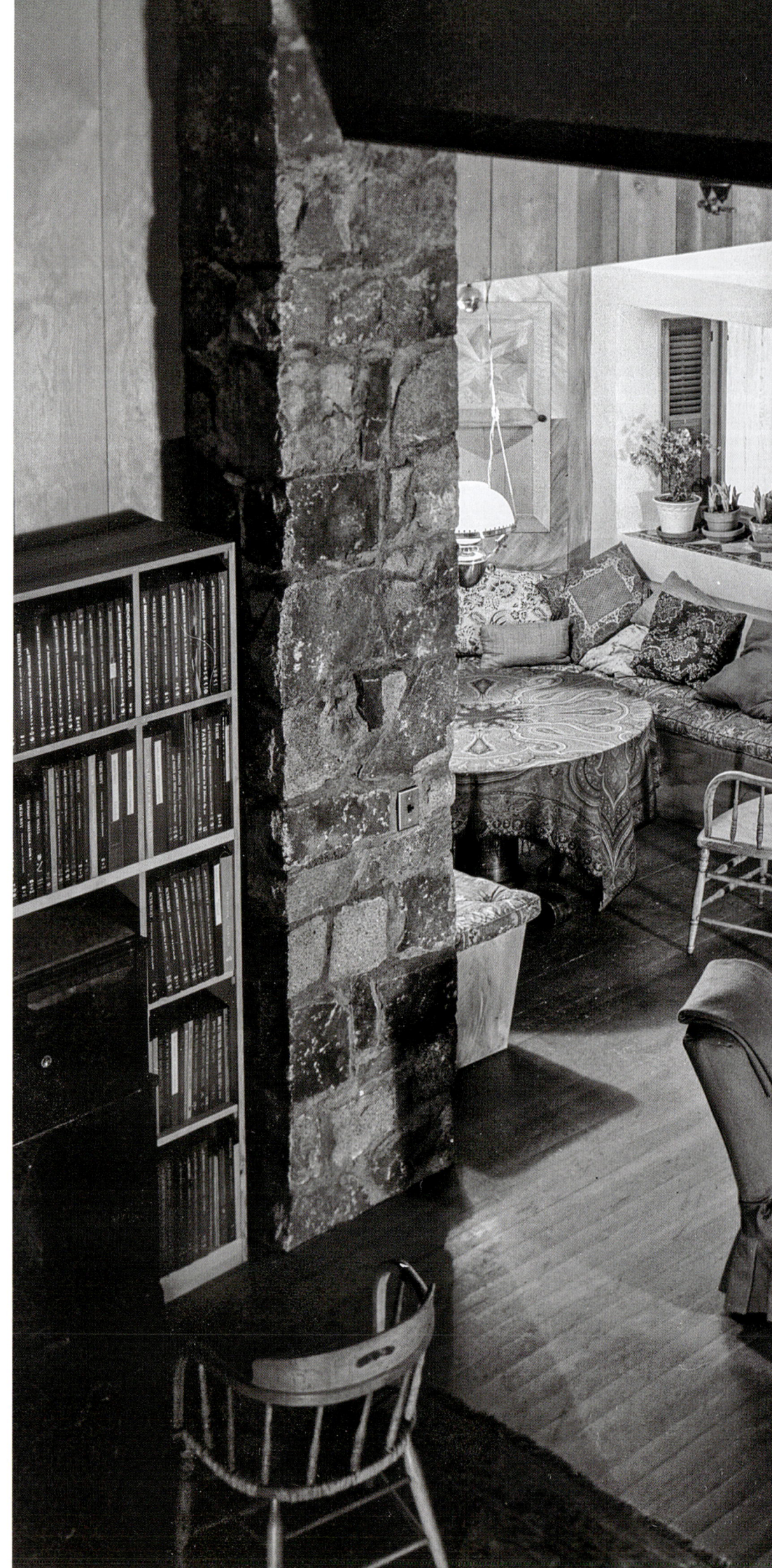

PAGE 63: Jerome Hill's ski house, credited to architects Wurster, Bernardi and Emmons, was the highest residence at the Sugar Bowl resort in 1947. RIGHT: Interior walls of the L-shaped living and dining room, three feet thick in some places, were made with local stone and finished Ponderosa pine shiplap, providing a striking background for Hill's extensive collection of modern American and French paintings. PAGE 66, CLOCKWISE FROM TOP LEFT: Jerome Hill sets out for a day of skiing; the stairs leading from the living room to Hill's study-bedroom and dressing room; deep powder snow at Sugar Bowl; paintings by Pierre Bonnard and Édouard Vuillard. PAGE 67: A Bonnard painting to the left of the fireplace, in an image that expresses Hill's interests in art and congenial entertaining.

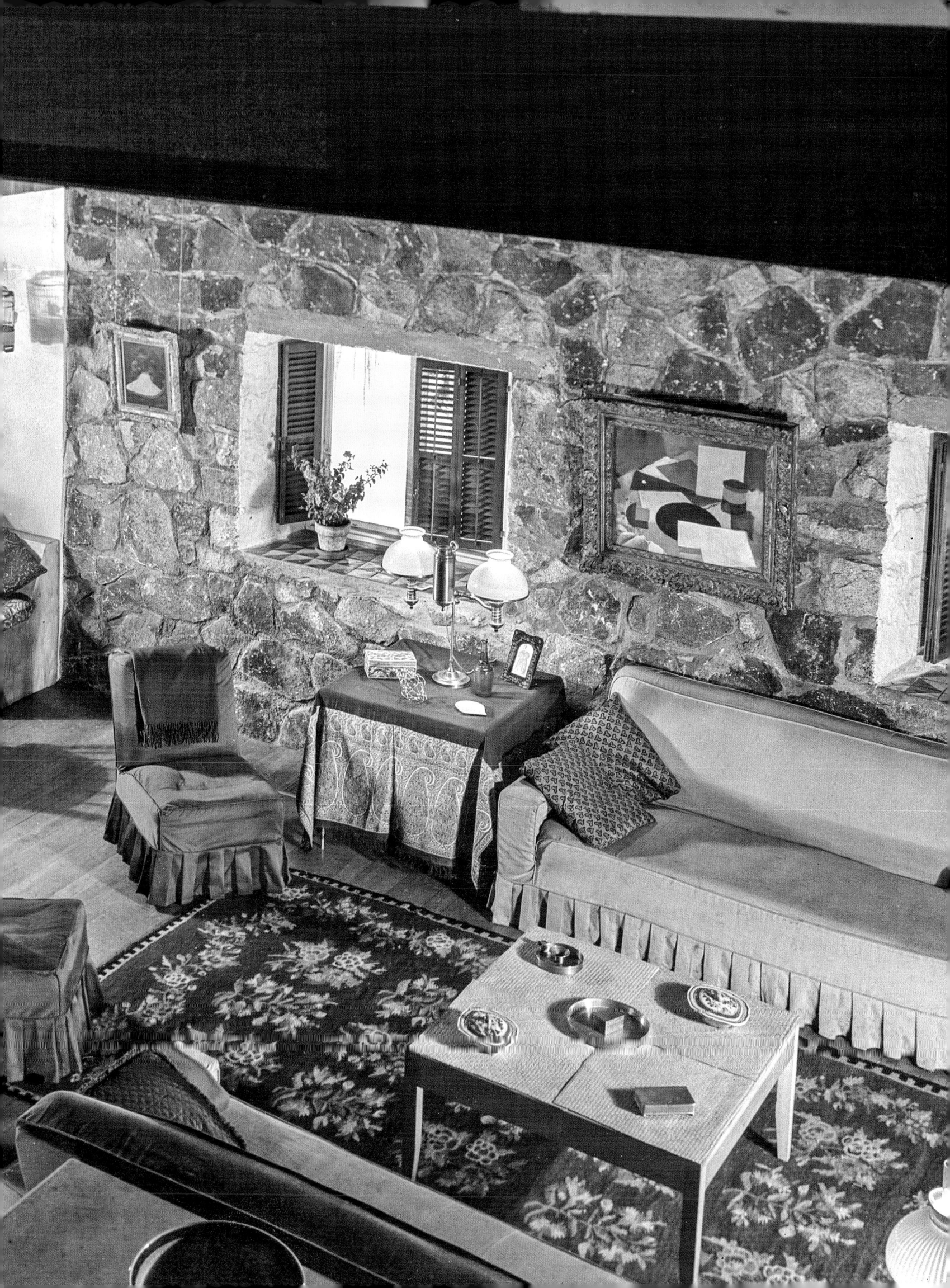

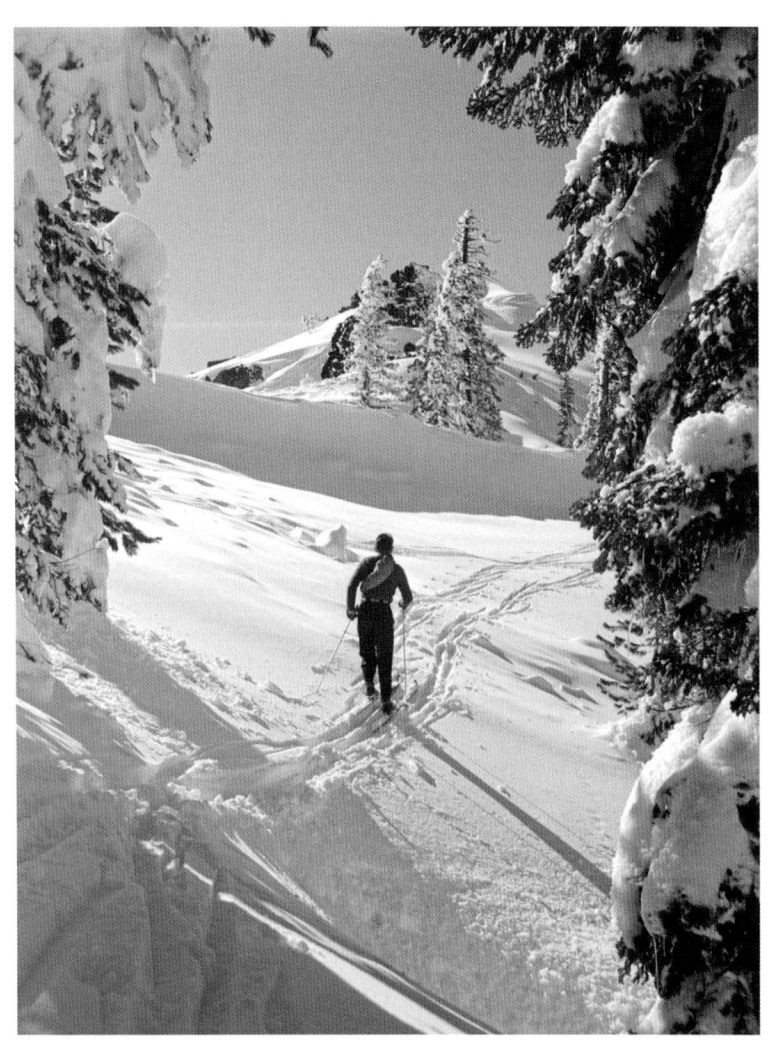
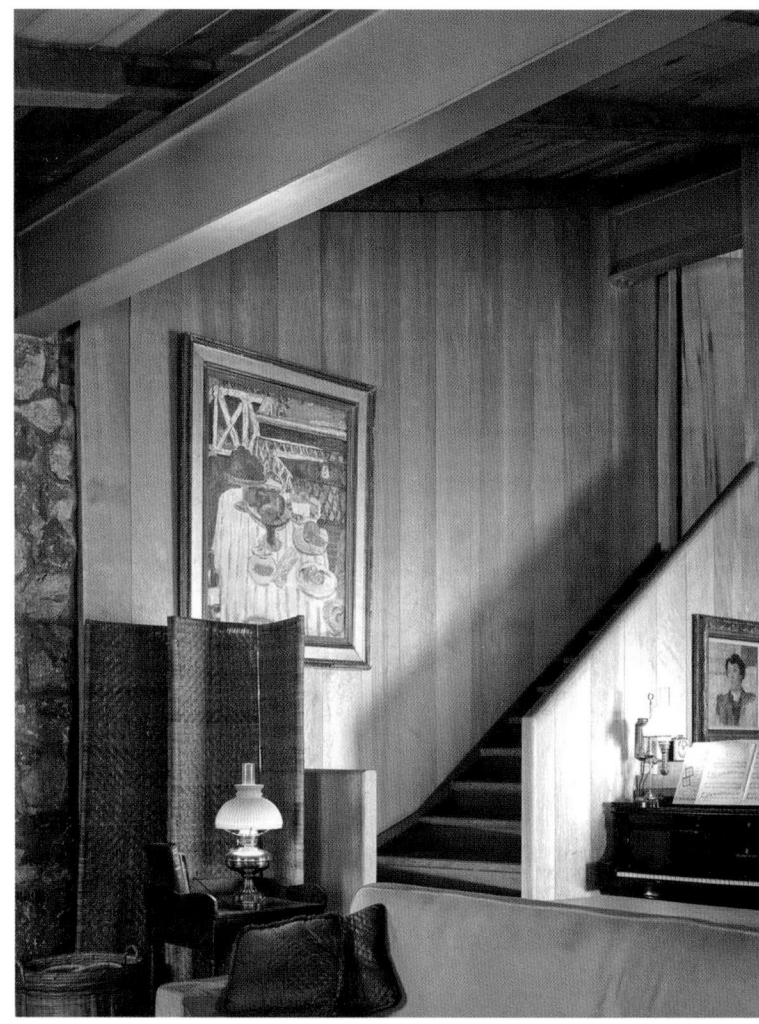
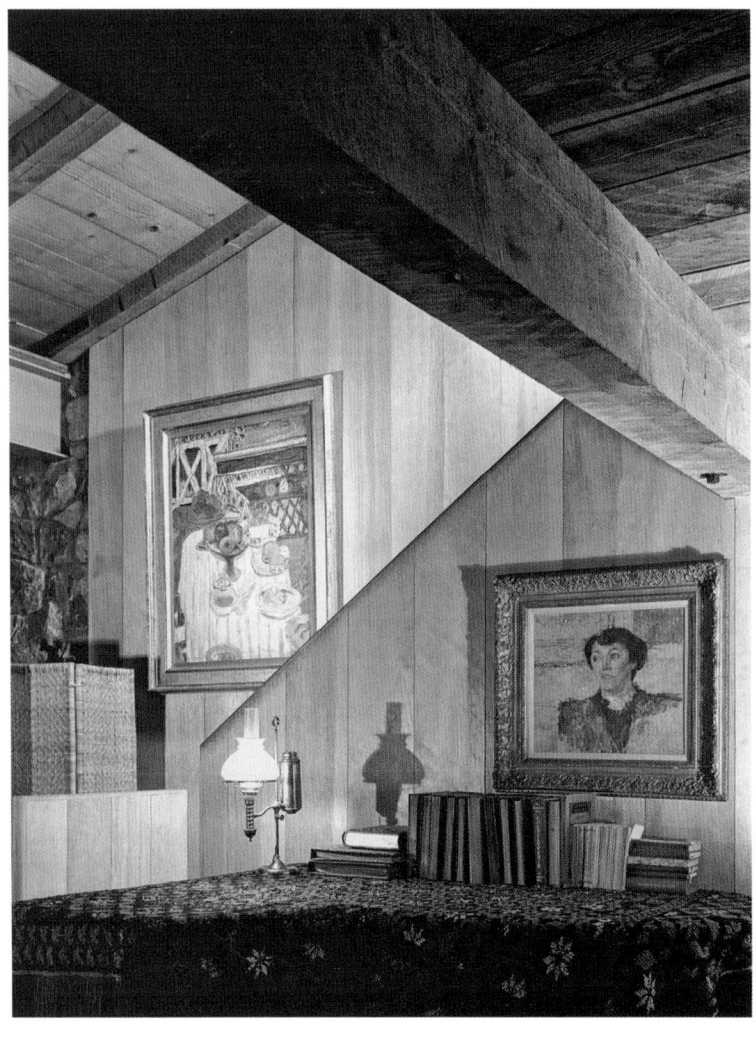
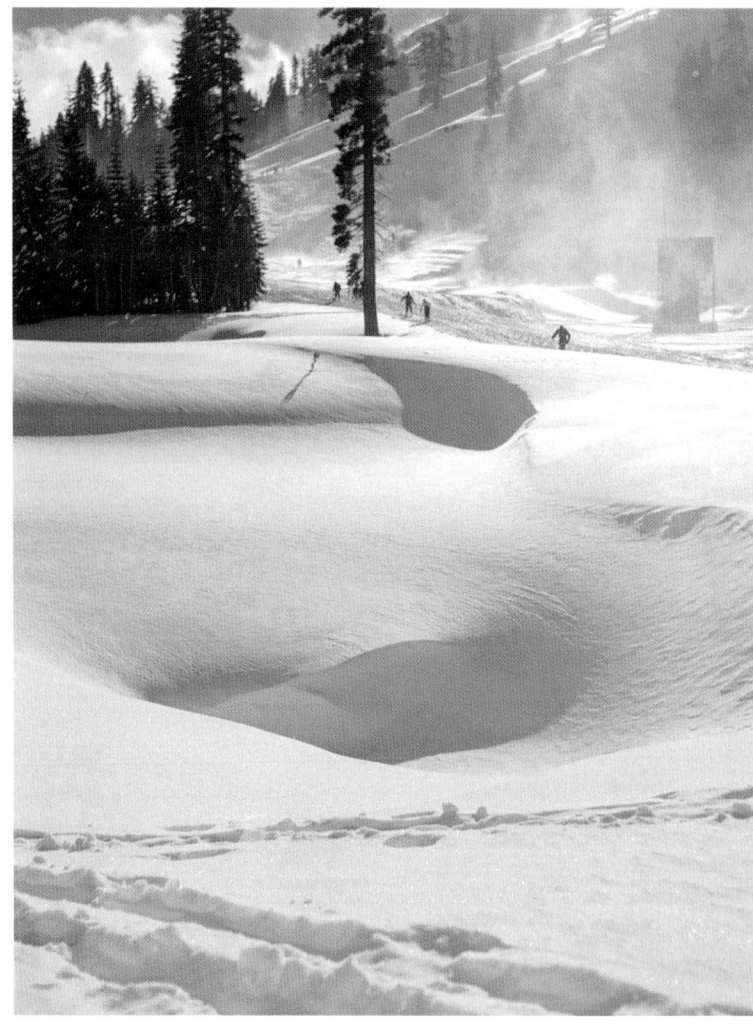

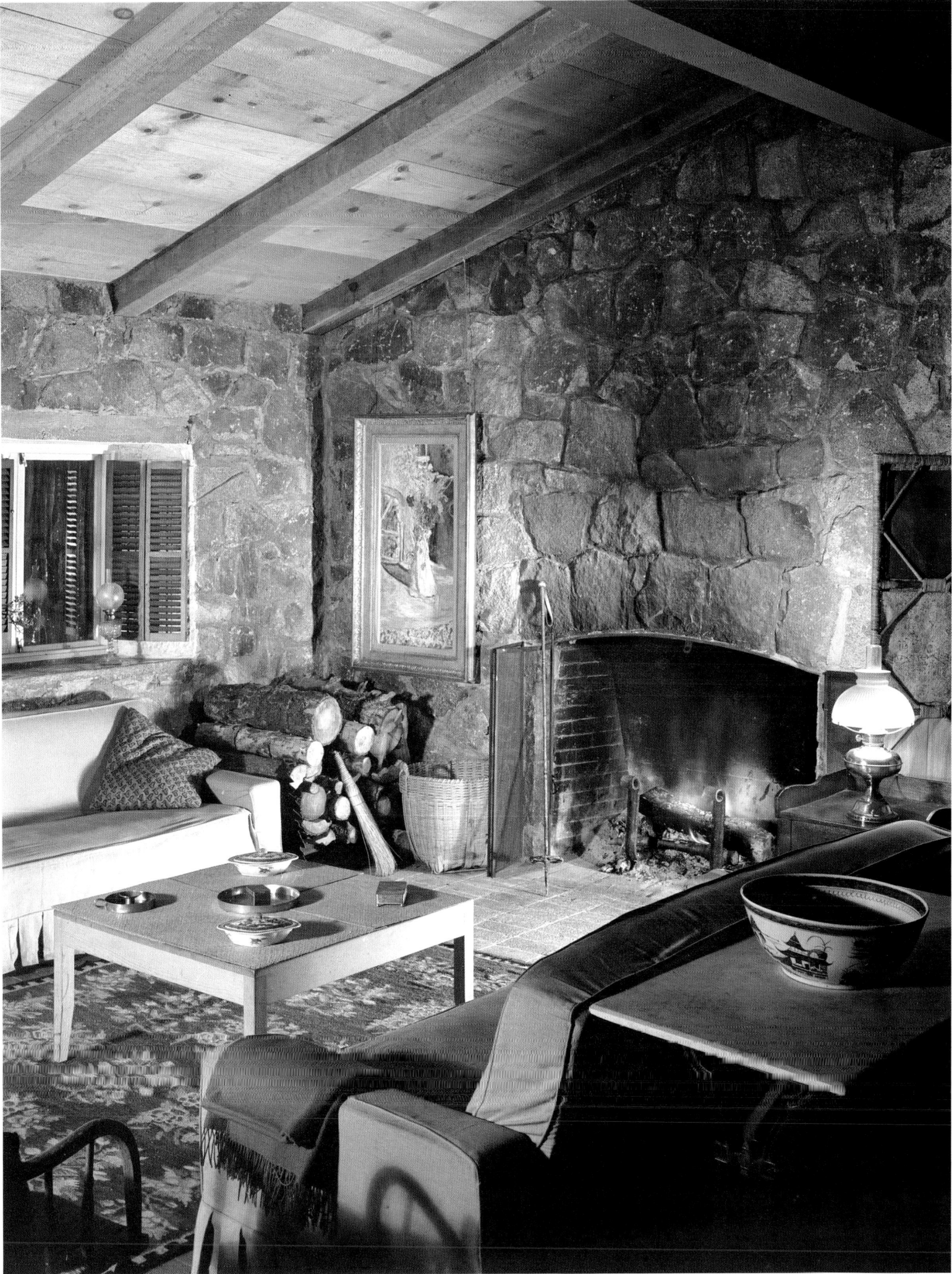

V. C. MORRIS GIFT SHOP

San Francisco, 1949

Frank Lloyd Wright designed the V. C. Morris Gift Shop—
purveyor of tableware and antiques—on Maiden Lane in San
Francisco in 1948. I recall that Mr. Morris had a successful shop
on the other side of the street before he commissioned Wright
to redesign this space at 140 Maiden Lane. Construction was
completed in 1949. I took these photographs on assignment for
Architectural Forum magazine, part of the Time Life empire.

The exterior was striking. The interior that Wright came up
with, however, didn't really work, in my opinion. There was a
prominent spiral ramp that resembled the later design Wright
used in the Solomon R. Guggenheim Museum in New York.
But I don't think his concept worked well at this smaller scale.
For one thing, it was impractical. There were display cases along
the ramp, and if somebody stopped to look at something, they
blocked the passage. The rest of the space was stunning. Hanging from the ceiling was a dish with vines pouring over its edges.
An arched tunnel served as the entryway. Items were displayed
on tables and ledges and behind porthole display windows, in
addition to the cases along the ramp.

Mr. Morris had just moved in when I took these photographs. He and I had been working together at night on
the photography. During one break, I commented, "It sure is
beautiful." Mr. Morris sighed and responded, "Yes. I just wish
somebody would buy something." He had gone into hock to get
this thing accomplished. It turned out well for him, and the
business thrived. After Morris and his wife died, a famous
silversmith took over the space but kept the Morris name for
the location. Later still, the space became an art gallery.   —*F.L.*

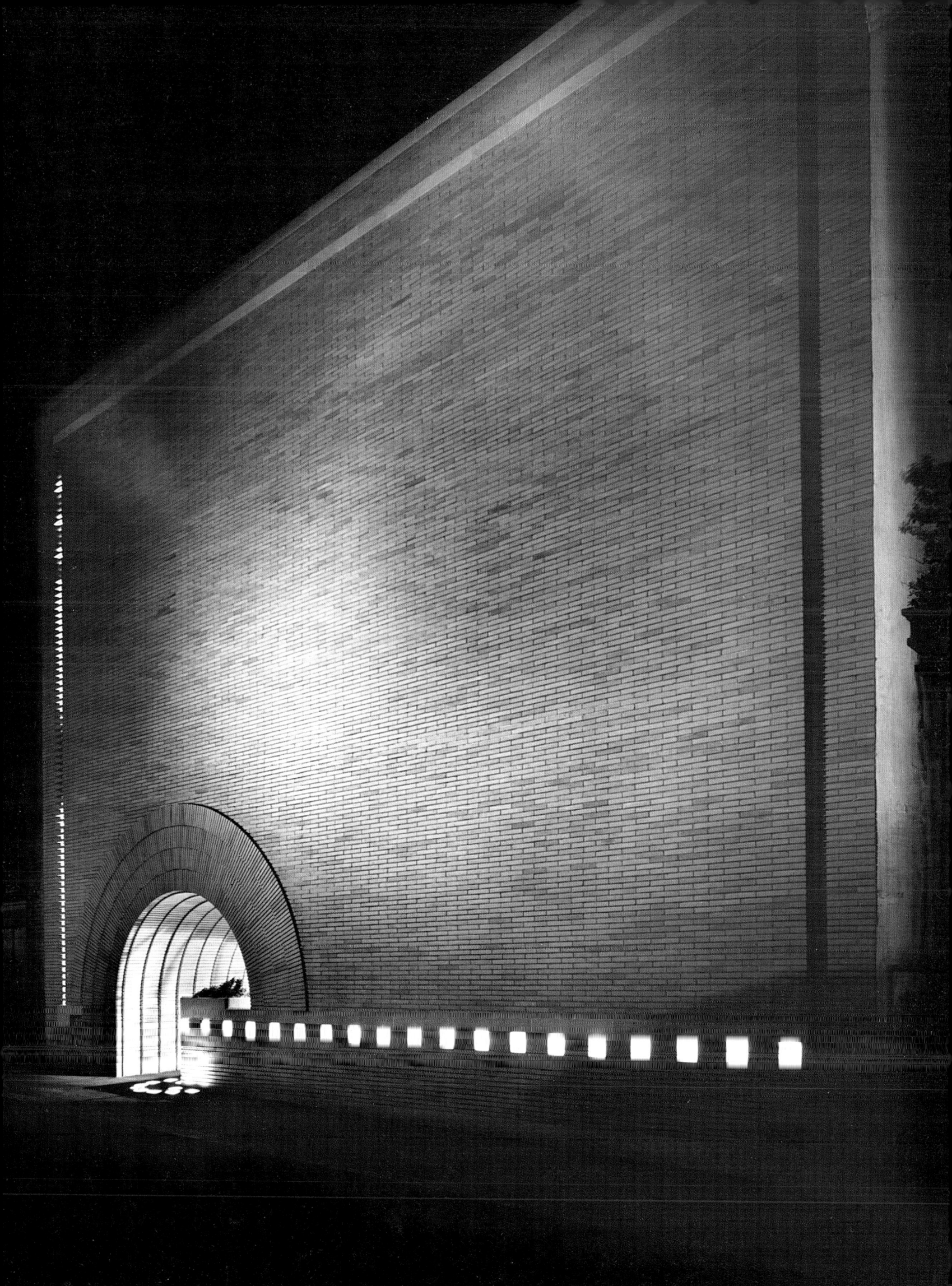

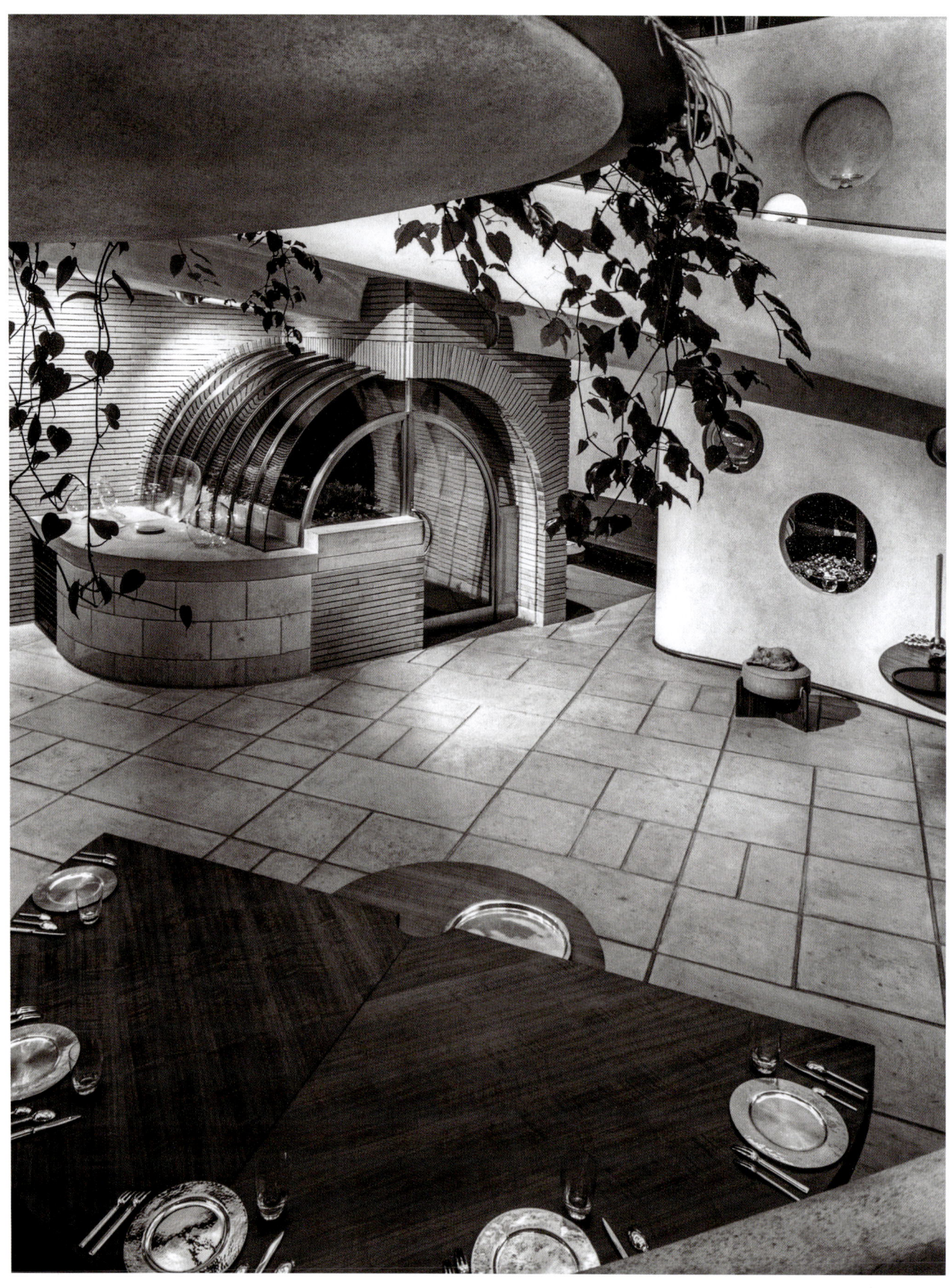

PAGE 69: Instead of a conventional storefront, architect Frank Lloyd Wright provided a blank wall of golden-yellow brick for the narrow Maiden Lane facade of the V. C. Morris Gift Shop, 1949. ABOVE: Customers entered through the archway into the main salesroom. OPPOSITE: The spiral ramp is similar in concept to that later designed by Wright for the Solomon R. Guggenheim Museum in New York City. The ramp was a concession to space constraints that precluded broad staircases or elevators.

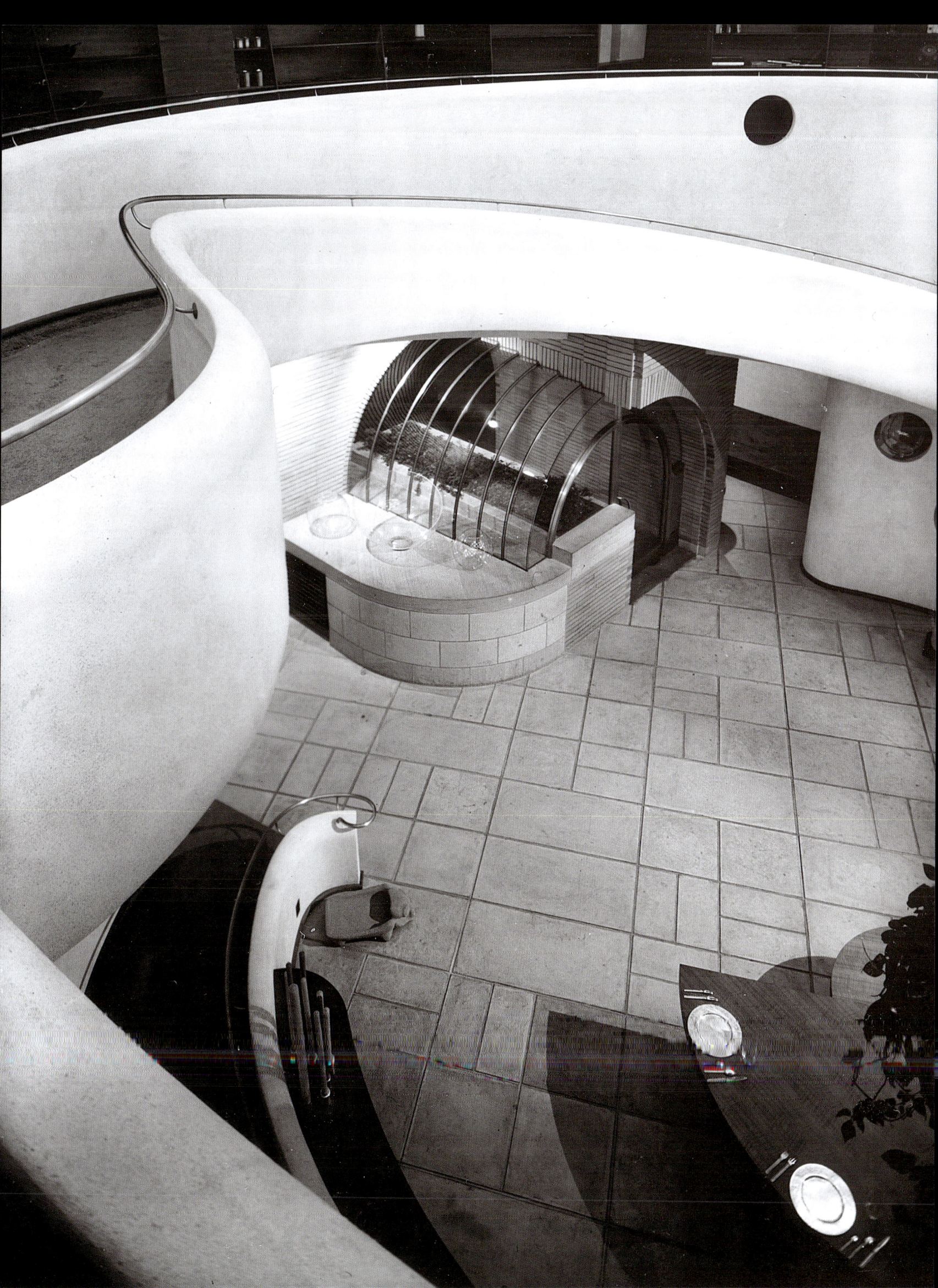

IV.

DOROTHEA WALKER
AND A HOST OF COLLABORATORS

Lyon's next big break again came courtesy of *House & Garden* and two women: one was Dorothea Walker, the Virgil-like guide for Lyon as he learned to navigate the circles of high society, and the other was Celia Tobin Clark, one of the grandest grande dames of California. The scene was Clark's magnificent estate, House-on-Hill, which was to be the subject of a spread in the magazine. In March 1948, Lyon got this plum assignment on the strength of his work at Whitney Warren Jr.'s house. But House-on-Hill, the emblematic country estate nestled atop hundreds of acres, was very different from Warren Jr.'s midcentury Telegraph Hill aerie. Lyon says, "Entering the property, I drove through miles of pastures lined with white fences. The road wound up and up and up to the summit where House-on-Hill was situated. The mansion overlooked all of Spring Valley lakes."[71]

Arriving at House-on-Hill, Lyon was greeted by Dorothea Walker, now with *House & Garden* in addition to her other job with *Vogue*, and Celia Tobin Clark herself. The two women were well acquainted with each other. Walker orbited high society most of her life, although she was not a member of it to the degree of a grande dame like Clark. Celia Tobin had been an "heiress to the Hibernia banking fortune"[72] and moved to the nucleus of society in 1904 when she married C. W. Clark, the son of W. A. Clark, the "copper king" and one of the most powerful, influential, and ruthless of the nineteenth-century American robber barons."[73] Writing about the Clark-Tobin wedding, the local newspaper reported that C. W. received $25,000 per month in "spending money."[74] (Today, that is more than $8.6 million per year for walking-around money.)[75] Celia and C. W. later divorced. In the settlement, she received five hundred acres of prime San Francisco Peninsula land. She chose noted architect David Adler (1882–1949), brother of Frances Elkins, to design the mansion that came to be called House-on-Hill.

When Lyon met Clark, she was deeply engaged in arts and intellectual pursuits. He found her charming. "She was from another era," Lyon says, "when young ladies were brought up to be great conversationalists. I was there with Dorothea Walker. Dorothea and Mrs. Clark had known each other socially for a long time."[76]

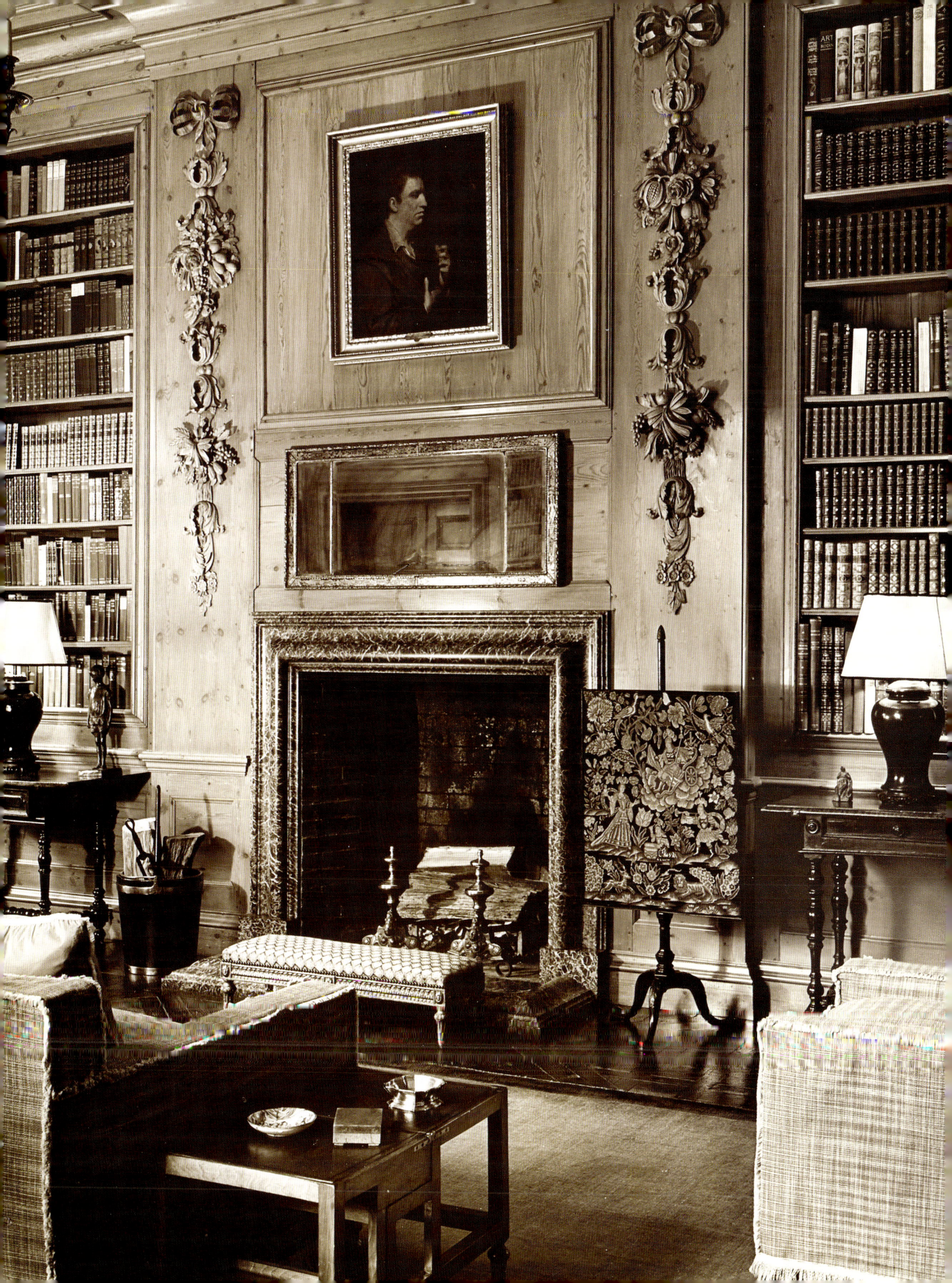

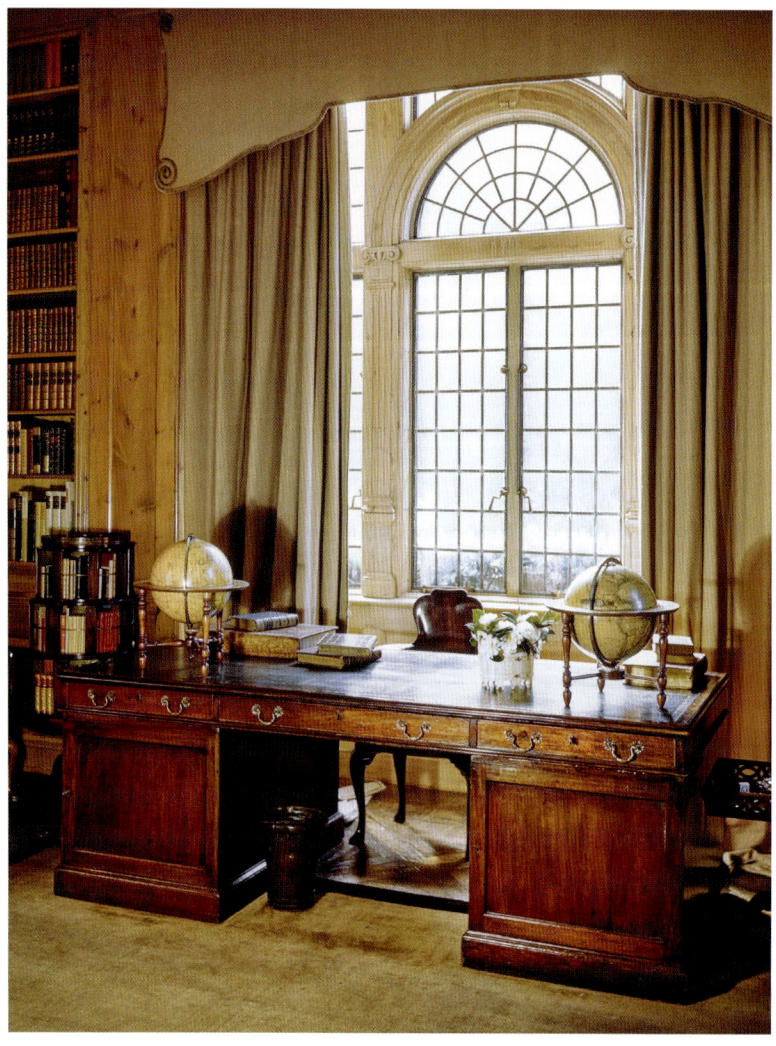

PAGE 73 AND LEFT: In 1948, Lyon photographed Celia Tobin Clark's Hillsborough country house, House-on-Hill, for *House & Garden*. Designed by architect David Adler in 1929, the house's library had tall bookshelves, parquetry floors, and a portrait of Samuel Johnson by Sir Joshua Reynolds over the fireplace.

This might have put Clark at ease with Lyon. She invited Lyon and Walker to lunch. Lyon recalls, "I had a wonderful time and really enjoyed talking to her. At that time, I didn't know much about her position in society or much about that level of society at all, but we had had a really nice chat together."[77]

The feeling must have been mutual. Lyon says, "Soon after, I got a phone call from Mrs. Clark's secretary. She wanted to know my mailing address. Shortly thereafter, I received an invitation to dinner at House-on-Hill. Dorothea called me on the phone and said, 'Fred, Fred, you are going to hear from Mrs. Clark.

She's going to invite you to dinner.' I said, 'I know. I got an invitation. I'm going to go.' I really liked talking to her."[78] The invitation was to Clark's biggest dinner of the year. Because it was Clark, it was the pinnacle of society dinners in Northern California. Lyon adds, "Dorothea tried to impress upon me how important this invitation was, but I really couldn't understand that at the time."[79]

The night of the party, it was storming. Lyon says, "I drove to the estate in my old coupe, with paint missing in spots."[80] Arriving at House-on-Hill, Lyon entered, as an invited guest, the rooms he had recently photographed. When dinner was served, the party was shown to "a long, long table, where at each place there was a filigreed silver frame with the menu in French."[81] Lyon didn't read French, so he "didn't pay any attention to it and amiably chatted with people left and right."[82] Lyon was about to commit his first gaucherie: "Then the fish course was served. I remember thinking, you would think she could afford red meat. I was hungry. I roared through mine. After everybody else had finished their fish course, the server came around and offered more. I took a second helping. This was a big faux pas; everybody at the table had to wait for their next course while I had my second helping of fish."[83]

After dinner, the party retreated to the library. Walker later described this as "the warmest and most welcoming room in the house," with parquetry from a castle in France, leaded windows, and built-in bookshelves that reached fifteen feet to the ceiling. Above the fireplace mantel hung a portrait of the writer Samuel Johnson by Sir Joshua Reynolds.[84] Lyon remembers, "A lot of people played bridge. I didn't, so I sat on a couch alone. There was a very friendly, folksy lady who plopped down on the couch next to me and asked me about myself. I was flattered that somebody wanted to know about me. I kept talking and talking. I guessed that because Mrs. Clark had invited me, people thought I must be okay."[85]

At the end of the evening, Lyon left with a parting gift. "As I drove away from the house, I noticed the gas gauge read full. I thought my gauge had broken. I never drove with a full tank, because I didn't have enough money to fill the tank. What I didn't realize with the grand houses was if you were a guest there and your car needed washing, they washed it during the party. Since it was raining, they couldn't wash the car, so they filled the tank."[86] He also remembers, "The next day, in the newspaper, there was a half-page article in the society section devoted to Mrs. Clark's dinner, and I was mentioned several times."[87] The woman he had chatted with was the editor of the society page of a San Francisco paper. He was starting to get noticed.

Dorothea Walker was a third-generation Californian whose grandfather came from England to California in the Gold Rush and made a fortune from his inventions and patents of machinery for the railroads. She was born in San Francisco in 1906, the year of the great earthquake.[88] Walker was fluent in three languages and once had been a dancer who had performed with the San Francisco Ballet.[89] Walker married a Navy officer and was living as a Navy wife in Honolulu during the buildup to the Second World War. When she discovered how little her fellow Navy wives knew about what went on at the huge naval base, she talked the base

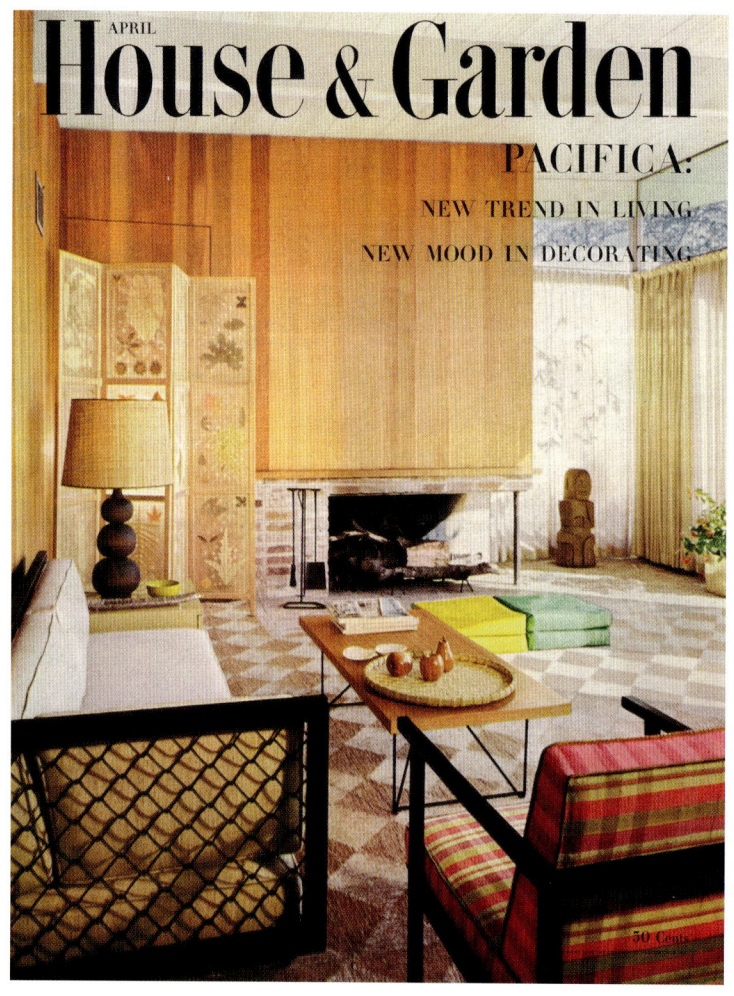

House & Garden

PACIFICA:

NEW TREND IN LIVING
NEW MOOD IN DECORATING

LEFT: Paneled living room in the John C. Dempsey house, Pacifica, designed by architects John Carden Campbell and Worley K. Wong. This was Lyon's first cover image for *House & Garden* magazine (April 1952). OPPOSITE: Frances Elkins embraced a stark, contemporary aesthetic for the interior of the Irma and Albert Schlesinger house in San Francisco's Pacific Heights neighborhood. Elkins offset what she called "hospital white" walls with black terrazzo flooring and red carpets. This image of Irma Schlesinger, standing with her gray poodle in the dining room, appeared in the April 15, 1952, issue of *Vogue*.

commander into letting her host a weekly radio program, called *Navy Wife*, that discussed base life from the spouse's point of view. After the Japanese attack on Pearl Harbor, Walker relocated to San Francisco, where she began to report on national radio. A chance meeting with *Vogue* editor Jessica Daves led to an assignment for a story about Bay Area movers and shakers. The *Los Angeles Times* reported, "The piece was so direct—she compared a prominent literary critic to a sick mouse and a composer to a baked potato—that she 'almost had to leave town.' But the magazine loved it."[90] Walker became the magazine's features editor, a position she held for twenty years.[91]

Lyon was now getting assignments from *House & Garden* on a fairly regular basis. Walker long had wanted to add *House & Garden* to her roster, and Lyon was keen to get into *Vogue*. Both were Condé Nast properties, so they decided to try to help each other. "Dorothea was a great one for maneuvering," Lyon says.[92] She put in a call to the powers that be at *Vogue* in New York. Lyon was soon getting assignments from that magazine, including a regular beat to photograph the fairy-tale-like San Francisco Debutante Ball at the Palace Hotel. These assignments yielded some beautiful fine art photography. Lyon had far less sway than Walker, but he spoke up for his friend to his editor at

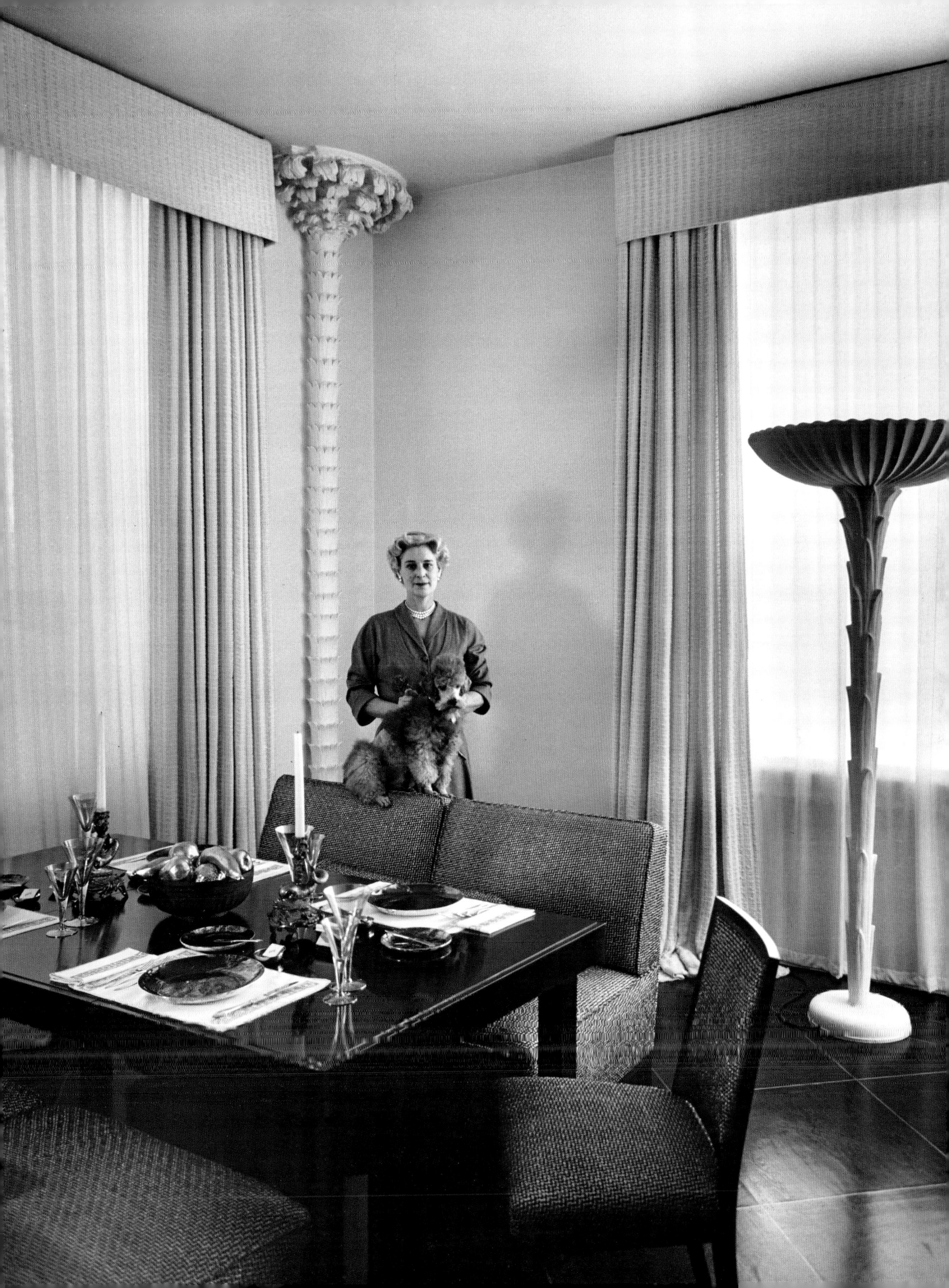

House & Garden in New York. Soon, Walker was a contributing editor there, a job she held until the magazine folded in 1993. Lyon remembers, "When I was on assignment with *House & Garden* and *Vogue*, I usually worked with Dorothea. She was smart and experienced, and we worked well together. The only thing I had to watch out for with Dorothea was her habit of accidentally having her foot or handbag in the frame. Looking through the back of a view camera, everything is upside down, and with wide-angle lenses it is dark and really hard to see in the corners. Aside from that, she was great to work with, and she was very patient with me because I was a gauche young man, and she eased me through lots of social situations."[93]

Thus, by 1948, Lyon had two accomplished women to guide him in the world of interior design: Dorothea Walker, who was like a fun aunt who showed him the ways of society, and Frances Elkins, whose significance in design he soon understood. "I quickly grew to be fascinated by Frances Elkins," Lyon says. "I saw that she owned her clients. She took me on a tour of her different projects. I recall going to Nan Kempner's parents' house in San Francisco. Nan's parents were great social figures."[94] These were Albert "Speed" Schlesinger, owner of one of Califor-

RIGHT: Architect Gardner Dailey's circular staircase in the Schlesinger house, 1951. Frances Elkins repeated the black of its ebony railings and the red of its carpeting throughout the residence.

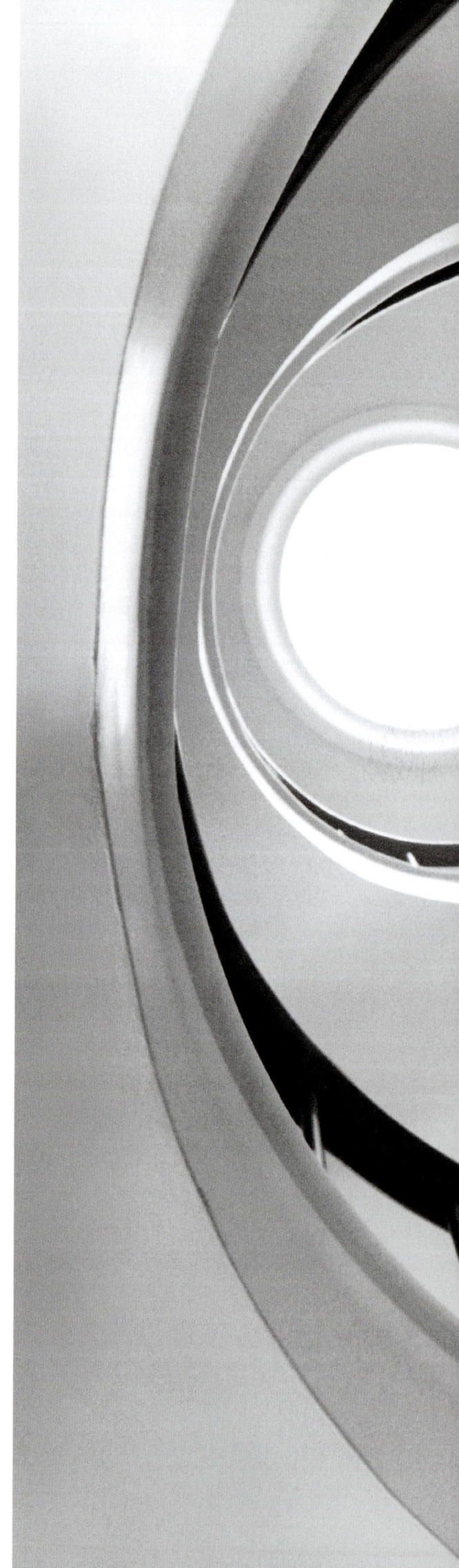

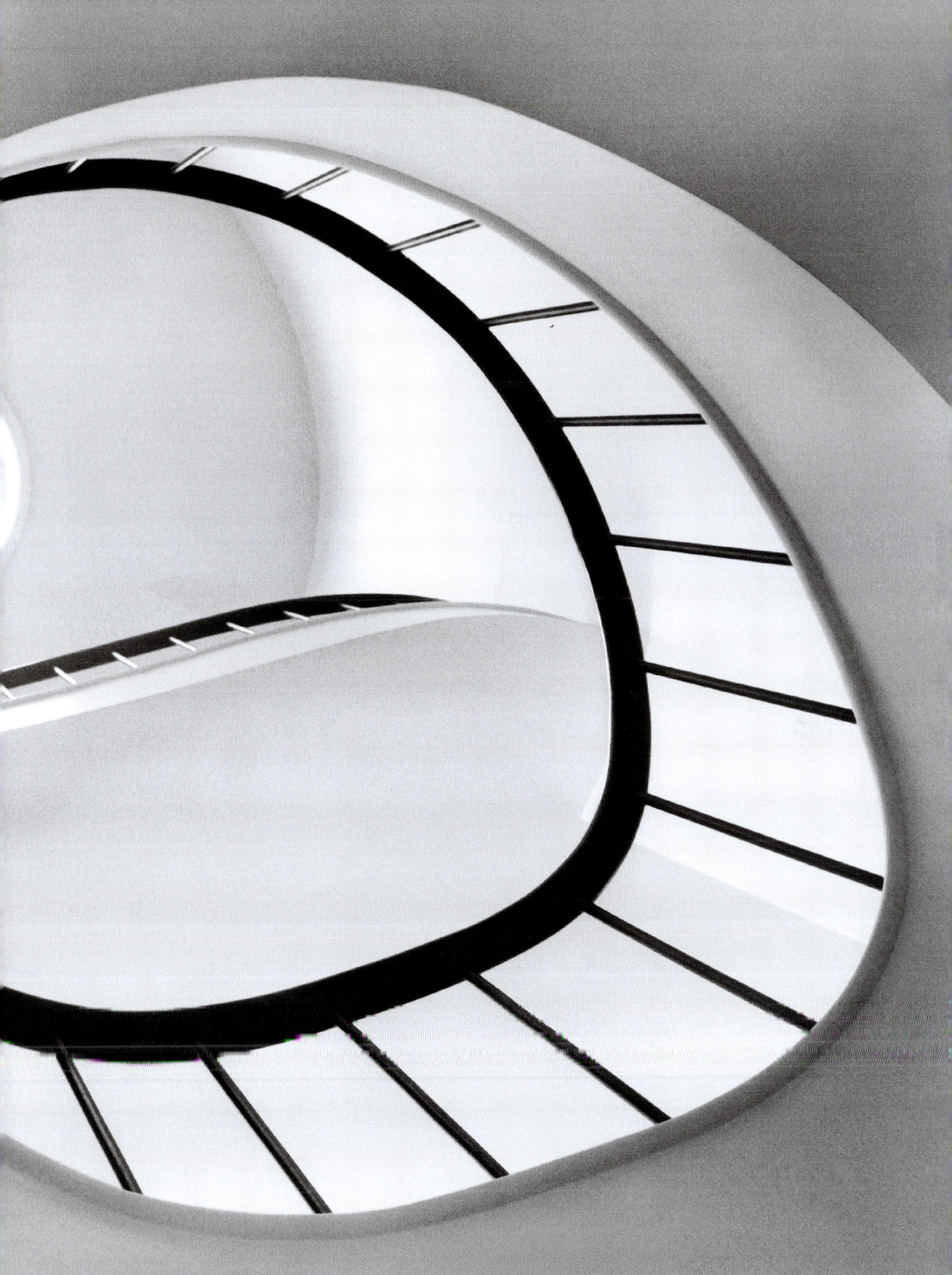

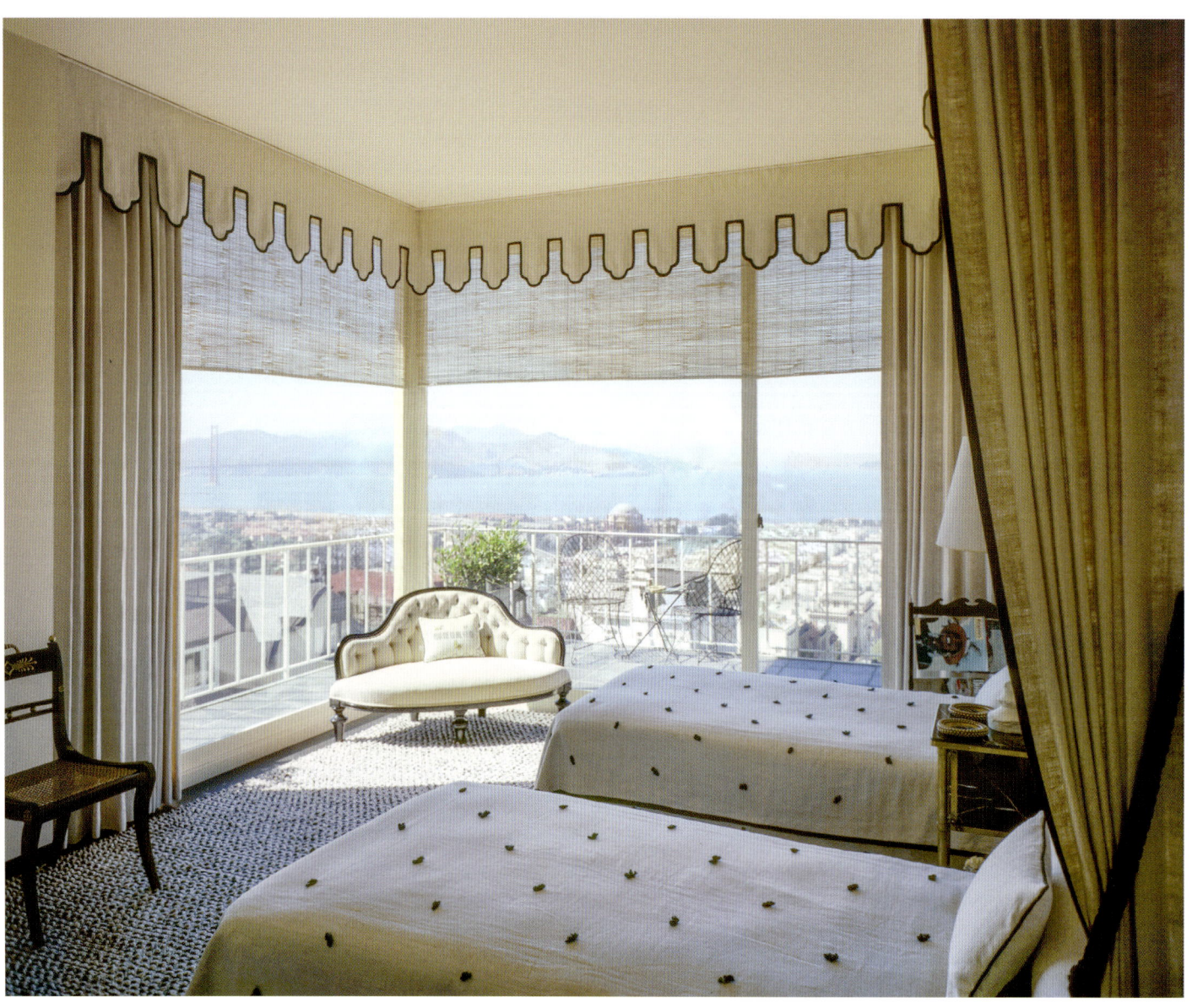

nia's largest Ford dealerships, and Irma Schlesinger, whom her daughter, Nan, called "an extraordinary fashion plate."[95] Lyon continues, "It was a Gardner Dailey House at the top of Broadway and Divisadero in Pacific Heights. In those days, if you wanted to cement yourself in San Francisco society, you had Gardner Dailey design a house, Frances Elkins decorate it, and Tommy Church as the landscape architect.

It was a foolproof combination."[96] He adds, "Dailey, Elkins and Church—I stayed alive by working amongst that trio for a long time."[97] Thomas Church (1902–1978) is considered the creator of the "modern California garden,"[98] characterized by elegance and native plantings in a harmony of "unity, function, simplicity, and scale."[99] Educated at the University of California, Berkeley, and Harvard University, Church

ABOVE: After Elkins died in 1953, Michael Taylor was engaged to design the bedroom of the Schlesinger's daughter, Nan Kempner. Photographed in 1957, the room's corner windows open onto a balcony overlooking the Golden Gate Bridge and the Palace of Fine Arts.

taught landscape architecture at Berkeley and opened his own office in San Francisco, where he practiced until nearly the end of his life. After six decades, Lyon still fondly remembers Tommy Church as "a warm guy with a wonderful, elegant wife. In the gardens Tommy always wore a button-down shirt with a tie and carried a battered leather briefcase. I don't think I ever saw him actually open the case, but I always remember the surreal contrast of Tommy in a garden with a leather briefcase."[100]

Elkins and Lyon last visited the Schlesingers' San Francisco house together in late 1951. The Schlesingers were traveling out of the country. No matter, Elkins had her own key. Dailey had designed the rectangular house to sit atop Pacific Heights on Broadway, one of the city's most spectacular locations. The unobtrusive gray-and-white facade gave no hint of the interior, with its fifteen-foot ceilings and stunning views of the Golden Gate Bridge and San Francisco Bay, and specifically designed by Dailey to accommodate the Schlesingers' collections, which included Ming porcelain, Chippendale and contemporary furniture, and African art.[101] Perhaps the most remarkable feature of the house was the free-hanging stairway, outlined by an ebony railing and red carpeted treads, that linked the

three stories of the house. *Vogue* called it an "architectural triumph."[102] Lyon remembers shooting the interiors for that feature in *Vogue* with Elkins in tow: "We swept in unannounced. As we went into the living room, there were shiny black hardwood floors and truly outstanding views from the windows. Dailey designed wonderful high ceilings and a circular staircase that I photographed. Nothing in the house was out of place; Frances Elkins had left a chart for the Schlesingers' maids indicating where to place the furniture, down to the ashtrays, and specified that the only flowers allowed were red and pink carnations, her late brother David Adler's favorite flowers."[103] Another visitor to the Schlesingers' home around this time was their daughter Nan Kempner's friend, an up-and-coming designer named Michael Taylor, who was greatly influenced by Elkins and always acknowledged his admiration for her work and its impact on American style.[104] The Schlesinger house was the final large commission Frances Elkins did before she died from cancer in 1953.[105]

Taylor's visit can be seen as a passing of the torch from Elkins to the next generation of designers. At the forefront were Michael Taylor, John Dickinson, Anthony Hail, and others. Fred Lyon worked with them all.

V.
THE WILD TALENT
OF MICHAEL TAYLOR

Fred Lyon describes the transition from Frances Elkins to Michael Taylor: "Frances had no competition at her level of work. It was so distinctive, fresh, and lively. In San Francisco, we have a lot of clients who insist their designers do the same dull, safe design: antiques, beige, gold, and drab. By contrast, Frances's work remains fresh. . . . She would work new things into her old designs. It was exactly what Michael Taylor did. He was a worthy successor."[106] Michael Taylor (1927–1986) has the distinction of having been described by Diana Vreeland, *Vogue*'s former editor-in-chief, as the "James Dean of interior design" and called "the best decorator in the United States" by Cecil Beaton.[107]

Noted San Francisco architect John "Sandy" Walker is a personal friend of Lyon's and another fan of Michael Taylor's work. Among Walker's most famous projects is the stunning Auberge du Soleil restaurant and boutique resort in Napa, which Taylor decorated. Auberge was a project that started around a dinner table at San Francisco's famed L'Étoile restaurant in the early 1980s. L'Étoile's owner, prolific restaurateur Claude Rouas, and his wife, Ardath, had paid

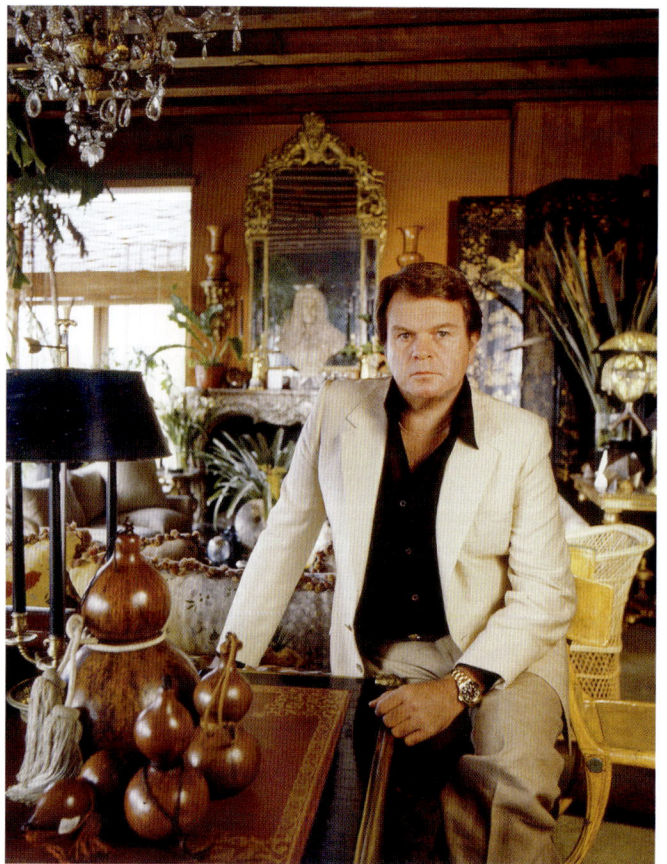

LEFT: Taylor's room setting at the Tour de Décors exhibition at the San Francisco Museum of Art, 1960. The installation marks Taylor's first significant use of *equipales*, the rustic Mexican furniture he came to favor and which he purchased at Cost Plus. In the background are a shell-framed mirror and a cast-stone console table of his own design. Taylor delineated the space with a cage of white-painted trelliswork.

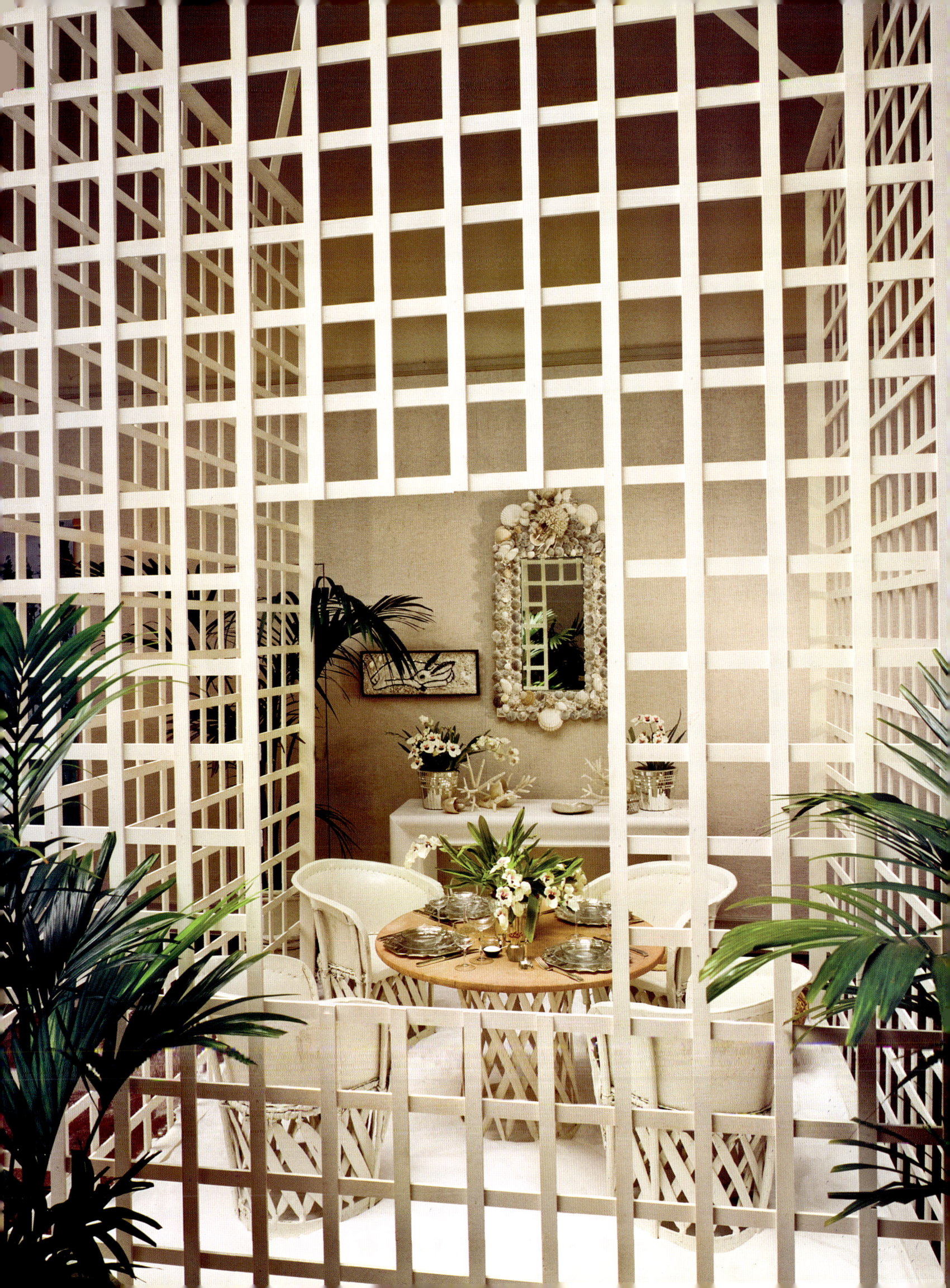

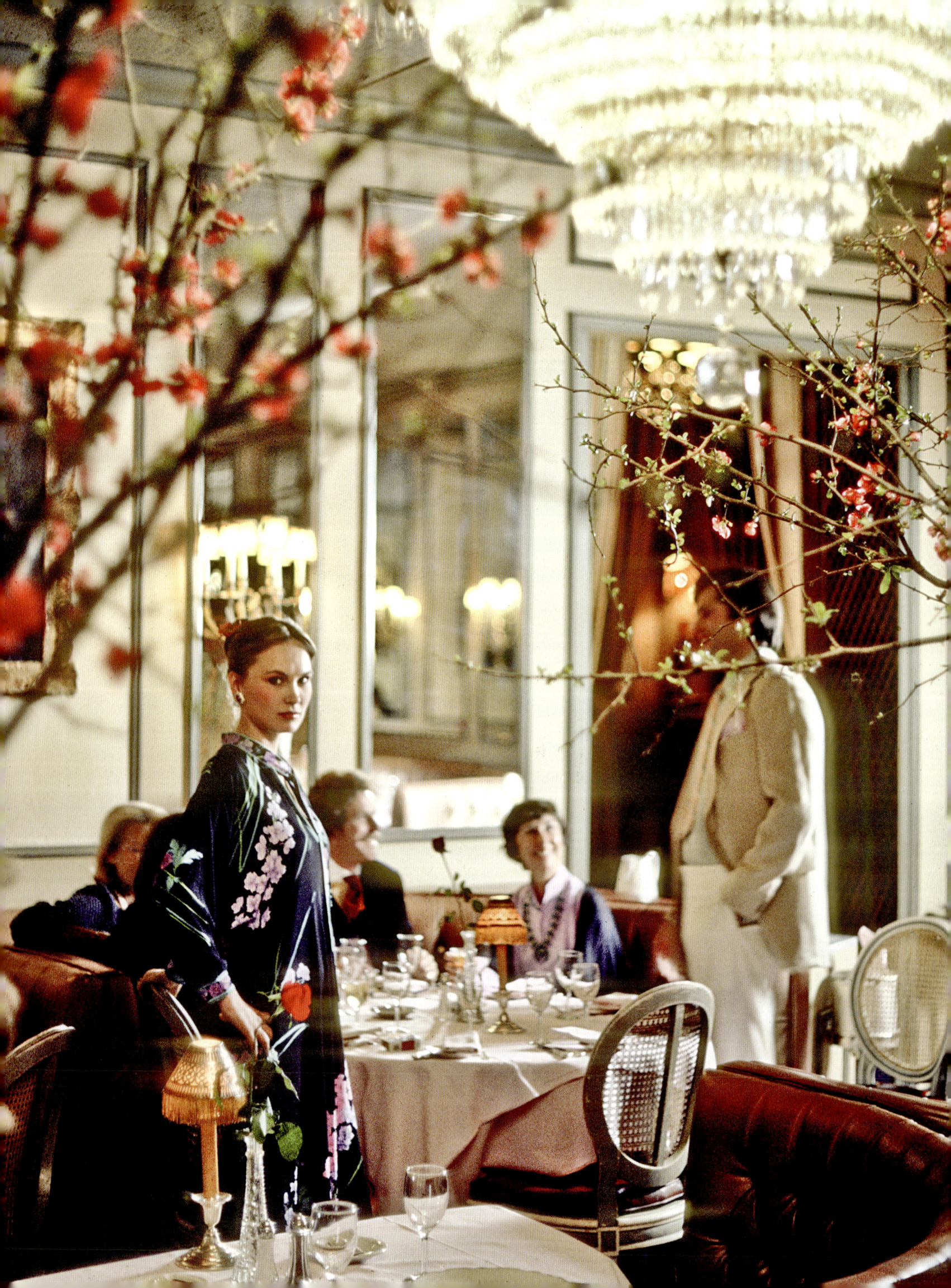

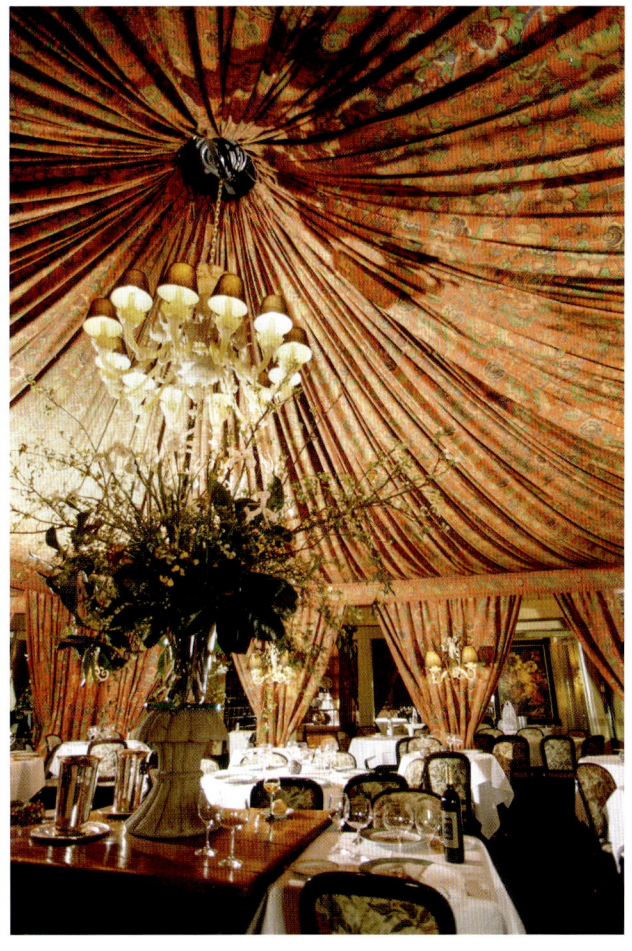

OPPOSITE: L'Étoile restaurant at the Huntington Hotel, Nob Hill, San Francisco, 1970. Although Michael Taylor designed the space, Fred Lyon says that some credit for its appearance must be given to its owner, Claude Rouas, and his wife, Ardath. RIGHT: Fleur de Lys, the Nob Hill restaurant owned by Claude's brother Maurice Rouas, was also designed by Taylor, 1970.

$120,000 to purchase sixteen acres of hillside land in Napa Valley's Rutherford appellation with sweeping views to the valley floor and the Mayacamas Mountains. The purchase included plans for an inn. The Rouases liked the property but not the plans.[108] At dinner one evening, the Rouases asked Walker to take a look at the grounds and come up with design ideas for a restaurant there. Walker worked closely with the Rouases, who, he says, "were very important in the creative aspects of the project."[109] Fittingly, the first space for Auberge that Walker designed was its restaurant, drawing his initial sketches while working at a table at L'Étoile. To run the new restaurant at Auberge, Rouas enticed New York master chef Masataka "Masa" Kobayashi

to become the executive chef. Kobayashi also had a hand in designing the Auberge kitchen. It was at this time that Ardath Rouas brought in Michael Taylor—who had decorated L'Étoile and the San Francisco restaurant Fleur de Lys, owned by Claude Rouas's brother Maurice—to work on the Auberge restaurant. Taylor enlisted his friend Kay Kimpton, owner of K Kimpton Contemporary Art in San Francisco, to supply much of the art for Auberge. (Walker and Kimpton enjoyed working with each other so much that they later married.)

Walker next turned his attention to adding residences to the property. He notes, "Our intention was to build fourteen condominium residence suites, one for each investor in the

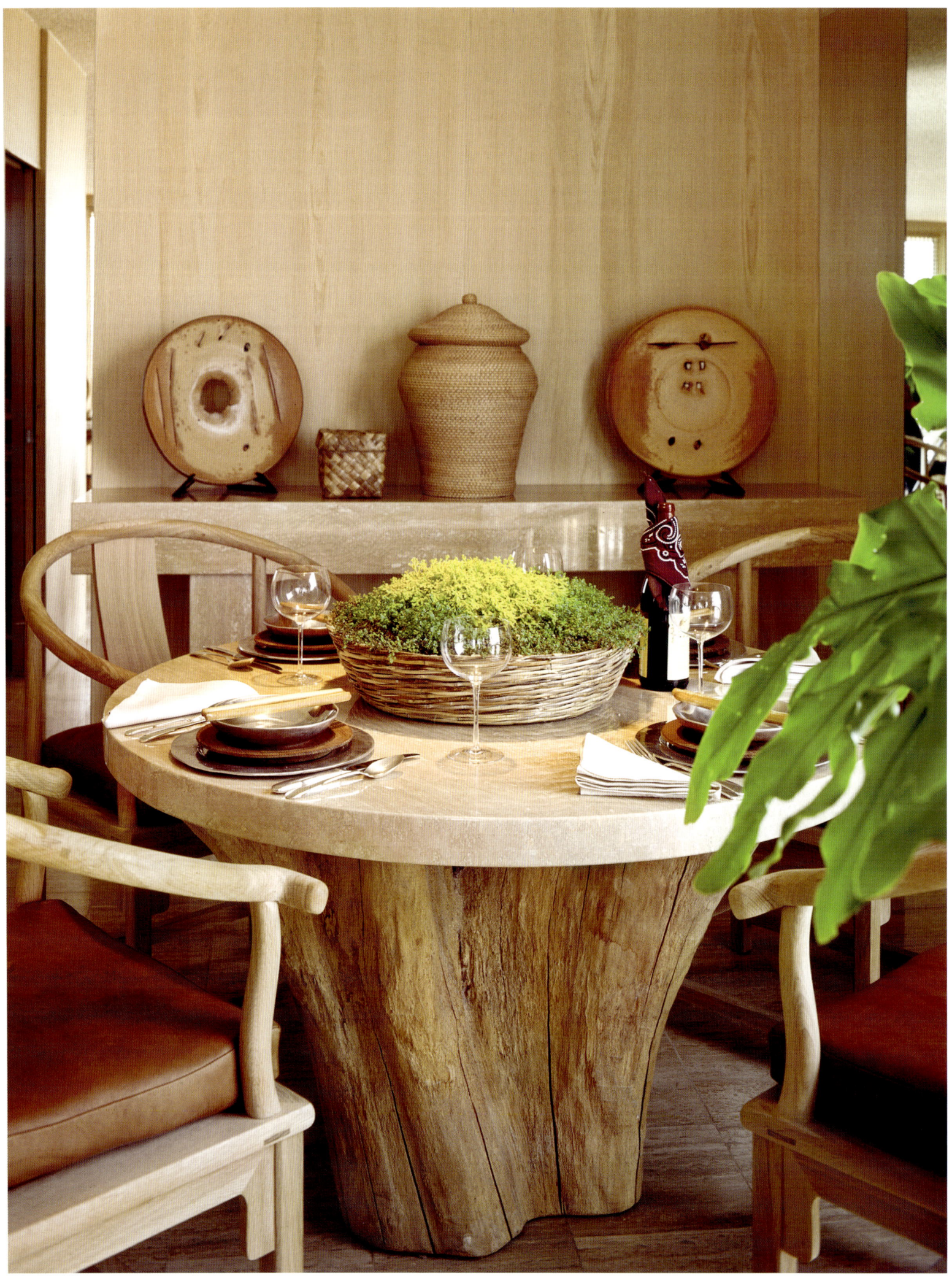

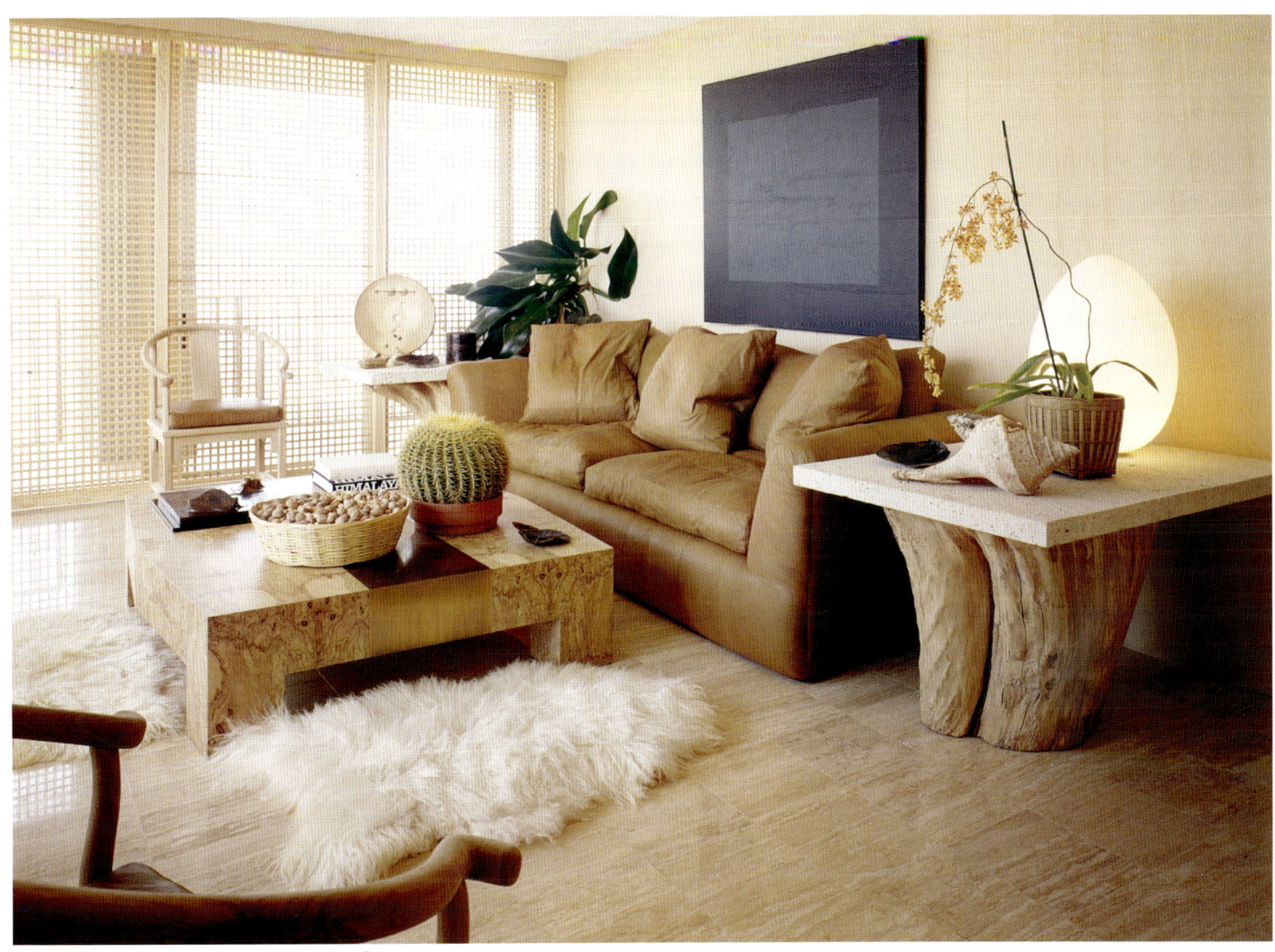

initial Auberge project."[110] While the restaurant project was underway, some of the initial investors pulled out. Walker then approached developer Robert Harmon to join the Auberge team. As the project progressed, Michael Taylor began to design the interiors for the suites, or *maisons* as they are called at Auberge. Walker and Taylor worked together in their usual manner. "Working with Michael was intense and always a collaboration," Walker remembers. "As the architect, I never just handed over a project to him to decorate. It was an ongoing collaboration, and Michael was usually involved from the beginning; indeed, Michael usually had the job first, and then he was influential in the client's decision about which architect to hire."[111] Remembering Taylor's commanding personality, Walker jokes, "At least I thought of it as a collaboration. He might not have thought about it that way."[112] According to Walker, "Michael didn't do a lot of drawings when we worked together. He could sketch well, but he didn't do a lot of it. Many of the well-known decorators at that time did not create drawings. The way Michael worked was by waving his hands in the air. We would try to interpret what he intended and draw it. For example, at Auberge, Michael had the idea that there should be strips of oak in the middle of the concrete flooring. He never drew up that design, but he described what he wanted and we tried to interpret that. That was the way a lot of things worked with decorators then."[113]

Walker says, "Michael was a very hot decorator. He had a direct line to *Architectural Digest*, which did a story on Auberge. That was a big boost for me."[114] Sandy Walker did not really need the boost. He comes from established families. His father is of the same family that started the famed Walker Art Center in Minneapolis. His mother and paternal aunt were involved early on with the San Francisco Museum of Modern Art. Walker grew up in the kind of society milieu where "people had architects." He says, "My grandmother had a house in Carmel that Frank Lloyd Wright designed. My mother had a house designed by William Wurster, and my aunt had a house designed by Gardner Dailey. Growing up, it seemed to me that everybody employed an architect."[115] Walker and Lyon go so far back that it is difficult for them to remember how they met. Walker thinks it was through Dorothea Walker—no relation, but a good friend of his family. She admired Sandy Walker's work and arranged for Lyon to photograph one of his creations for *House & Garden*. This happy symbiosis would occur often with these three people.

For architects, often their client's initial relationship is with the decorator or landscape architect. Reflecting on the power that some decorators can wield, Walker says, "Michael Taylor brought a lot of work to me. I grew up knowing the landscape architect Tommy Church, and he also suggested me to his clients, and I got a lot of work through him, too."[116]

Lyon photographed Taylor's work from almost the beginning of the decorator's career, in 1954, when he was in partnership with Frances Mihailoff. Lyon told Diane Dorrans Saeks, "We shot everything Michael did, for *House & Garden* and *Vogue*, and in the sixties and seventies and into the eighties he had an enormous amount of work.... Those were the days of the decorator-as-despot. Michael was bold and terribly outspoken and his clients were completely in awe of everything he said and did. But his rooms for each client were elegant, sometimes eccentric, and always highly individual."[117] Taylor, described as "almost troublingly handsome . . . denied himself nothing and thought his clients should do the same.

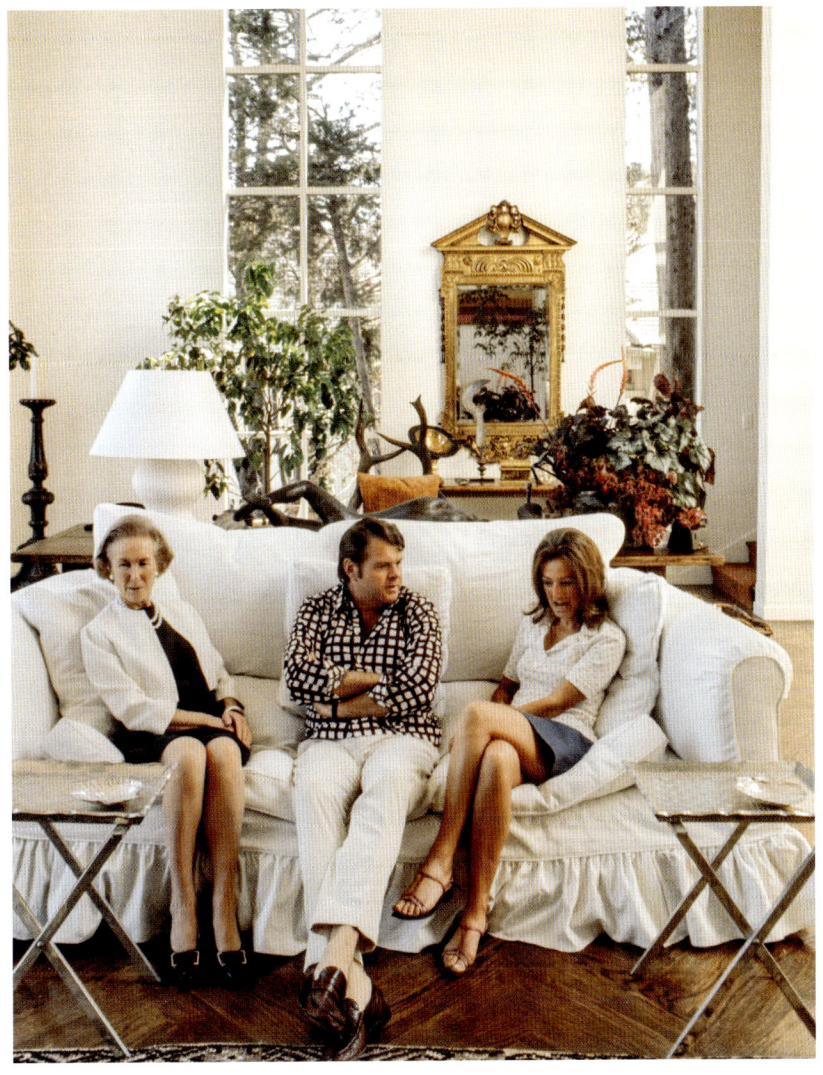

Or rather he thought they should deny him nothing if he agreed to come down from the mountain to do their houses."[118]

Taylor's clients had to be patient. Lyon says, "Michael Taylor was out of control. He'd gossip with clients all day long. These ladies married exceedingly well but many were neglected by the captains of industry they had married. An amusement for them was to retain a high-end decorator. Michael Taylor was tall and handsome and could be very amusing at his best."[119] Taylor never kept to a schedule. Days before a shoot, a lady in Aptos called Dorothea Walker to say that Michael Taylor had not quite com-

pleted her interior design. Walker advised the owner to say that Lyon was coming soon to photograph the space. Lyon says, "Michael came and finished it in record time. He was very good at fixing things for the camera.... With a big painting, he'd make blemishes on walls disappear. This time he just picked up the phone and called gallery owner John Berggruen to borrow a painting for the day. The owner eventually bought it. Michael Taylor was the hottest thing in California, and enormously influential in decorating then and now.... He was one of the first superstar decorators, restless, imposing, always exploring new design ideas."[120]

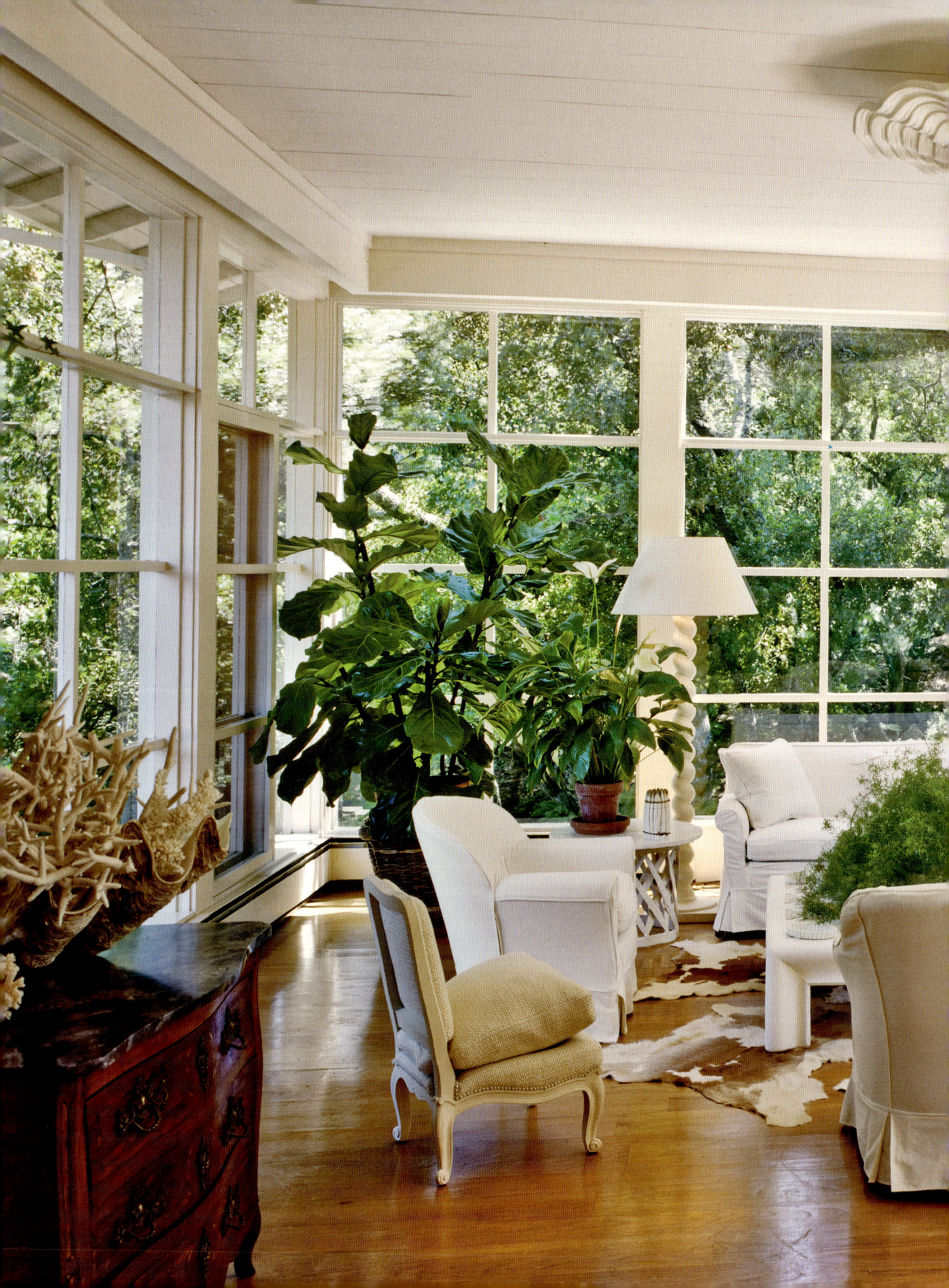

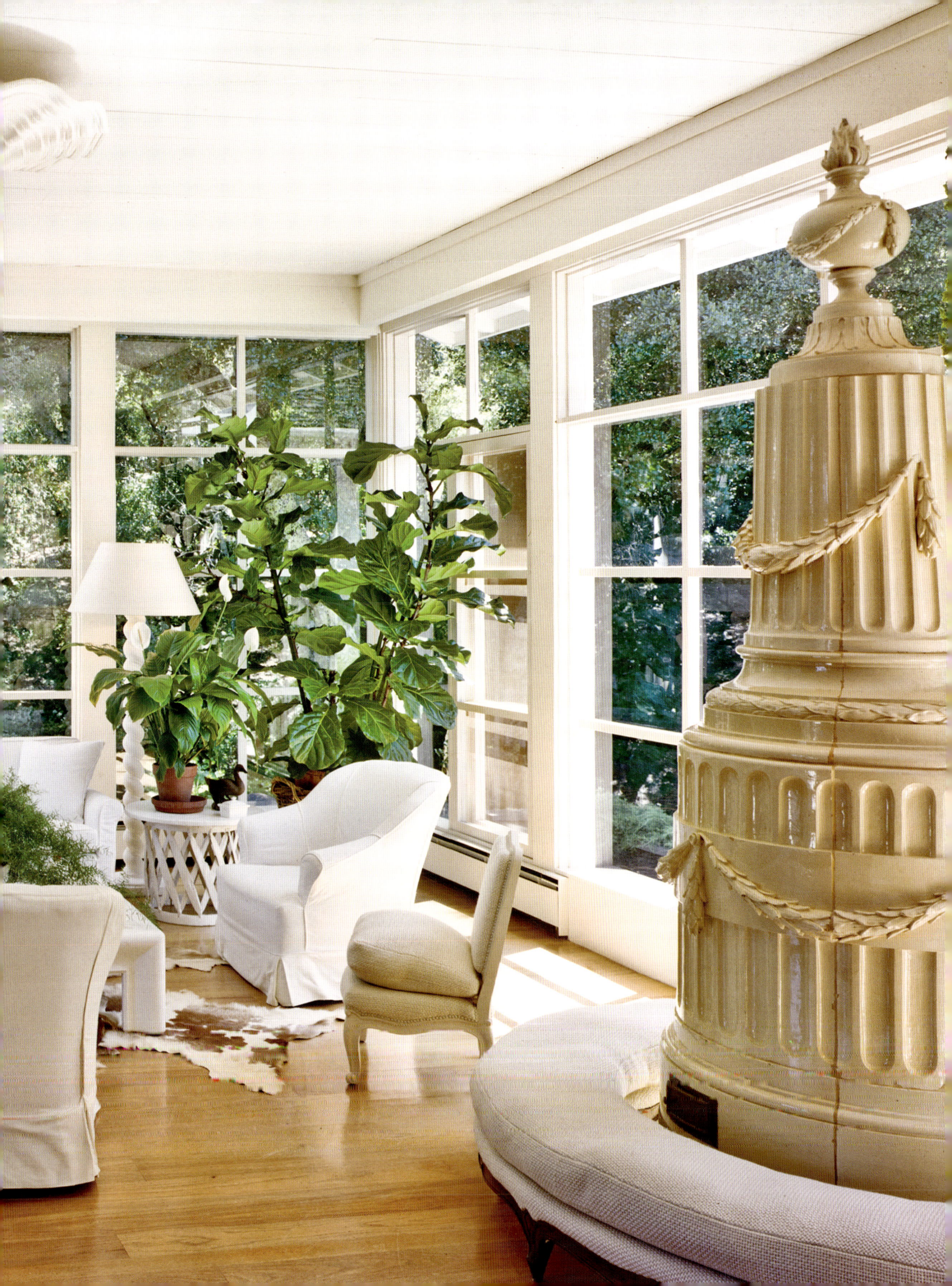

MICHAEL TAYLOR SHOWROOMS

San Francisco, 1957–1960

During much of his career, Michael Taylor maintained distinctive shop spaces in downtown San Francisco. His first shop was located at 430 Post Street, on the ground floor of the St. Francis Hotel. He shared this space with his business partner, the designer Frances Mihailoff. A few years later, each decided to establish a separate business. Michael stayed in the Post Street location until 1956, when he moved his shop to a large space one block away, at 556 Sutter Street.

From time to time, Michael created complete room settings in his downtown shops. Sometimes they were tributes to designers he admired, including one homage to Syrie Maugham. At other times, Michael created settings to explore ideas he was considering, such as spaces with pieces from Western Art Stone, leather-upholstered chairs, and a huge piece of driftwood or a tree trunk. He used these kinds of pieces for texture and scale.

It was part of Michael's design genius to mix pieces, including very costly antiques paired with items he purchased from Cost Plus. Michael was very big on sourcing objects from that store, which had a terrific buyer named Gale Taffinder. Michael, like John Dickinson, was very open to using nontraditional sources. They both encouraged their suppliers to acquire more fanciful objects. Michael bought inexpensive wooden stools from Mexico, with leather stretched across their seats. He took these stools to an auto painting shop, where they masked off the leather tops and spray-painted the stools a glossy white enamel. They looked fantastic. Michael also had an enthusiasm for cast plaster. You would see cast-plaster furniture in his showrooms, as well as in the spaces of many of his clients.

In 1969, Michael purchased a mansion in the Sea Cliff neighborhood, overlooking the Pacific Ocean and Golden Gate Bridge. He closed his Sutter Street space and operated out of his home, where he held court with his clients.

—F.L.

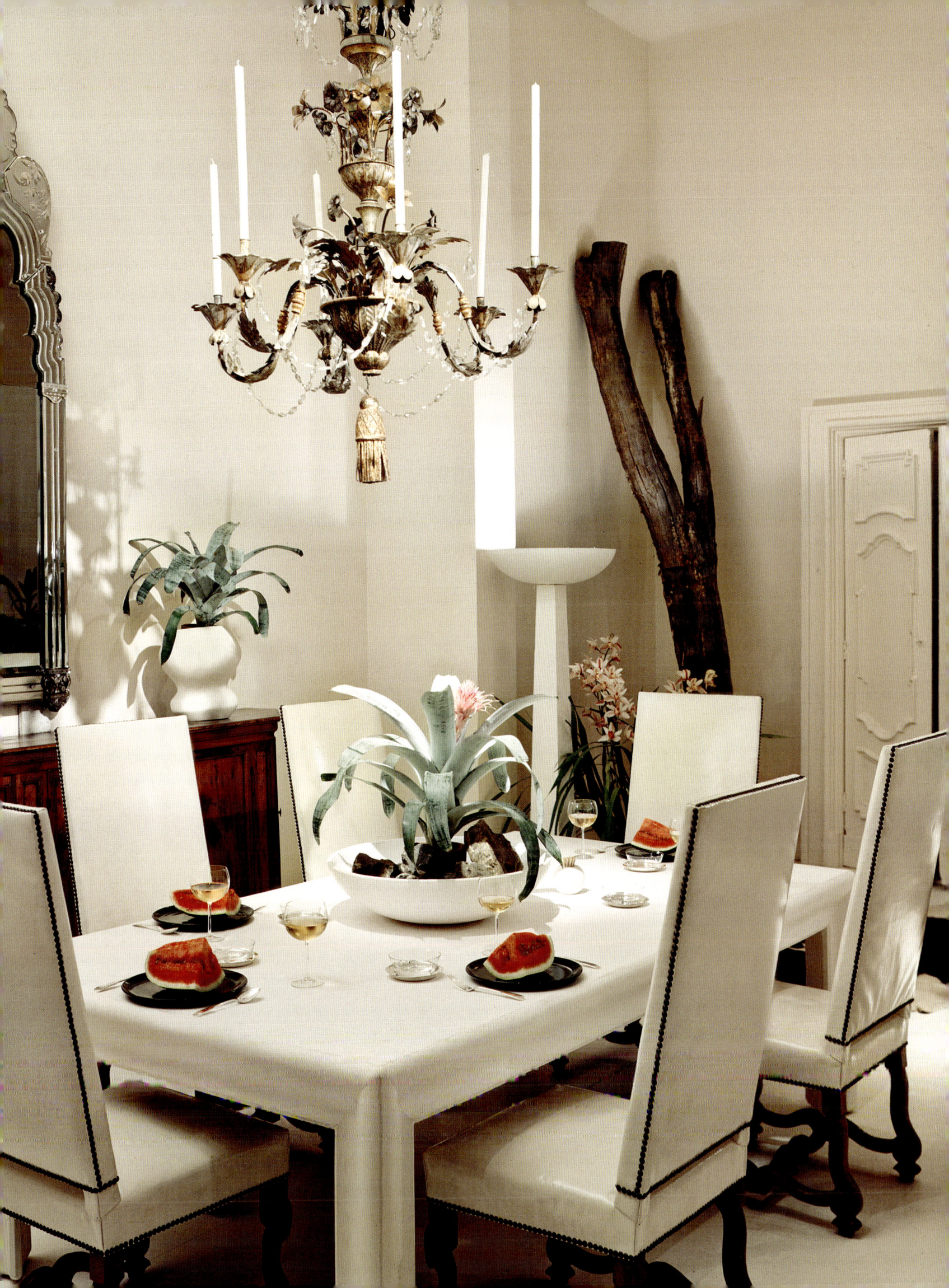

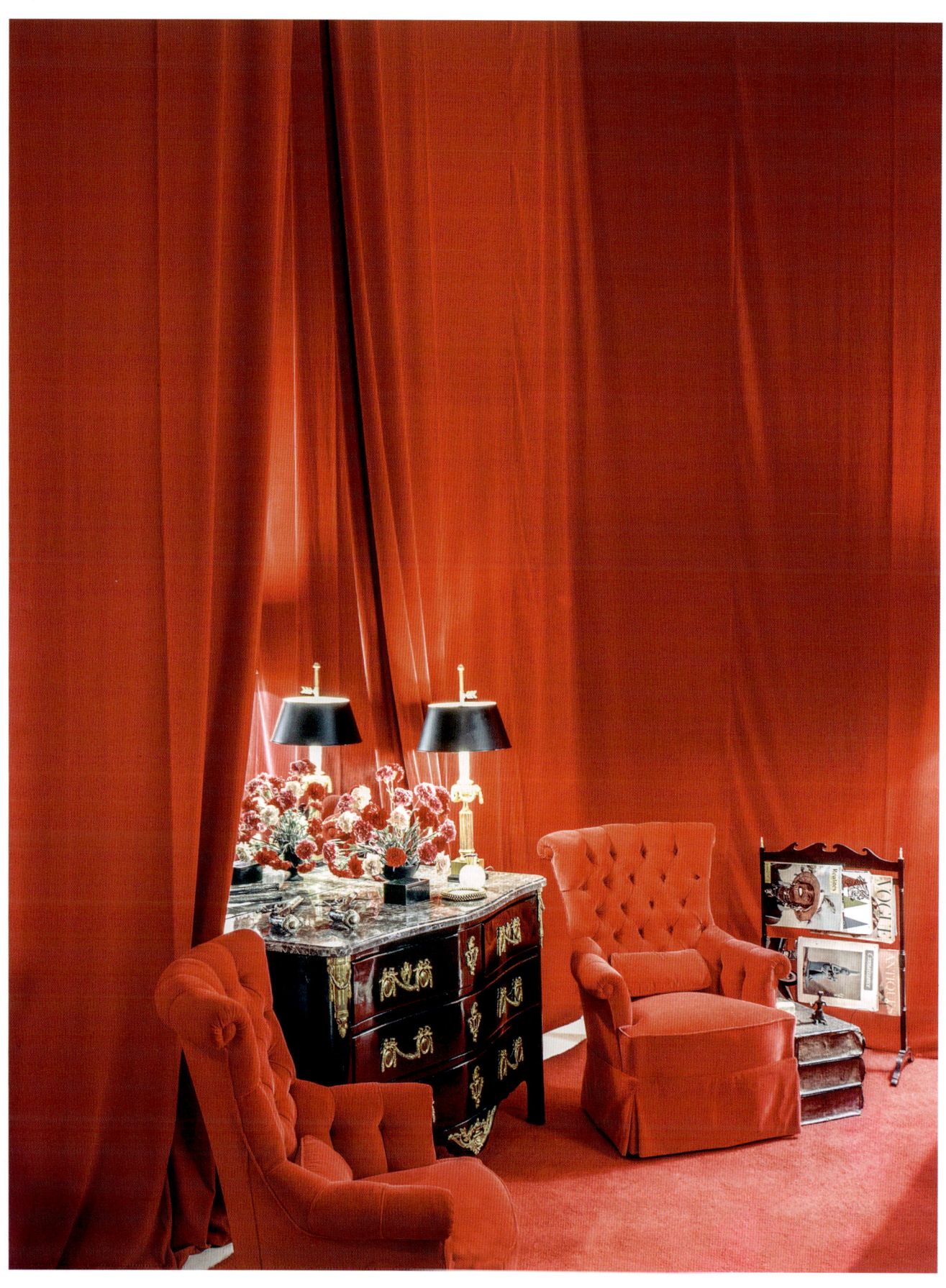

PAGE 93: A white dining room setting at Michael Taylor's showroom at 556 Sutter Street, San Francisco, 1960. ABOVE: Detail of a living room setting in Taylor's showroom, 1957. Red velvet hangs from the high ceiling. OPPOSITE: View of the same living room, which was centered on a bold cast-plaster fireplace, 1957. The model provides scale for the dramatic room.

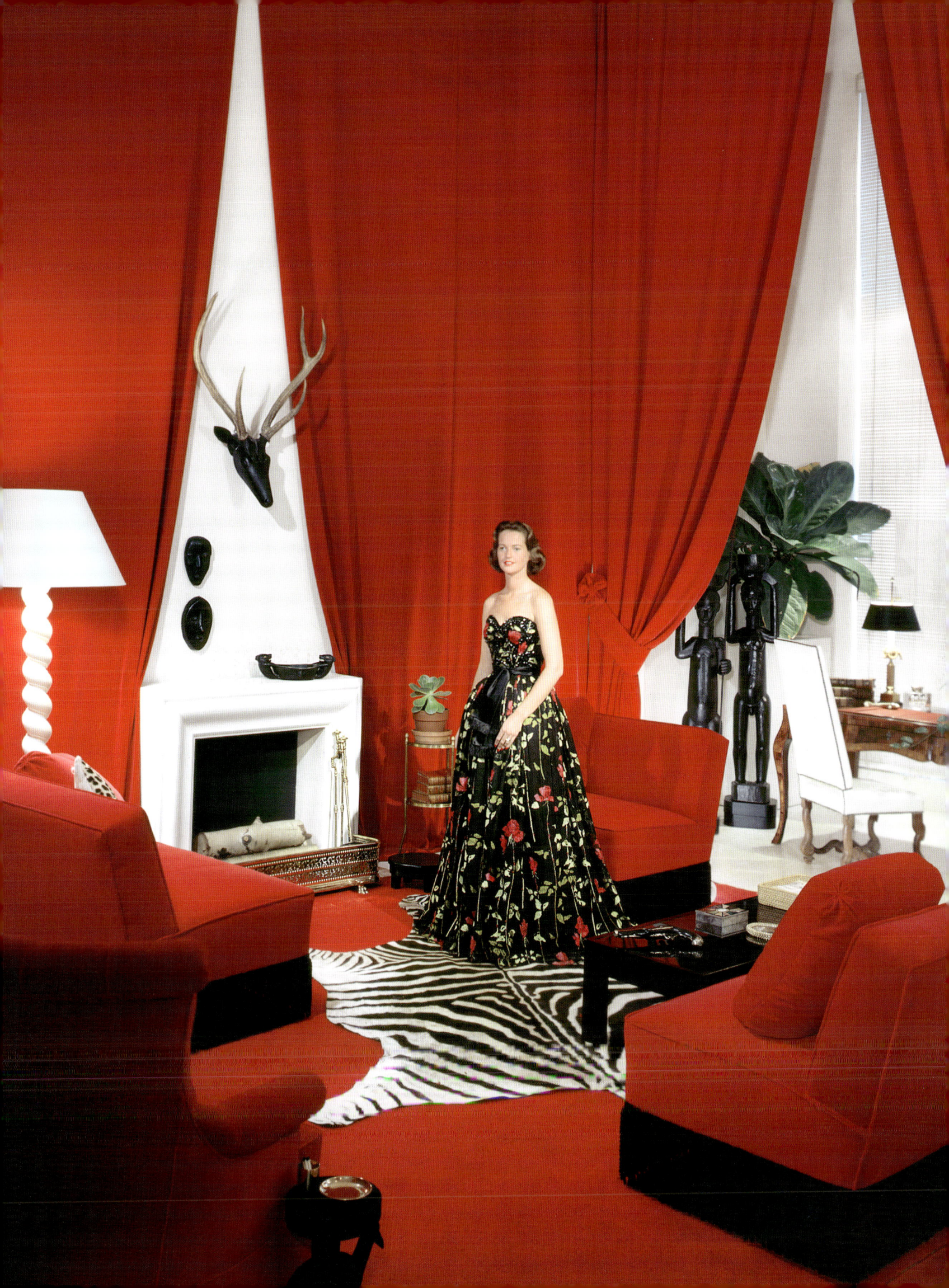

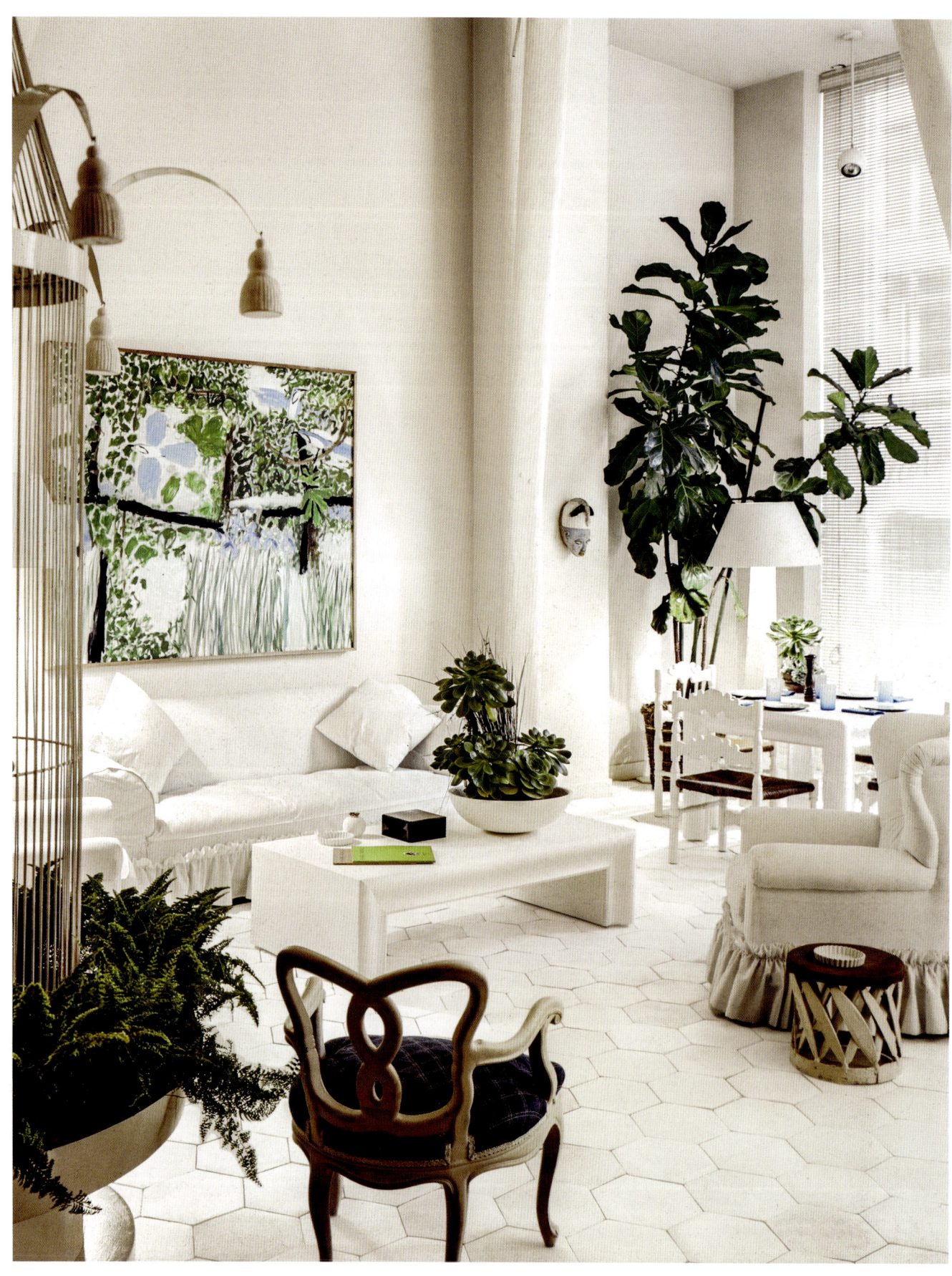

ABOVE: A sunroom setting at Taylor's showroom, 1960. *Scrub Jays* (1957), a painting by Bryan Wilson, stands out in the all-white interior. This image was used for the cover of the August 1960 issue of *House & Garden*. OPPOSITE: Bedroom setting at Taylor's showroom, 1959. The room is a study in white: from the hexagonal glazed terra-cotta floor tiles to the eighteenth-century Portuguese bed hung with oyster-white spun nylon to the cast-stone table designed by Taylor. The Spanish baroque mirror frame is gilded wood.

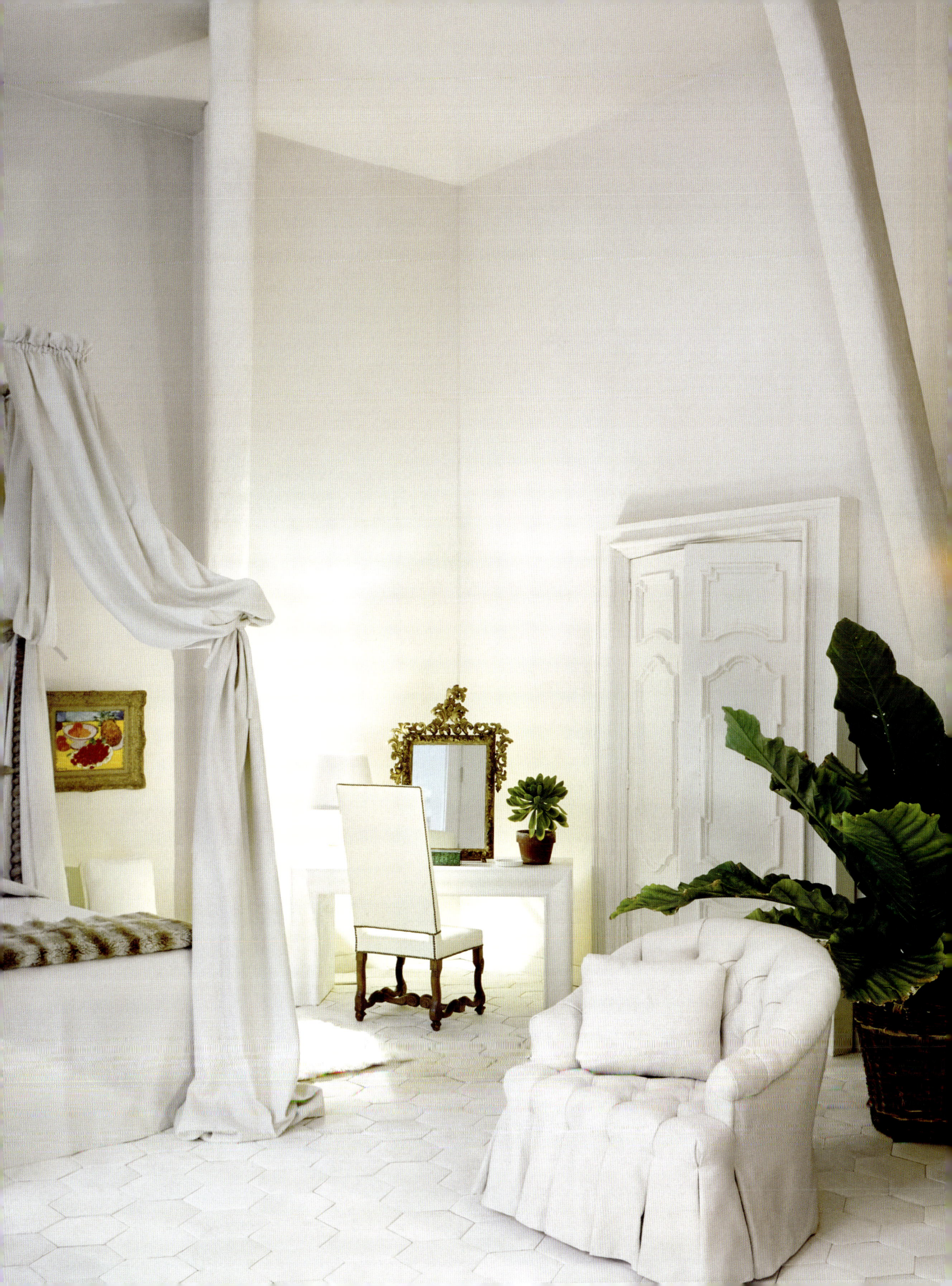

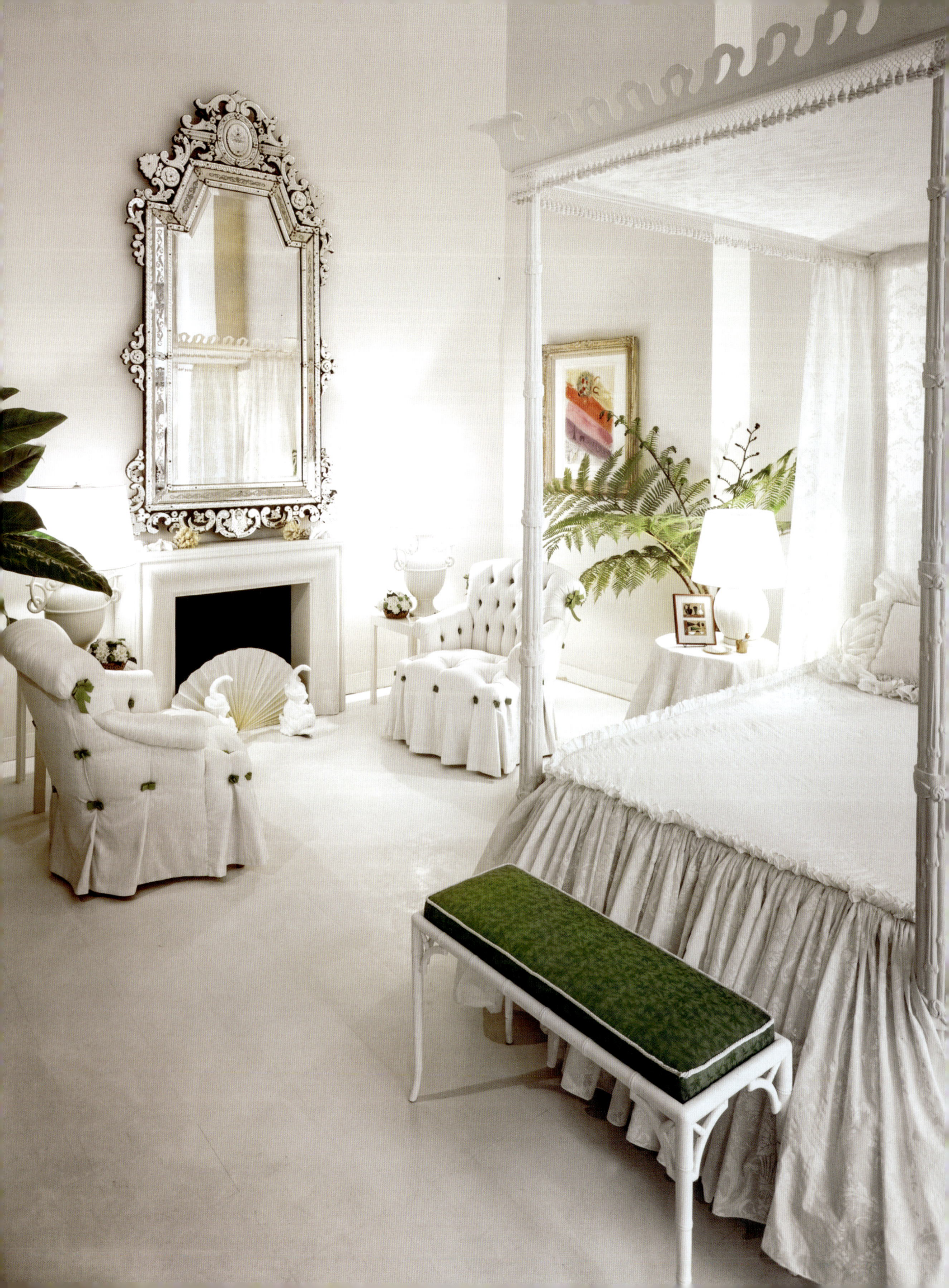

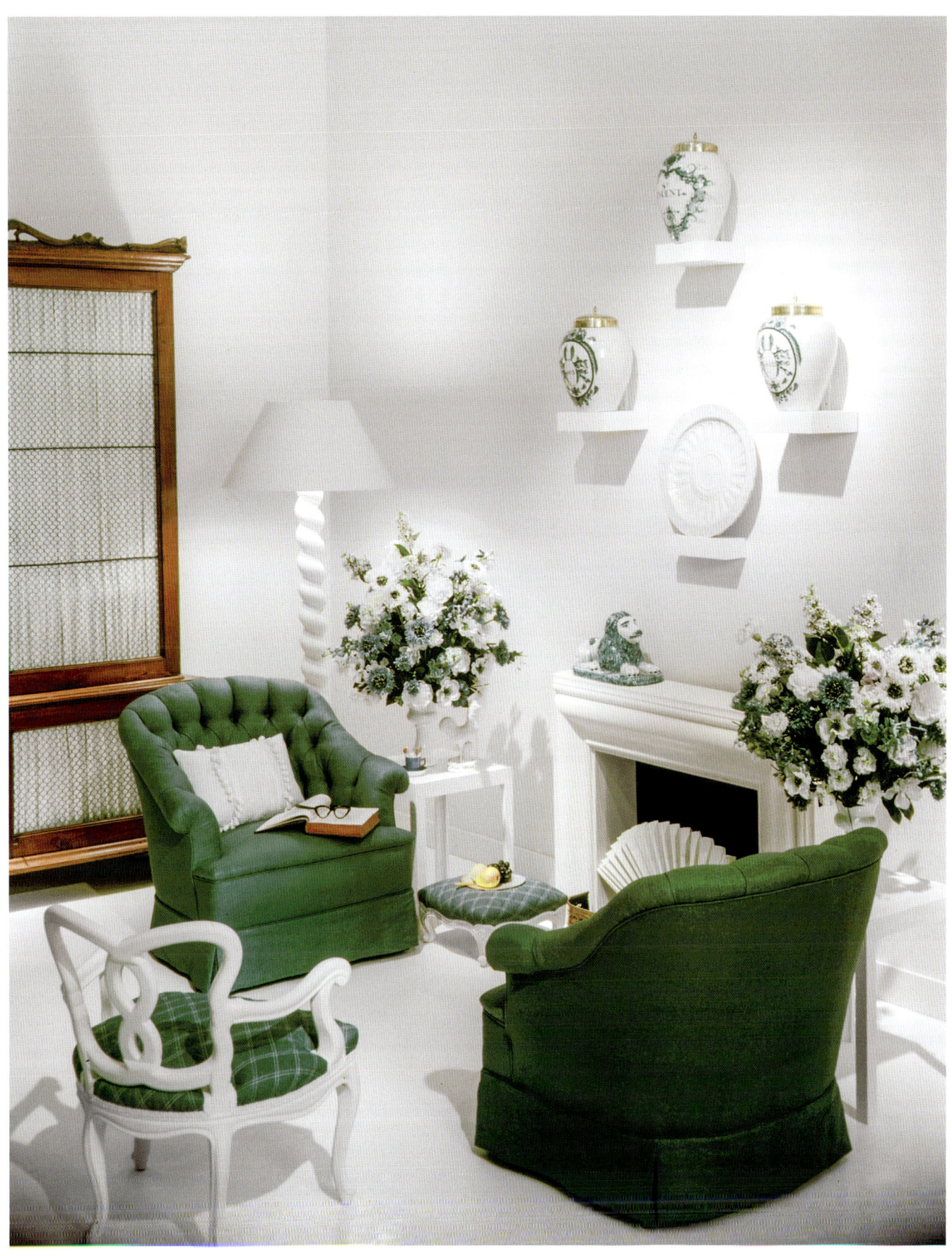

OPPOSITE: Bedroom setting at Taylor's showroom, incorporating furniture from his Syrie Maugham collection, 1959.
ABOVE: Detail of Taylor's showroom, 1959 A pair of green upholstered chairs enlivens the white space.

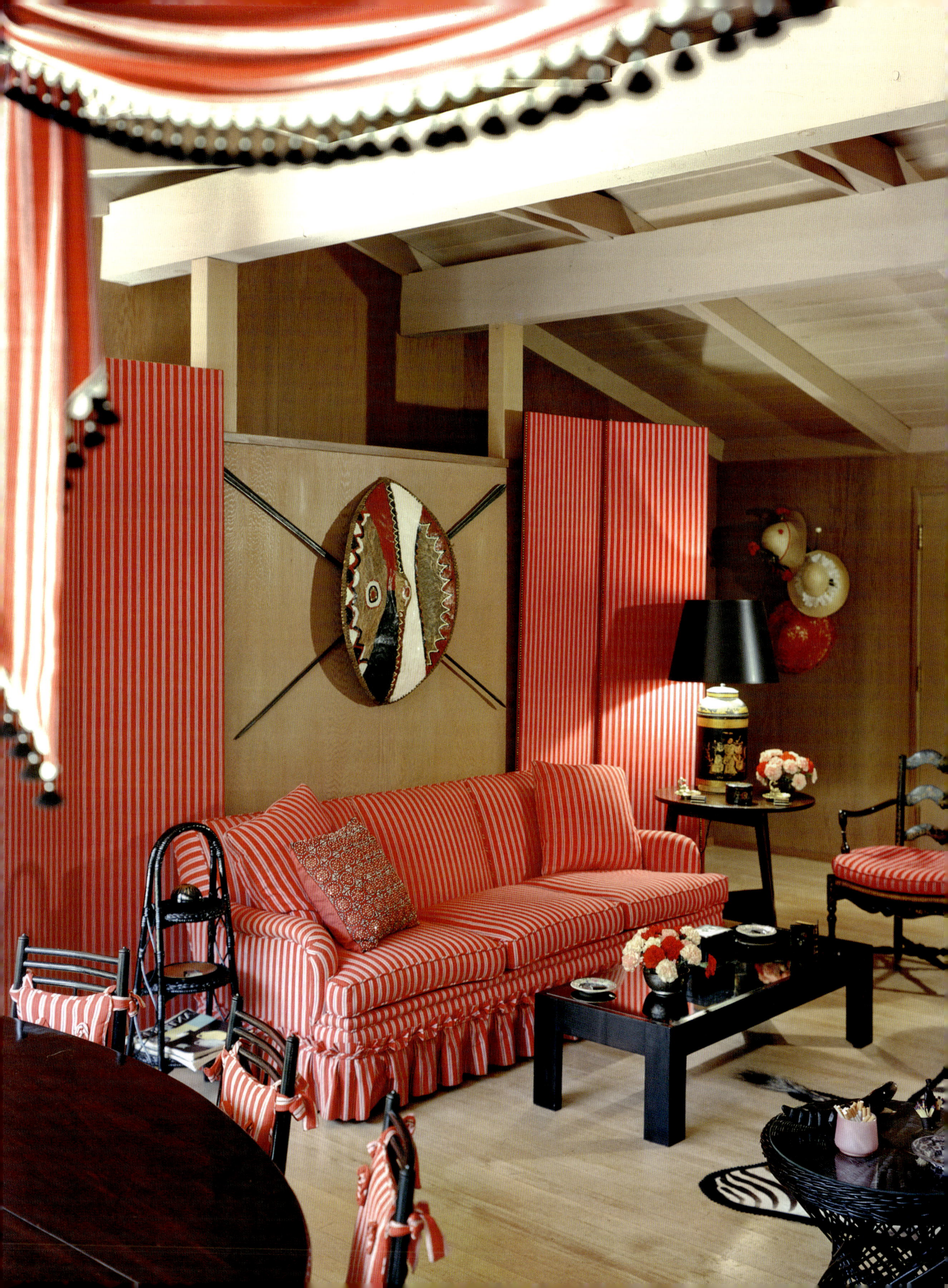

IRMA AND ALBERT SCHLESINGER HOUSE
Atherton, 1958

Michael Taylor decorated the Atherton house of Irma and Albert Schlesinger in 1958. Frances Elkins had decorated their San Francisco house in 1951. After she died, it was natural for the couple to turn to Michael, who was Frances's spiritual heir and a good friend of the Schlesingers' daughter, Nan Kempner.

To photograph the interior spaces, I brought natural light into the rooms by placing reflectors on the outside of the windows. To soften the light, I covered the windows with diffusion cloths. I also used a blue photo bulb in some of the lamps to equalize color. We had to be very careful when using those bulbs because they burned very hot and sometimes they burned out the lamp socket, which understandably aggravated the homeowners.

The design of the Schlesingers' Atherton residence, a respite from their life in San Francisco, was influenced by a passion for big game hunting. Trophies, zebra-skin rugs, and African mementos were displayed in the trophy room, as well as in most other rooms of the house. A thatched-roof bar was the highlight of the barroom, off of the trophy room. These photographs were published in the July 1959 issue of *House & Garden*.　　　　—F.L.

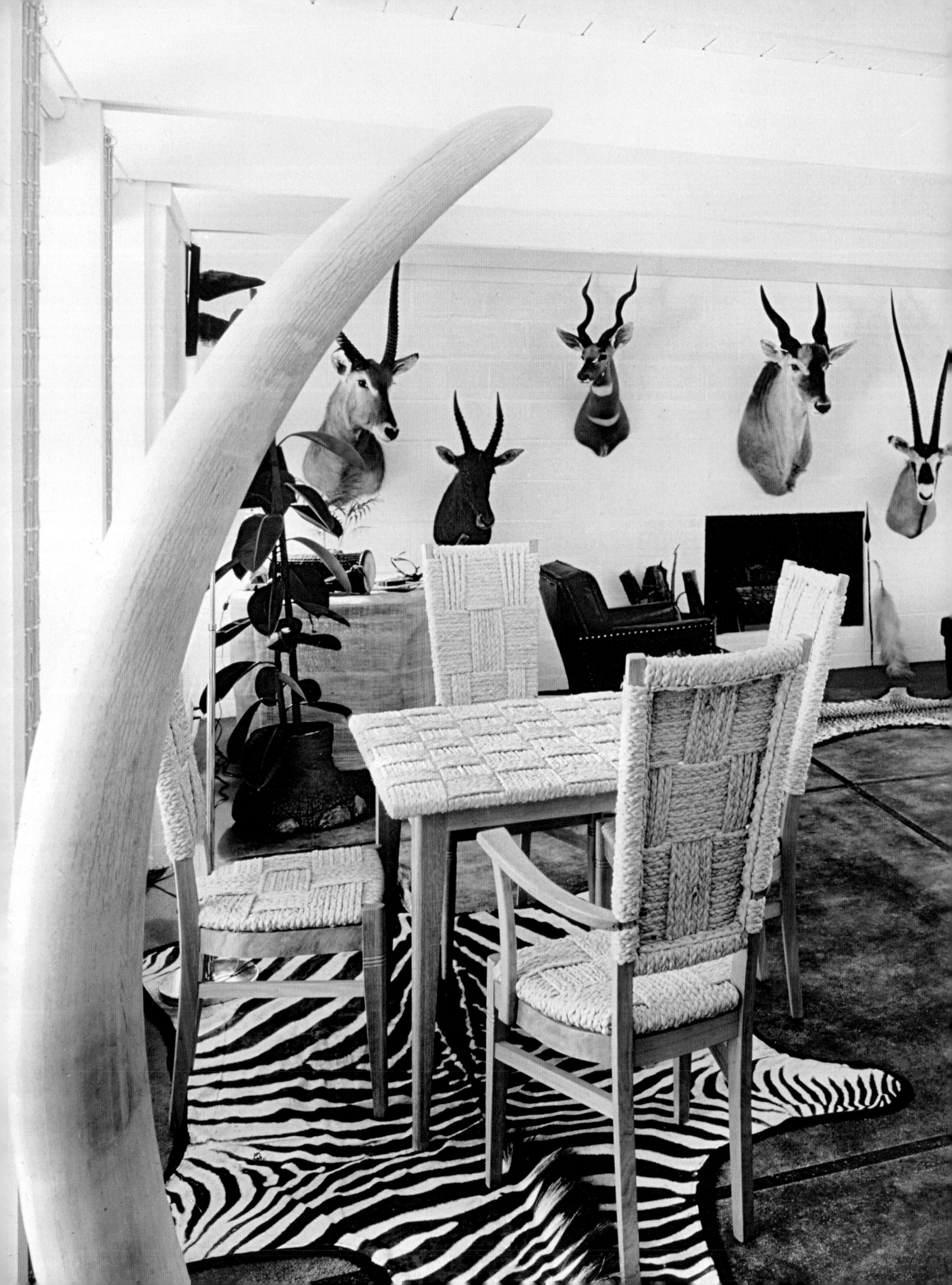

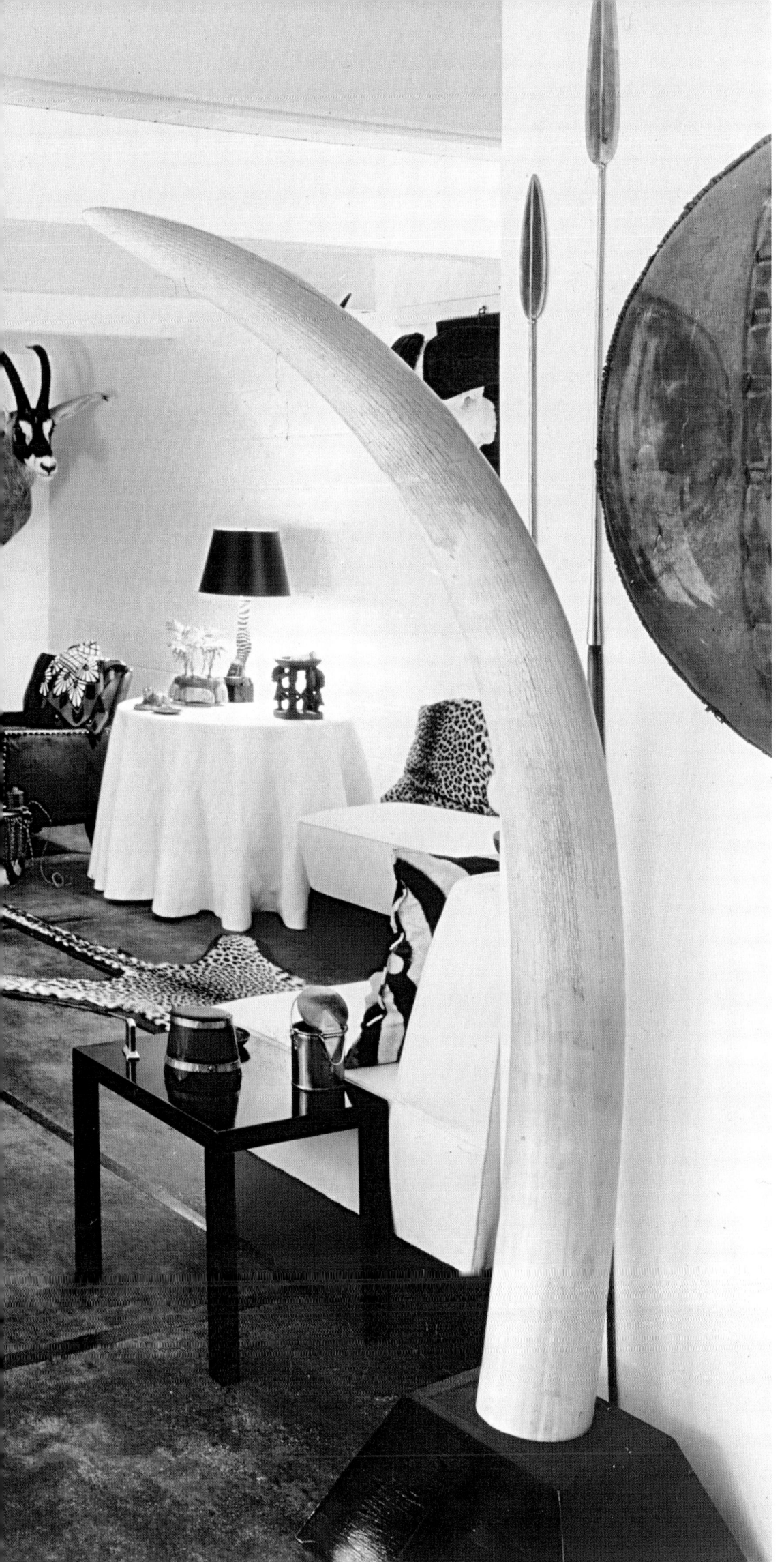

PAGE 100: Living room of the Schlesinger house in Atherton, 1958. Michael Taylor used red-and-pink-striped cotton for the upholstery and screen panels. Over the sofa are a Maasai shield and crossed spears. An eclectic collection of furniture includes a French provincial ladder-back chair and eighteenth-century dining chairs that Taylor stained black. LEFT: Albert "Speed" Schlesinger's trophy room, which exemplifies the big-game theme used throughout the house.

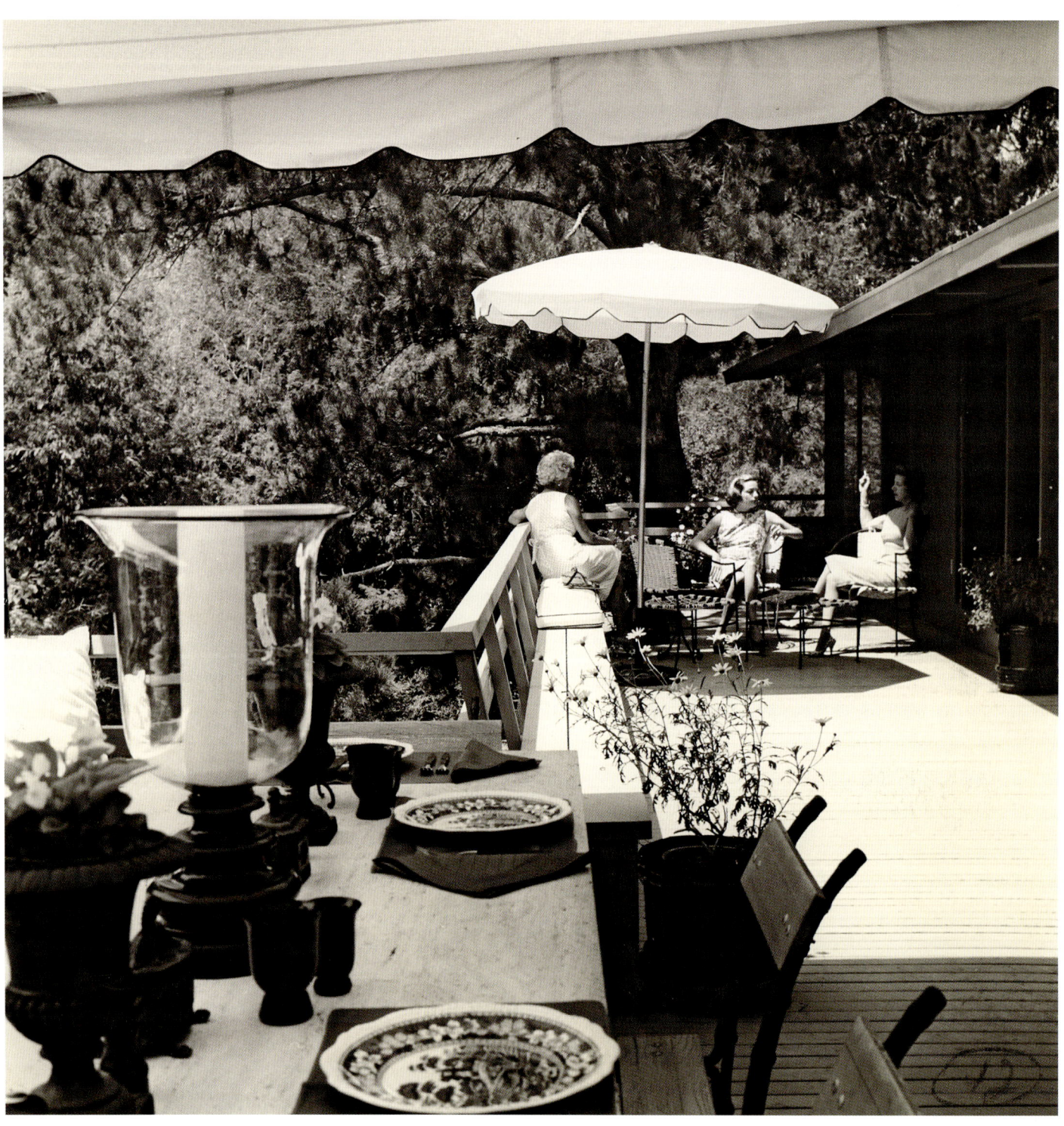

ABOVE: Irma Schlesinger and friends relax on the deck off the living room, 1958. OPPOSITE: In the Schlesingers'
bedroom, the corkscrew posts of the bedframes echo the horns of the antelope heads mounted on the walls.

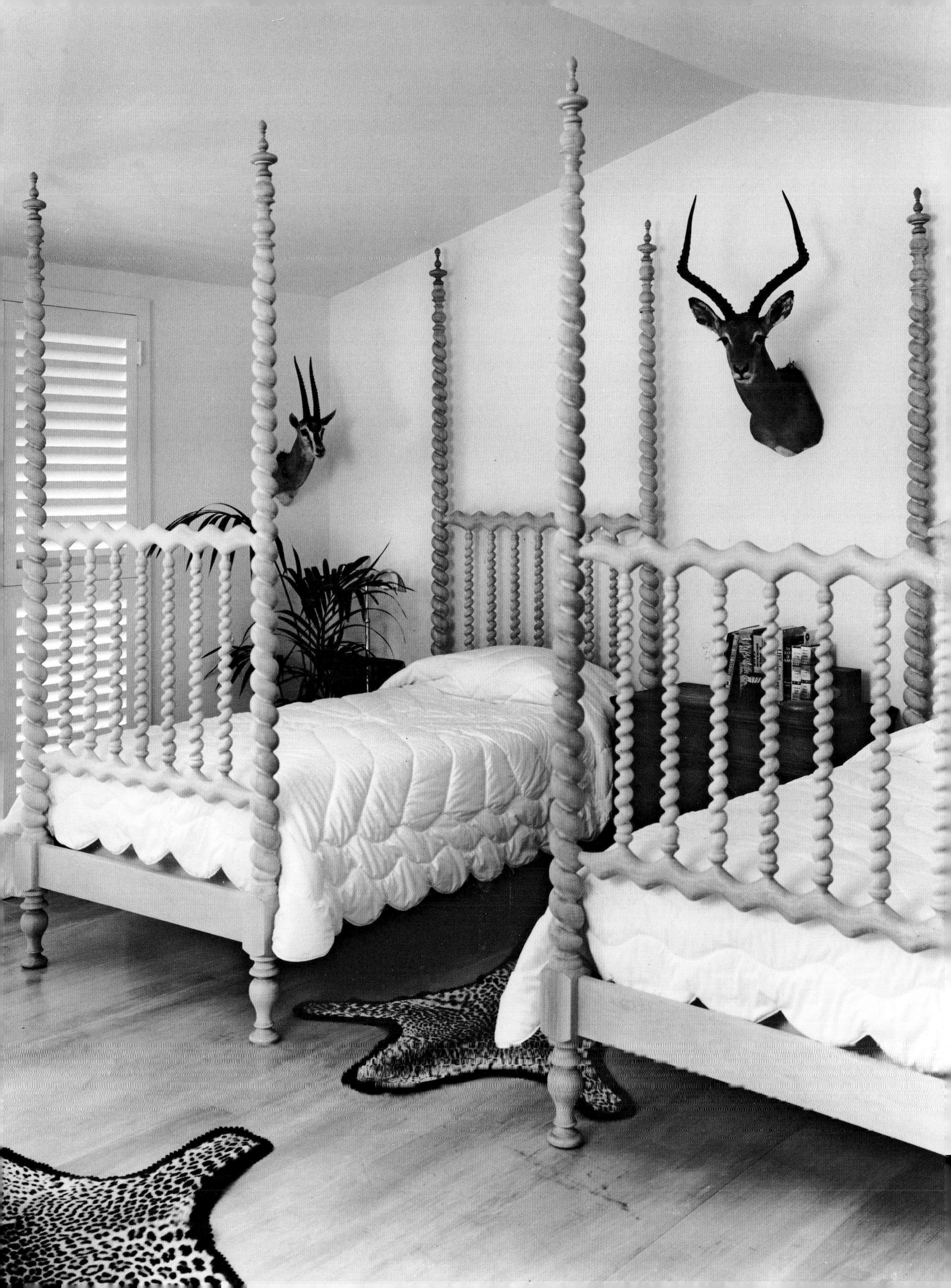

GERRY AND WILLIAM ROBERTS HOUSE
Woodside, 1965

Michael Taylor loved to come on photo shoots for his projects. He would redecorate in front of the camera, which was frustrating for me, but the results were glorious. Even when he made me furious, Michael was funny and a joy to be with.

There was lots of black and white furniture with sunlight streaming into some of the rooms, which was a challenge to photograph. Other rooms had very little natural light. Most of the rooms had tremendous scale, with very high ceilings. The spaces could accommodate visually the beams and braces that Michael had made for this house and placed throughout.

The bedroom-study of the two college-age brothers had a circular fireplace in the center of the room with a plaster hood. Only Michael would create a design like that. Another bedroom was accessed from the hallway through a Dutch door. Nobody else was doing that either. The house was situated in a sylvan area in Woodside and had lots of surrounding space. There was a large indoor-outdoor room that Michael ingeniously integrated into the house. The family seemed to spend much of their time in that space.

I think these photographs, taken for the January 1966 issue of *House & Garden*, show exactly where Michael's head was at that moment. The absurdity of the flokati rugs and the zebra upholstery—that was how his mind worked. I appreciate his talent even more as I review these images decades later.   —*F.L.*

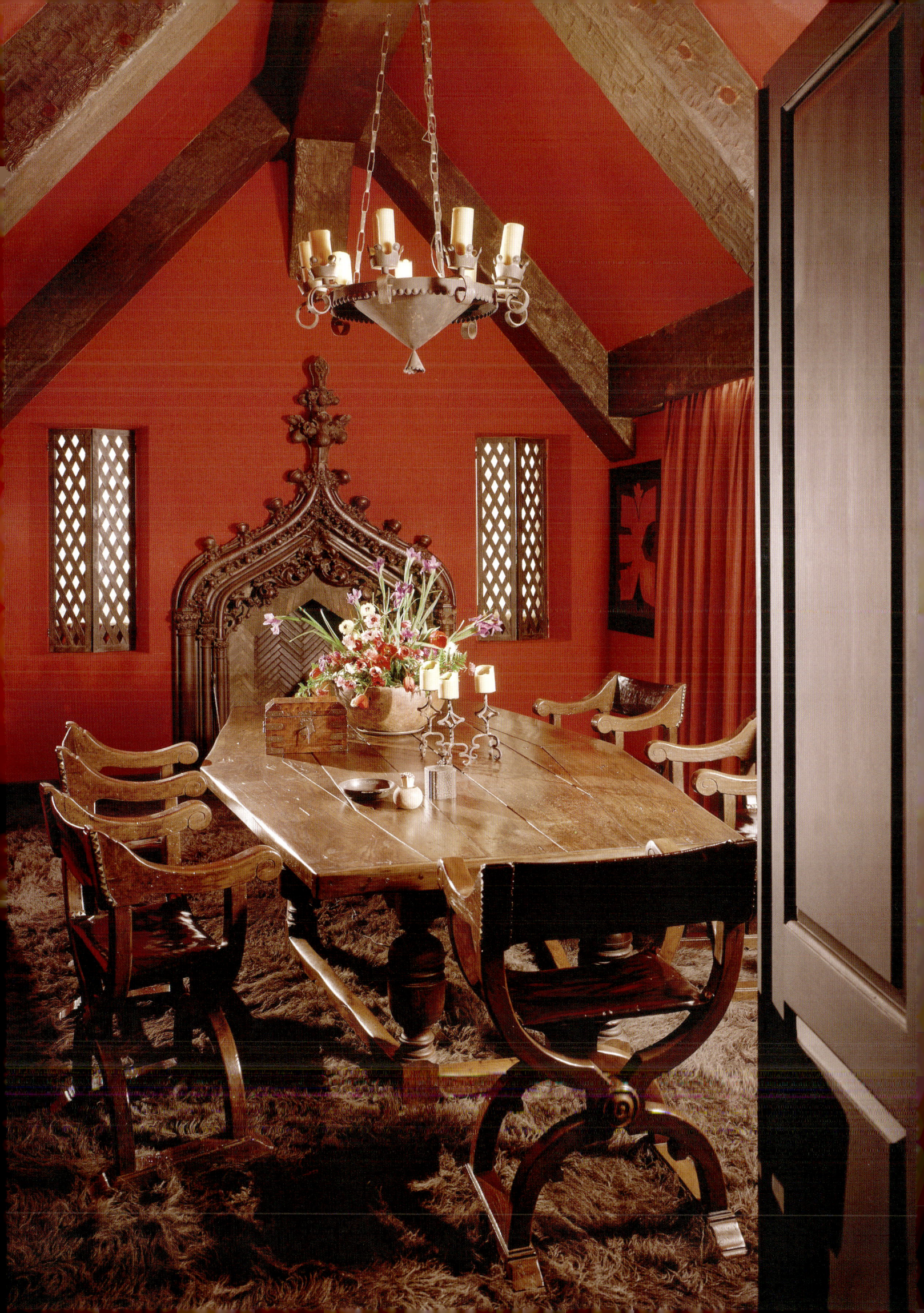

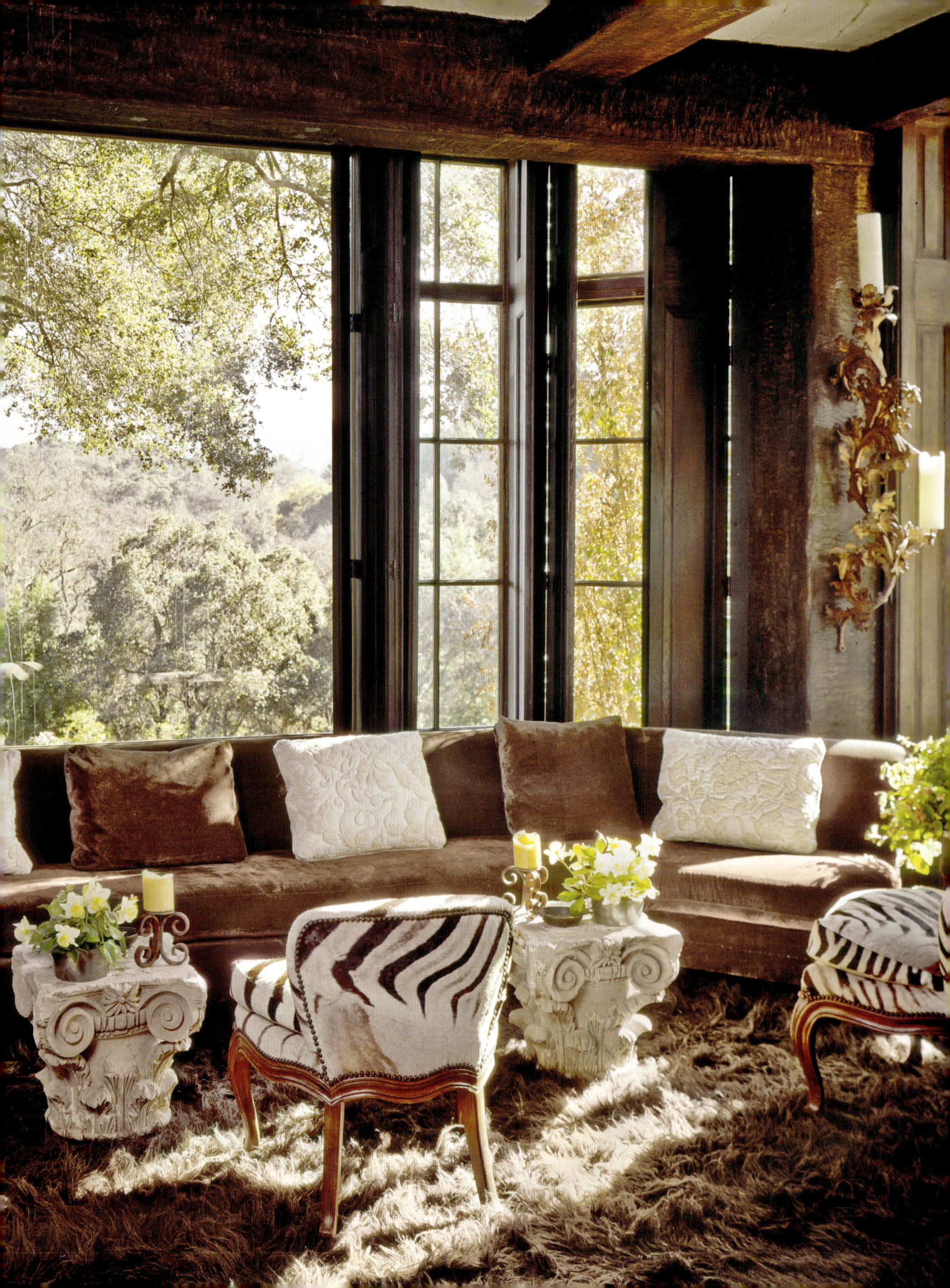

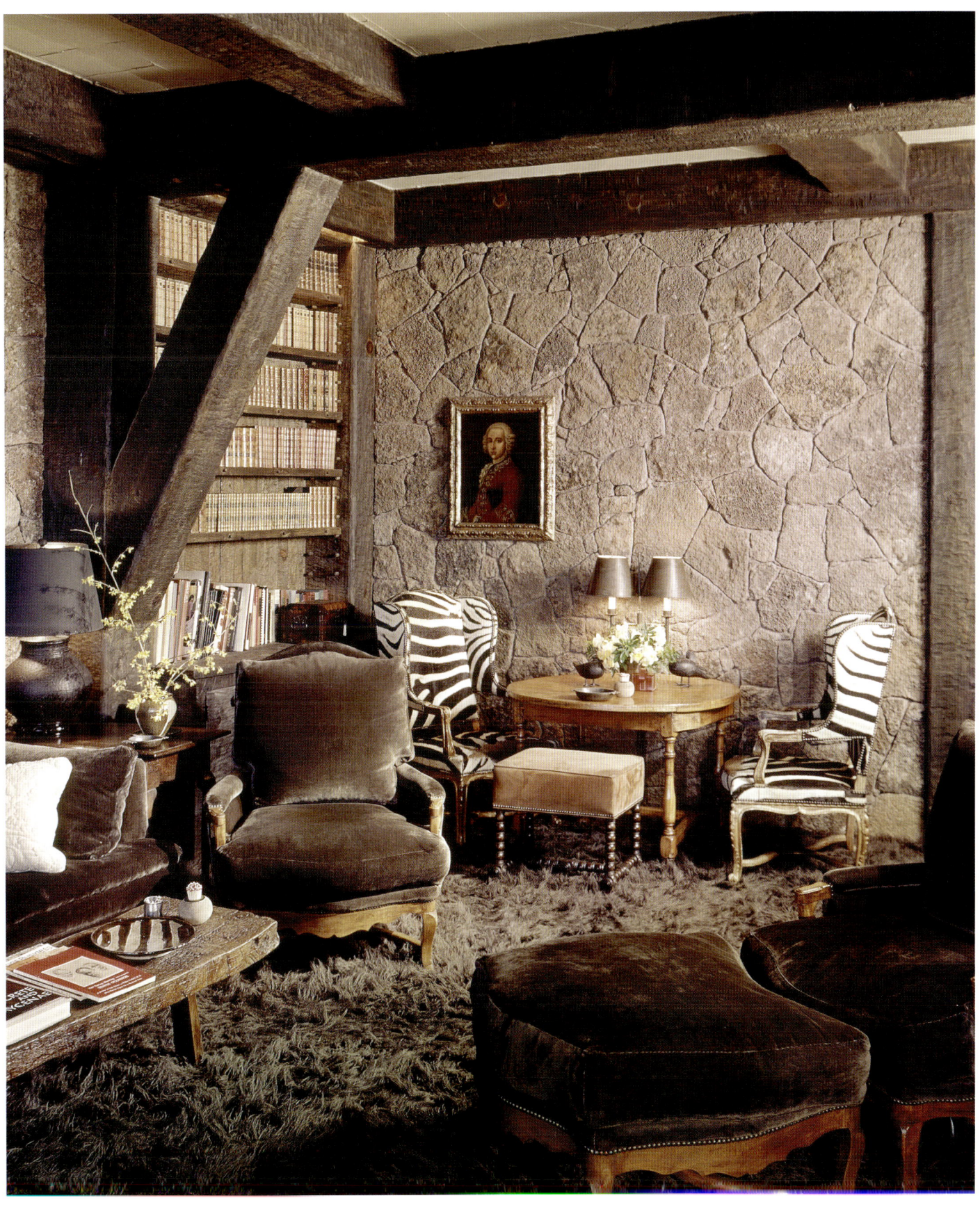

PAGE 107: Michael Taylor used red burlap to cover the walls and ceiling of the dining room in the Gerry and William Roberts house in Woodside, 1965. Jacobean style dining chairs pair well with the Gothic Revival fireplace; overhead is a Mexican tin chandelier. OPPOSITE AND ABOVE: The living room overlooks bucolic terrain. The furnishings are eclectic: a wraparound sofa covered in chocolate-brown velvet, Mexican stone capitals used as tables, French chairs with zebra-skin upholstery, and a Greek goat-wool rug. Stone walls are framed with rough-hewn beams.

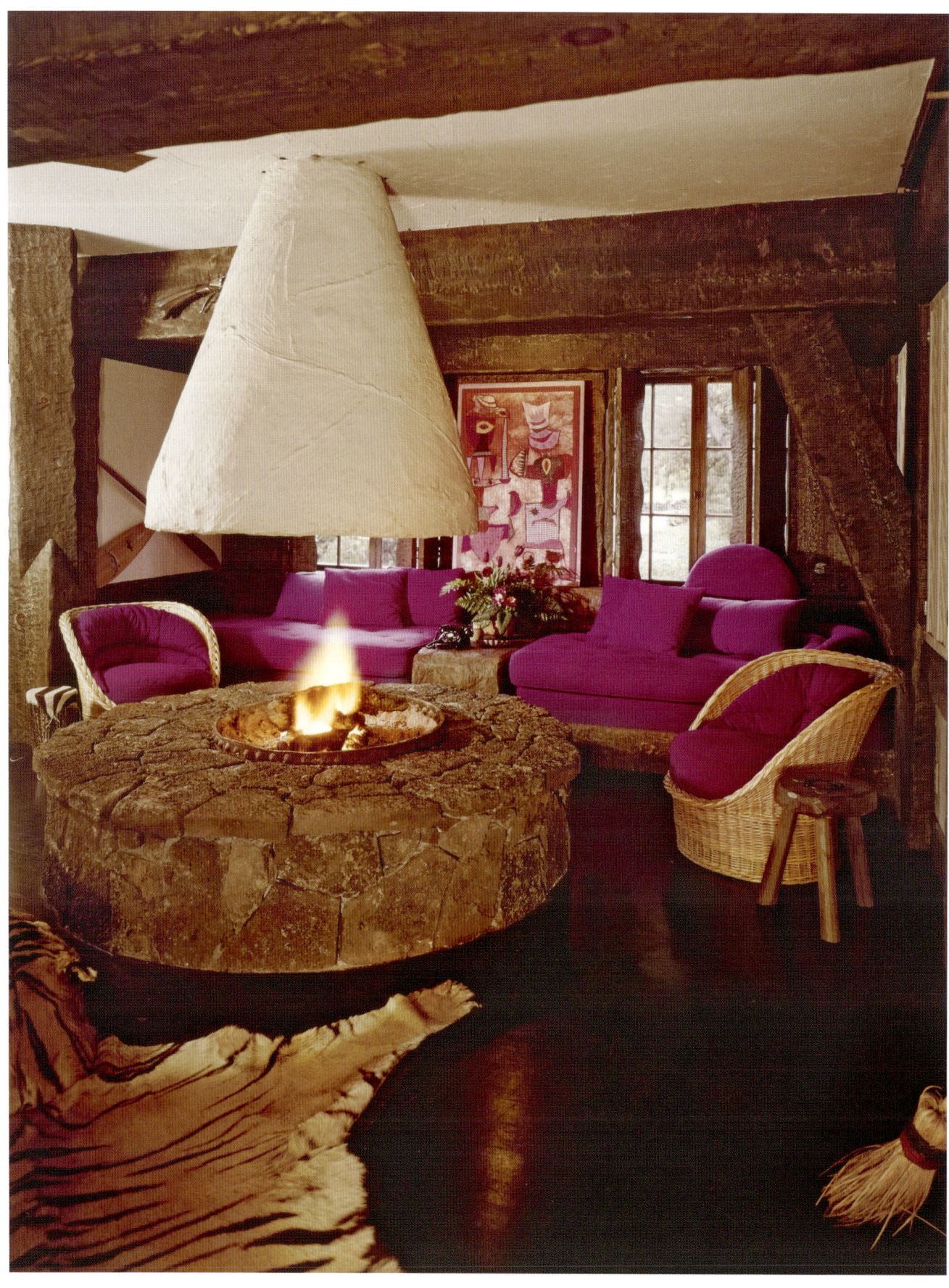

ABOVE: Two small bedrooms were combined to create an L-shaped bedroom and study for college-age twins. A plaster-hooded firepit of rough stone sits on a polished black floor. Wicker chairs and built-in beds, which double as sofas, supply seating options.
RIGHT: The primary bedroom and sitting room use brighter colors and tones than the rest of the house.

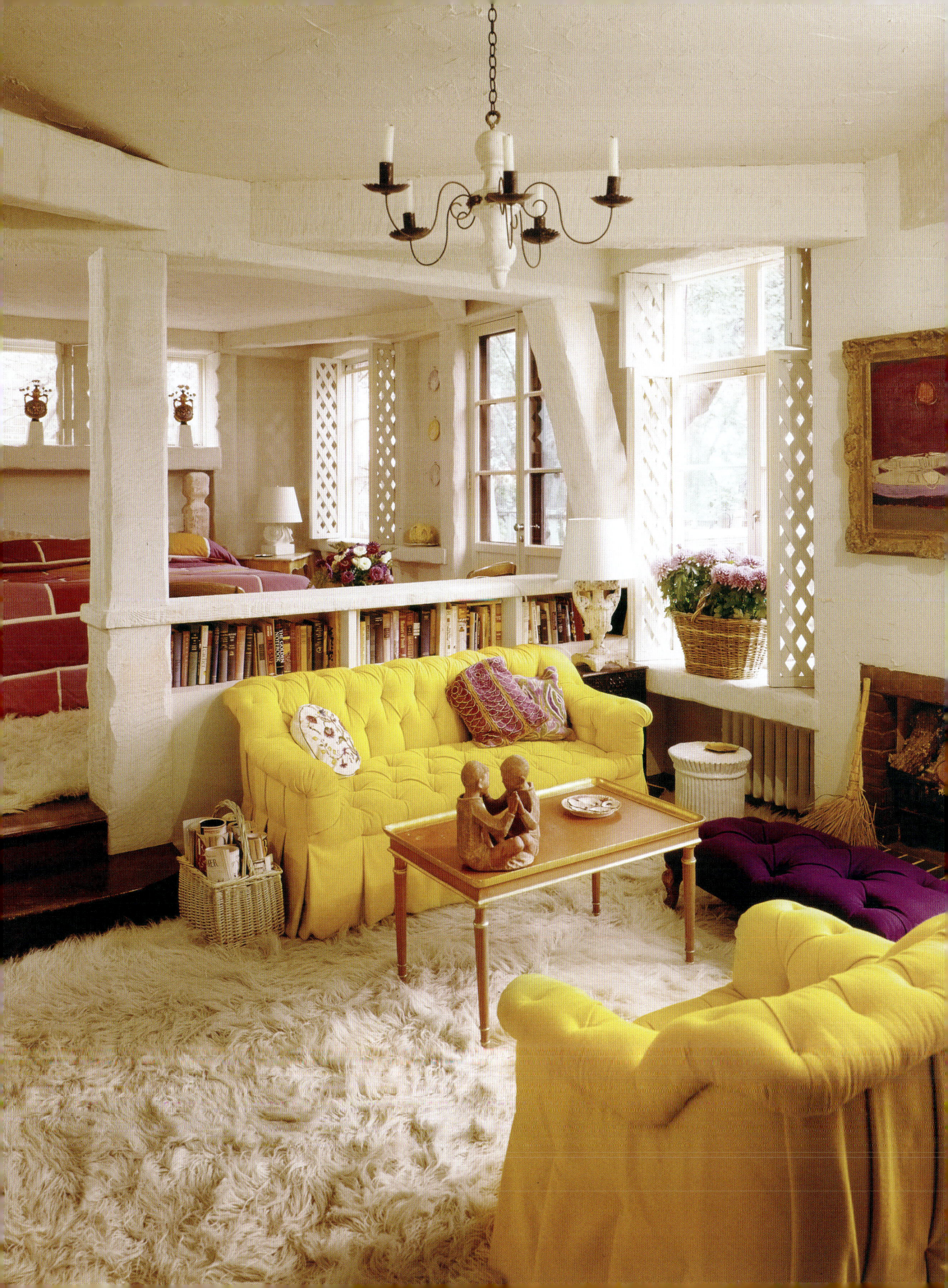

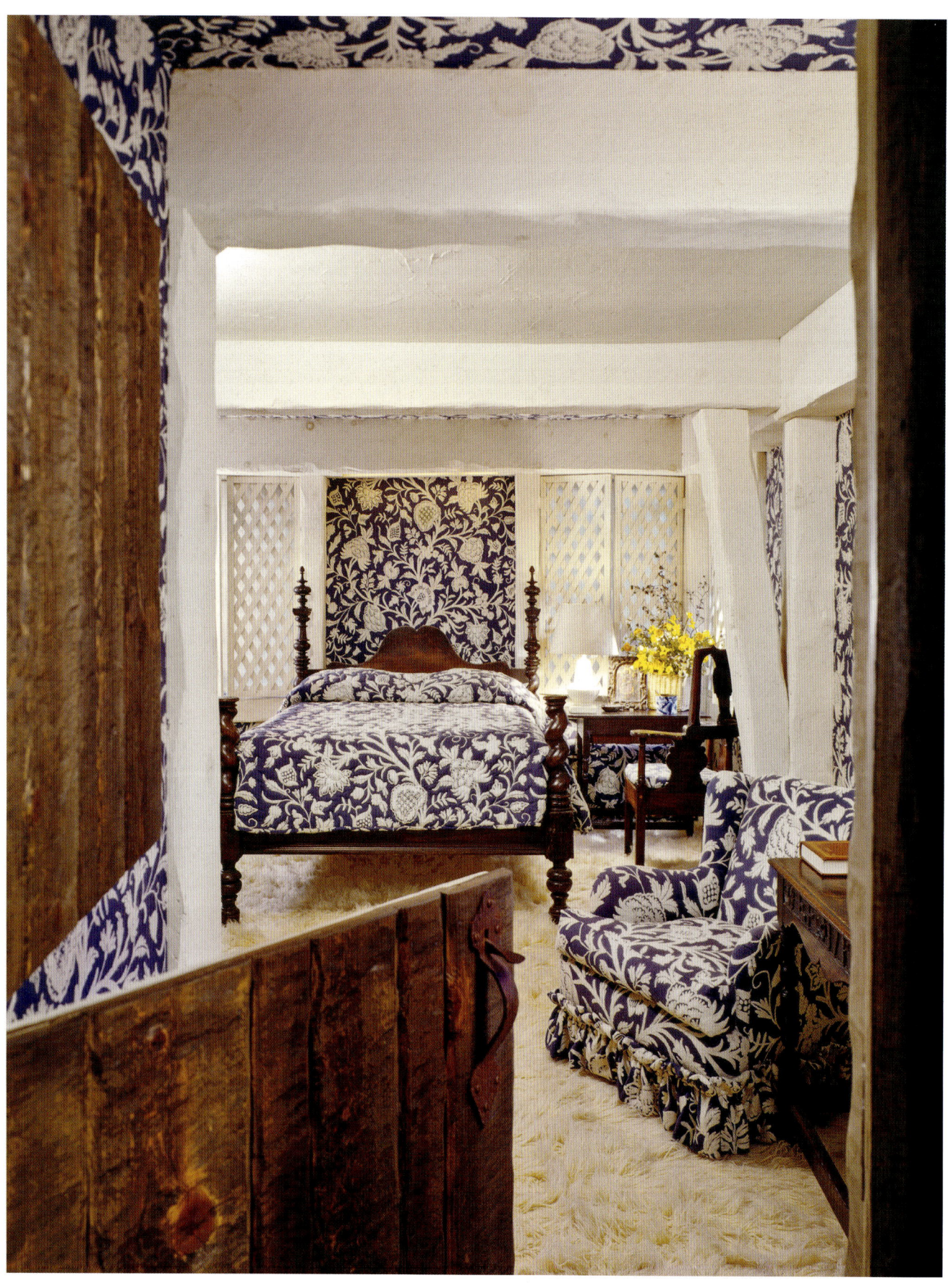

ABOVE: The lattice shutters and timber trim of a guest room are painted bright white, in contrast to the unpainted oak Dutch door. Crewel-embroidered fabric covers a chair, walls, part of the ceiling, and the four-poster bed. OPPOSITE: This indoor-outdoor room with its framework of stone and rough timbers was a favorite space for the family.

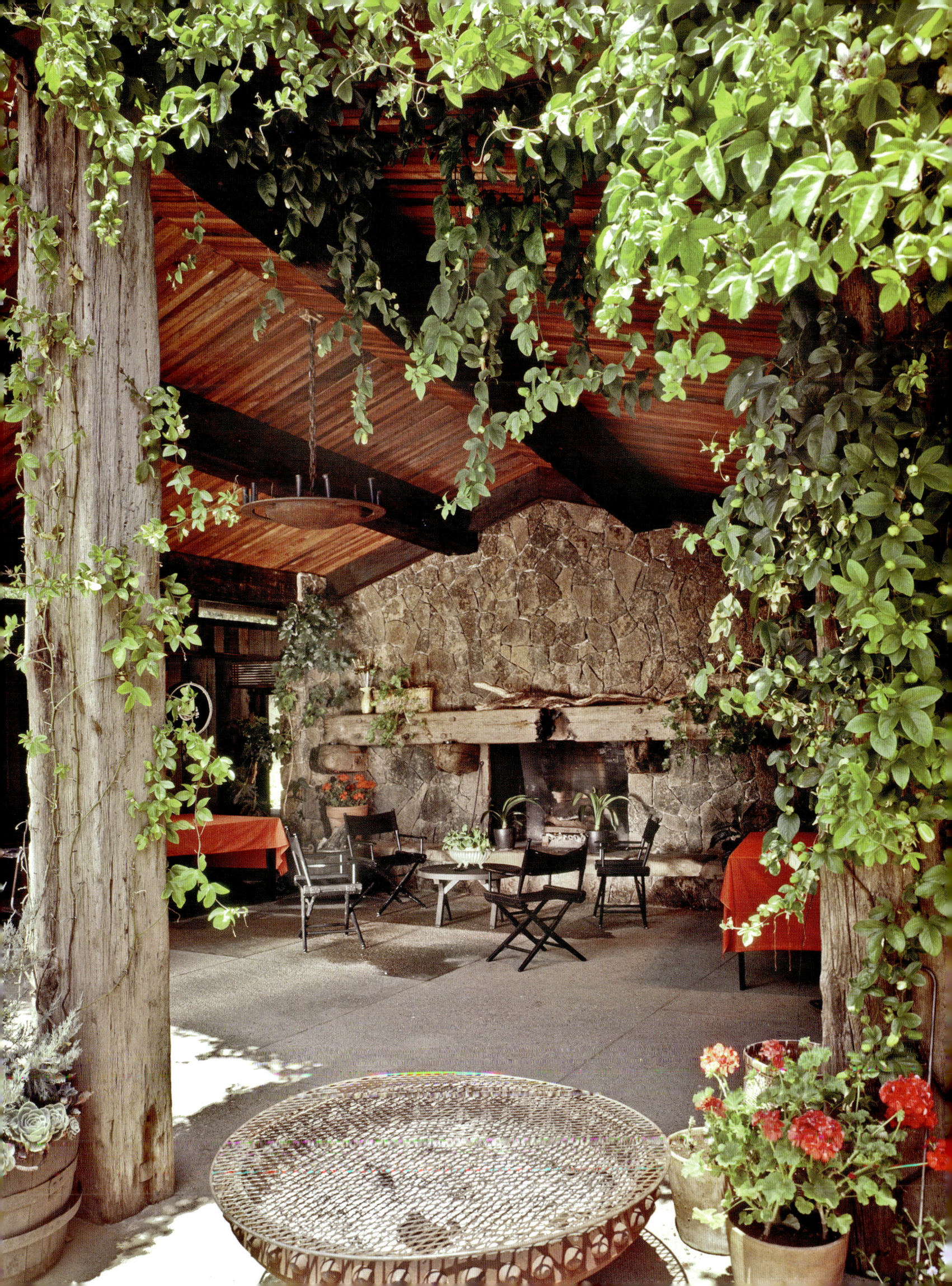

MARYON DAVIES
LEWIS HOUSE
San Francisco, 1966

In 1963, Michael Taylor decorated the Pacific Heights residence of Maryon Davies Lewis. I took these photographs a few years later for a 1968 issue of *Time* magazine.

As a subtitle for an article on decorators, *Time* once used "Shuffling the Goodies," referring to the way decorators used similar (or the same) objects from project to project. While photographing the Lewis living room, I was amused to discover that I had taken images of the identical desk and the Coromandel screen elsewhere. This type of screen had been a favorite piece of Frances Elkins, who installed them in most of the great houses she did, usually placing it behind a sofa so it would float out into the room. I had seen a similar overmantel mirror and upholstered chair in other Taylor projects as well. The pelmets in the game room are similar to ones that Elkins liked to use, reflecting once again the influence she had on her protégé. Adding to the exuberance of the game room, Michael upholstered the Venetian chairs in vivid shades of silk and added lemon-yellow upholstered club chairs.

In any case, the decoration had a traditional yet youthful flair for the young Mrs. Lewis. I remember that she was besotted with Michael and had invested in his business at one point.   —*F.L.*

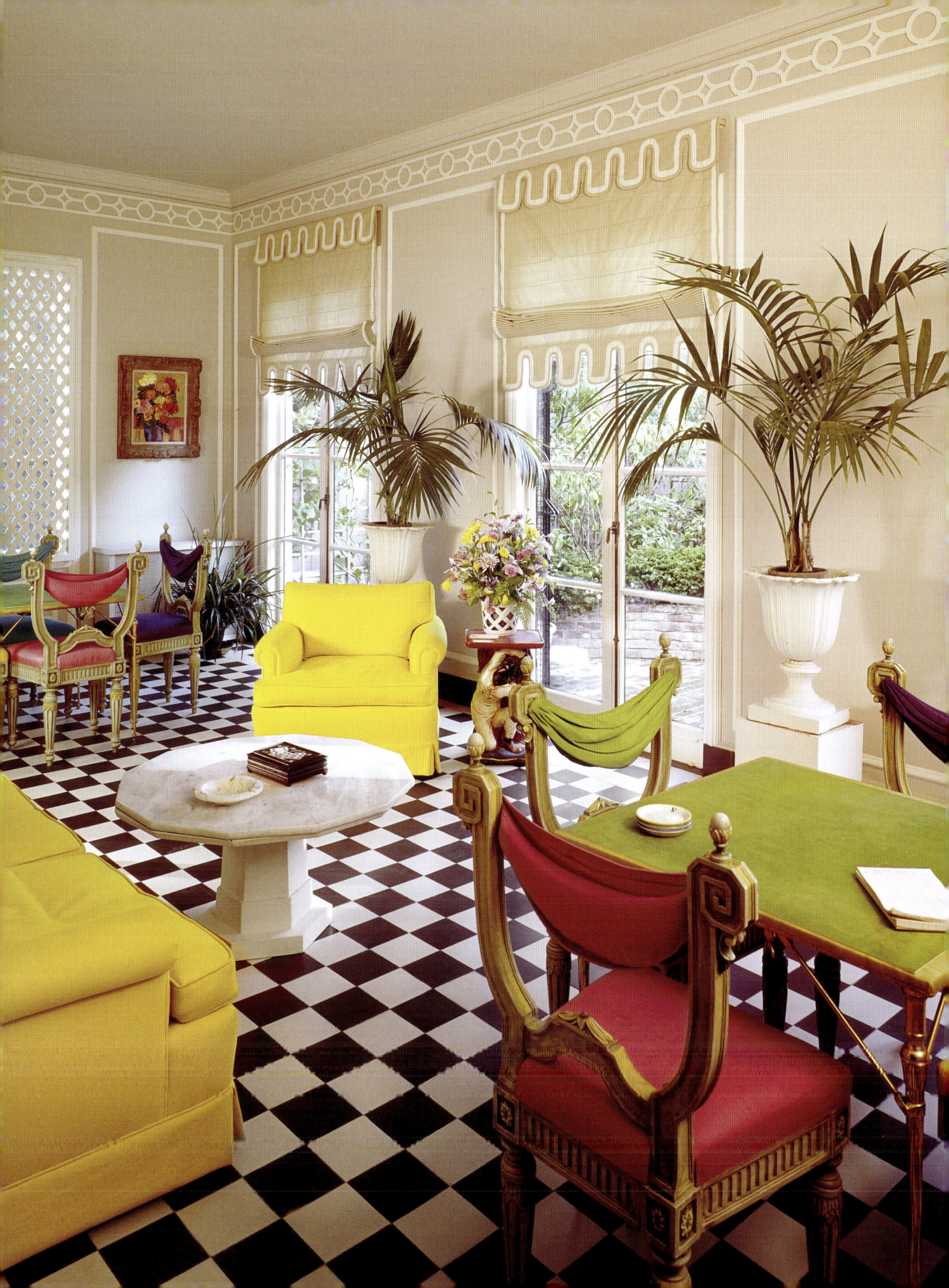

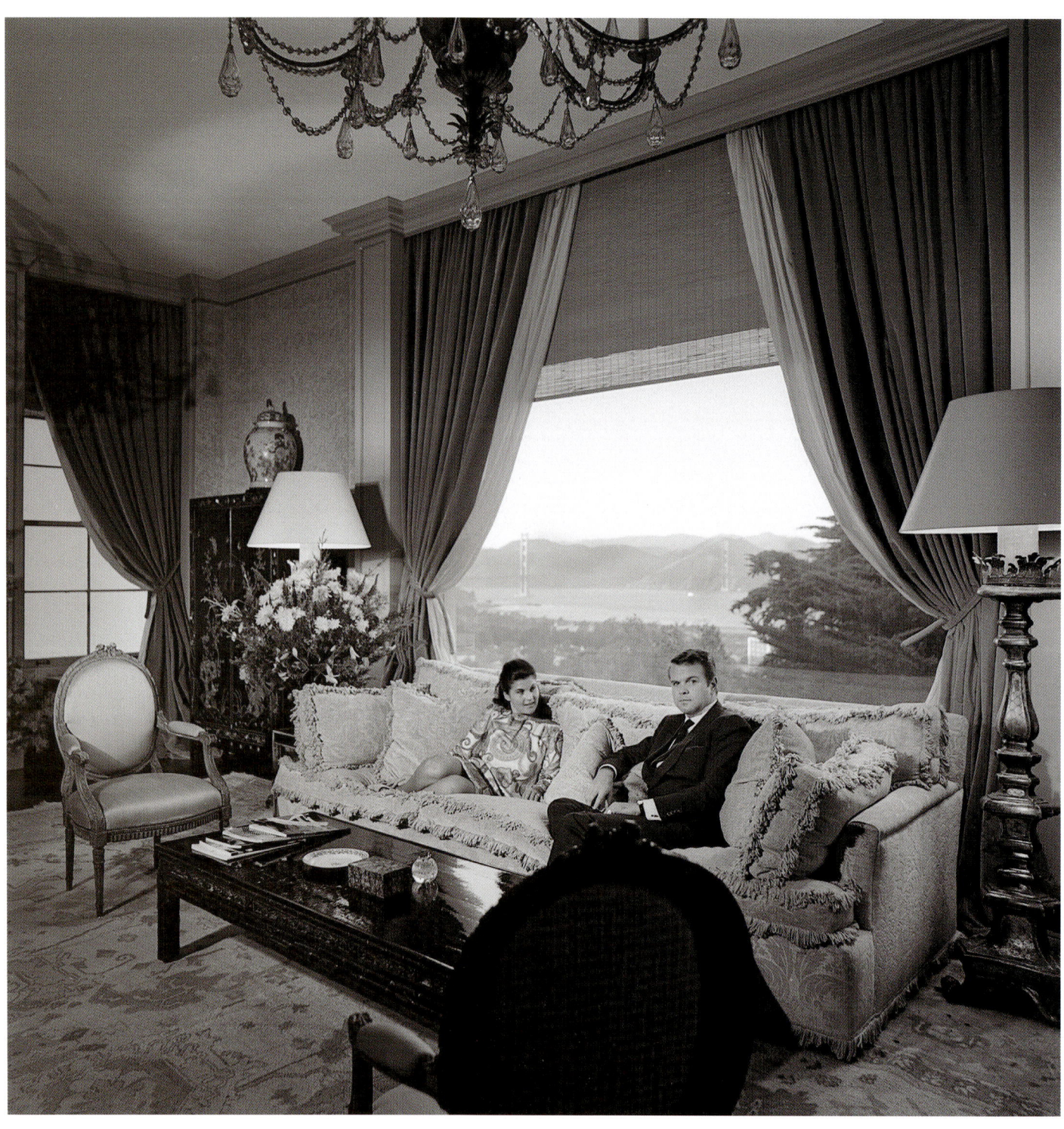

PAGE 115: Cardroom of the Maryon Davies Lewis house, Pacific Heights, San Francisco, 1966. Pale-gray walls offset furnishings in a range of colors. The suite of eight eighteenth-century Venetian chairs, upholstered in green, purple, raspberry, turquoise, and yellow silk, is set around two brass card tables. ABOVE: Lewis and Michael Taylor in her living room. OPPOSITE: Taylor upholstered the living room walls and sofas in pearl-gray embossed linen velvet. The Turkish Oushak carpet has hints of raspberry, the same color as the velvet curtains.

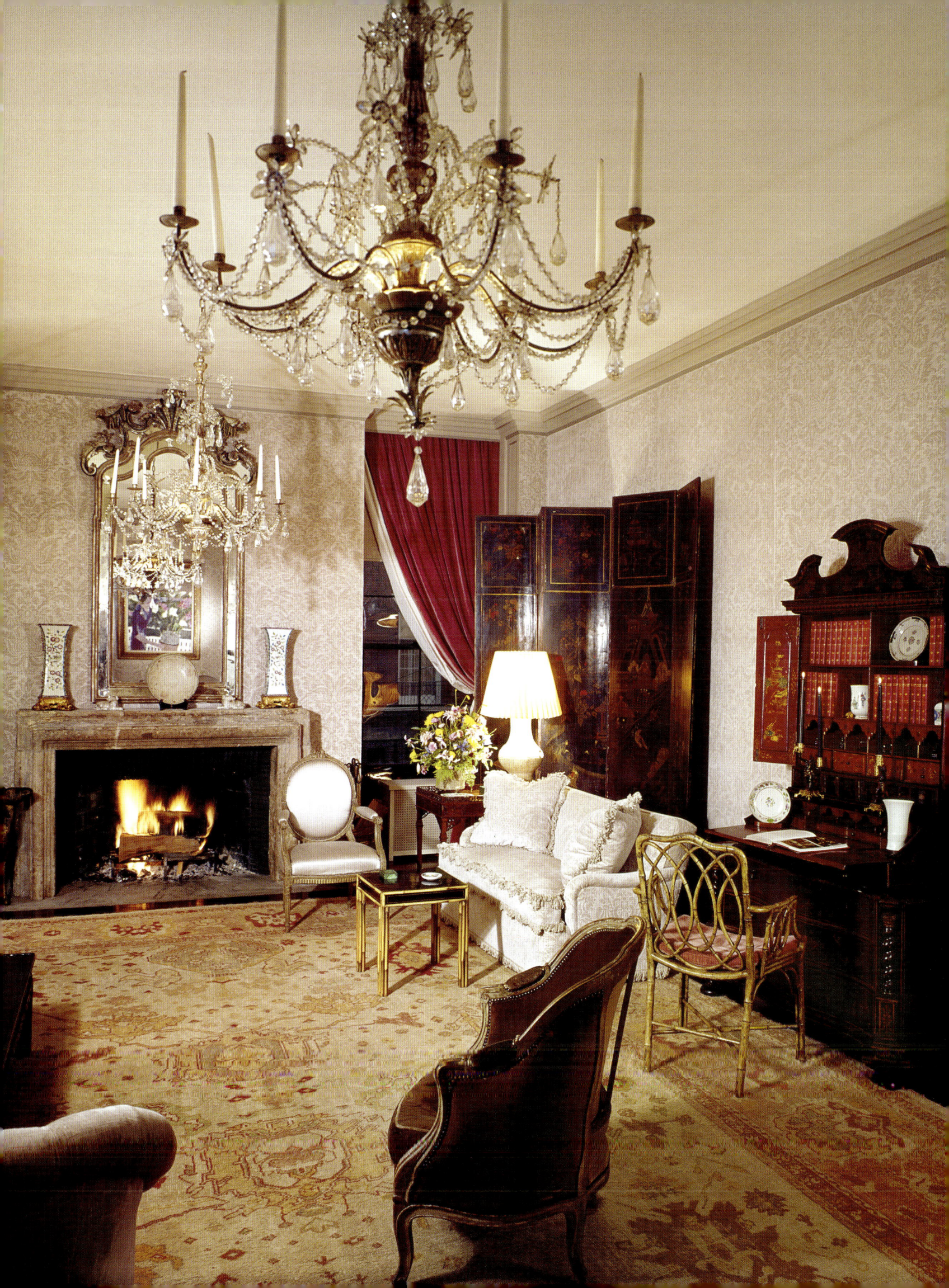

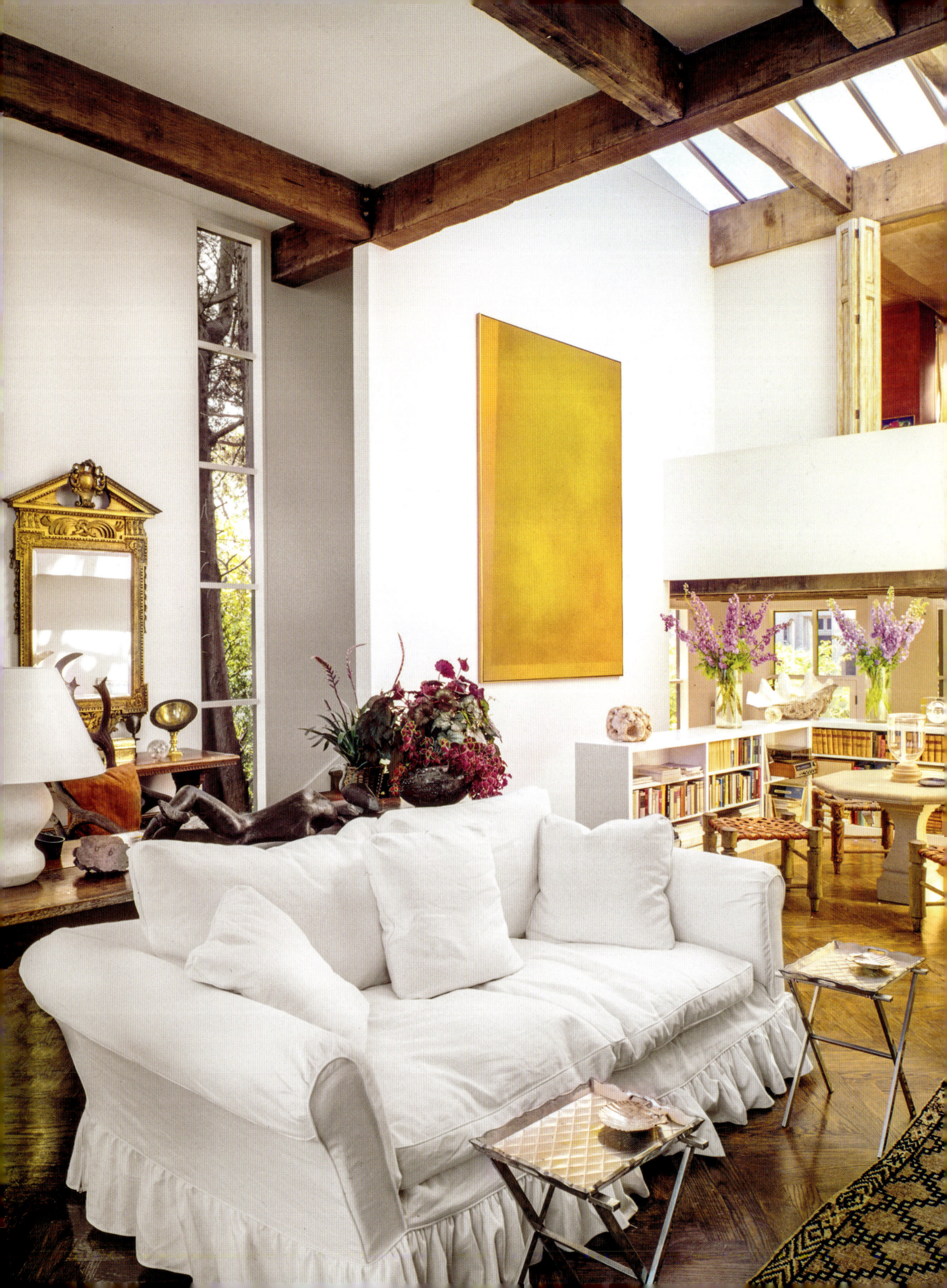

PAT AND SANDY
WALKER HOUSE

San Francisco, 1970

My friend architect Sandy Walker designed this house for his wife and himself. The spaces were beautiful and had natural light throughout. The couple hired Michael Taylor to decorate. Dorothea Walker (no relation to Sandy) wanted to photograph the house for *House & Garden* (the story appeared in the October 1970 issue). The problem was that Michael would never get around to finishing the project. I ran into Sandy at a party and told him Dorothea was being badgered by her editors for photographs of the place. Sandy agreed to press Michael.

The day of the photo shoot, Michael arrived with a truckload of furniture and art by the abstract expressionist Kenneth Noland; he loved Noland's work. Michael and his crew moved all of Sandy's furniture outside and put in their own furniture and art. I took a photograph of Sandy and his wife sitting outside on their couch, looking completely spent. Michael would set up a room, and I would photograph it. Then Michael would set up another room, and I would photograph that. It was exhausting for everybody.

These photographs show some typical Michael Taylor touches—original works of art paired with slipcovered furniture and tin tables from Cost Plus; an antler chair, a favorite of the designer; and a white plaster lamp from Western Art Stone. *—F.L.*

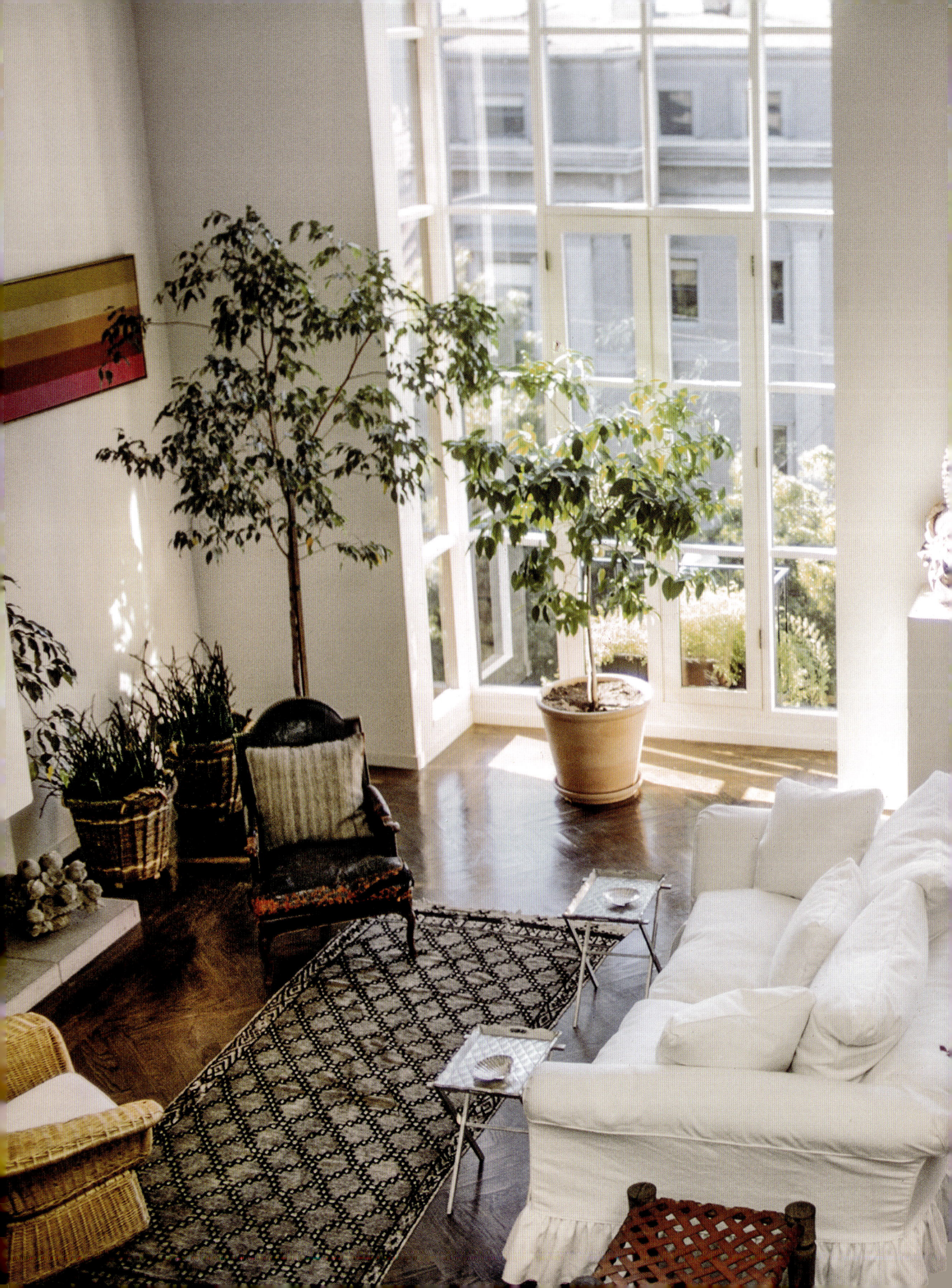

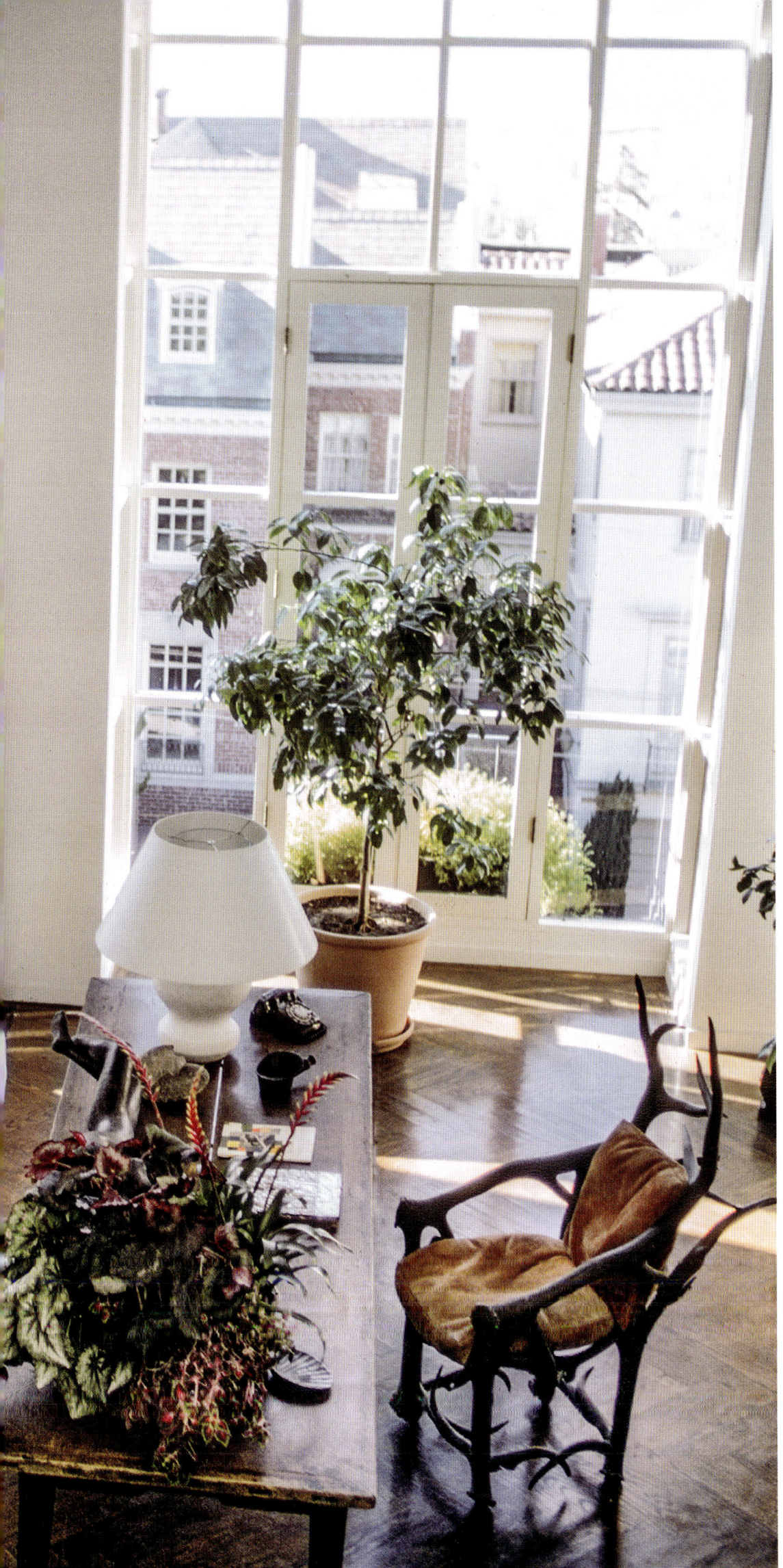

PAGE 118 AND LEFT: Living room of the Pat and Sandy Walker house, Pacific Heights, San Francisco, 1970. The high space, with its sixteen-foot beamed ceiling, was situated at the top of the house. Wicker armchairs, baskets, a white slipcovered sofa, plaster lamps, an antler chair, and Mexican tin tables are signature Michael Taylor elements. The interior was photographed by Lyon for the October 1970 issue of *House & Garden*.

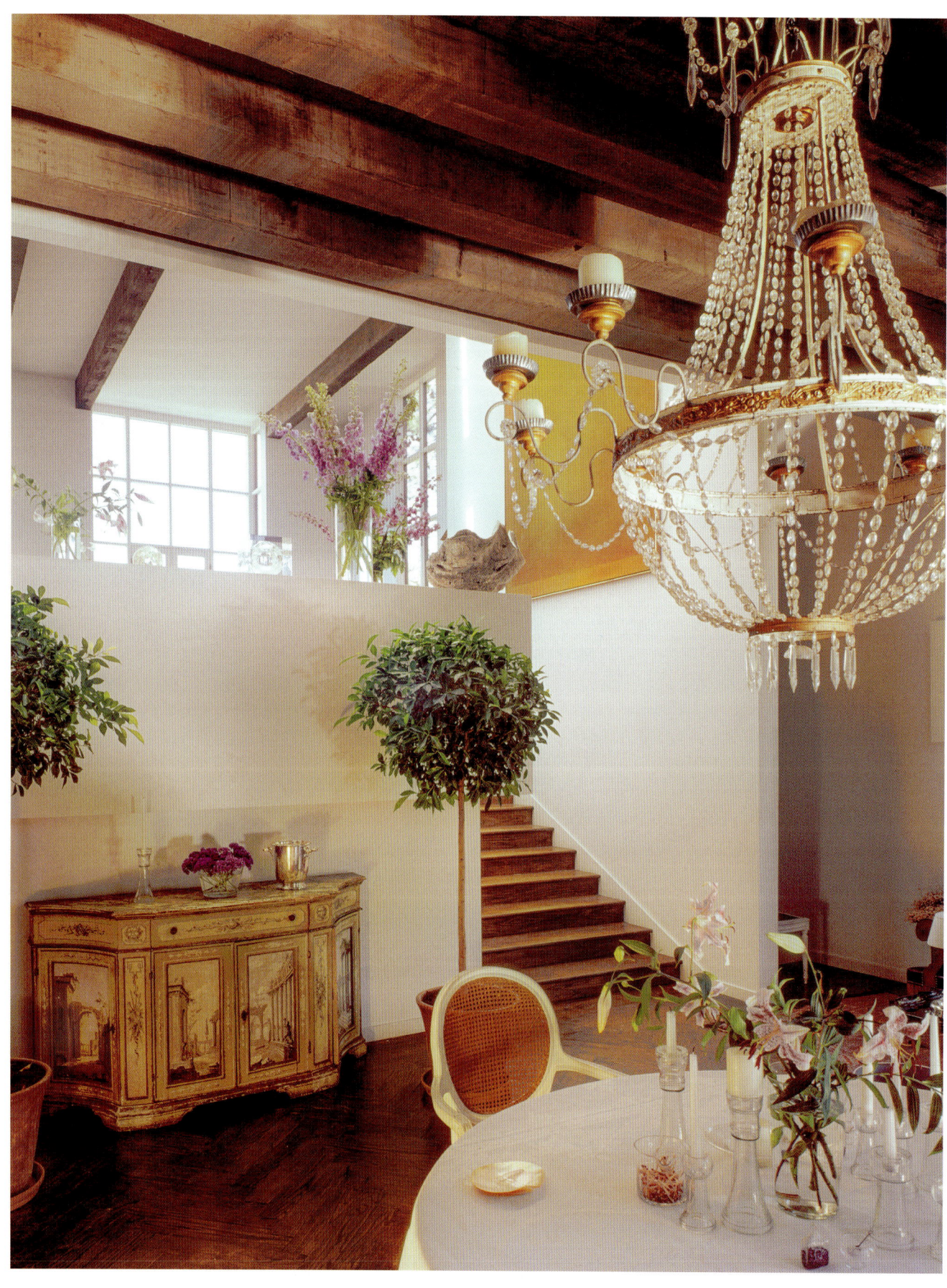

ABOVE: The dining room with steps leading up to the living room. OPPOSITE:
A Kenneth Noland striped painting runs the width of the living room.

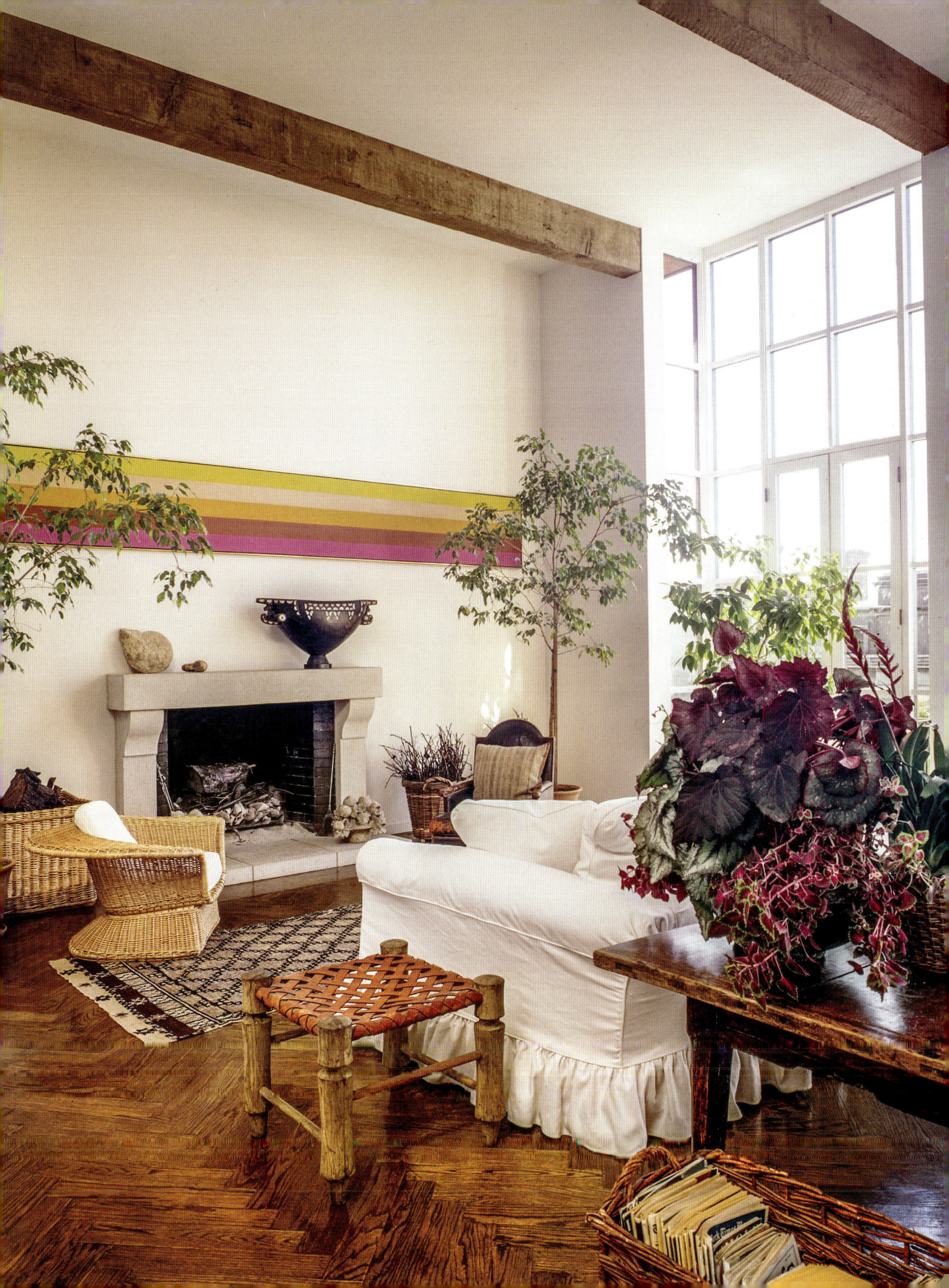

AUBERGE DU SOLEIL
Rutherford, circa 1984

The Auberge du Soleil bar and restaurant, and later the accommodation spaces, illustrated the successful partnership between Michael Taylor and Sandy Walker, the project's architect. Auberge's founder, Claude Rouas, wanted intimate indoor spaces that overlooked the valley. Michael and Sandy really delivered.

The shape of the millstone that Michael placed at the entry foreshadowed the round barroom. On the wall over a nestled banquette in the latter room, Michael installed a woven pannier, which was used by grape harvesters to carry the fruit they picked. An antique cultivator, used in vineyards to turn the soil, hung nearby. Michael placed seashells in the cultivator. Each object was unique and gave texture to the background.

The reception area had polished concrete floors with an overscale grid of wood planks, and pillars of timbers (with bark still intact) punctuated the dining and drinking spaces—an ingenious use of materials. Each room had a distinct character, but they related wonderfully to each other and were stitched together by Michael's dexterous handling. On the outside deck, the canopy slats and railing posts are grape stakes. That's a Sandy Walker touch. They were the right size, abundant in the Napa Valley, and complement Michael's decorative work inside. —*F.L.*

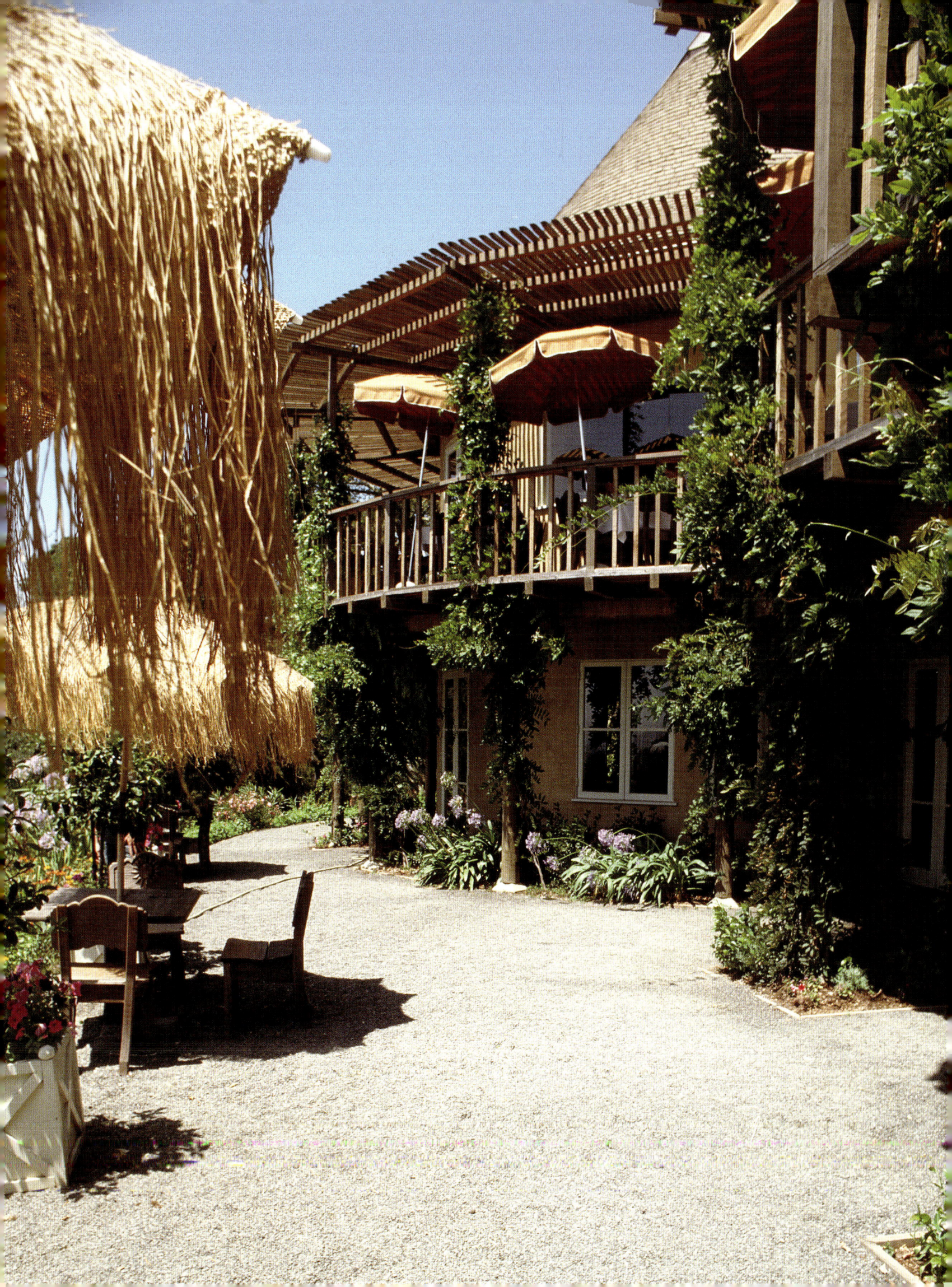

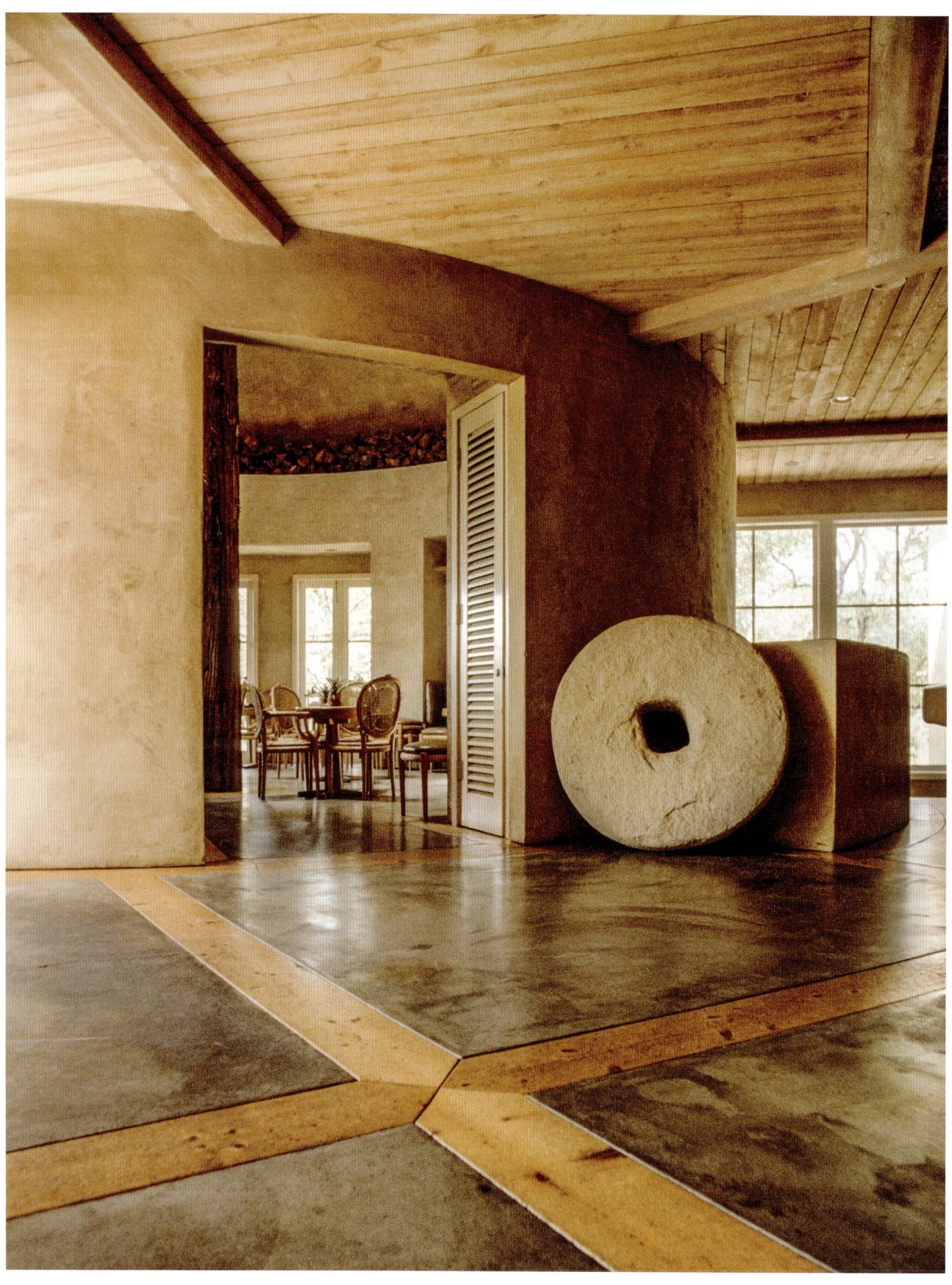

PAGE 125: View of the outdoor dining terrace at the Auberge du Soleil, Rutherford, Napa Valley, ca. 1984. The slats of the terrace roof are repurposed grape stakes. ABOVE: The entrance lobby with a view into the bar. A large millstone dominates the space. OPPOSITE: Taylor furnished the bar with natural wood tables and cane-backed chairs. The central tree trunk with its bark intact adds drama and evokes the surrounding landscape.

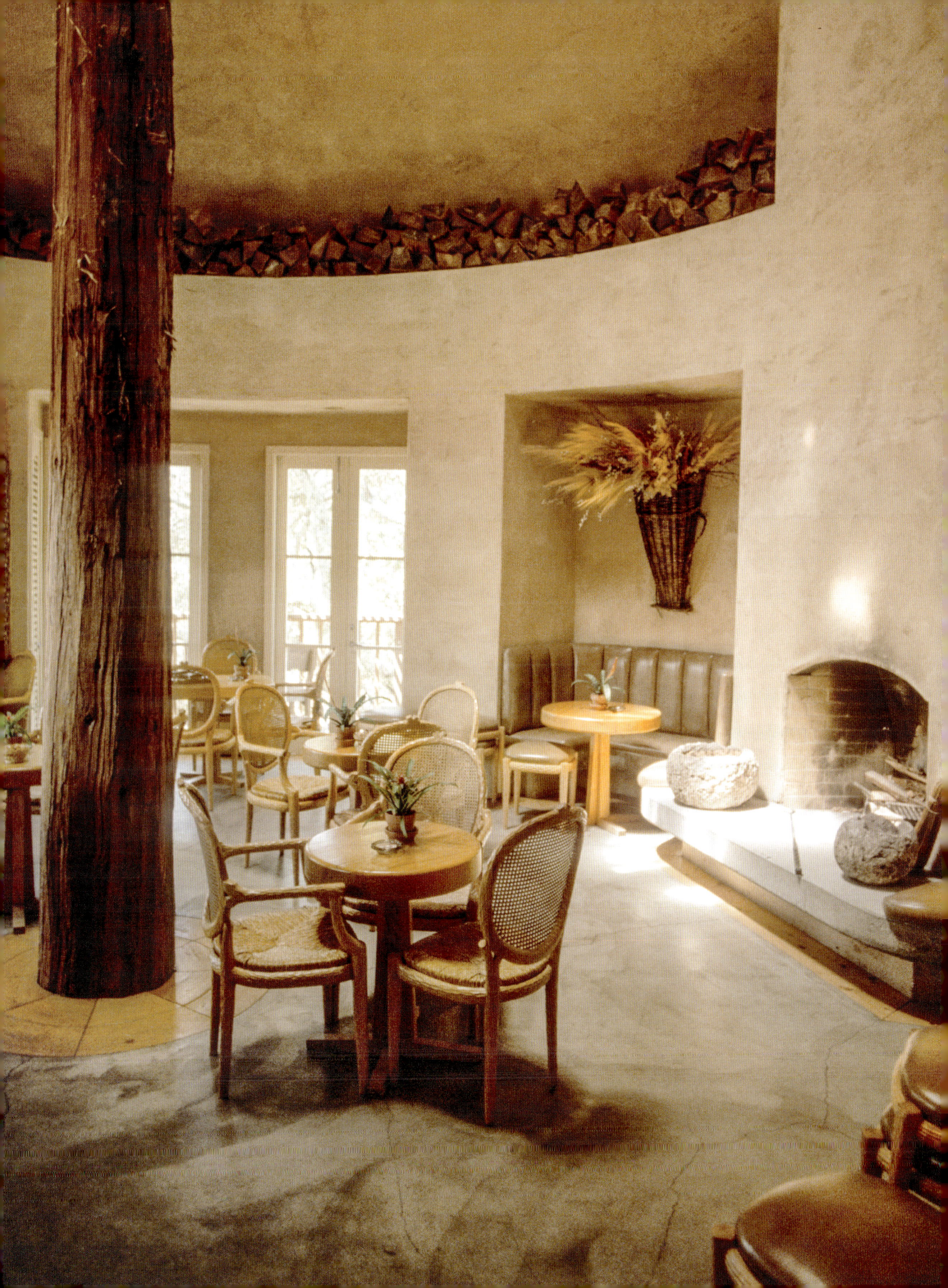

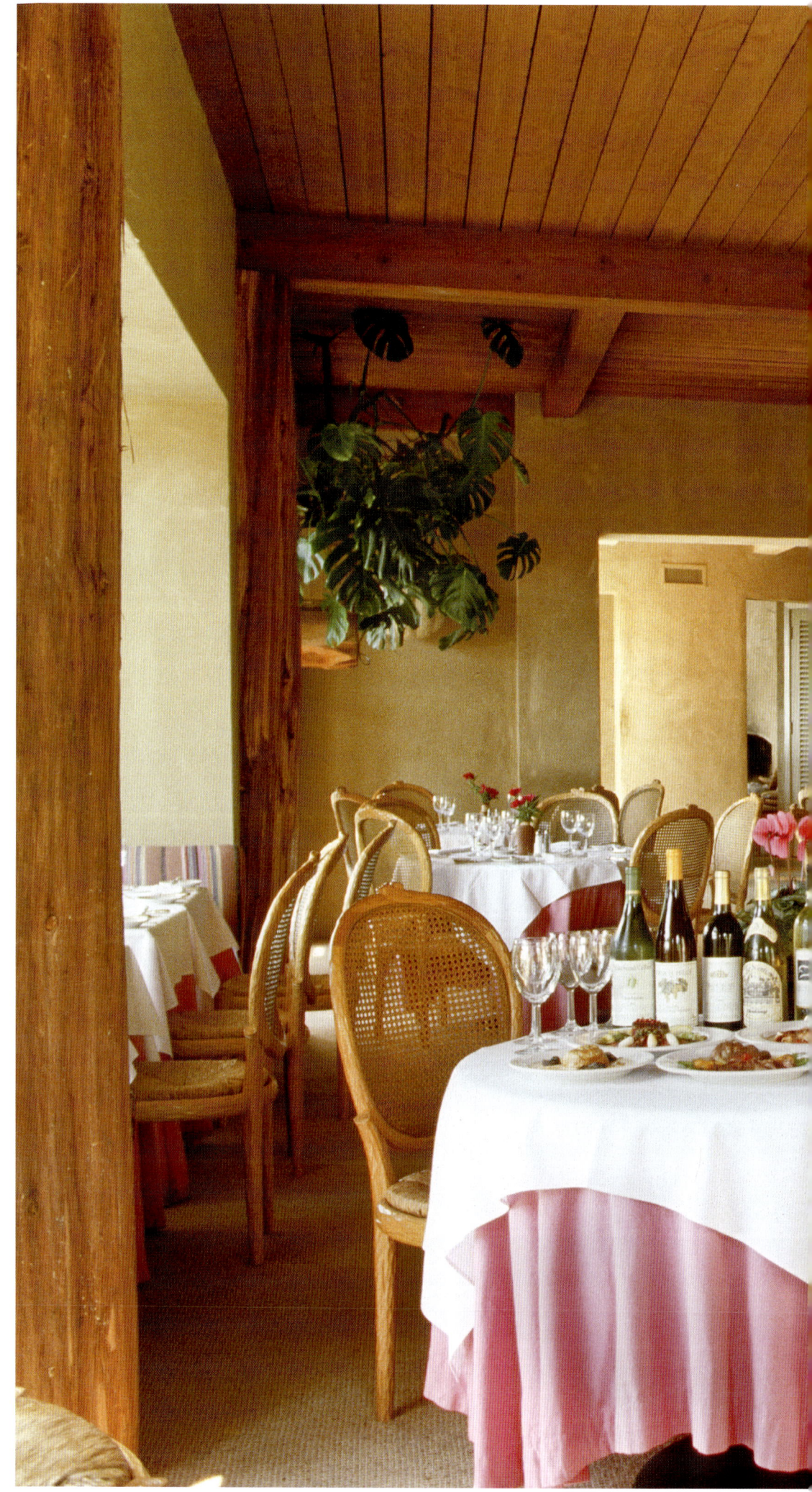

RIGHT: Taylor designed the dining room to accommodate a variety of seating arrangements around both round and square tables. PAGE 130: Banquettes were upholstered in multicolor striped fabric. PAGE 131: The dining terrace with its sweeping view of the Napa Valley.

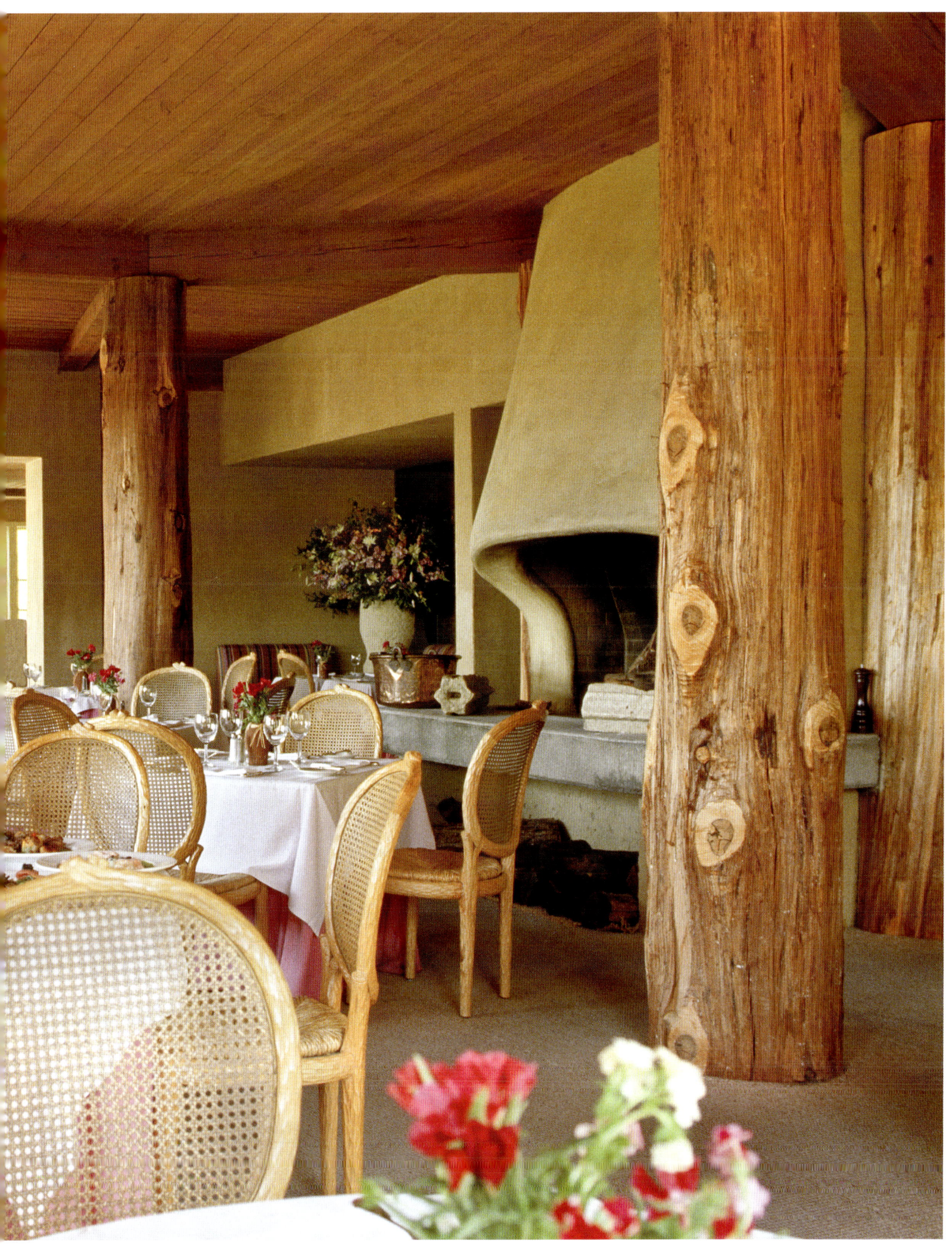

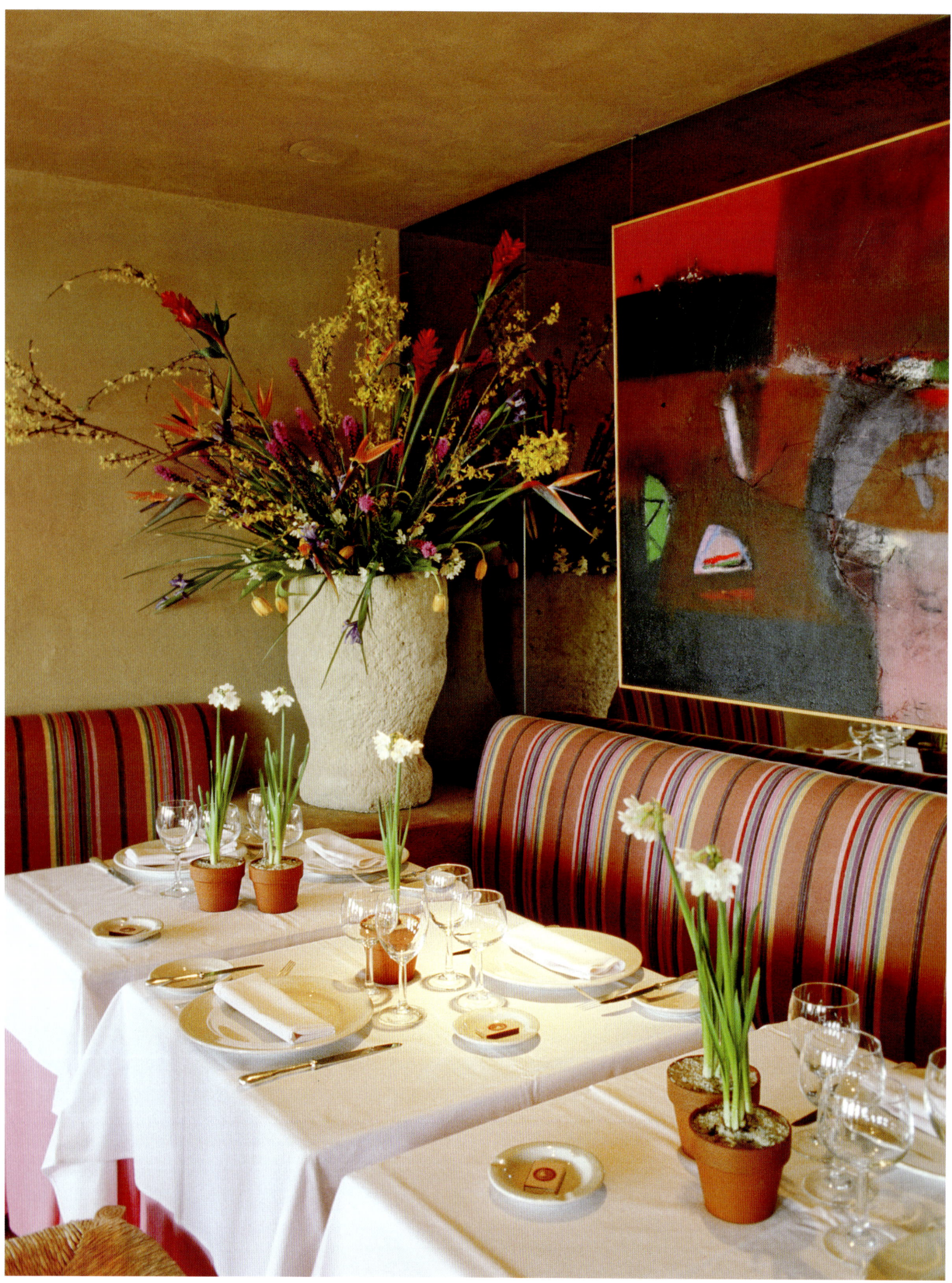

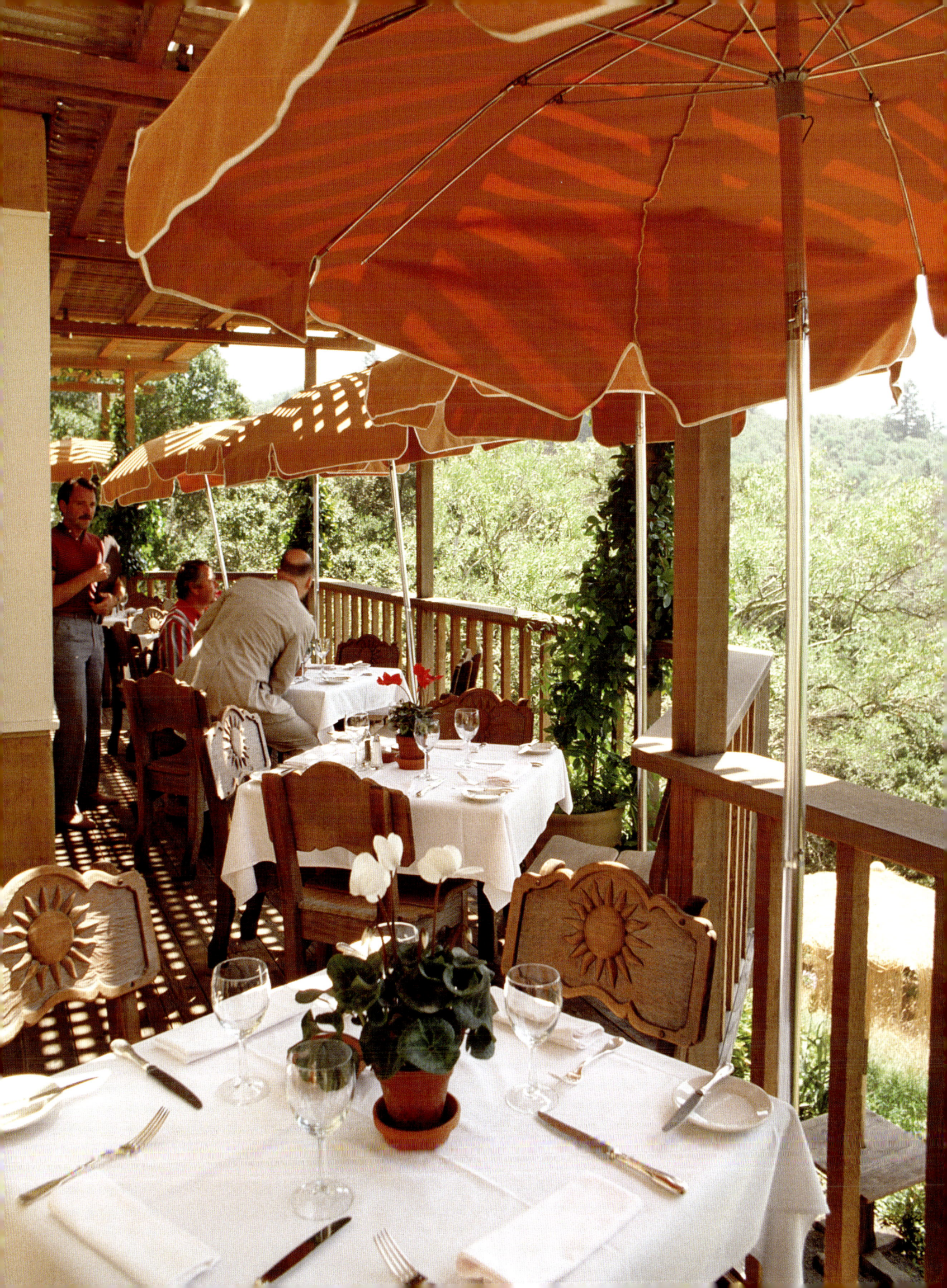

VI.
ELEGANT ANTHONY HAIL
AND INVENTIVE JOHN DICKINSON

met Tony Hail when he was working for Michael Taylor, decorating a house for my parents on Russian Hill," recalls architect Sandy Walker. "Fred photographed that house. When Tony went out on his own, I got several jobs through him. It often starts with the decorator or the landscape architect, who then suggests the architect."[121] Although he is not as well known as Taylor and some others, Anthony Hail (ca. 1925–2006) is considered "the decorator's decorator." He trained in architecture at the Harvard Graduate School of Design. Hail then served as an architectural assistant during the renovation of the White House under President Truman and later worked with furniture designer Edward Wormley. His style is firmly classic and neoclassical, even throughout the heyday of the Modern Movement.[122] Lyon calls Hail "the ultimate gentleman with reserve and European polish."[123]

Taylor's and Hail's near contemporary John Dickinson (1920–1982) was another decorator Lyon admired and whose work he photographed. Although he was not as famous as Taylor, Dickinson "remains a cult figure among the cognoscenti."[124] The *New York Times* wrote, "Dickinson's talents were acknowledged by his peers.

The San Francisco decorator Tony Hail occasionally collaborated with him, though he [joked]: 'You couldn't take just a little of John Dickinson. It was all or none.'"[125] He was known for the "tailored modernism" of his designs and his inventiveness.[126] "Much of his work combined a subtle sense of sophistication with a touch of humor."[127] A good example of Dickinson's inventiveness is the series of tables he produced that were inspired by a find from an inexpensive import store. Inspired by the contrast they presented with chic modernity, Dickinson produced his own tables in plaster, reinforcing the table legs with metal rebar. The tables were a hit and used by other decorators, including Michael Taylor. They were heavy, which discouraged clients from rearranging his furniture placement, a characteristic that most decorators appreciate. They were also somewhat fragile. The pieces that remain are highly sought after. Dickinson was building on his earlier experience creating storage pieces that were a "brick-for-brick copy of a Victorian townhouse that looks entirely realistic because the stone pattern is printed on its facade, and doorway and window frames are painted on by hand."[128] Furniture manufacturer Drexel made and sold these pieces.

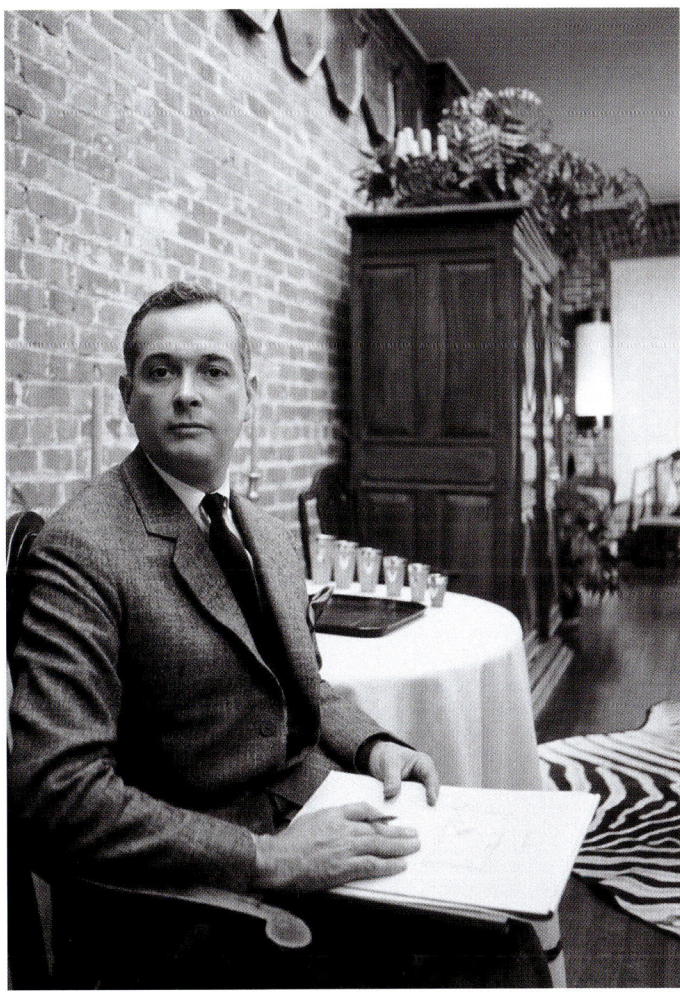

Lyon met Dickinson when the designer was just starting out in the business, at the E. Coleman Dick design studio in San Francisco in the 1950s. Lyon says, "I was considered one of the best interior photographers around, if only because I was one of the only ones doing that kind of work. John had done a handful of rooms around San Francisco and wanted me to shoot them. The problem was he couldn't afford me, and I couldn't give him a special rate because other designers would hear about it and I would have to give them the same deals."[129] Lyon came up with a solution: "I told John, 'Hire me for one day, and let's do as many rooms as we can.' Somehow, John managed to get seven rooms camera ready at the same time. There was a hallway here, a bedroom there, a guest room in somebody's house, seven different rooms in seven different houses, mostly Victorians, around San Francisco. It was very hard, but we got it done. And the photographs helped him."[130]

Dickinson was terrifically inventive, especially with his own interiors and possessions. Lyon recalls, "John had a beautiful black Jaguar with cane side panels. It was really distinctive. I asked him who customized his car. He told me he did it and proceeded to show me exactly how he managed it. John had a very narrow and small garage. He positioned the cane paneling along the side of the car in the garage and placed ply

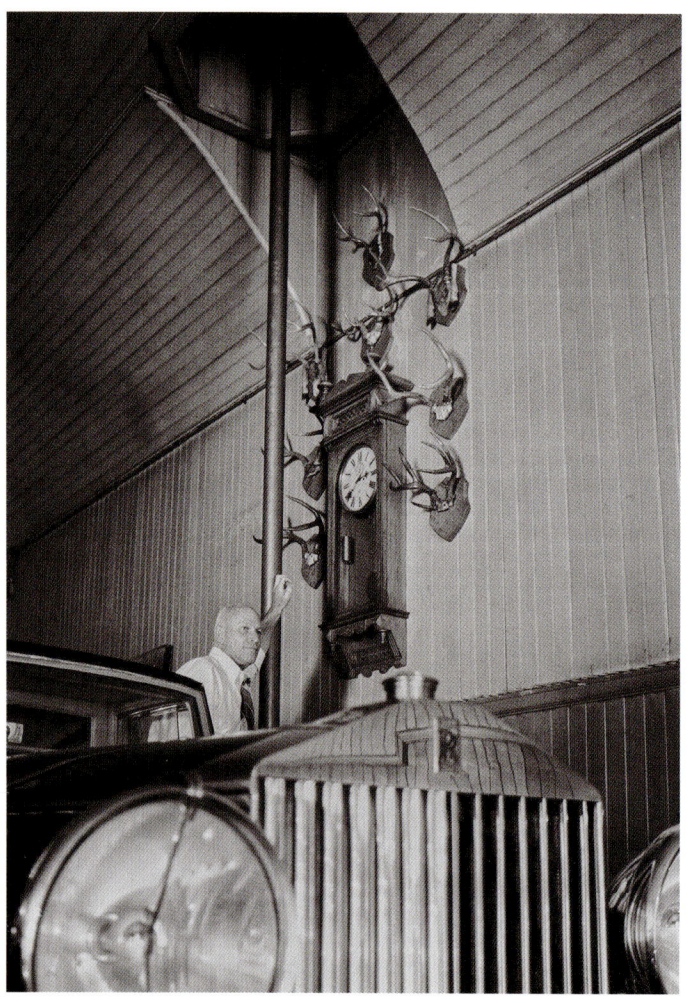

wood sheets along the side of the garage. He then filled sandbags that he positioned between the plywood sheet and the paneling to hold the cane in place while the epoxy holding it to the car dried. This was the kind of creativity John brought to his work, too."[131]

A *San Francisco Chronicle* article quotes Lyon as saying, "John Dickinson was another one-of-a-kind artist. . . . His approach was comparable to [1930s French designer] Jean-Michel Frank. He took unconventional materials and treated them like gemstones."[132] The article noted, "Dickinson gained notoriety for his odd use of skeletal imagery and unusual materials. Huge, white pine coffee tables that looked like spools of thread, galva-

nized metal furniture and lampshades made of buckets were classic Dickinson innovations."[133] In the article, Lyon also says, "These things looked terrific and startling. At the height of his fame, in his firehouse home, he sprayed cheap plastic figurines that looked like African statuary all white, and they looked smashing. He was unafraid."[134] In another article, Lyon says Dickinson "combined carnival heads from the Old Spaghetti Factory with a grand Art Nouveau dining table, and plaster tables. . . . He could take humble materials like straw, leather, plaster, pine planks, or galvanized metal and have them crafted in the most luxurious manner so that they seemed precious. He was a true original."[135]

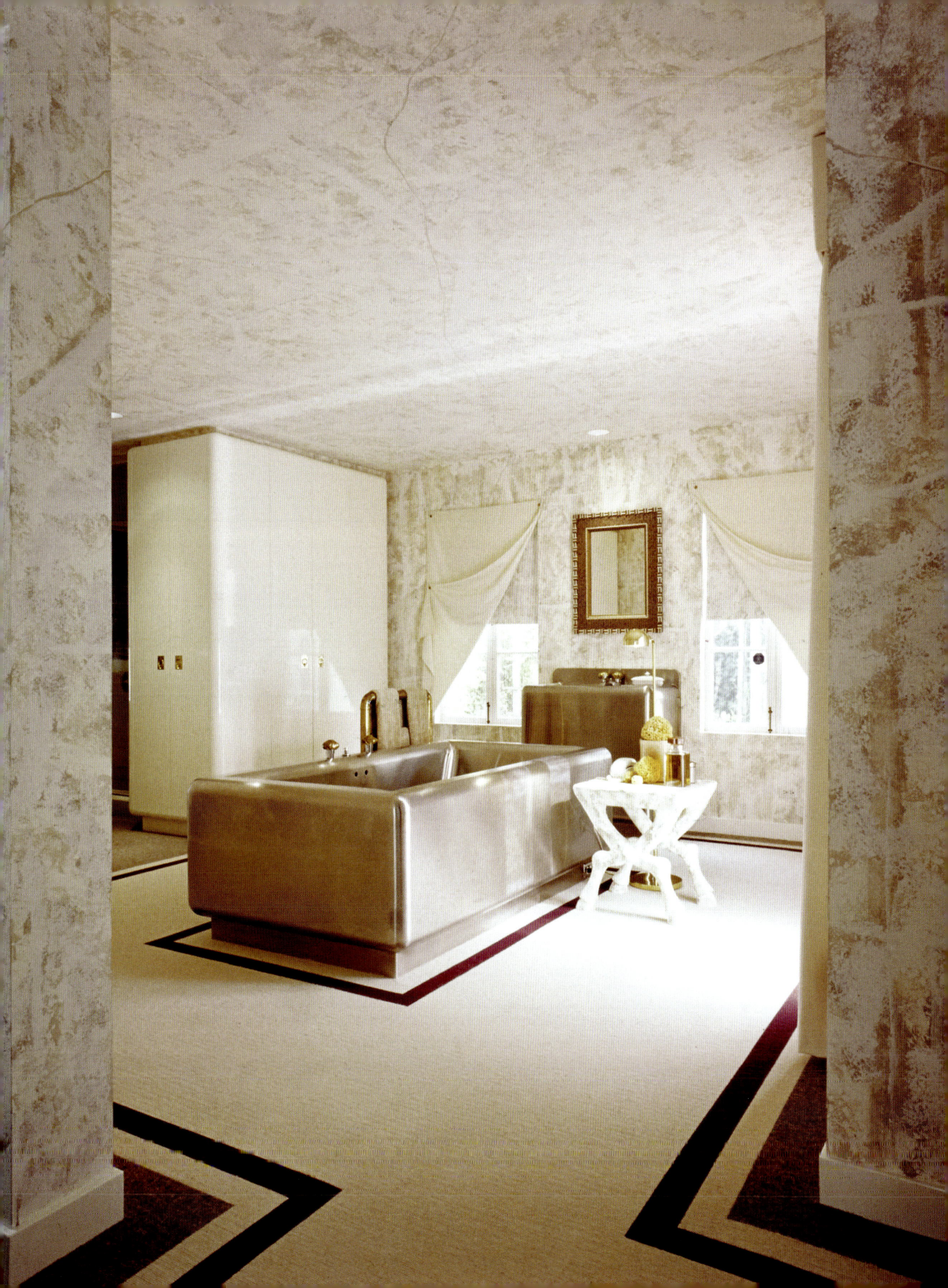

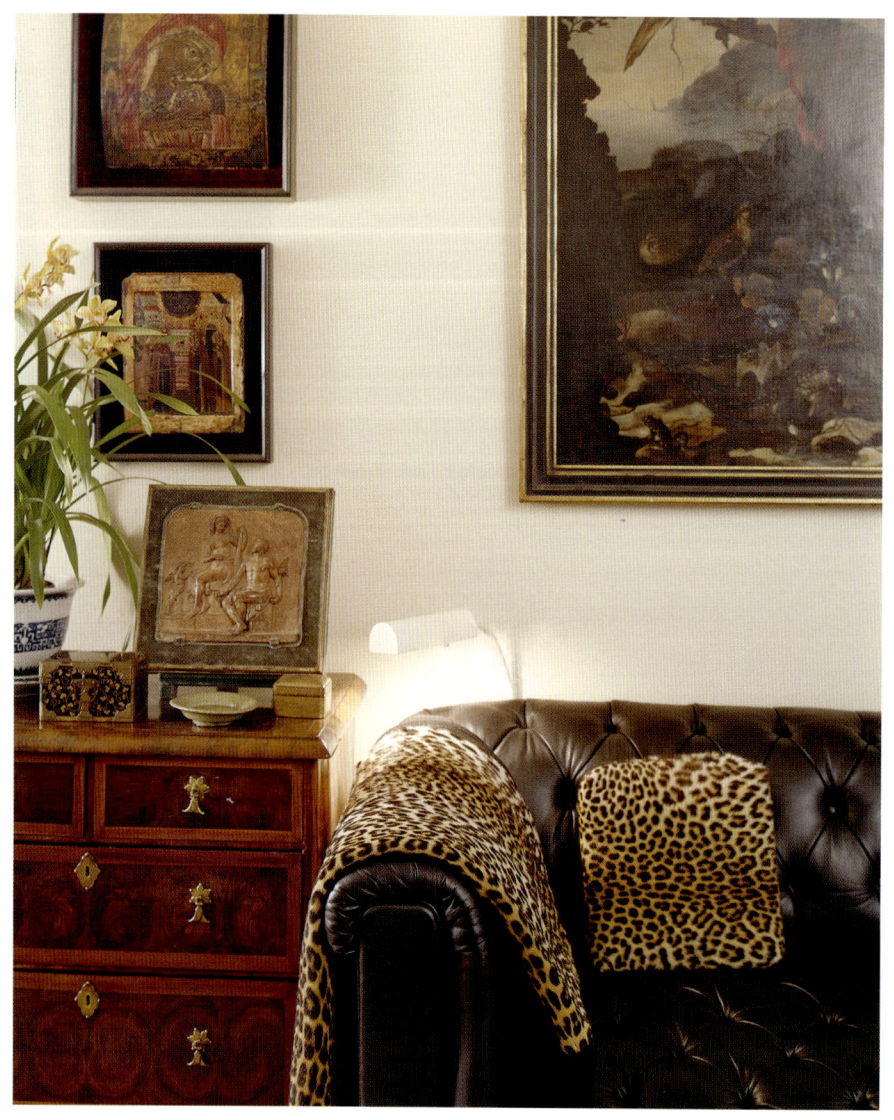

ANTHONY HAIL RESIDENCES
San Francisco, circa 1969 and 1972

Anthony Hail became famous for taking good objects, antiques, and rare books and arranging them flawlessly. His rooms had subtle color and the kind of luxury that was totally understated. Some of these qualities come through in my photographs of his residences. I photographed three of his homes in San Francisco: a small, elegant Telegraph Hill apartment near his work studio, both of which featured in issues of *Vogue* (1958 and 1960, respectively); a town house on Russian Hill, which appeared in *House Beautiful* (1968); and his glamorous apartment on Nob Hill, which appeared in both *Architectural Digest* (1972) and *Town & Country* (1987). Hail's noted eclecticism, as seen in all of his residences (two illustrated here), translated into tranquil spaces.

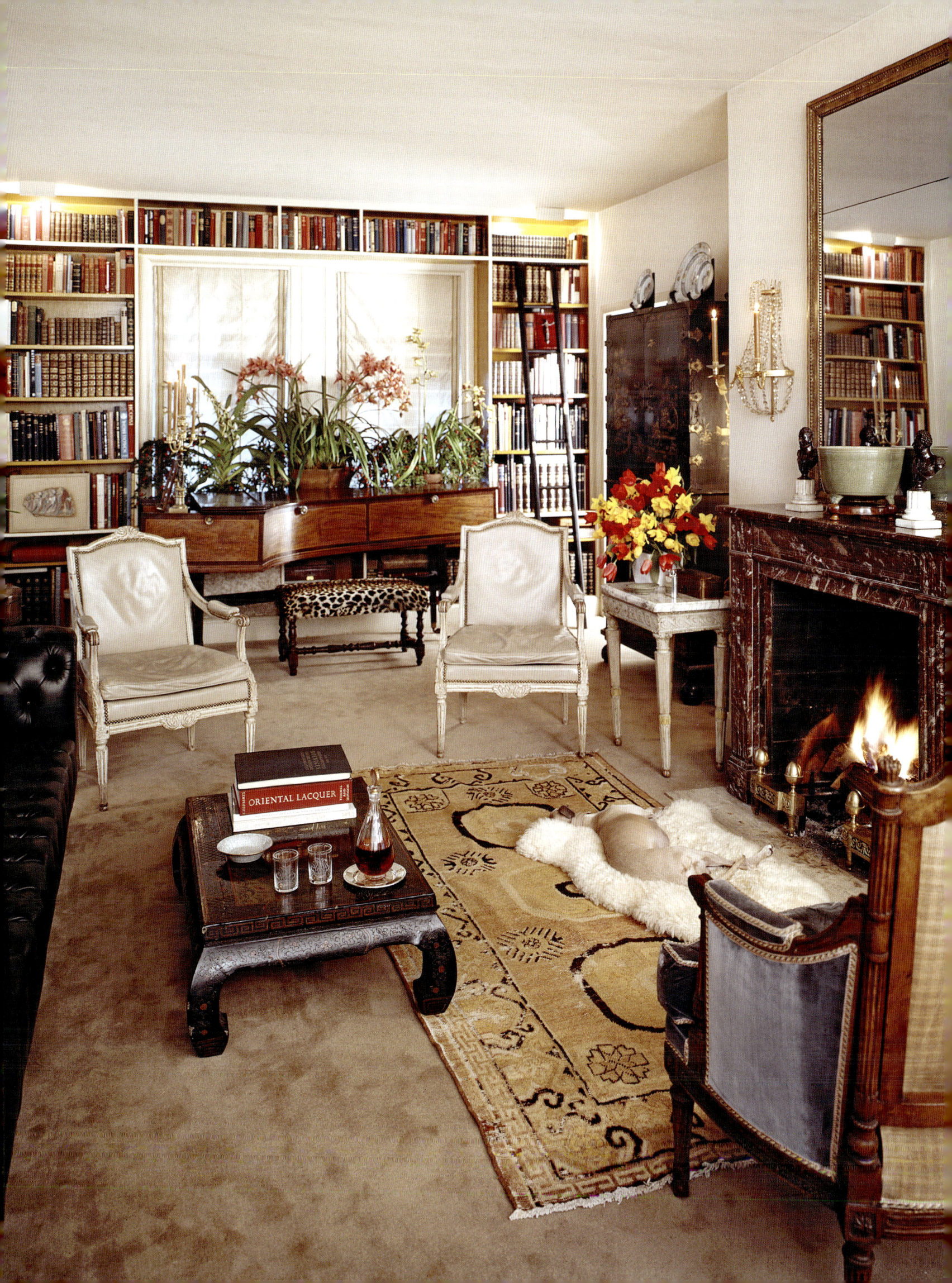

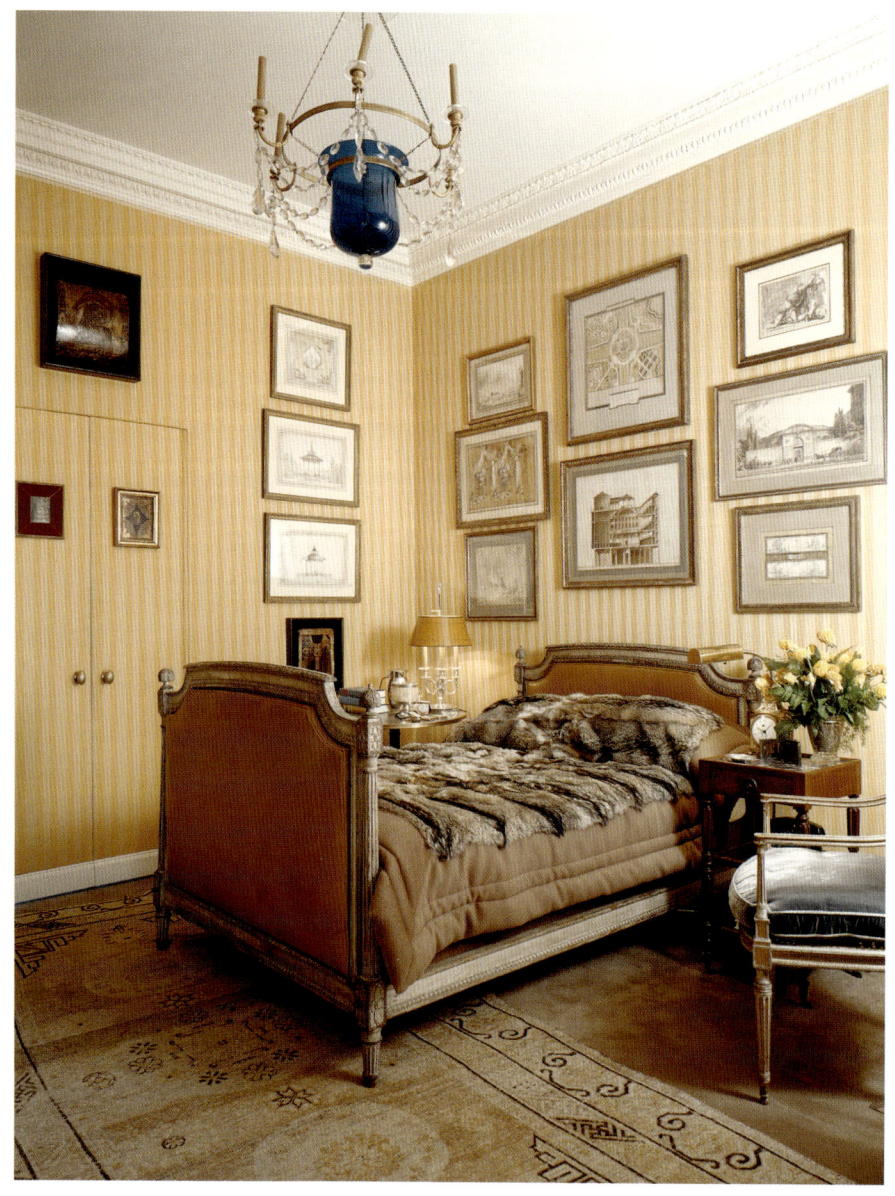

I met Tony soon after he arrived in San Francisco, near the start of his career. In 1958, Dorothea Walker and I worked on the first shoot of one of his residences. The magazine exposure likely was a boost to his career. Early on, Tony worked with Michael Taylor to decorate the house of the parents of my friend the architect Sandy Walker. Sandy met Tony on that project, and Sandy says that Tony helped *his* career by recommending him to his clients. In some ways, San Francisco is a small town.

—F.L.

PAGES 136 AND 137: The living room of Anthony Hail's town house, Russian Hill, San Francisco, ca. 1969. The house was designed by architects Charles Porter and John Robert Steinwedell. ABOVE: Hail's bedroom in his Nob Hill apartment, next door to the Huntington Hotel, 1972. The walls are upholstered in striped silk. The neoclassical chandelier is Russian, and the Louis XVI bed is French. OPPOSITE: Living room of Hail's Nob Hill apartment, which he shared with his partner, Charles Posey, 1972.

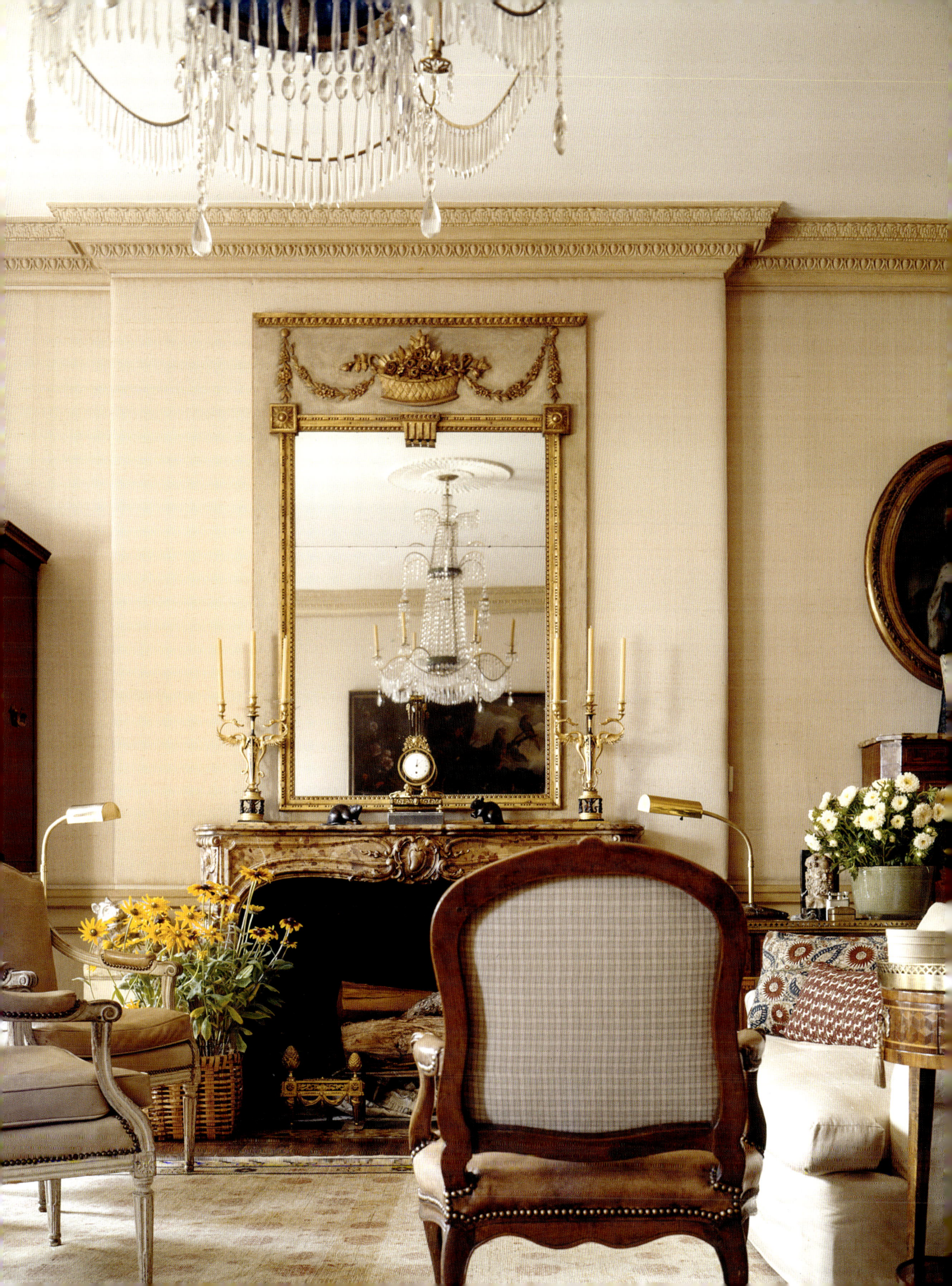

GUIGNÉCOURT

Hillsborough, 1961 and 1964

The Eleanor and Christian de Guigné III estate in Hillsborough—whose mansion was designed by architects Walter Bliss and William Faville and completed in 1916—spread out over forty-seven acres, which included lawns, gardens, and trails designed by Tommy Church.

Tony Hail took on the main redecoration of Guignécourt in the early 1960s and was careful to preserve its classical elements. The ballroom featured excellent Hail decoration. He filled it with elegant tables and chairs. At one end of the ballroom was a huge Coromandel screen and a gigantic philodendron. I think Tony had been influenced a lot by Billy Baldwin in arranging furniture.

The pool pavilion, designed by Charles Porter and John Robert Steinwedell, was added decades after Bliss & Faville did the main house. Porter and Steinwedell, who formerly worked for Gardner Dailey, also did my Napa house—a somewhat different project! I took these photographs as a favor to them, in order to showcase their work at the estate. The pool pavilion really completed and complemented the existing architecture. It became a focal point for the de Guignés' entertaining on occasions when the grand ballroom wasn't called for. The pavilion was certainly inviting and elegant. It was the site of many fun-filled times.   —*F.L.*

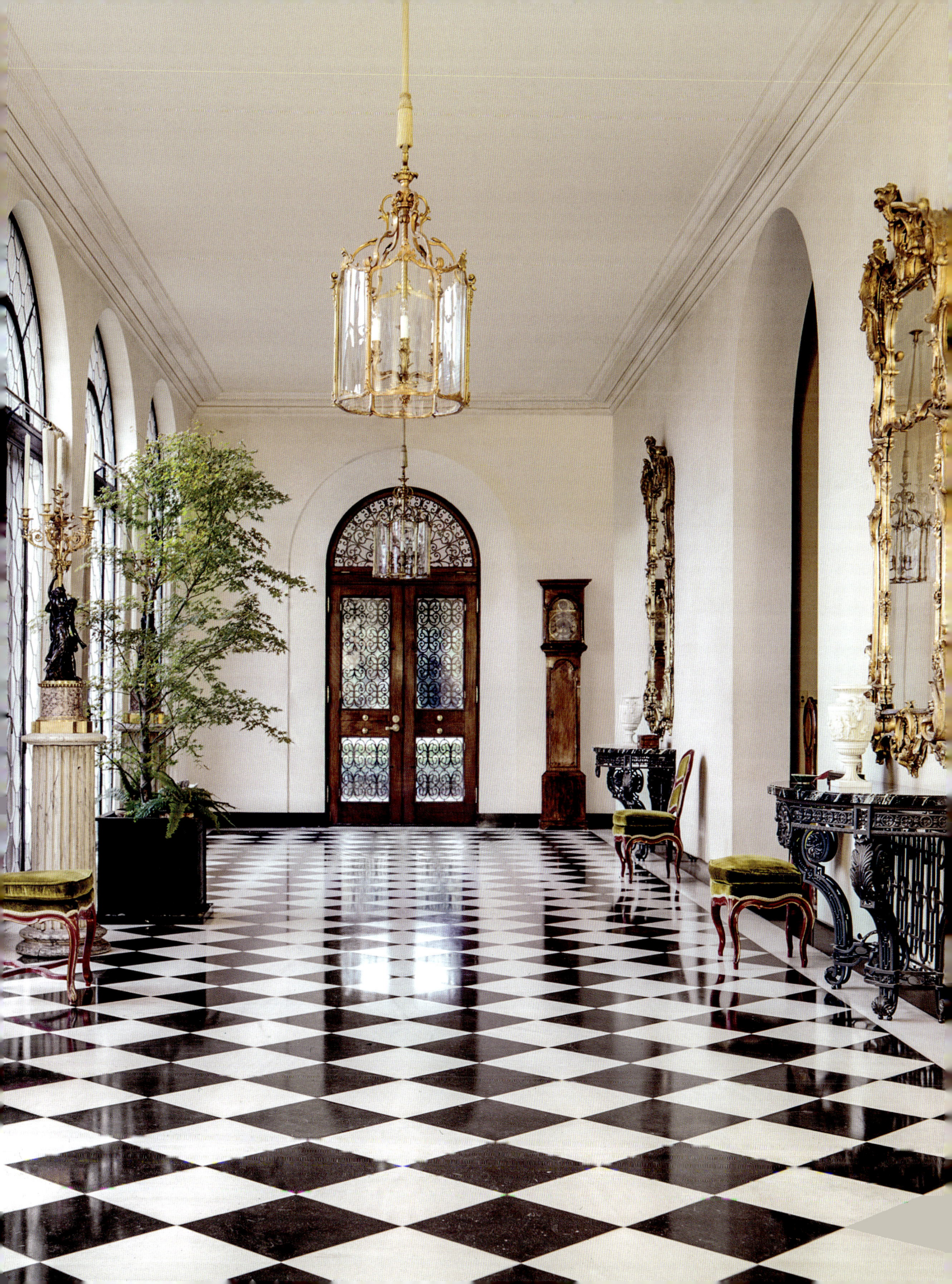

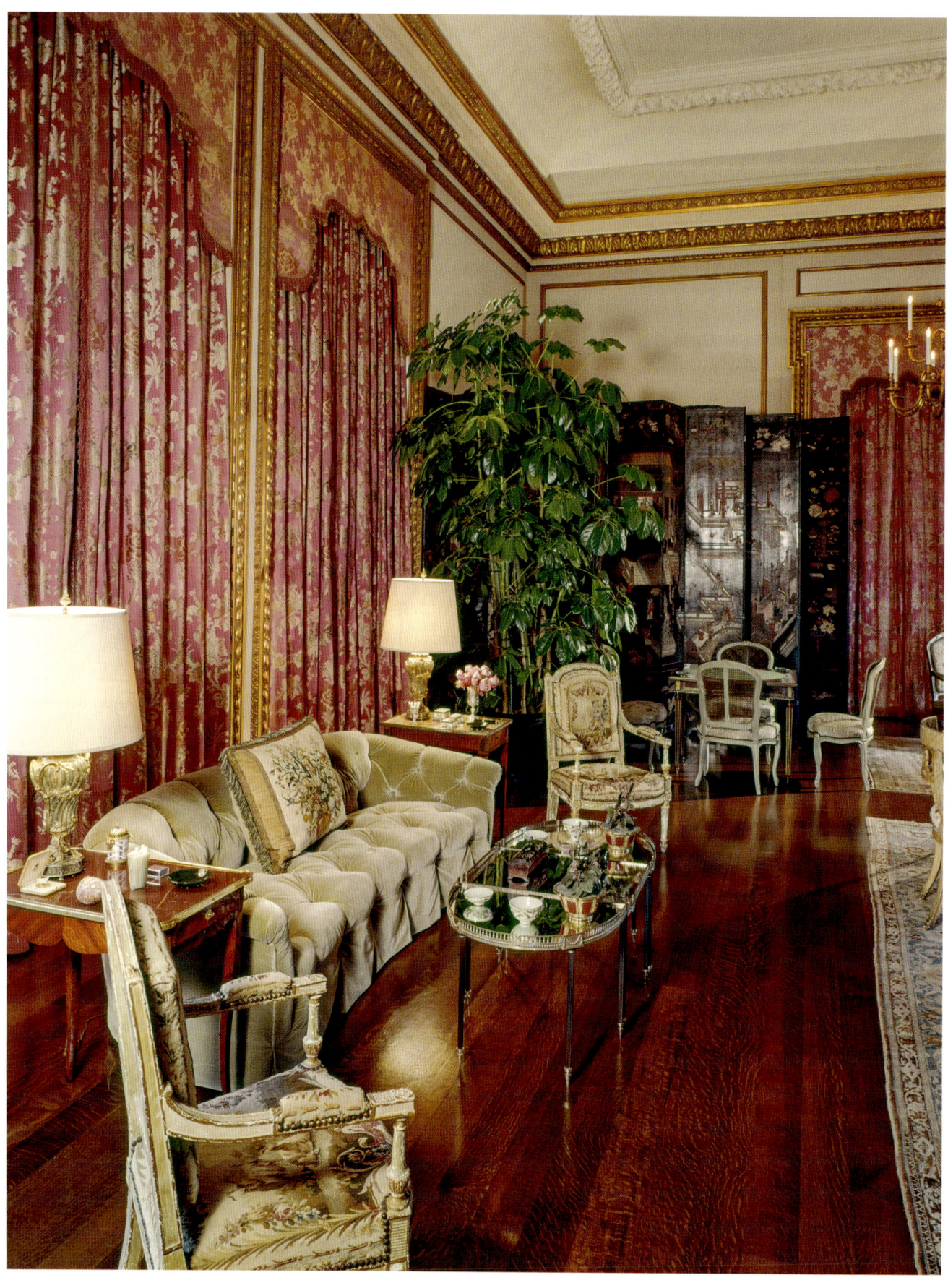

PAGE 141: The entrance hall of Guignécourt, the Eleanor and Christian de Guigné house in Hillsborough, 1964. Built in 1916 by architects Bliss & Faville, the residence reflects the grandeur of the Gilded Age. ABOVE AND OPPOSITE: Two views of the ballroom, which also served as a formal drawing room. Anthony Hail's pale-green velvet sofa takes its place among traditional Asian and European furnishings: a twelve-panel Coromandel screen, Imari porcelain jars, a late nineteenth-century Tabriz carpet, and eighteenth-century Directoire chairs, 1964.

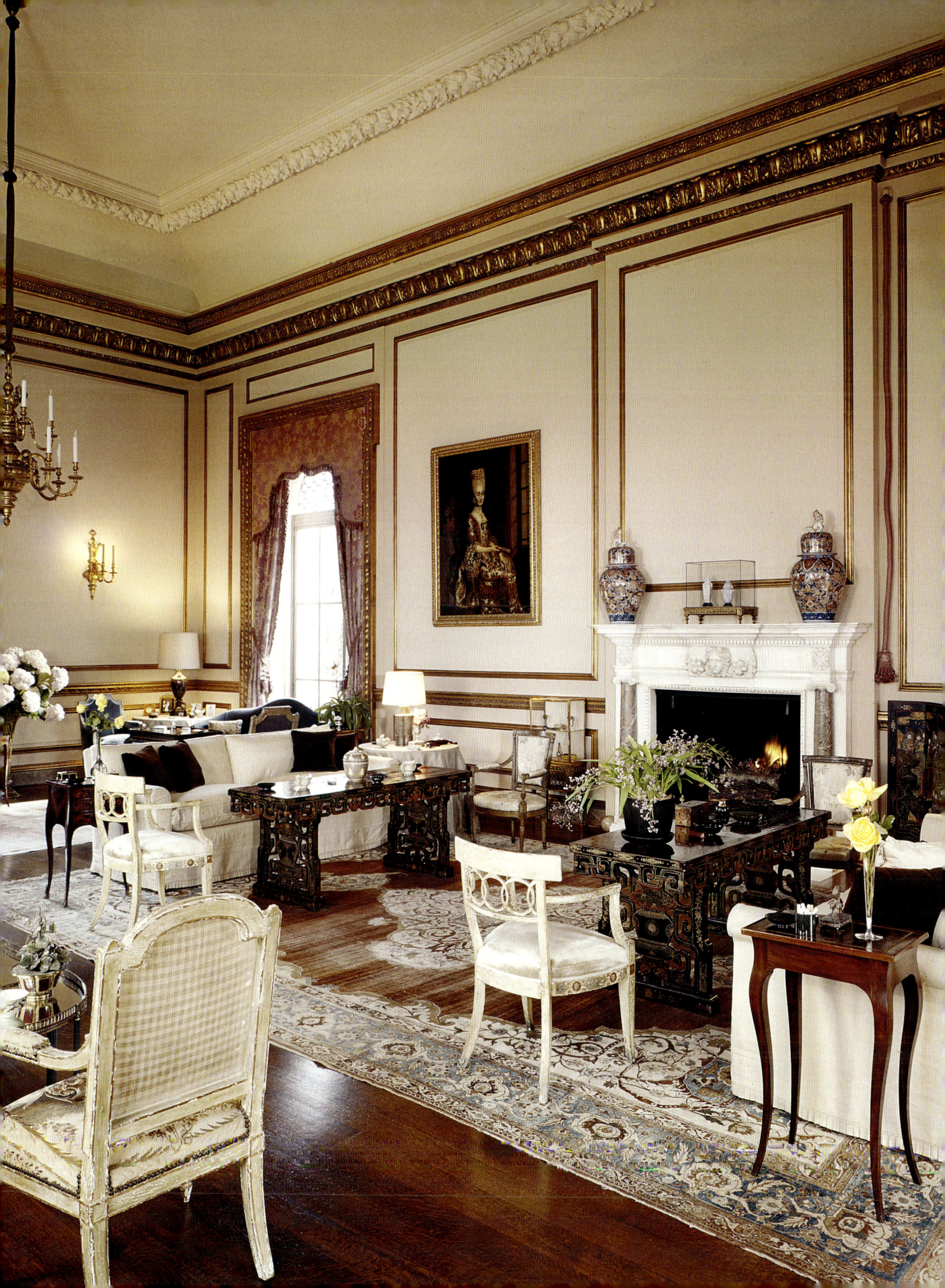

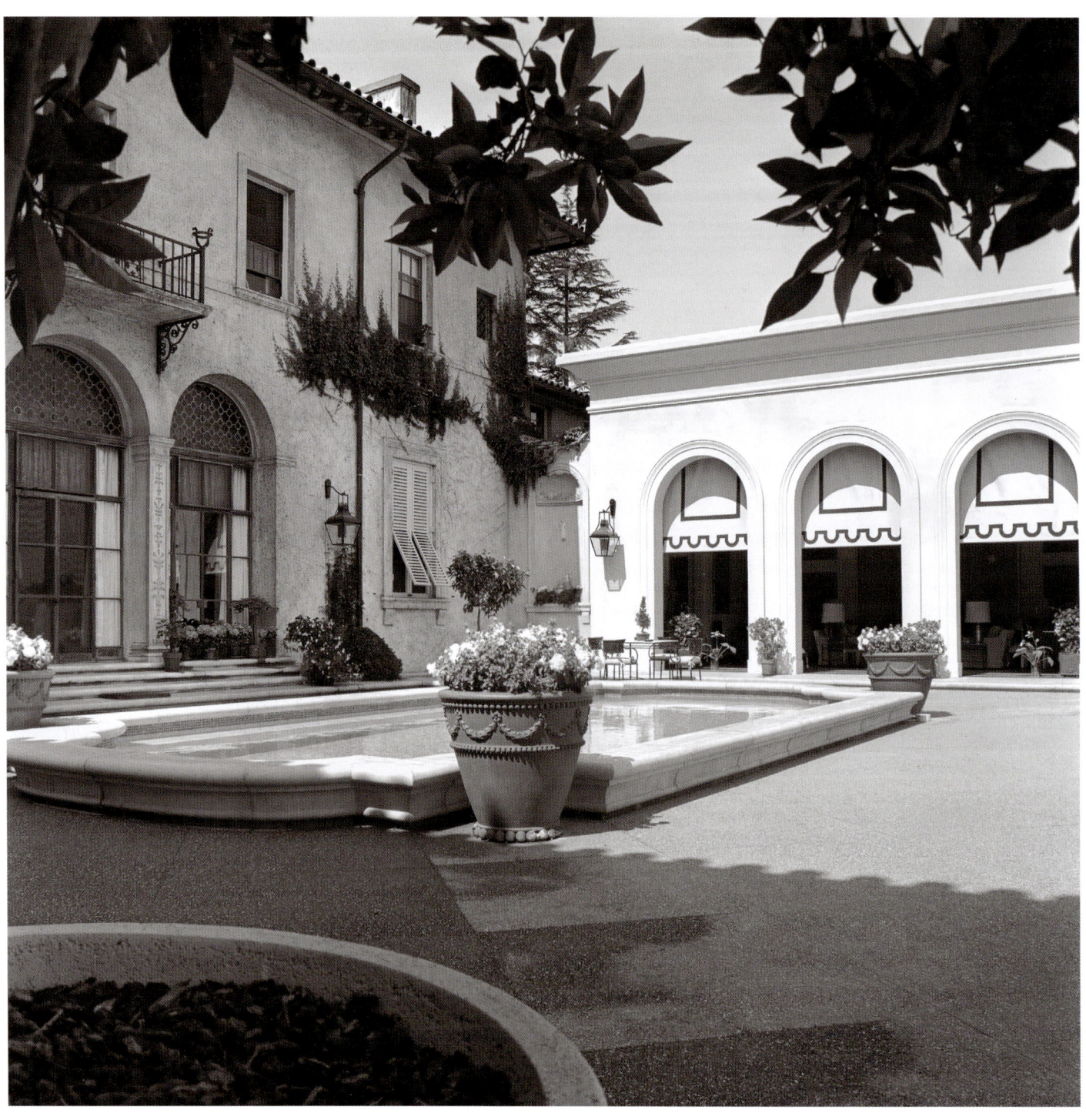

ABOVE: In 1960, architects Porter and Steinwedell designed a loggia-like pool house with arched openings (*right*) to harmonize with the de Guigné's Florentine-inspired pool, 1961.
OPPOSITE: Eleanor de Guigné with one of her dogs in the pool courtyard, 1961.

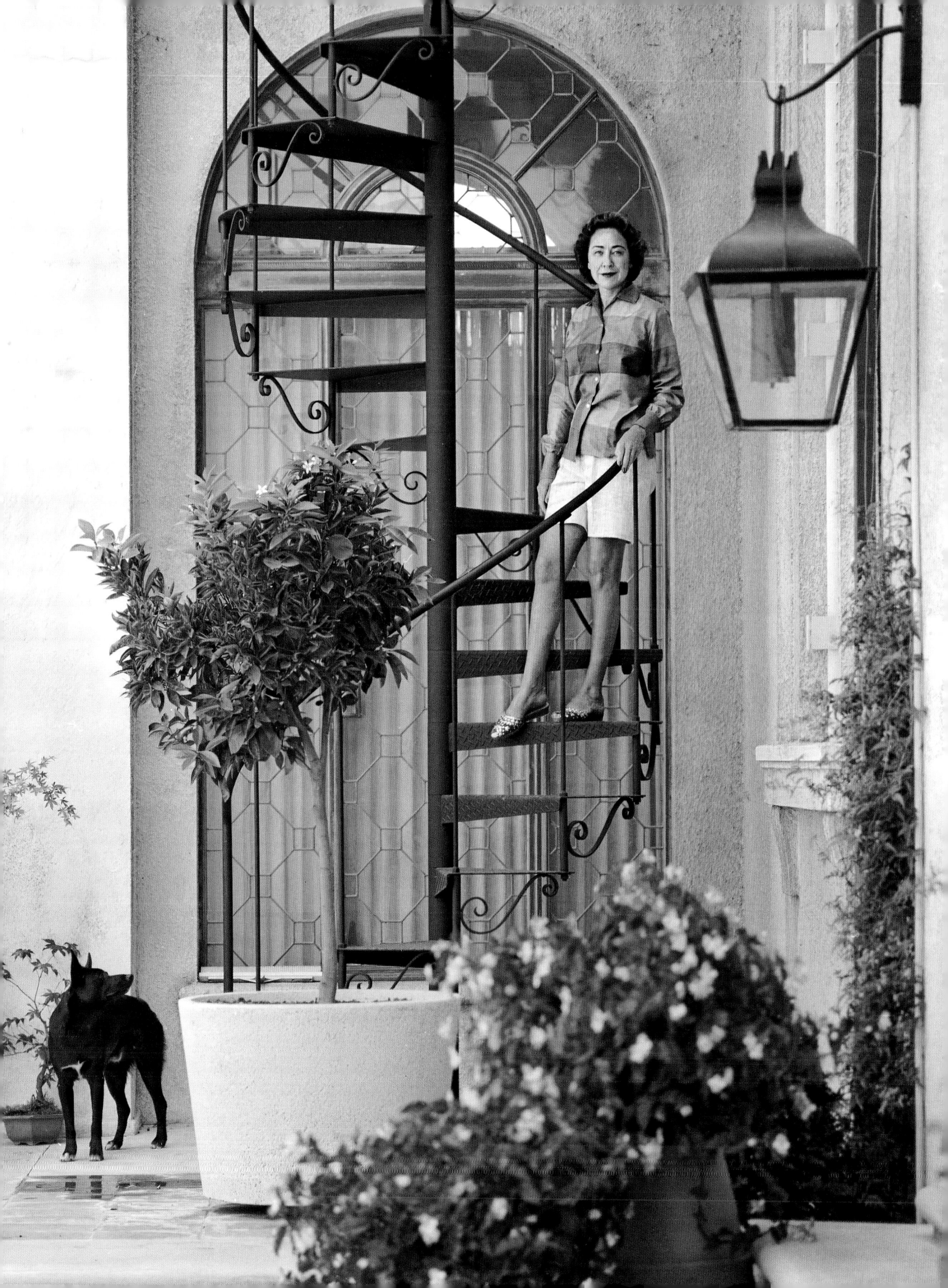

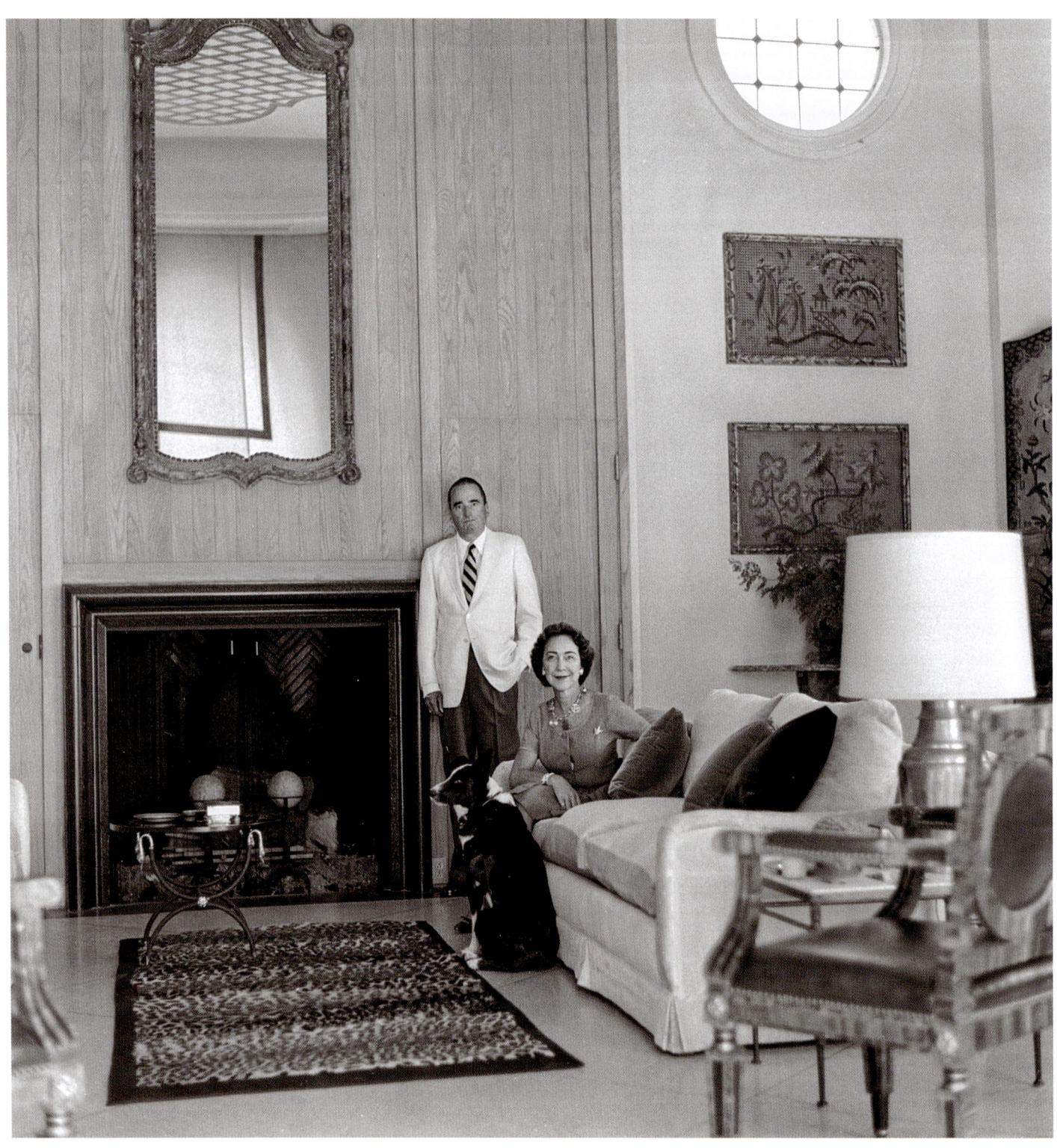

ABOVE: The de Guignés by the fireplace inside the pool house, 1961. Hail filled the interior with Italian furniture and decorative wall panels with Chinese motifs. The sofa was upholstered in beige linen velour, with pillows in chocolate and orange silk velvet.
OPPOSITE: Soon after the original decoration was completed, Hail updated the interior to give it a more Chinese look, covering the walls with eighteenth-century wallpaper depicting a mountainous landscape. At one end of each sofa is an antique Chinese table, 1964.

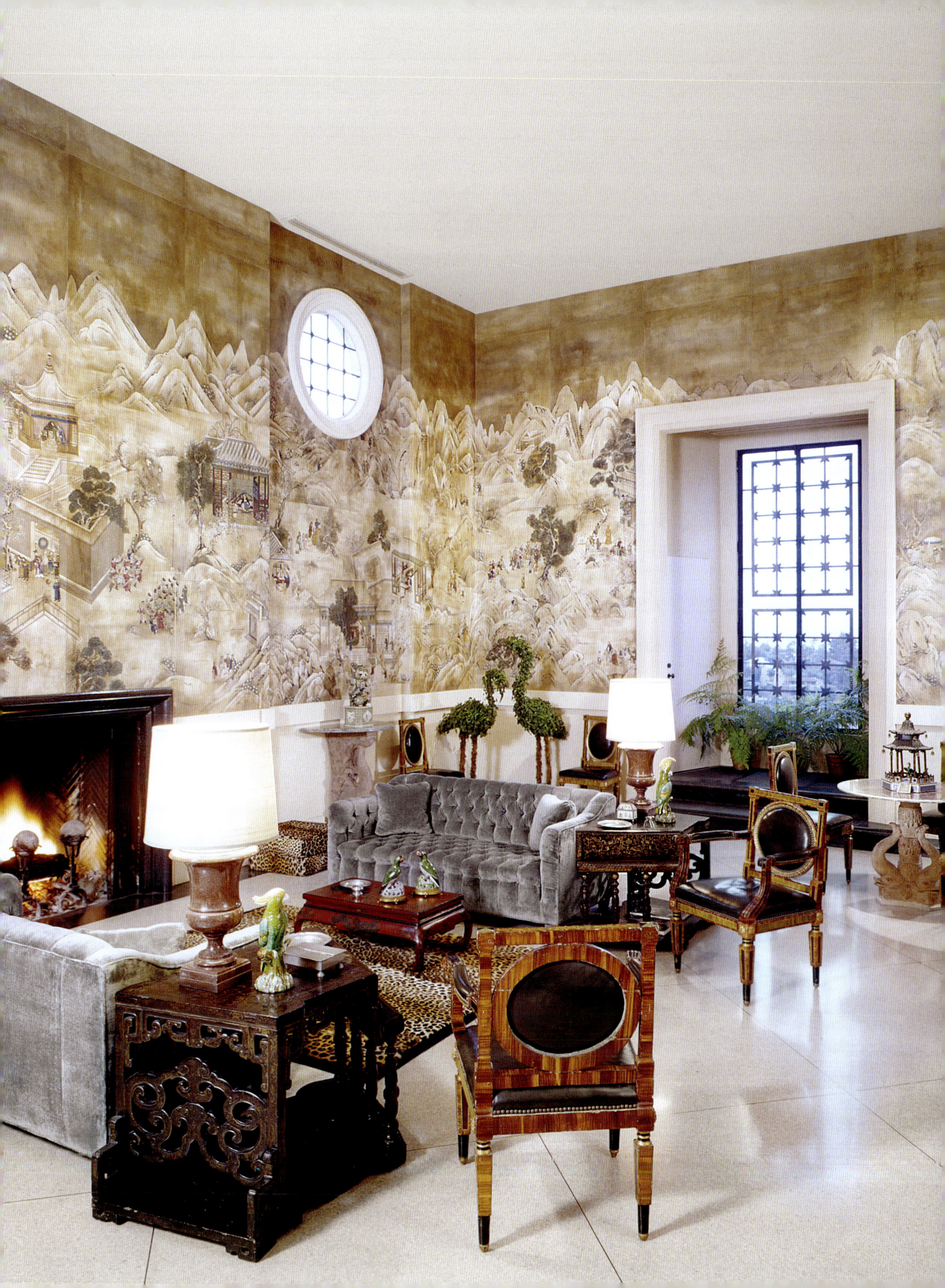

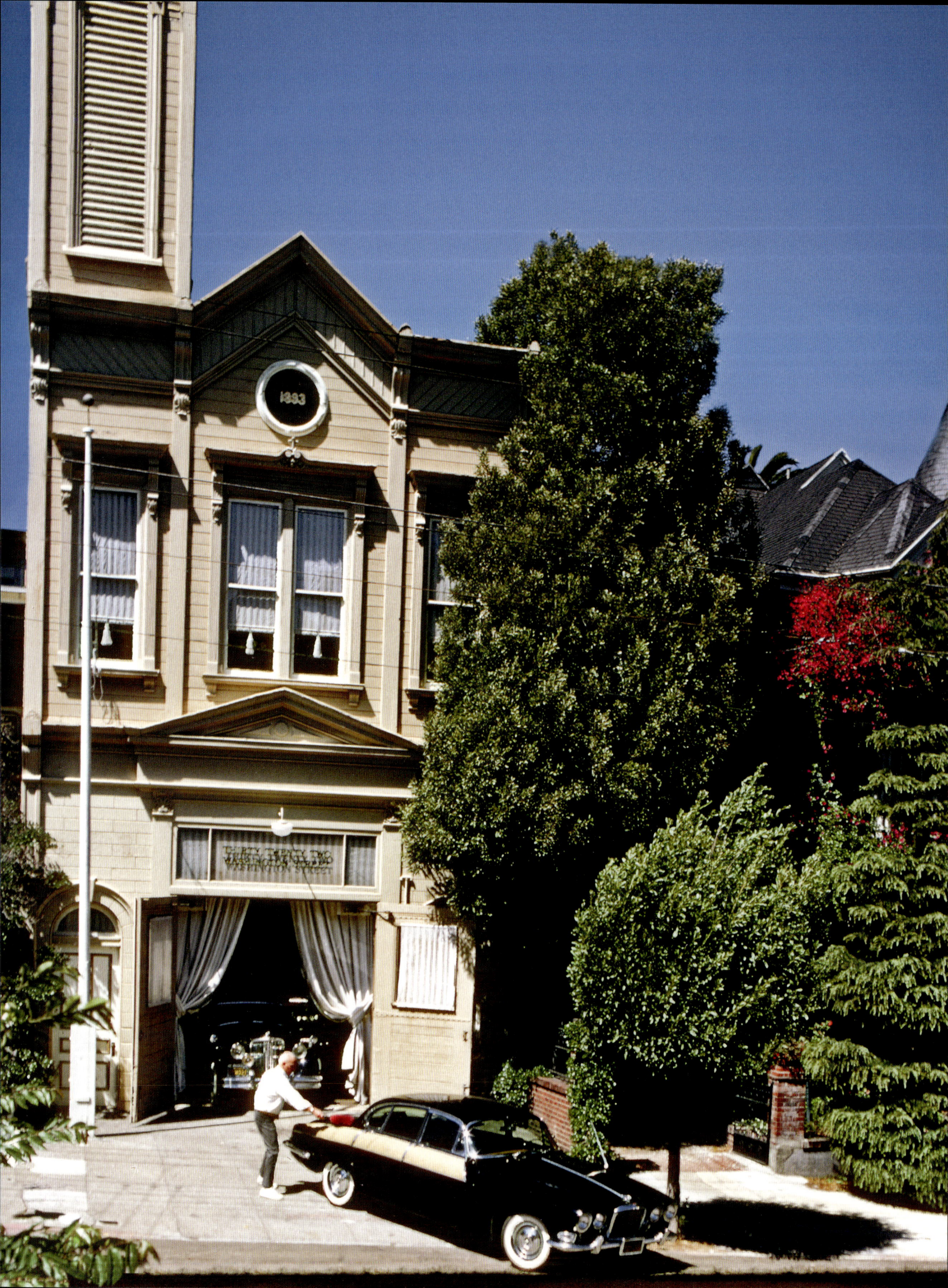

JOHN DICKINSON HOUSE

San Francisco, 1973

John Dickinson turned a former firehouse in Pacific Heights into his own residence. The space was hard to work with because it had been designed to accommodate fire engines on the ground floor, with dormitory accommodations for firefighters on the second floor. There was a separate cookhouse in the back. These spaces turned into canvases for John's immense creativity.

On the ground floor, where fire engines were once housed, John kept a Rolls-Royce and a Jaguar that he customized himself. The main room of the residence was on the second floor, facing the street. The large table in this room served as John's work desk and dining table. The dining chairs were kept against the walls when he wasn't entertaining. The plaster walls throughout the upstairs were original to the structure and had a wonderfully mottled patina—most striking against the shiny white enamel of the wainscoting. John made a pedestal for the wildly sculptural fireplace, which defined the prime seating area.

In the back of the second floor were the kitchen, dressing room, and bedroom. John created the kitchen from scratch. The room had a white plaster mirror, which was lovely but probably not very practical for a kitchen. The dressing room was fitted with a wall that resembled a street elevation, with the building facades on hinges that opened to reveal his closets. It was fanciful *and* it worked. That is pure John Dickinson.   —F.L.

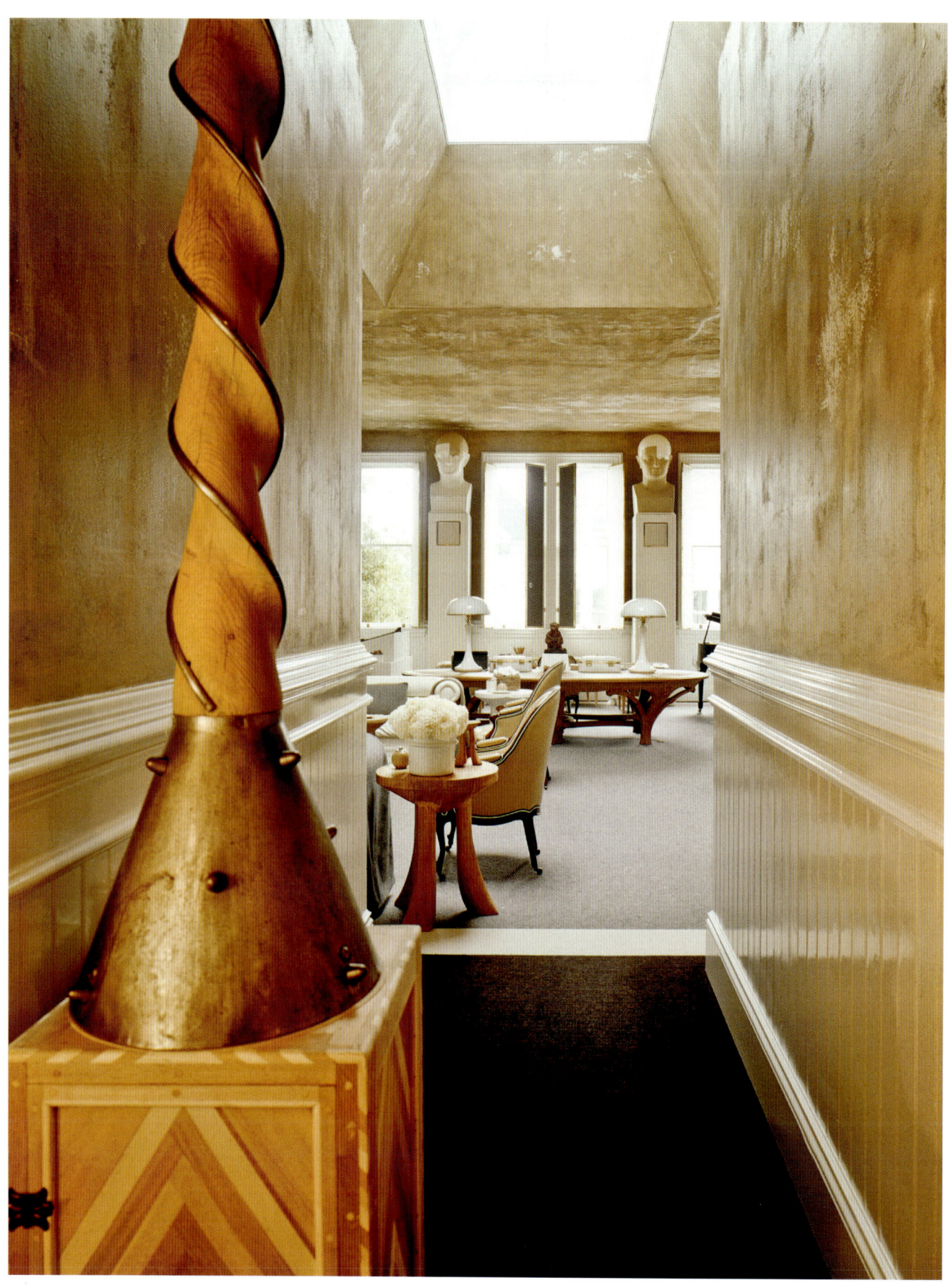

PAGE 148: Exterior of John Dickinson's 1893 converted firehouse residence, Pacific Heights, San Francisco.
ABOVE: View toward the living room, with narwhal-tusk sculpture in foreground. RIGHT: Dickinson kept the living room walls and ceiling exactly as he had found them, but painted the original brown dado white.

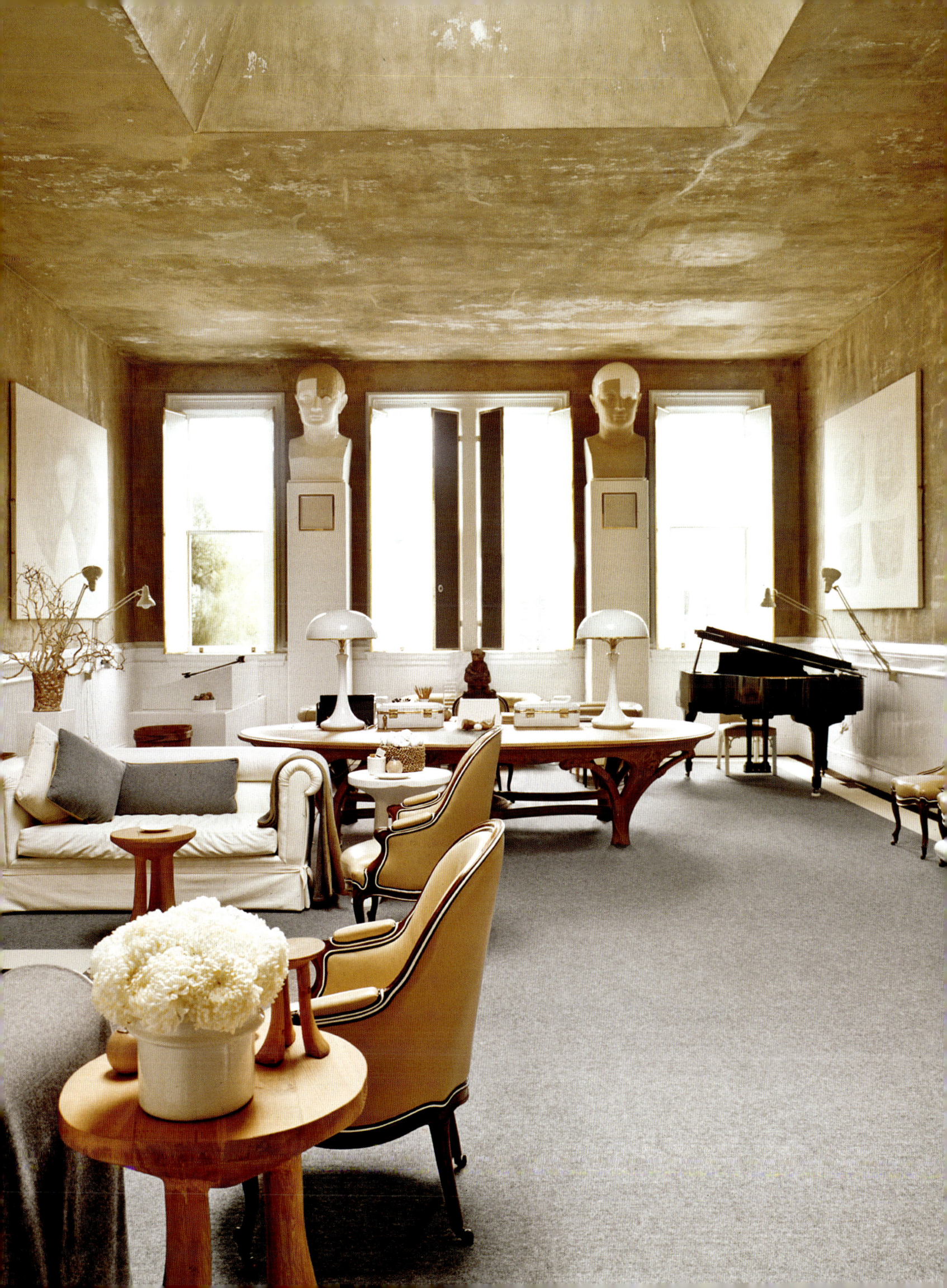

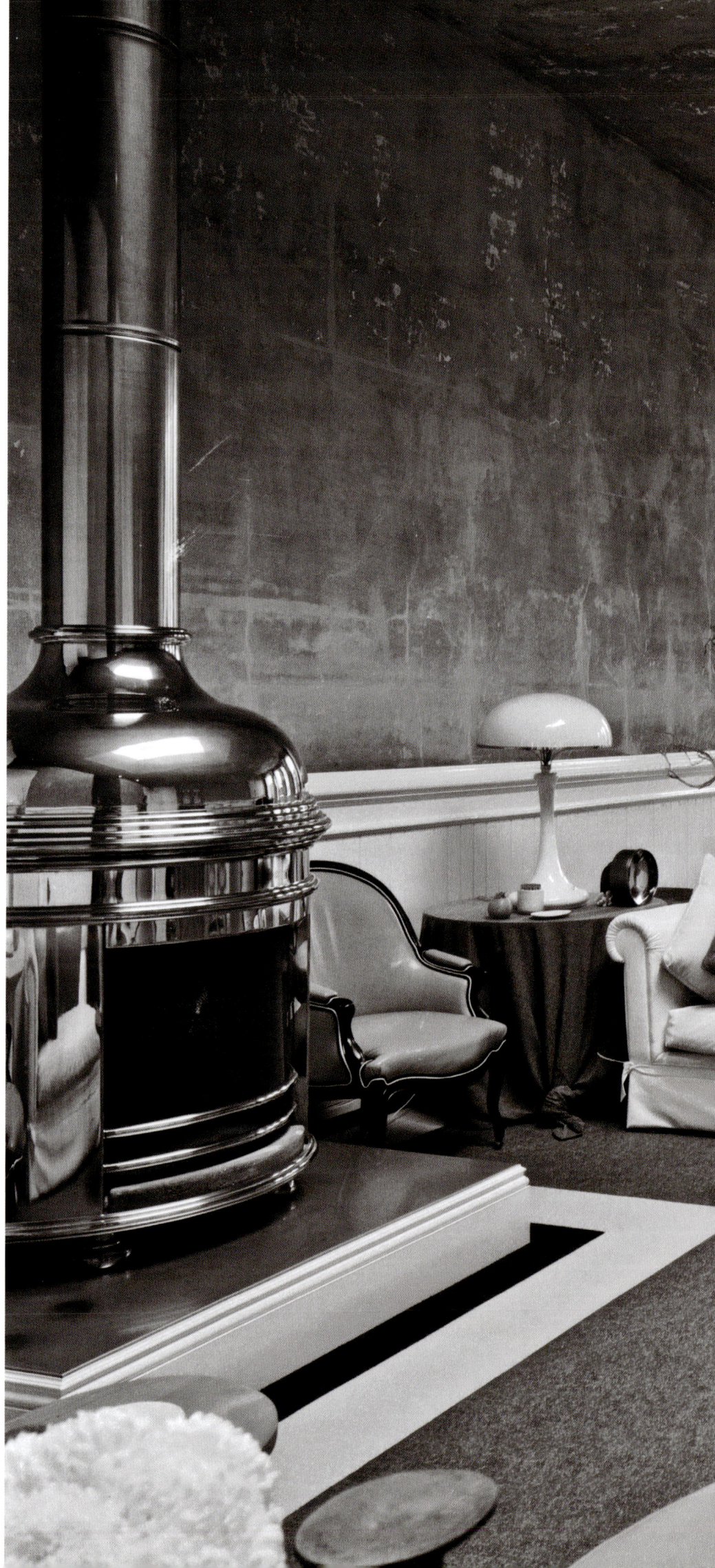

RIGHT: Living room, with the main seating area arranged around the woodstove on its raised base. PAGE 154: Art Nouveau table with Victorian chairs covered in leather matching the wall color. PAGE 155: Dickinson designed the wood stove, which took a year to execute.

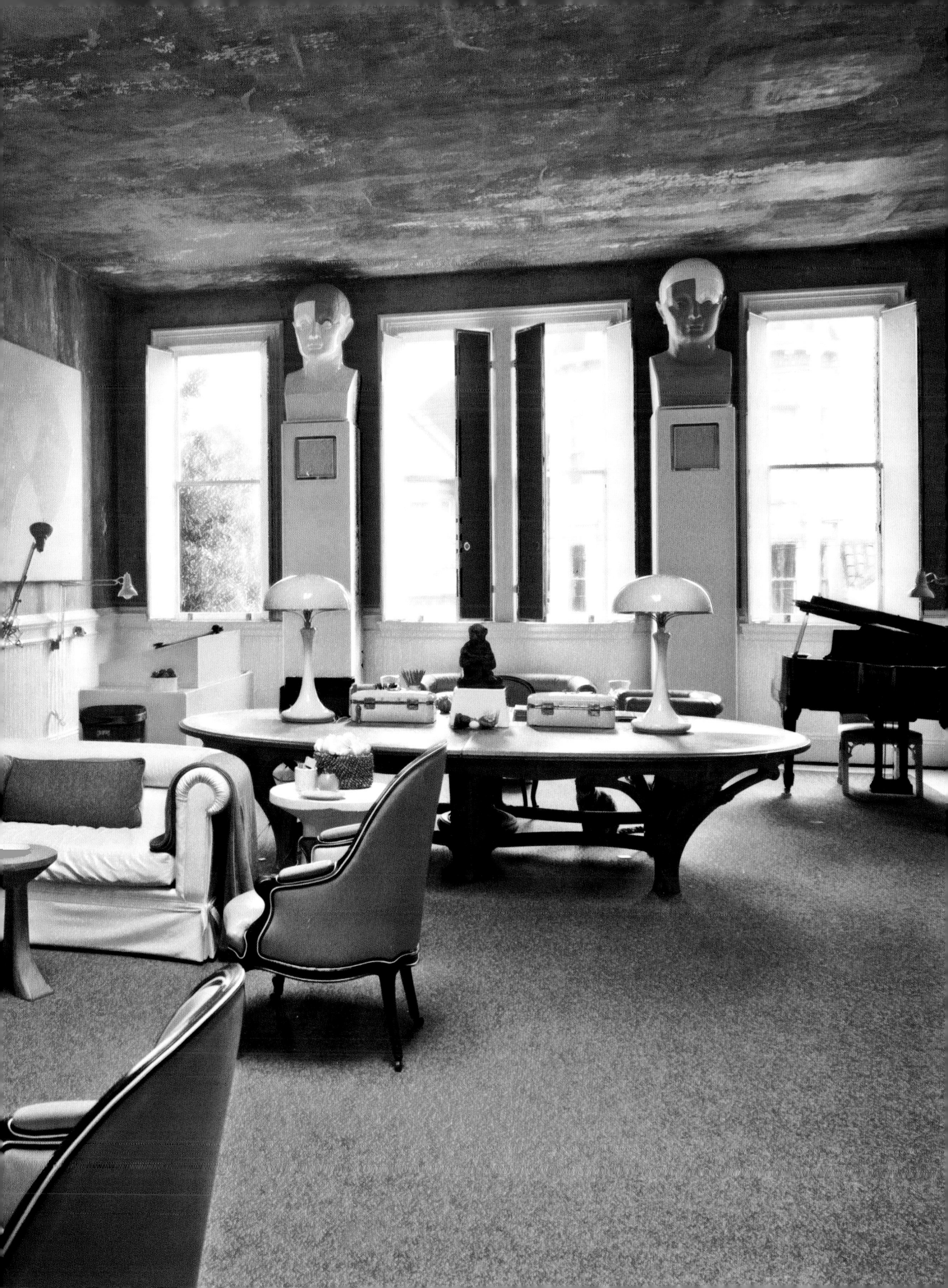

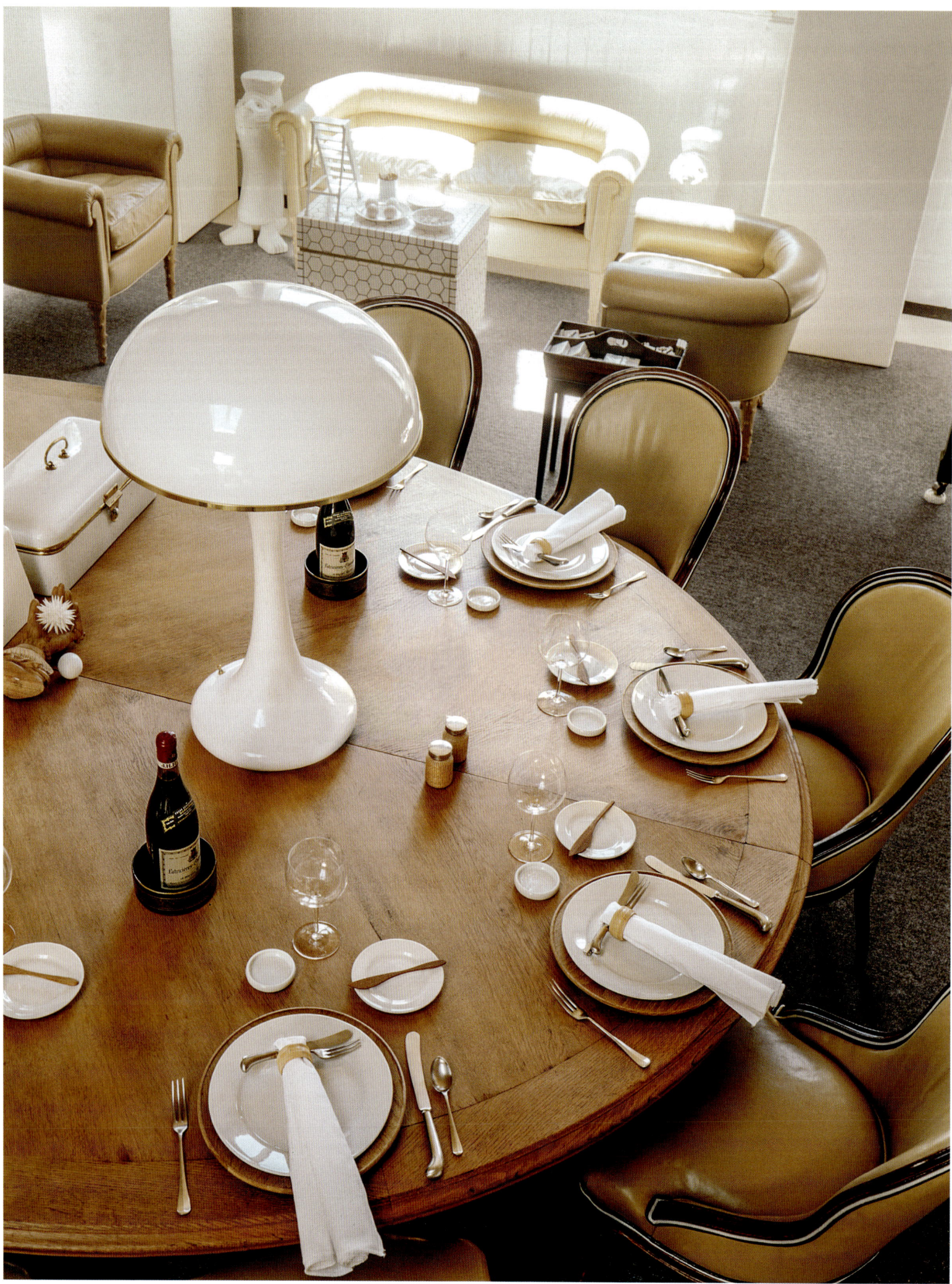

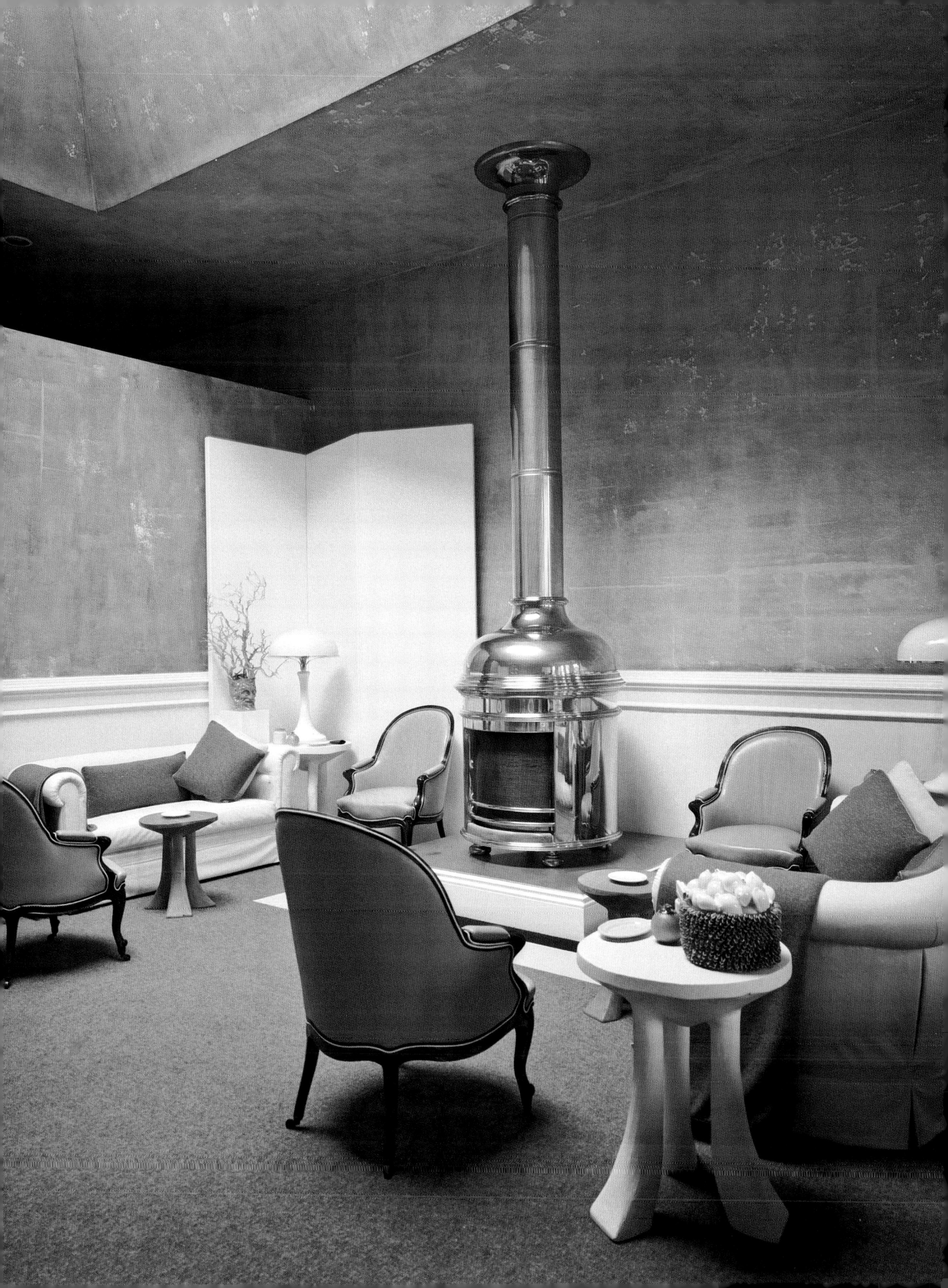

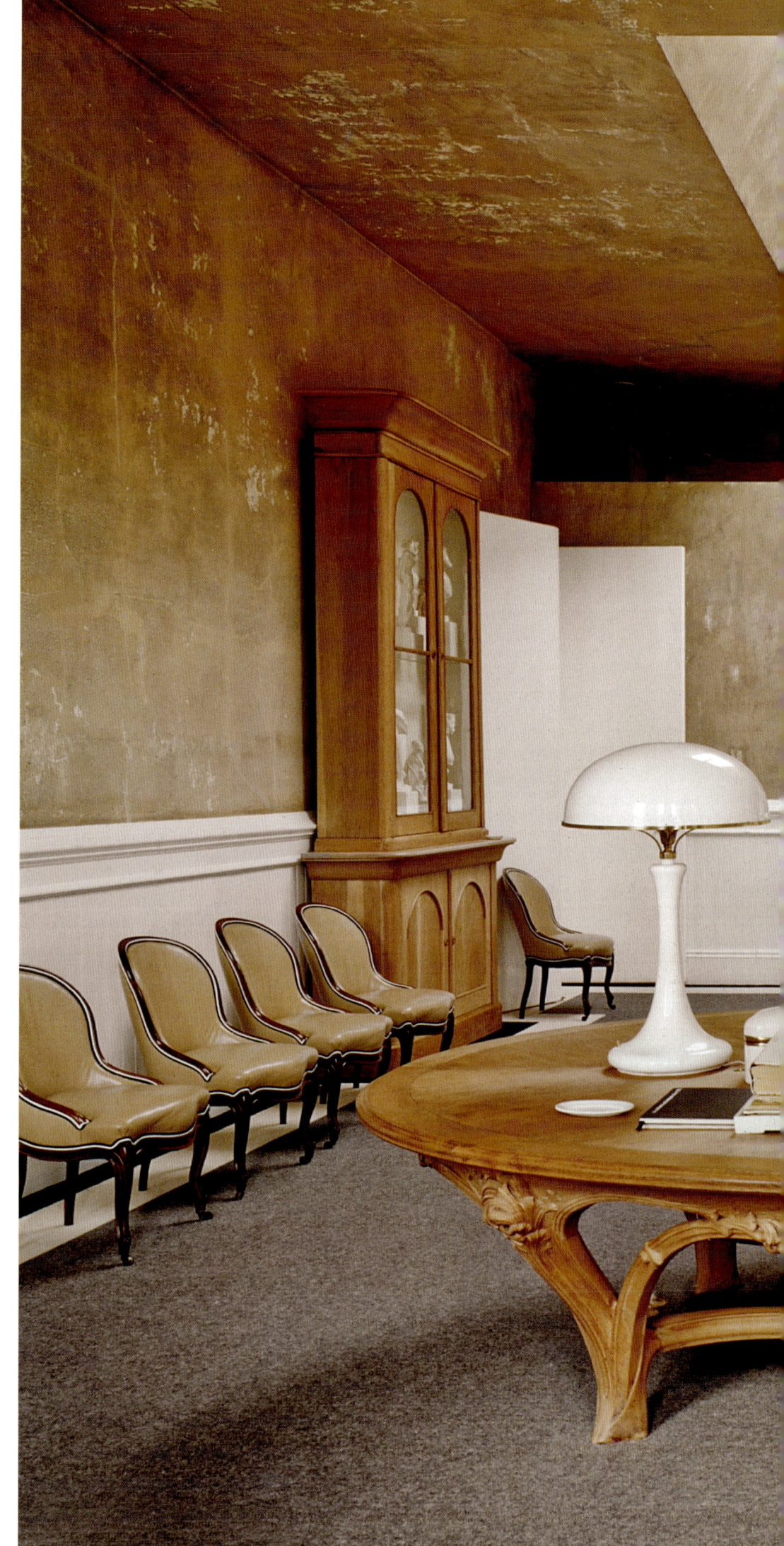

RIGHT: Dickinson used the Art Nouveau table in the foreground for both work and dining. PAGE 158: Closet doors in Dickinson's dressing room evoke a streetscape of town houses. The facades open outward to reveal storage. PAGE 159: The bedroom walls were covered with black vinyl resembling horsehair, and the carpet was dark brown. French doors opened onto a balcony that overlooked the rear garden. Dickinson designed the faux-bamboo bed, which has a wood-grain painted finish.

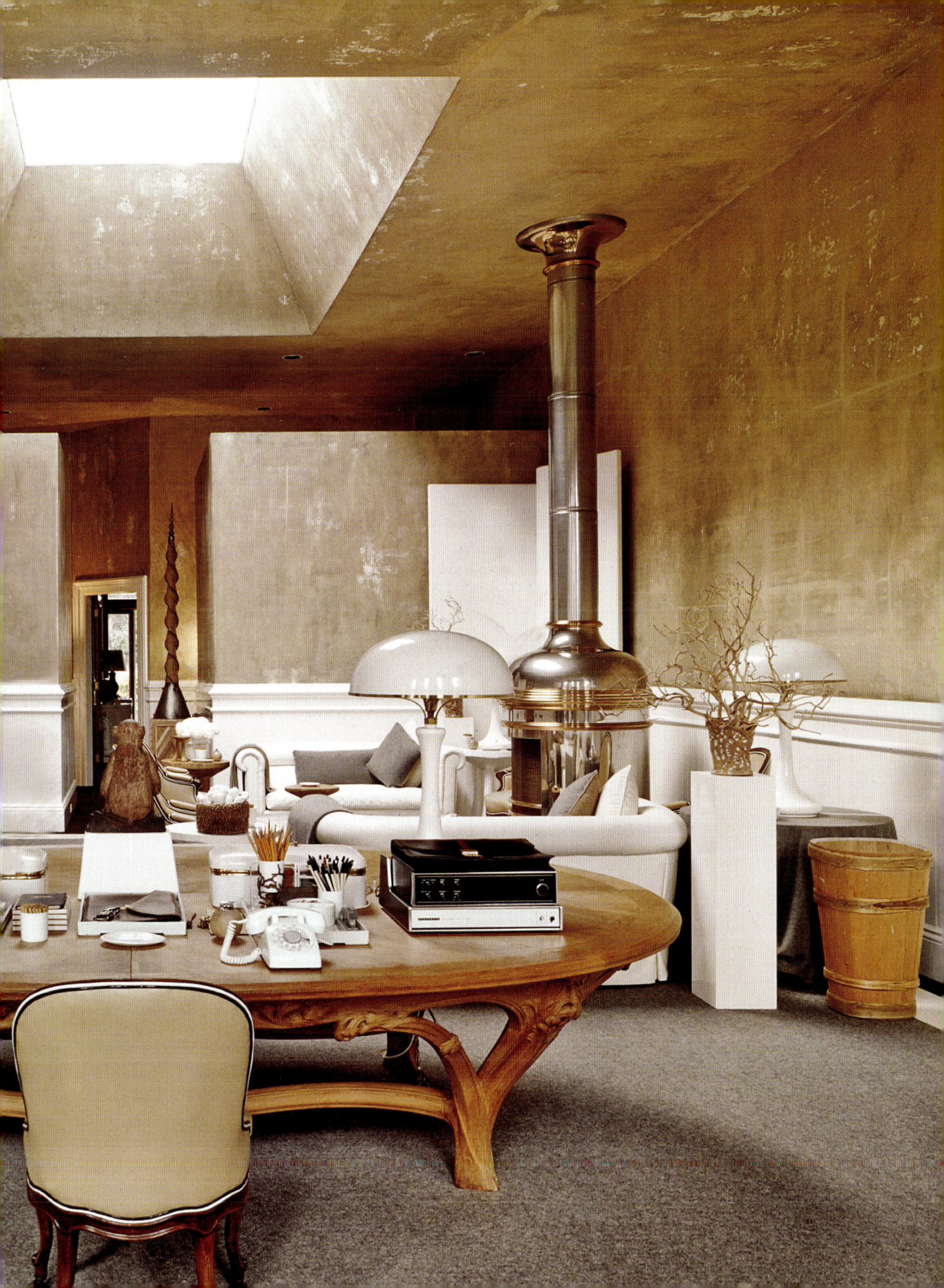

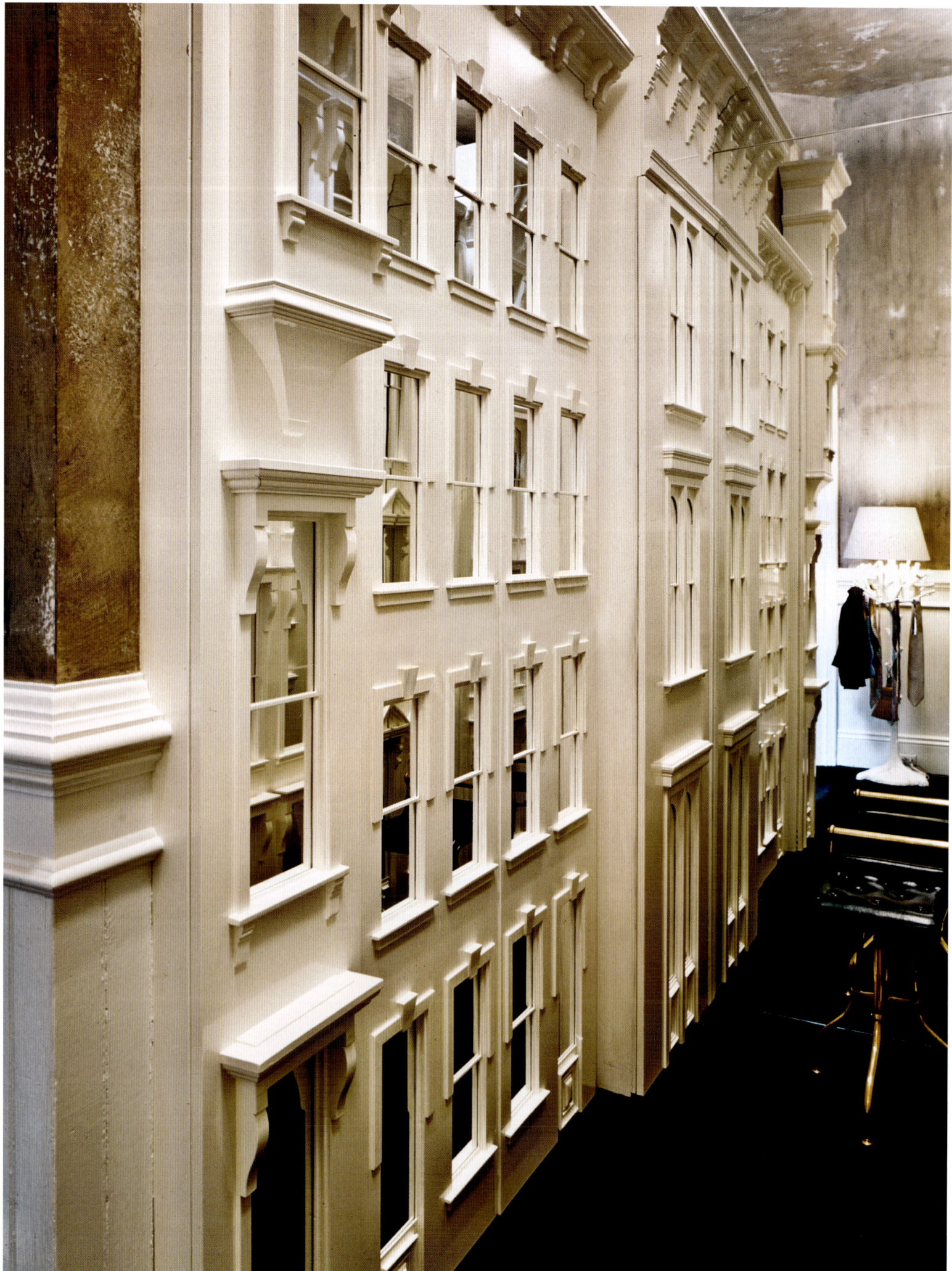

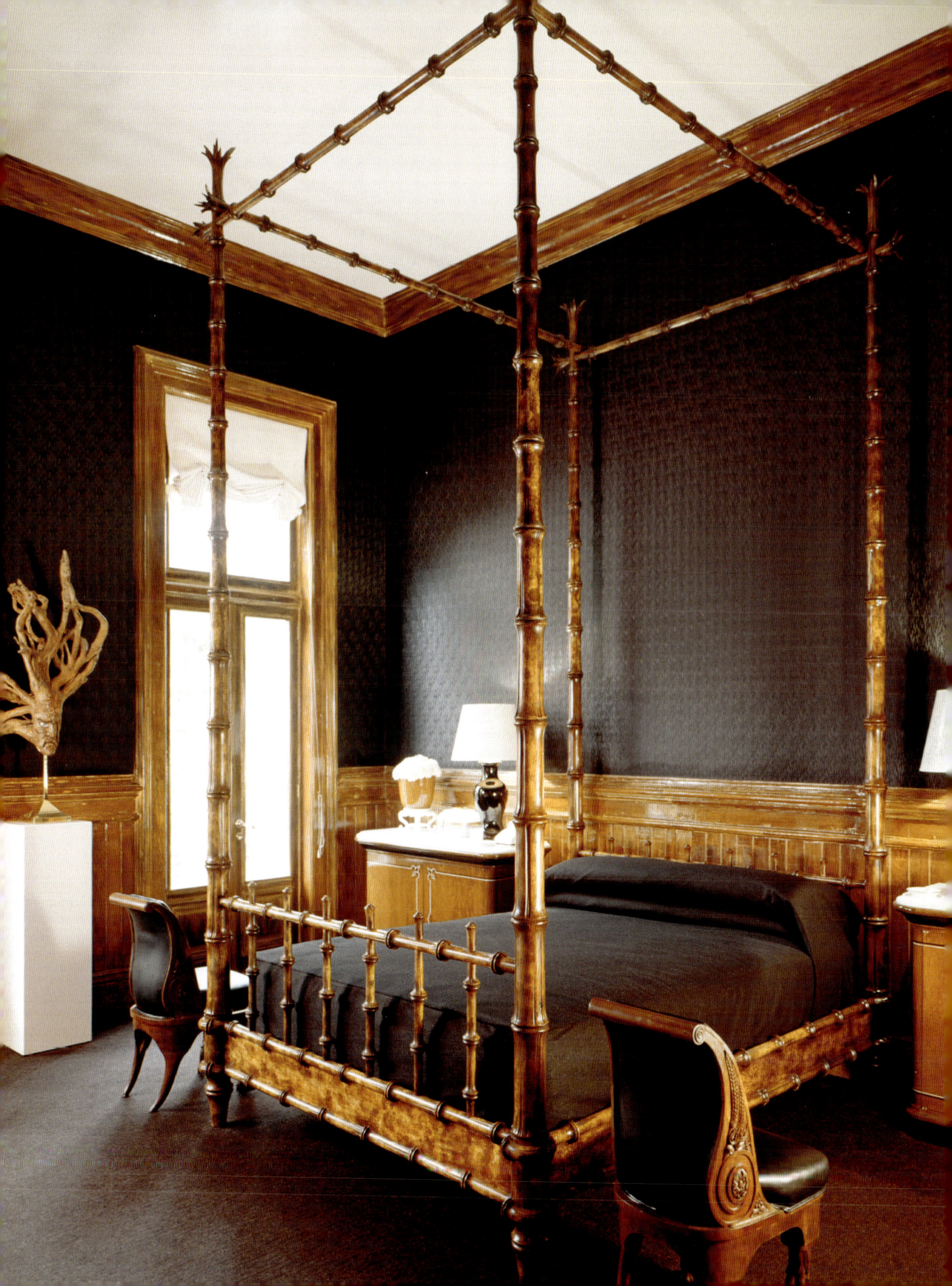

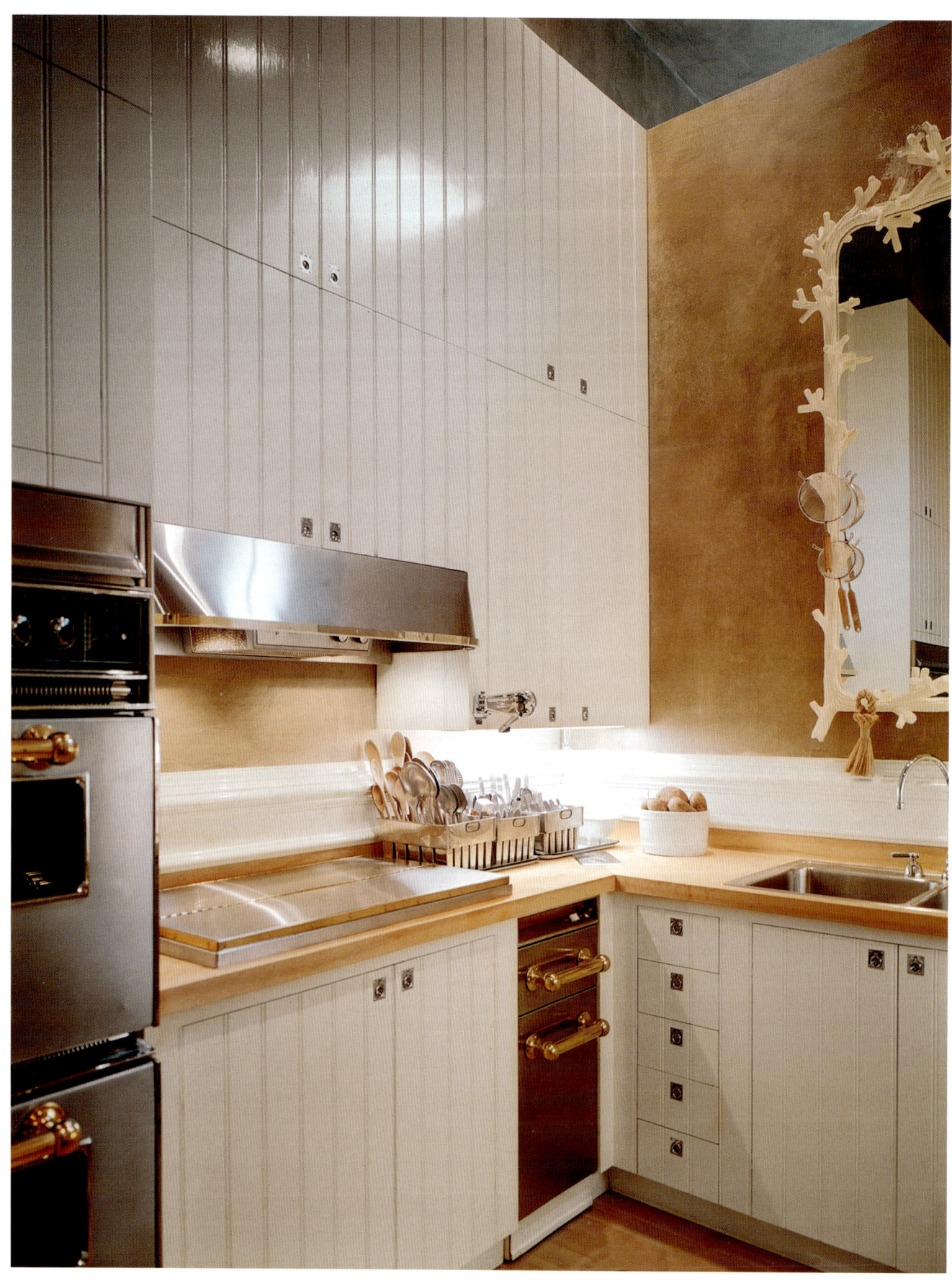

ABOVE: The substantial brass pulls on the kitchen appliances make reference to fire poles. OPPOSITE: At the center of the garden are a rustic table and chairs with wood seats carved to suggest cushions. A topiary sunshade—made from ivy climbing on a steel armature—stands in the middle of the table. This image was taken in 1970, at an earlier shoot than the other images.

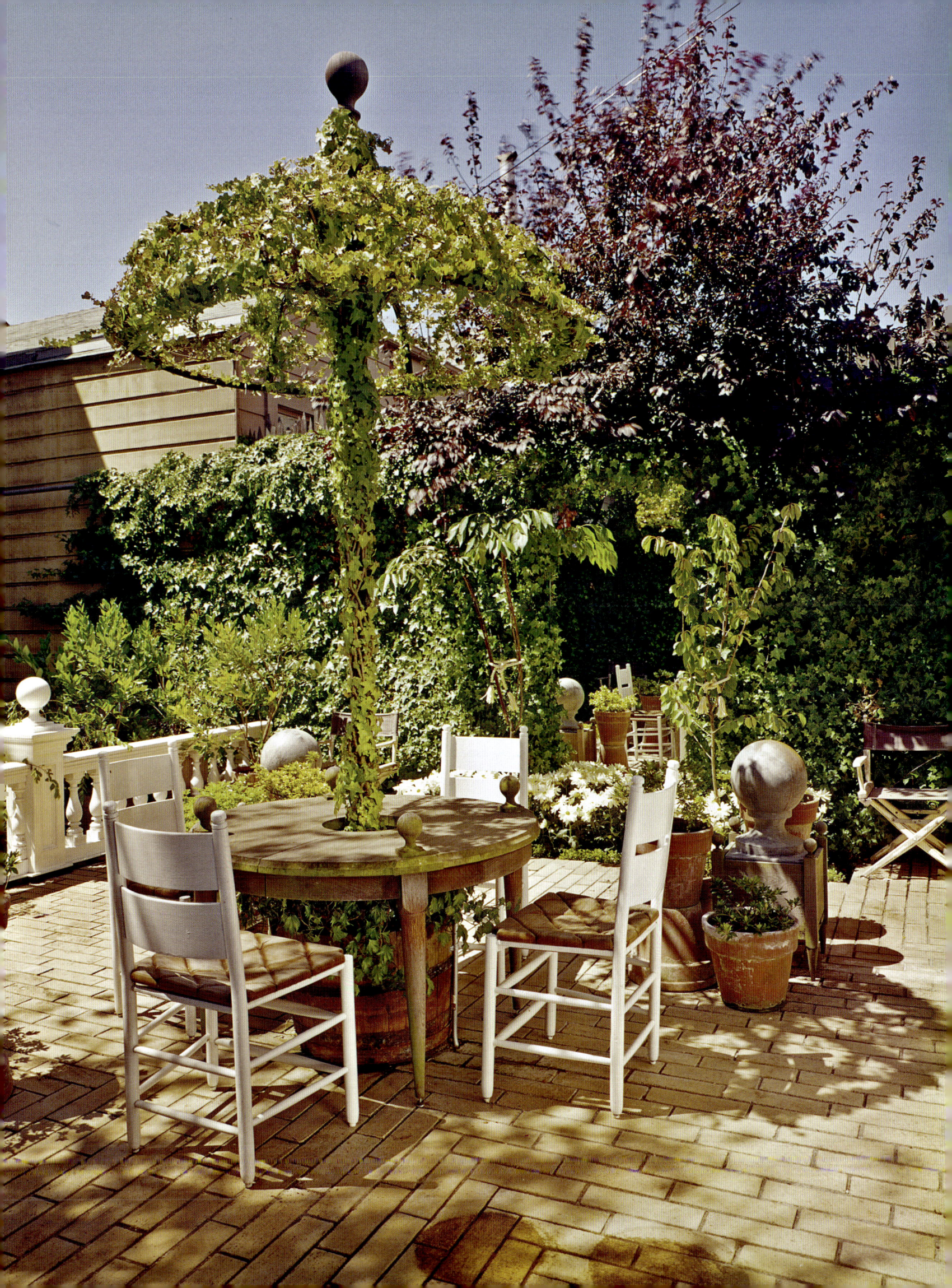

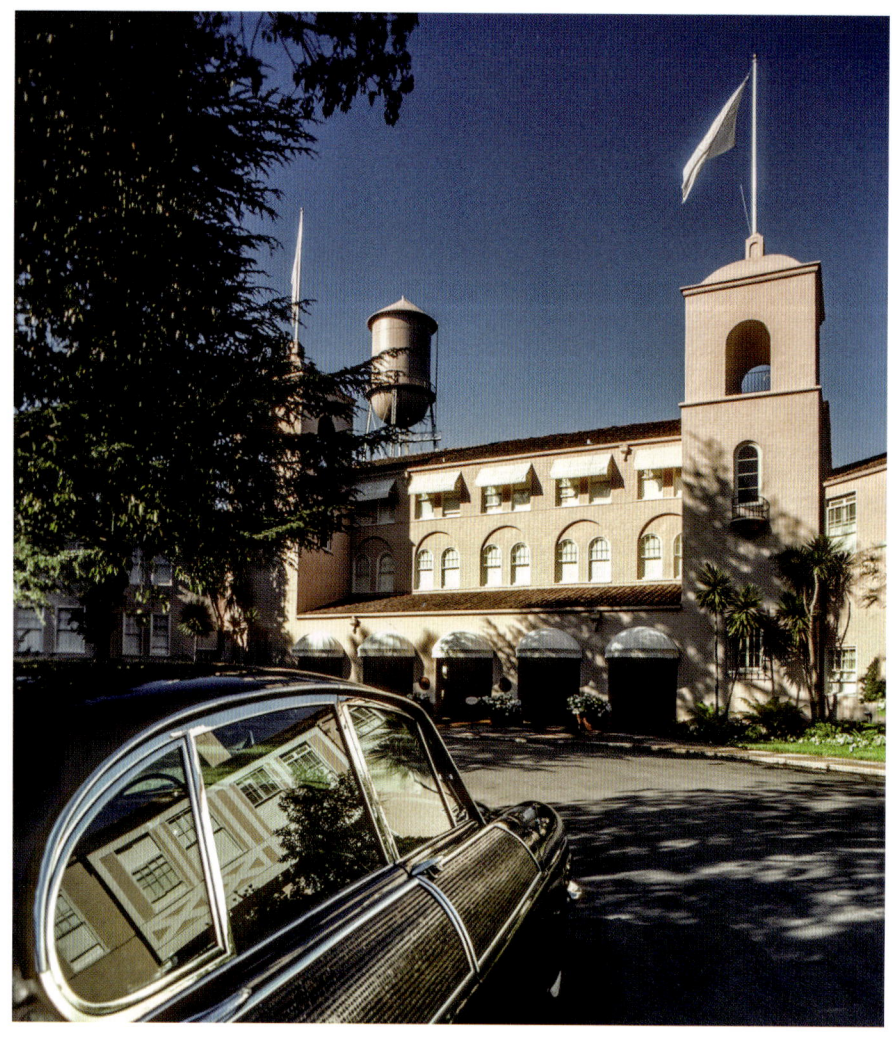

SONOMA MISSION INN

Sonoma, 1980

Edward Safdie was trying to bring the Sonoma Mission Inn at Boyes Hot Springs back to life—it was going to be torn down. He snapped it up and inveigled John Dickinson to do a budget job on fixing it up, from the public spaces, restaurant, and bar area to the bedrooms. John did an economy job that was unbelievably good. He attacked it with great verve and used inexpensive materials. It took pure design excellence to make it work.

In the photograph of one of the bedrooms, there is a container of gladioli on the floor. John was not one to use flowers or plants in his interiors, so this was obviously the addition of someone else. The tables, banquette, and window shades in the small bar area are pure Dickinson. Sadly, this space did not exist like this very long; it was changed by the succeeding owner.

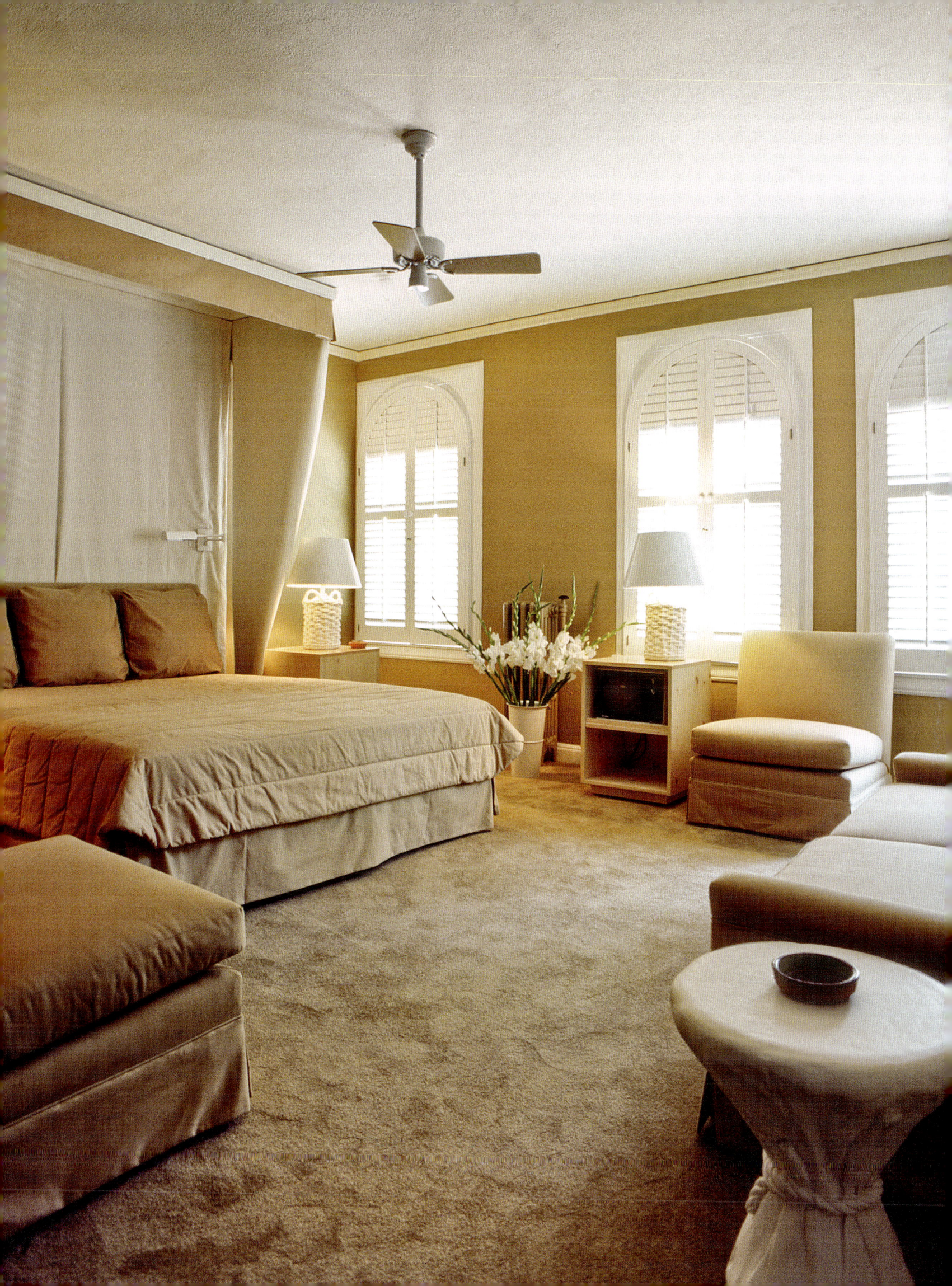

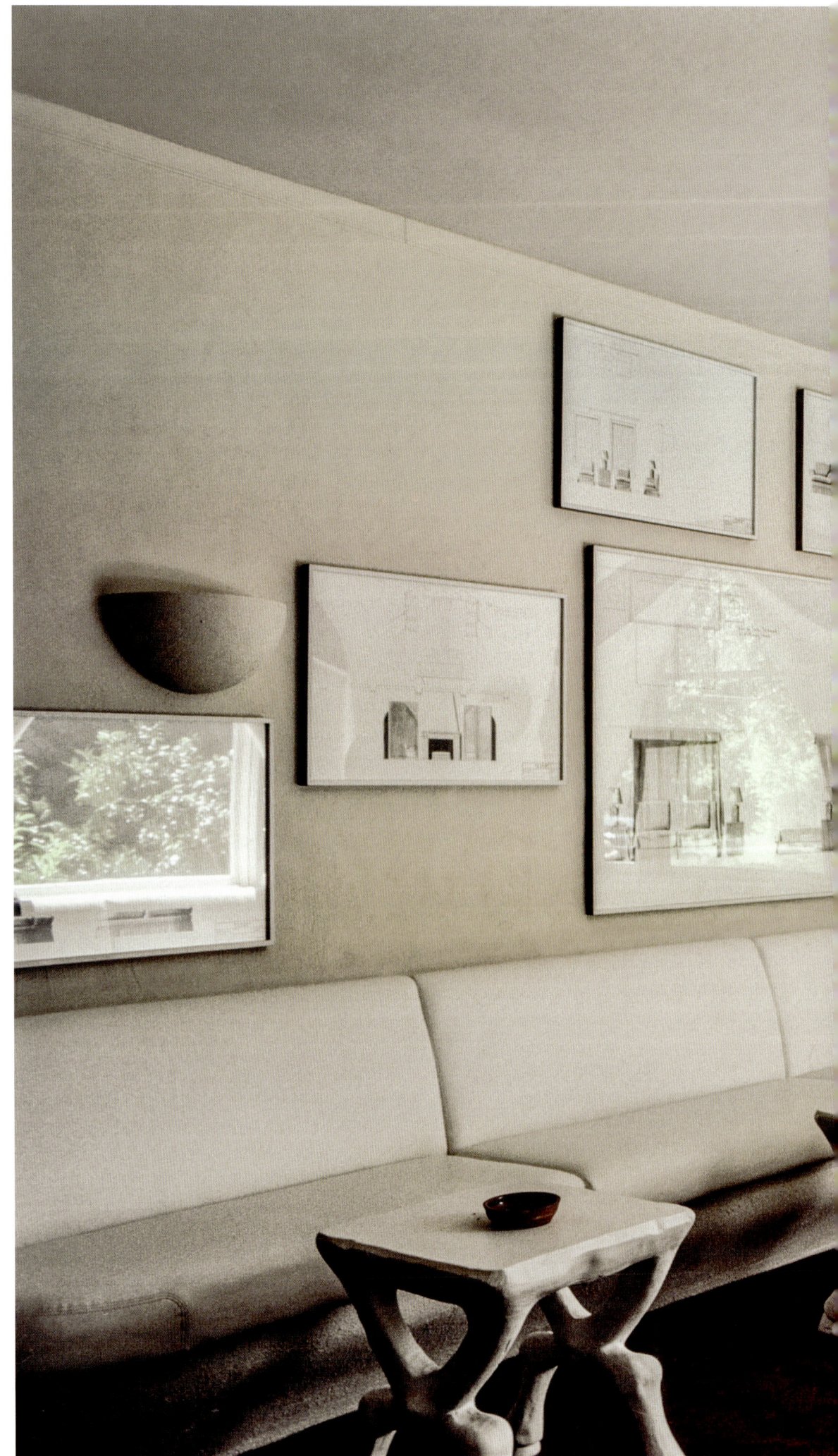

PAGE 162: Entrance facade of the Sonoma Mission Inn, Sonoma, 1980. John Dickinson selected the pink color of the building's exterior; the designer's Jaguar is in the foreground. PAGE 163: A bedroom at the Sonoma Mission Inn. RIGHT: The small bar area featured hooved tables designed by Dickinson.

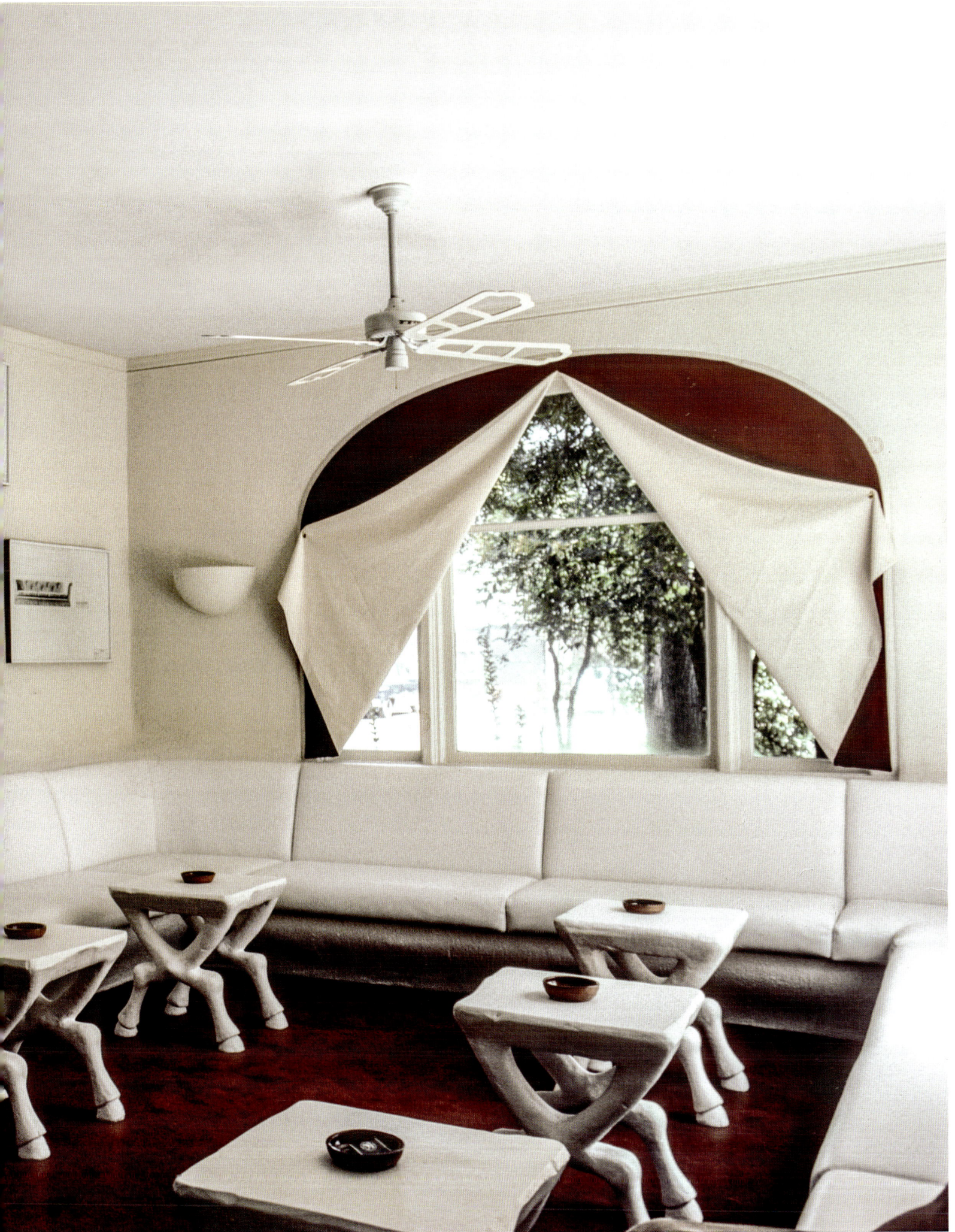

VII.
SKIDMORE, OWINGS & MERRILL:
From Wild Bird to the Bank of America Building

Fred Lyon's eye for interiors was far-reaching. It took in not only penthouse apartments, mansions, and country residences but also corporate settings. He had a long association with the premier architecture, interior design, and engineering firm Skidmore, Owings & Merrill (SOM) that began when Lyon photographed Wild Bird, the notable cliffside dwelling that the firm's cofounder Nathanial Owings designed for his wife and himself. This assignment for *Time* magazine in 1959 led to a long and fruitful relationship with

SOM that years later would have tremendous personal significance for Lyon.

Charles Pfister (1939–1990) earned a degree in architecture from the University of California at Berkeley and trained at the Rudolph Schaeffer School of Design in San Francisco. In 1965, Pfister joined Skidmore, Owings & Merrill, where he developed a reputation for design that featured understated opulence. During his time at SOM, he created the Pfister Lounge Collection for furniture maker Knoll as a side project. In 1971, Lyon photographed his work on Cyril Magnin's apartment at

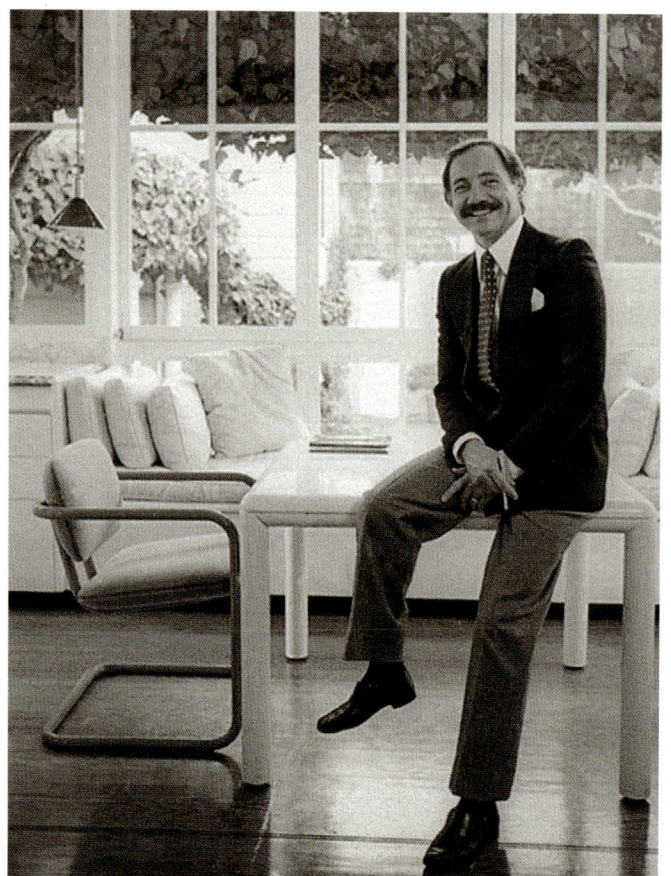

LEFT: Charles Pfister at home, Telegraph Hill, San Francisco, 1971. OPPOSITE: Living room in the Cyril Magnin apartment atop the Mark Hopkins Hotel, Nob Hill, San Francisco, 1971. Pfister designed the room to accommodate the tapestry by artist Mark Adams.

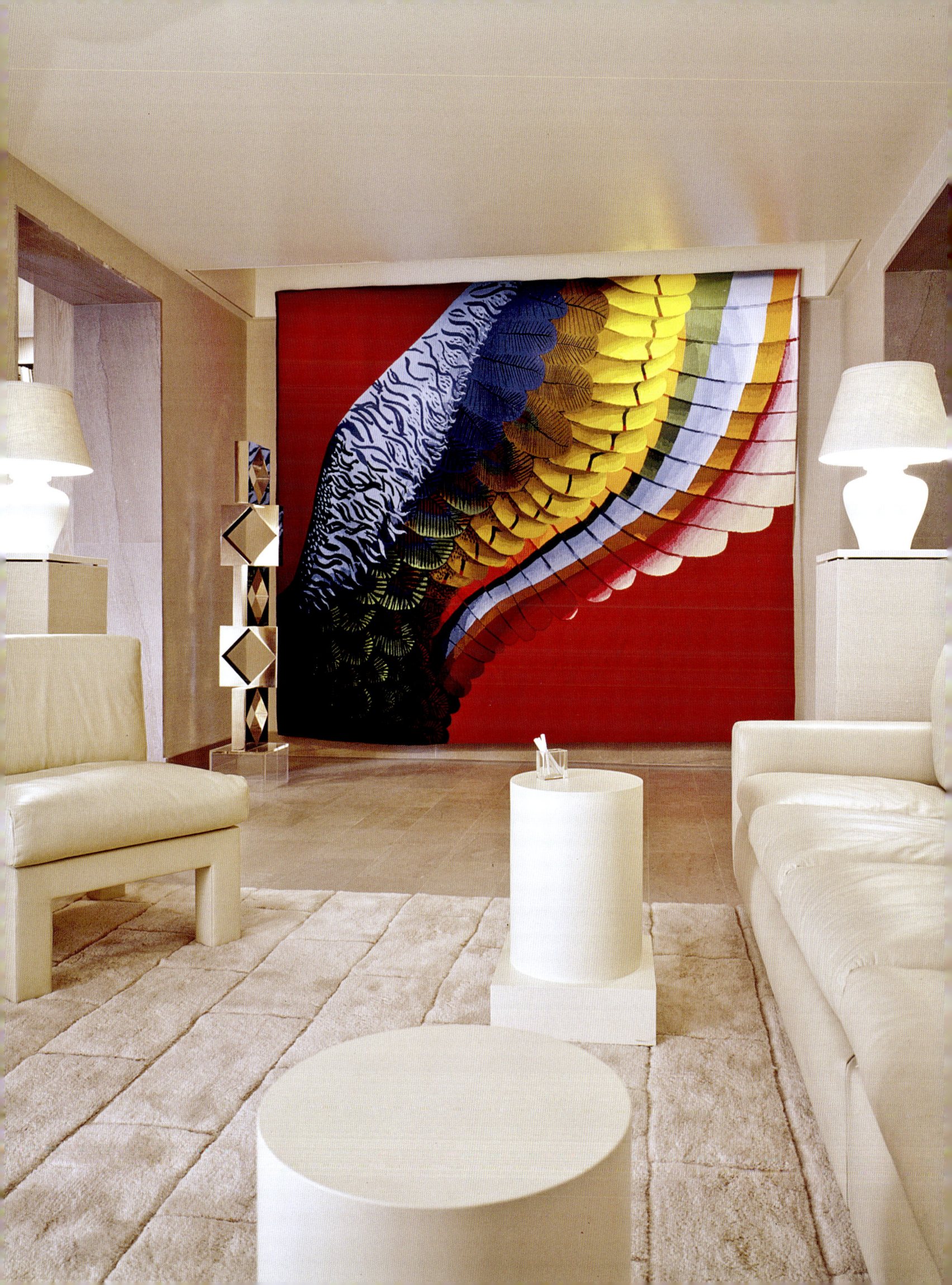

the top of the Mark Hopkins Hotel, a project for SOM. In 1981, he left SOM to establish his own firm, Pfister Partnership, with offices in San Francisco and London.[136] Pfister's business and life partner, designer Jeffry Weisman, characterized Pfister's hallmark as "luxurious materials used with great discipline."[137] His firm "produced interiors for corporate offices, hotels and boutiques in the United States and in Europe that often combined antique furniture with modern detailing."[138]

One important assignment Lyon did for SOM was to photograph the interiors of one of the firm's most important projects, the towering fifty-two-story Bank of America Building in San Francisco, at the time of the building's unveiling in 1969. Photographing this prestige project was a plum job for Lyon but also taxed his skills. The look and feel of the interiors of this massive building were the responsibility of Margo Grant Walsh (b. 1936), at that time a fast-rising interior architect at SOM still only in her mid-thirties. This was one of many significant projects that Walsh, a force of nature in the design world, undertook in her distinguished career. Walsh had been born on a Blackfeet Indian reservation in Fort Peck, Montana, and worked her way to, and through, the University of Oregon, where she earned a degree in interior architecture. Later, Walsh would reside in a landmark co-op on

RIGHT: Sunroom in the Magnin apartment. The building's rooftop ornaments are visible through the windows.

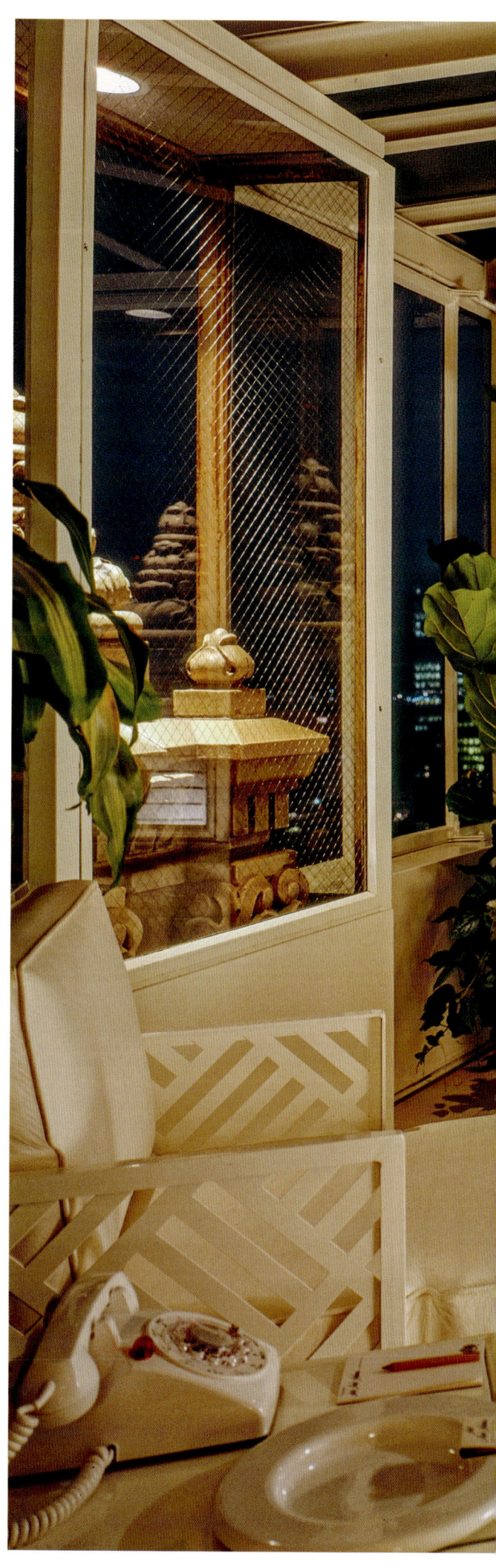

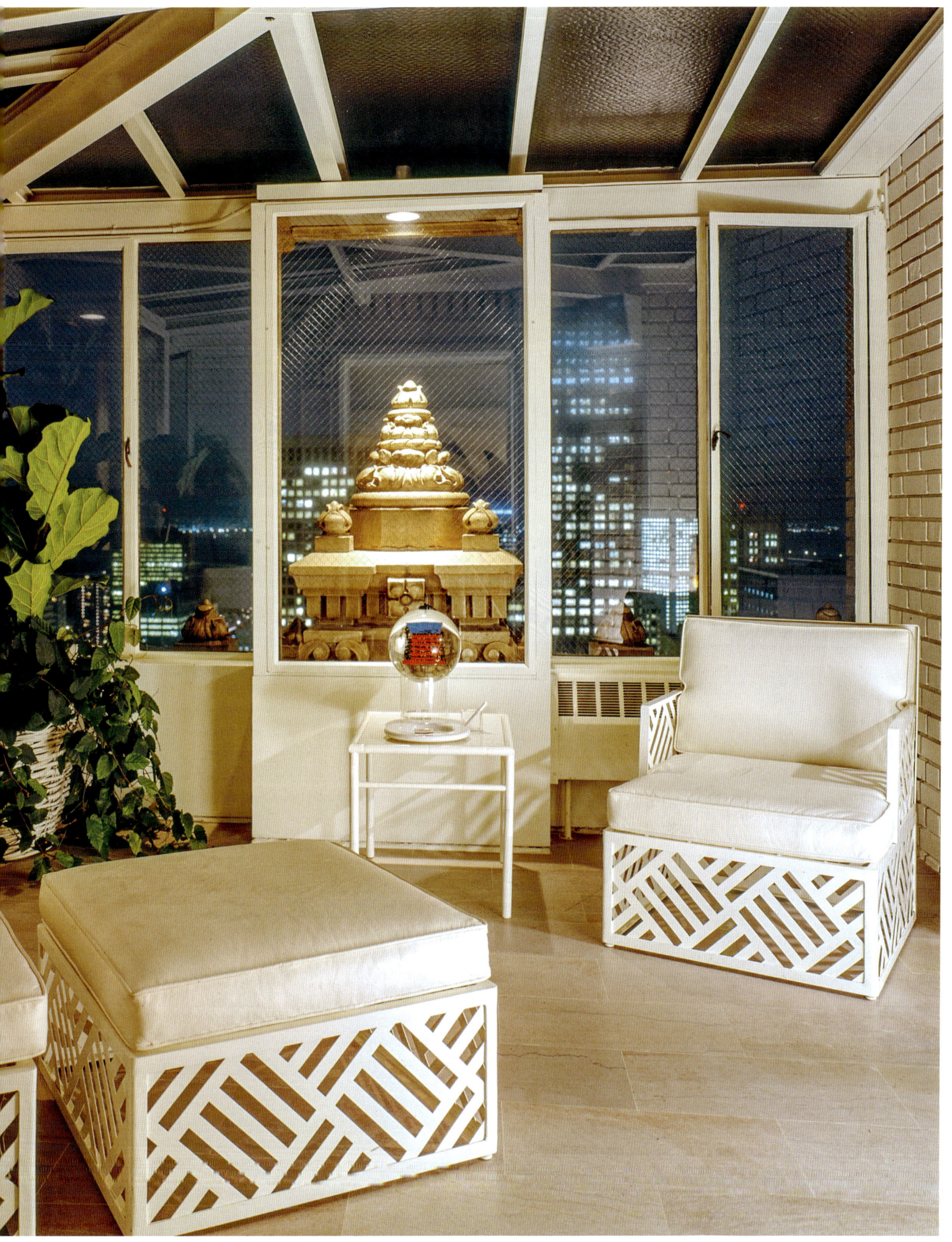

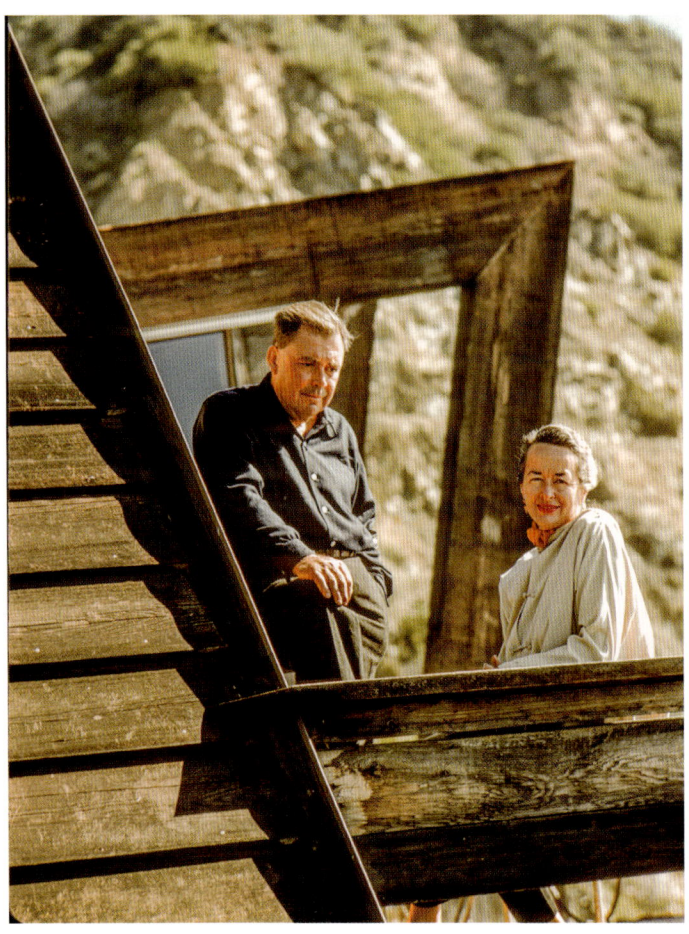
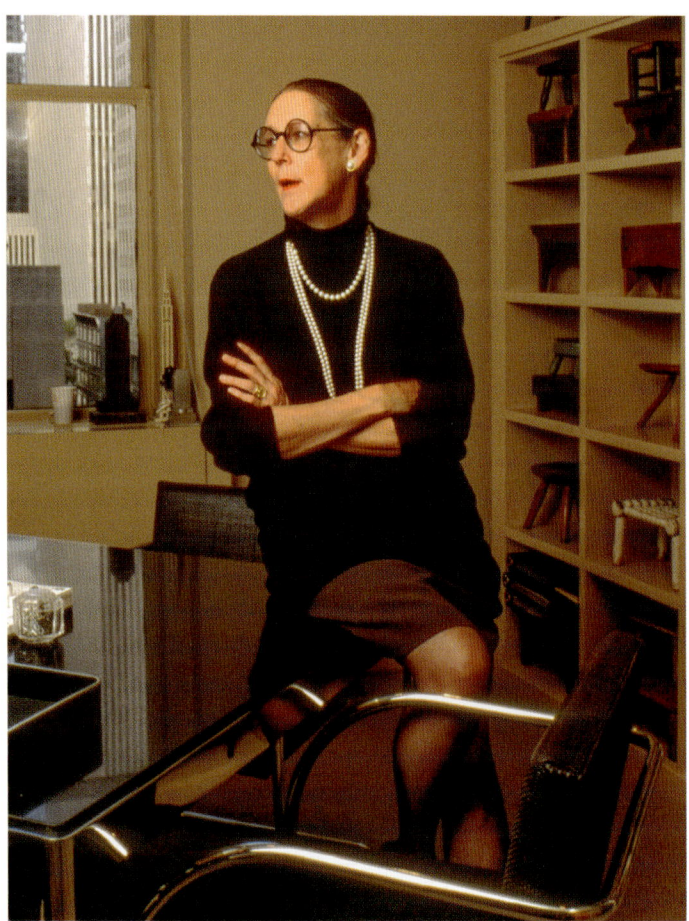

the Upper East Side of Manhattan. In between, she traveled the world designing the interiors of noteworthy buildings for SOM and later Gensler and Associates.

To help her with the Bank of America World Headquarters project, Walsh brought on Penelope "Penny" Whelan (b. 1943), a young Midwesterner who had studied at the University of Michigan School of Architecture and Design. Penny Whelan (later to become Penny Rozis) was new to San Francisco, and this was her first big job. Walsh and Whelan grew to become very close. After the bank staff moved in, Whelan was responsible for directing the photography of the private offices of the most senior executives and other special areas such as the international floor and the boardroom in the

new granite-clad tower high above the San Francisco Financial District. "These were the photographs that the Bank of America cared most about," says Walsh, Whelan's boss at that time.[139] Walsh says that SOM worked with only a very short list of photographers, and Lyon was one of them. It was a big job for both Whelan and Lyon. Whelan had to art direct the photography of a space that exceeded three hundred thousand square feet and select the areas for Lyon to photograph from among fourteen floors of newly built and decorated office space.[140]

Penny Rozis says, "A photo shoot is a team effort between the designer and photographer. The work involved is very detailed."[141] She had to direct the photographer, select the spaces to photograph, and approve the photographs. Rozis remembers,

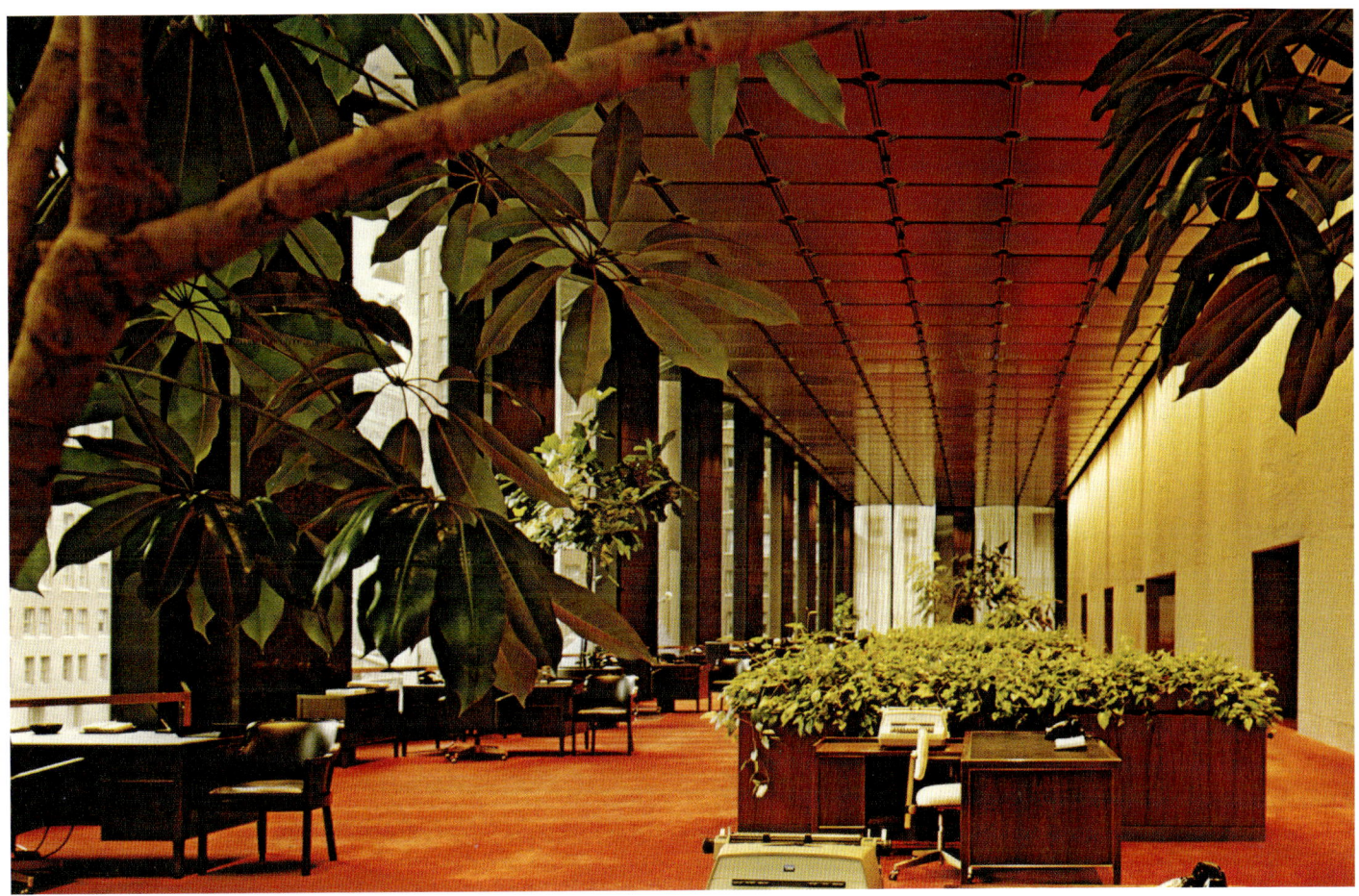

"We worked on the weekend so we would not disturb the bank staff and executives and so they would not interfere with our pictures. Most of the floors were open plan and composed of row after row of desks."[142] Lyon was challenged to make these scenes interesting. Rozis says, "The International floor was a much more dramatic space with soaring ceilings. Fred made stunning images of this space that the SOM partners and clients at the Bank of America loved."[143] It was labor for both Lyon and Rozis, but fun. She says, "Despite the weekend hours and the usual mental toil that goes with planning shots and physical exertion from moving furniture, art, and even desk tchotchkes, I remember the entire shoot being a pleasure. We worked hard and laughed a lot."[144]

OPPOSITE LEFT: Margaret and Nathaniel Owings at their house, Wild Bird, Big Sur, 1959. Owings, a founding partner of the architectural firm Skidmore, Owings & Merrill (SOM), designed the house. OPPOSITE RIGHT: Margo Grant Walsh in her office, New York City, 1974. ABOVE: International department at the Bank of America Building, designed by SOM, San Francisco, 1971.

WILD BIRD
Big Sur, 1959

Margaret and Nathaniel Owings named their stunning A-frame house, which was poised at the edge of a cliff, Wild Bird. Nat was a founder of the architectural firm of Skidmore, Owings & Merrill (SOM). I worked with SOM, photographing some of their large projects including the Bank of America Building in San Francisco. My wife, designer Penny Rozis, got her start at the firm. These photographs predate all of that, of course. They were taken for the December 28, 1959, issue of *Time* magazine.

The structure fit so unobtrusively into the landscape that my attempts to photograph it from an airplane failed to show it off well. Nat designed the house to blend in with its environment and not stand out—from land, sea, or air. I had to take a long view from the land to visually describe how the house was sited. Although it was perched on a cliff, the house was only a few hundred feet off of Highway 1. Nat had built a small pool at the end of the approach road, near the entry drive. The structure was surrounded by a series of cantilevers that provided each bedroom with a deck that looked out onto

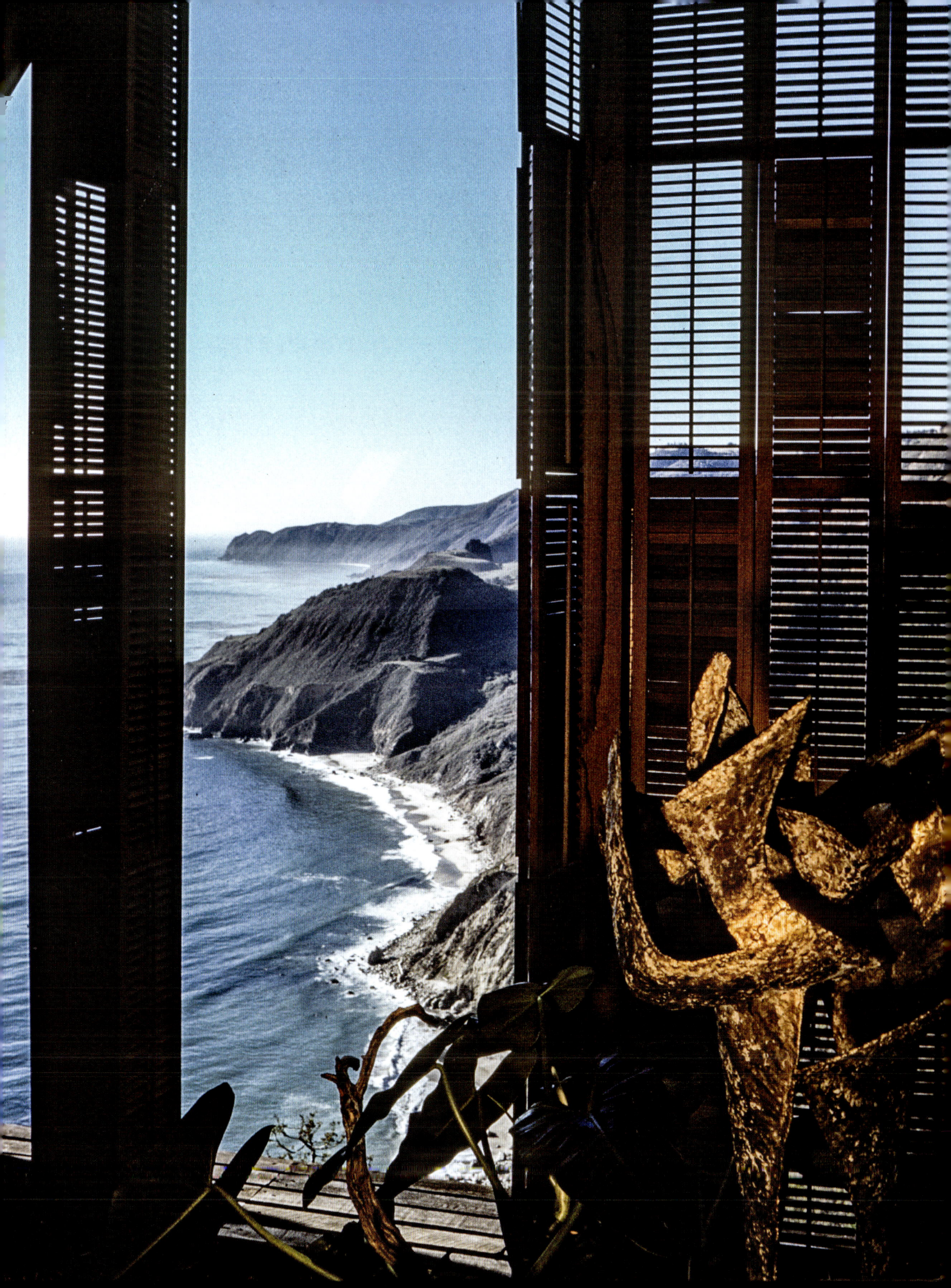

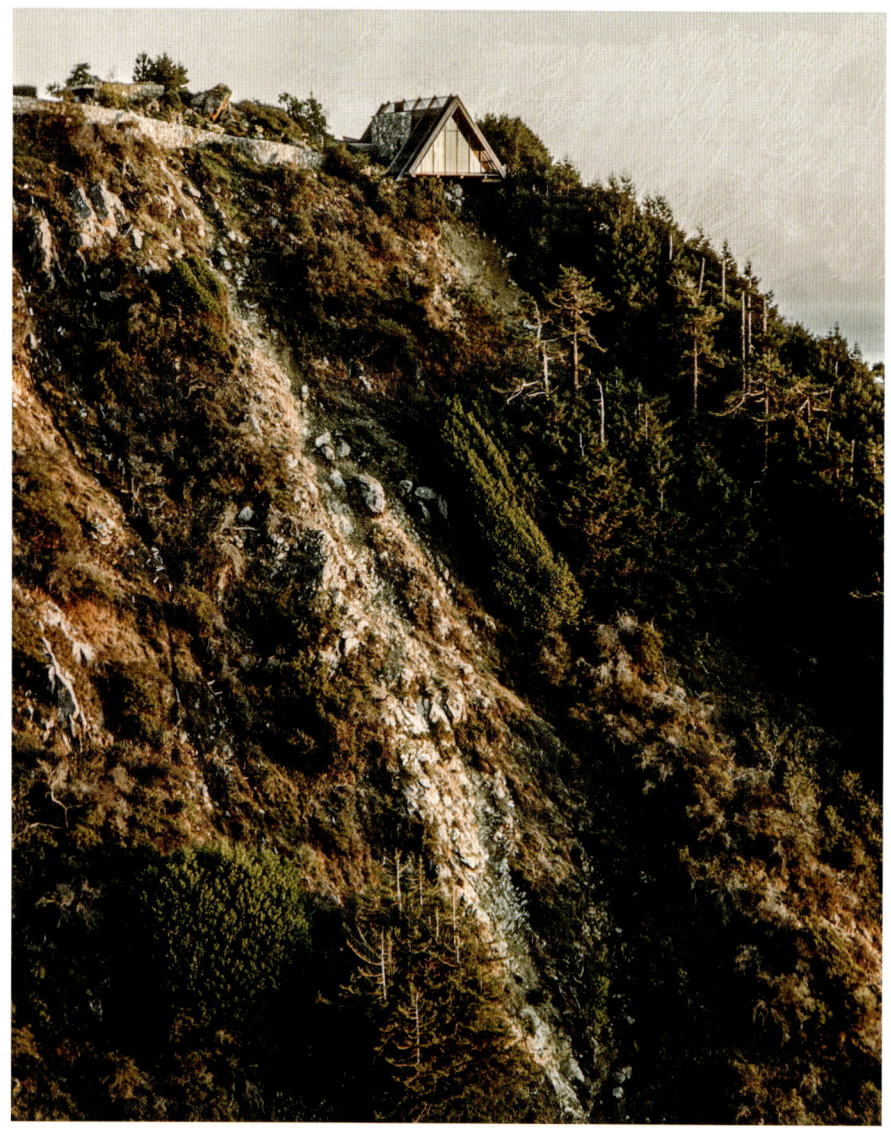

the ocean. The patio and living room had spectacular views of the ocean. Every window looked out onto either the Pacific or the rugged Big Sur landscape. The roof beams are of repurposed redwood timber.

Margaret was an artist and a conservationist. I think she made some of the artwork seen in these photographs, and the house certainly felt like it belonged to someone who loved nature. The photography took so long that I had to stay overnight with the Owingses. At that time, there was nowhere nearby to lodge. The couple were lovely hosts. She was an elegant lady; he was a bear of a man—both were funny and terrifically warm.　　　　　　　　　　　—F.L.

PAGE 173: View from Wild Bird looking north along the coast, 1959. ABOVE: The house is sited dramatically, six hundred feet above the Pacific Ocean. OPPOSITE: The concrete structural beams have abstract patterns molded into them.

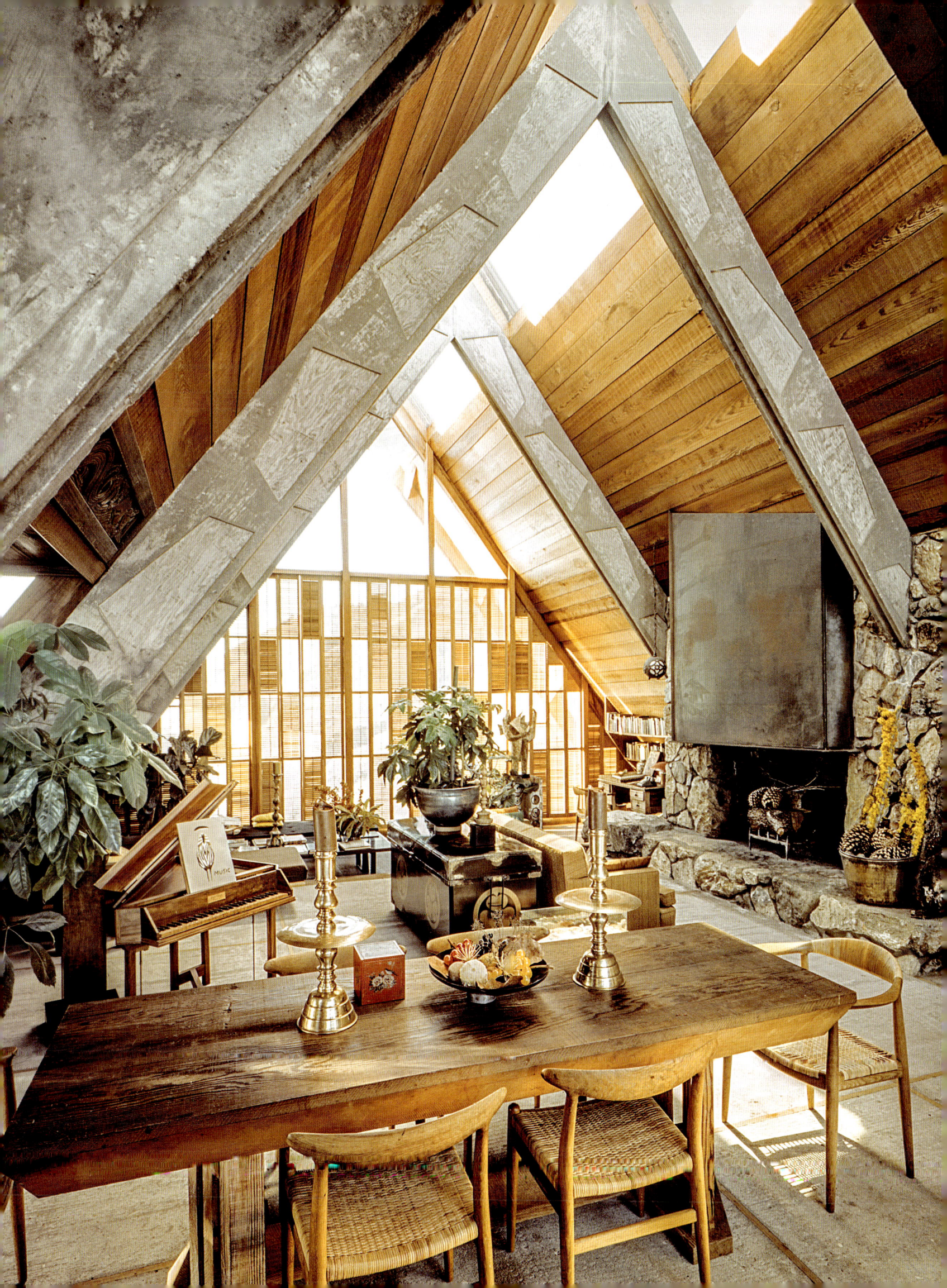

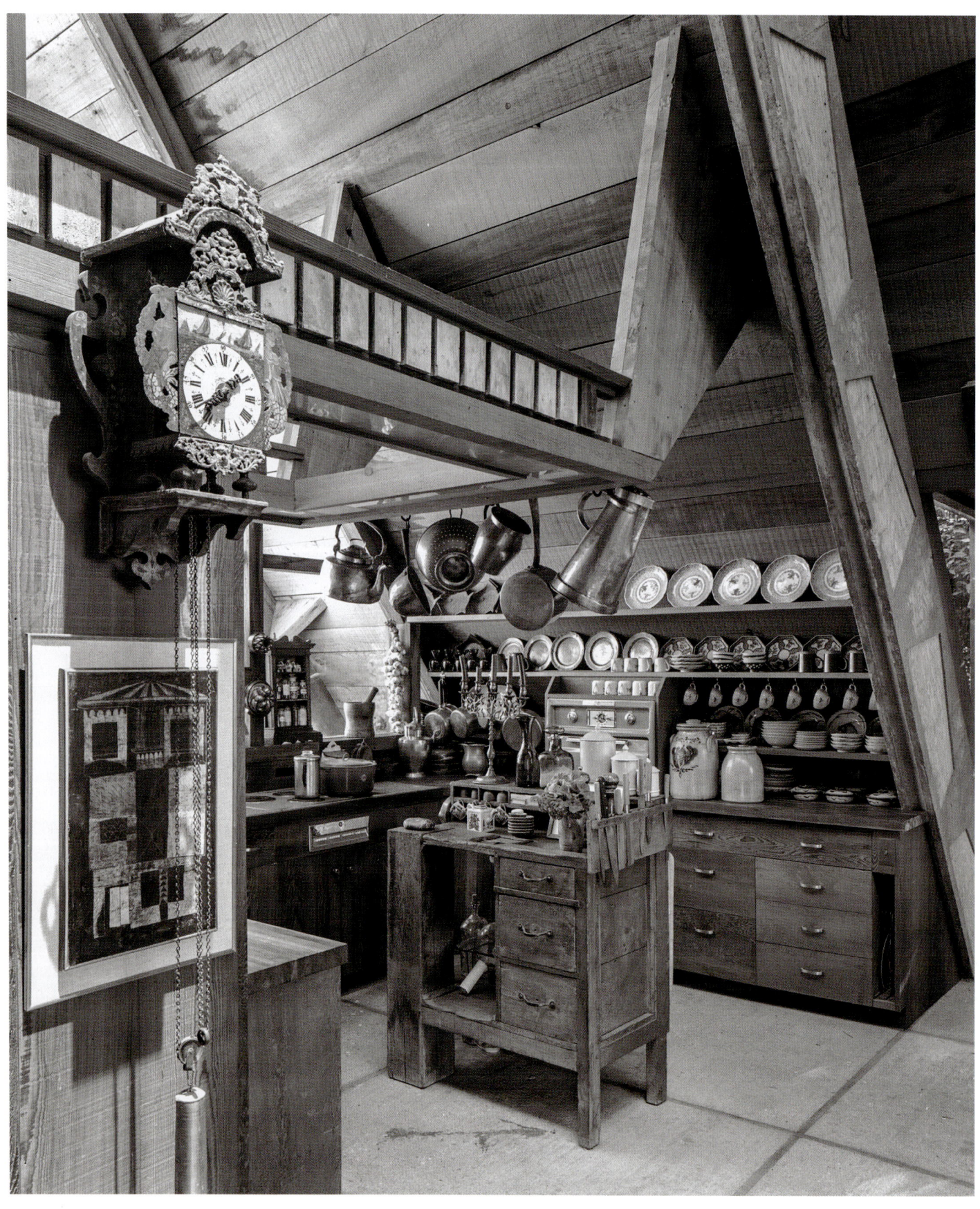

ABOVE: Kitchen. OPPOSITE, CLOCKWISE FROM TOP LEFT: Guest bedroom; living room fireplace;
pool beside the entry drive; nighttime view into the house.

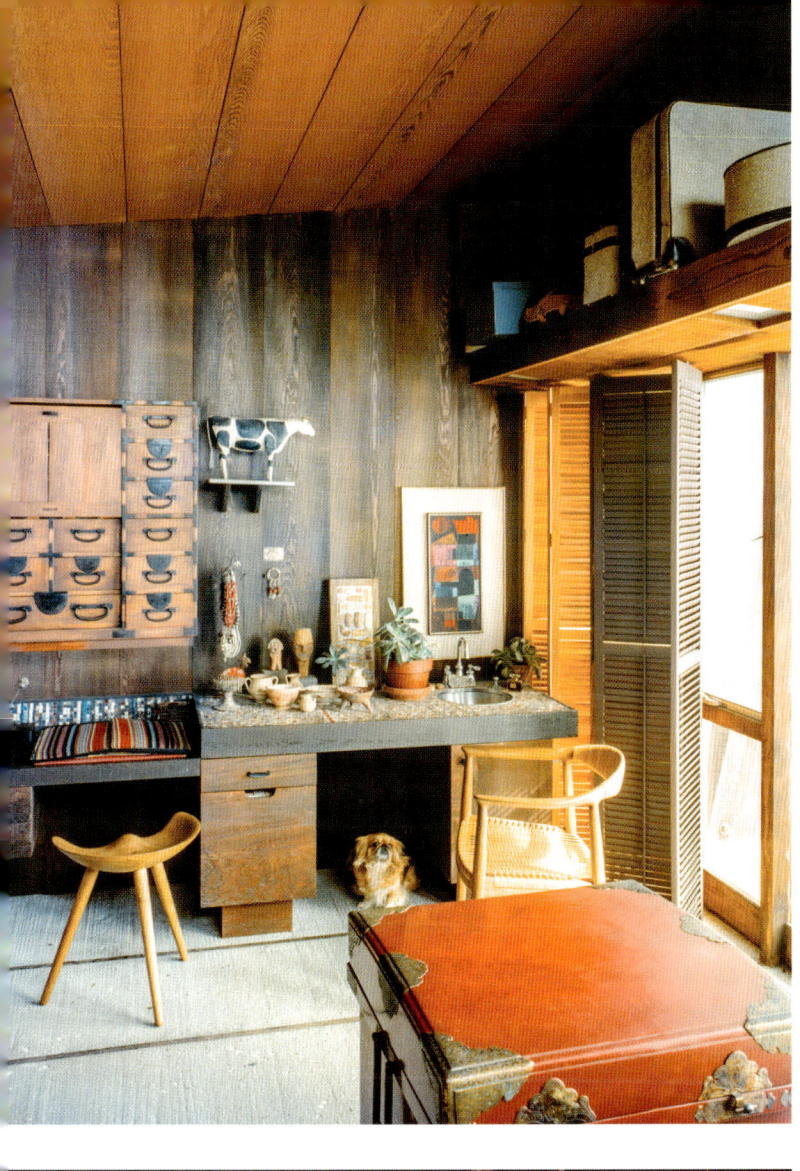
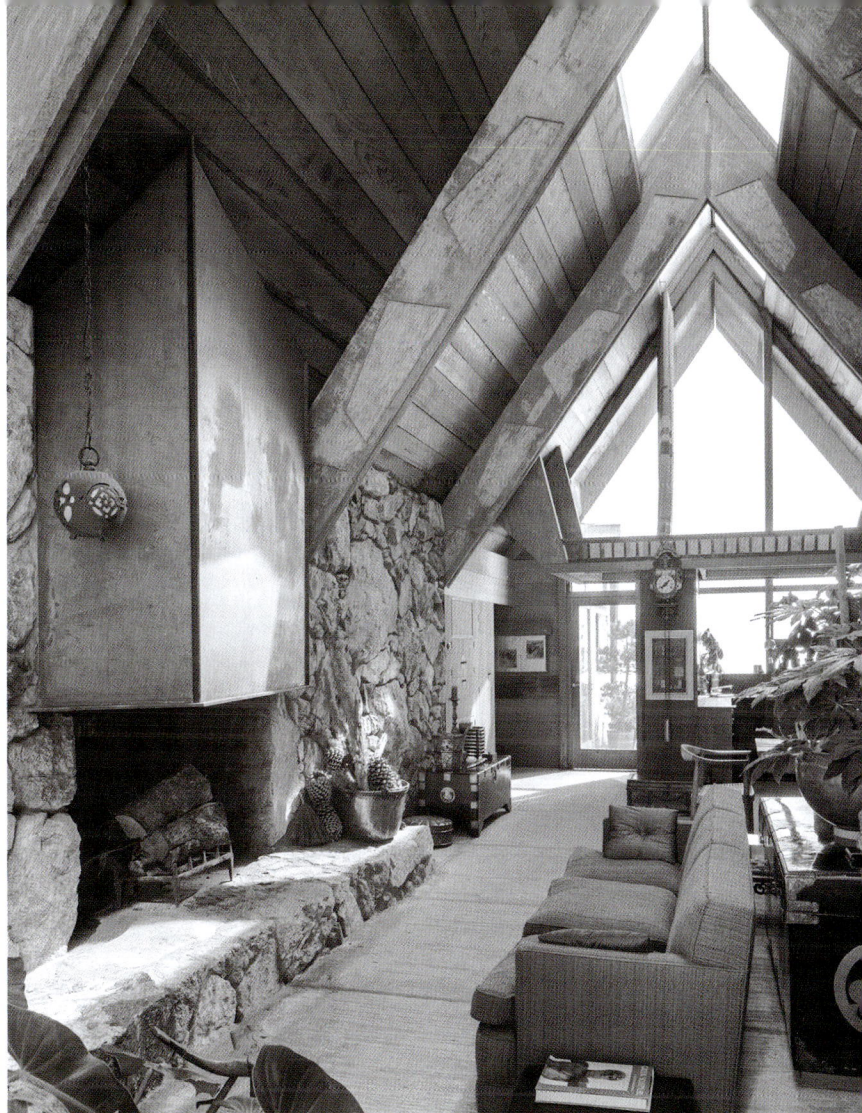
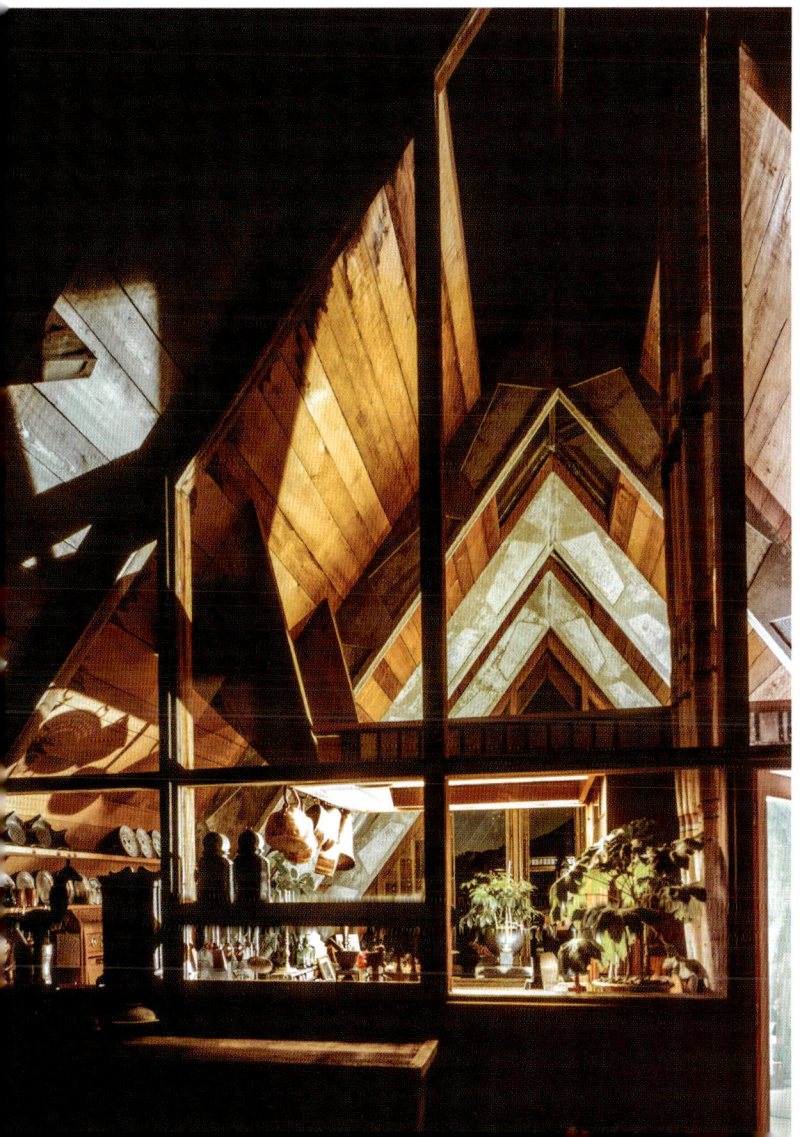
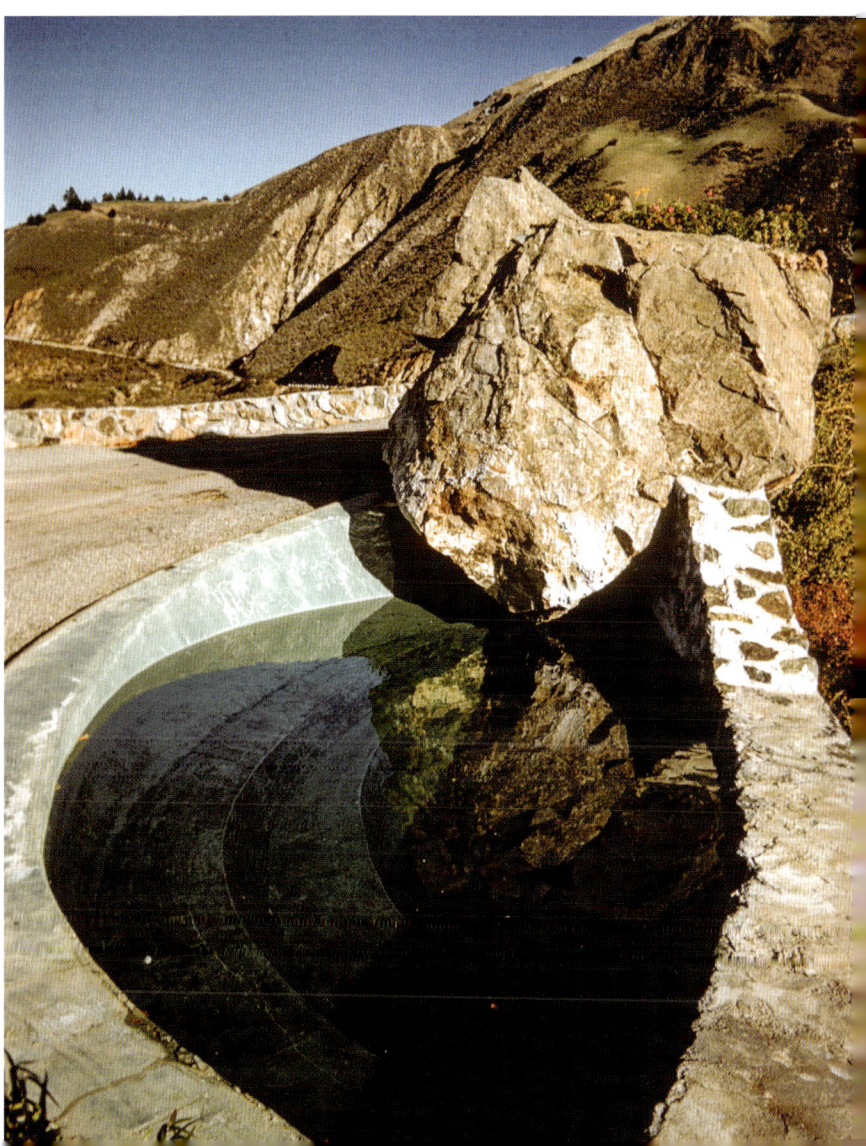

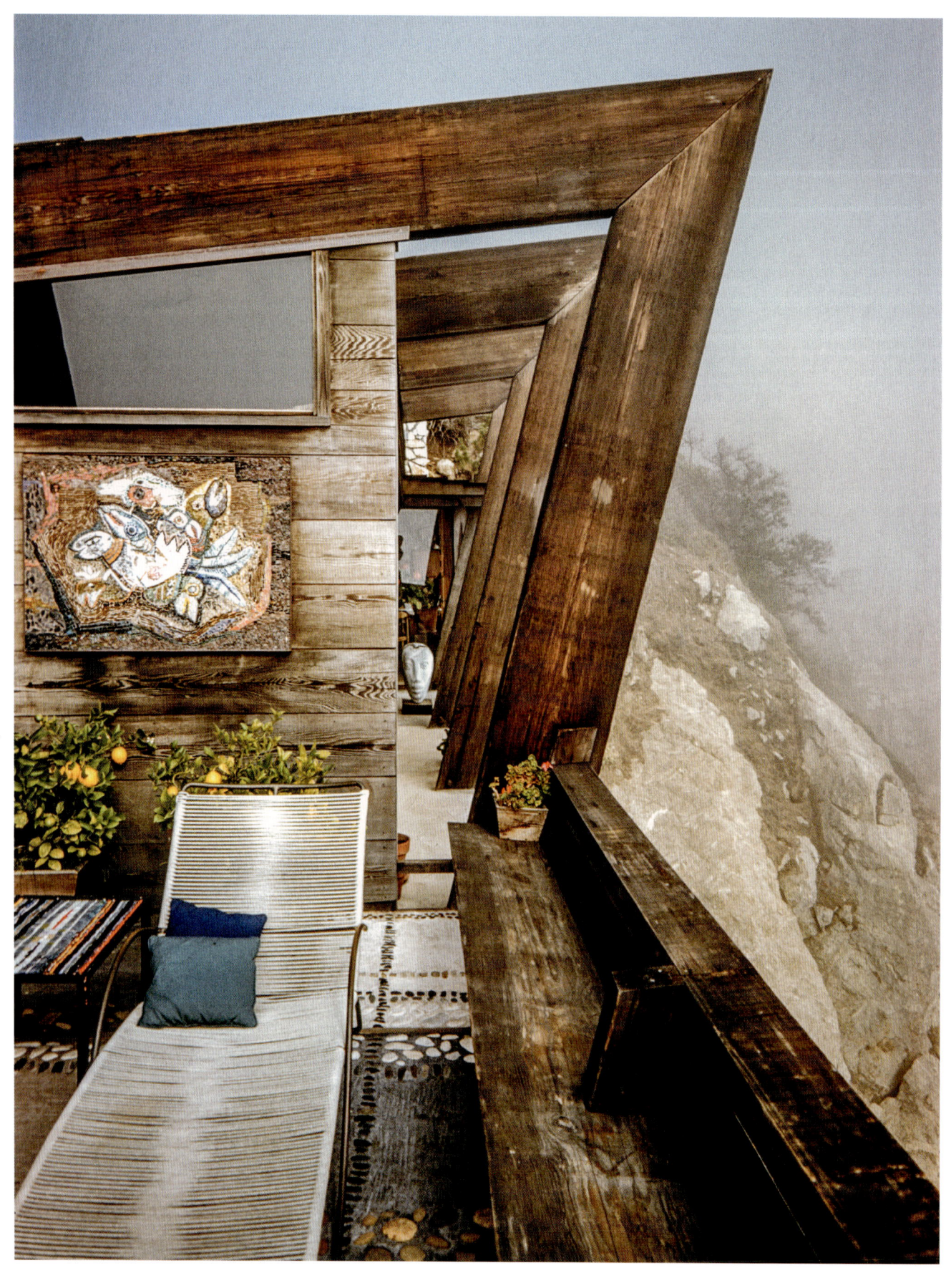

ABOVE: A sequence of joined beams runs along the edge of the patio.
RIGHT: Exterior view with stone chimney.

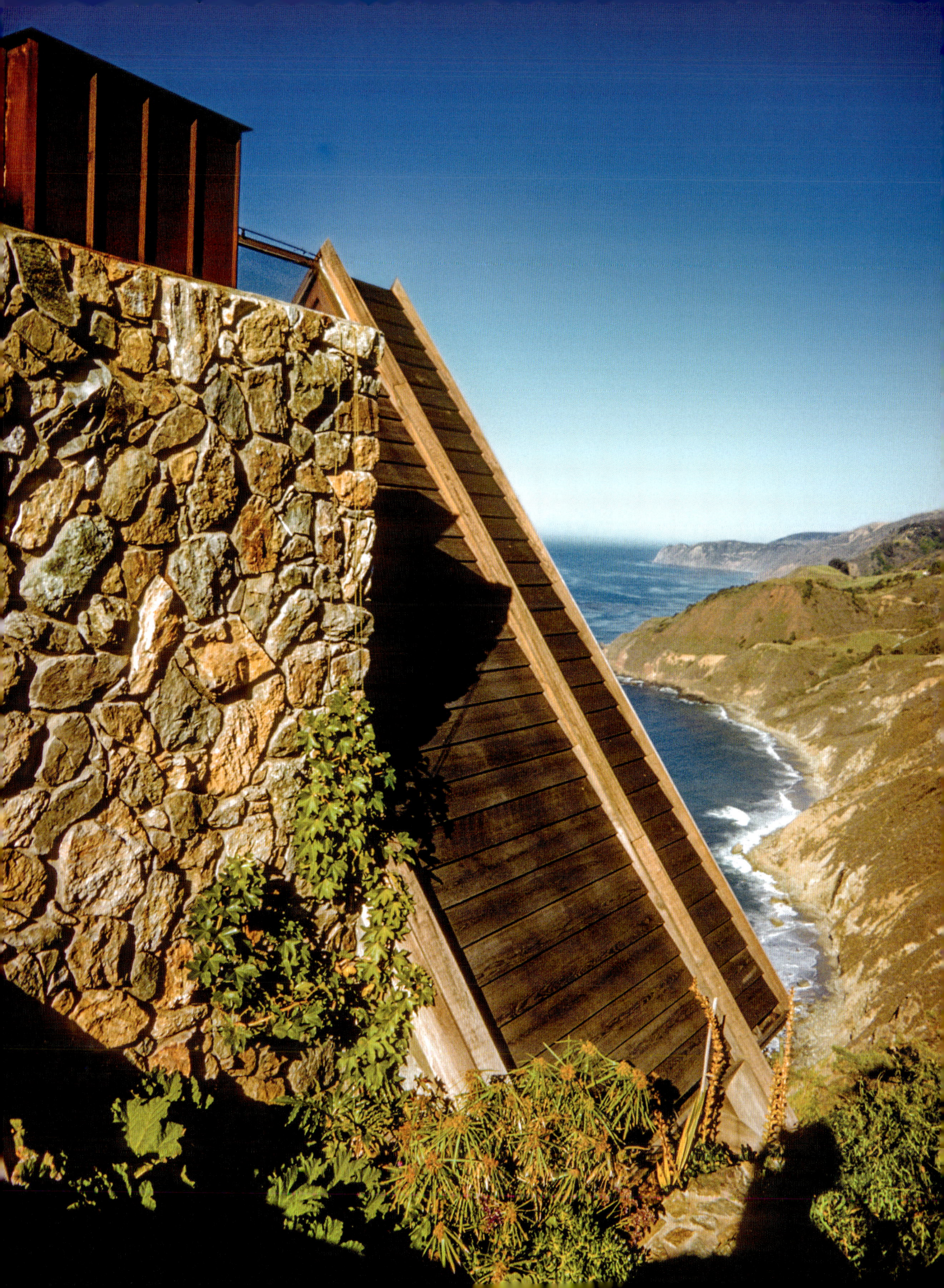

VIII.
HOLIDAY AND HIGH SOCIETY

n 1950, Fred Lyon married that "skinny blonde kid" he used to photograph, the fashion model Anne Murray. They set up house together in Sausalito, just north of the Golden Gate Bridge. If a photographer marrying his model seems to be a cliché, for the Lyons it was the basis of a long and successful union. The couple's charm and talents contributed to their elegant midcentury lifestyle. It seems inevitable that Lyon, still young but now increasingly established in his career, would begin to mix with the best photographers, including interior and lifestyle photographers, of his generation. He did so in his work for *Holiday*, the travel/lifestyle magazine that was the best of its kind by far. In its prime, it was the last word in sophisticated and literate travel. Featuring broad sheets of high-quality paper, at fifty cents per issue, it was not cheap, but readers got far more than they paid for. *Holiday*'s large, eleven-by-fourteen-inch format was similar in size to *Life* and *Look* magazines, which offered a large canvas for images. The photography was directed by picture editor Frank Zachary, who had worked

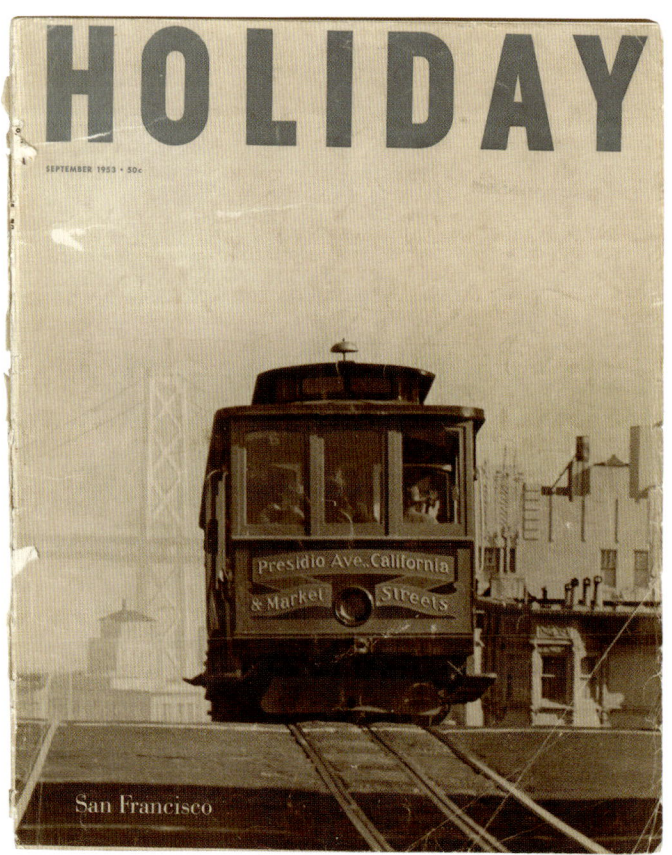

LEFT: Cover of *Holiday* magazine (September 1953). The issue featured photography by Slim Aarons, Robert Capa, and Fred Lyon, among others. OPPOSITE: Grant Avenue in San Francisco's Chinatown, Chinese New Year, ca. 1954.

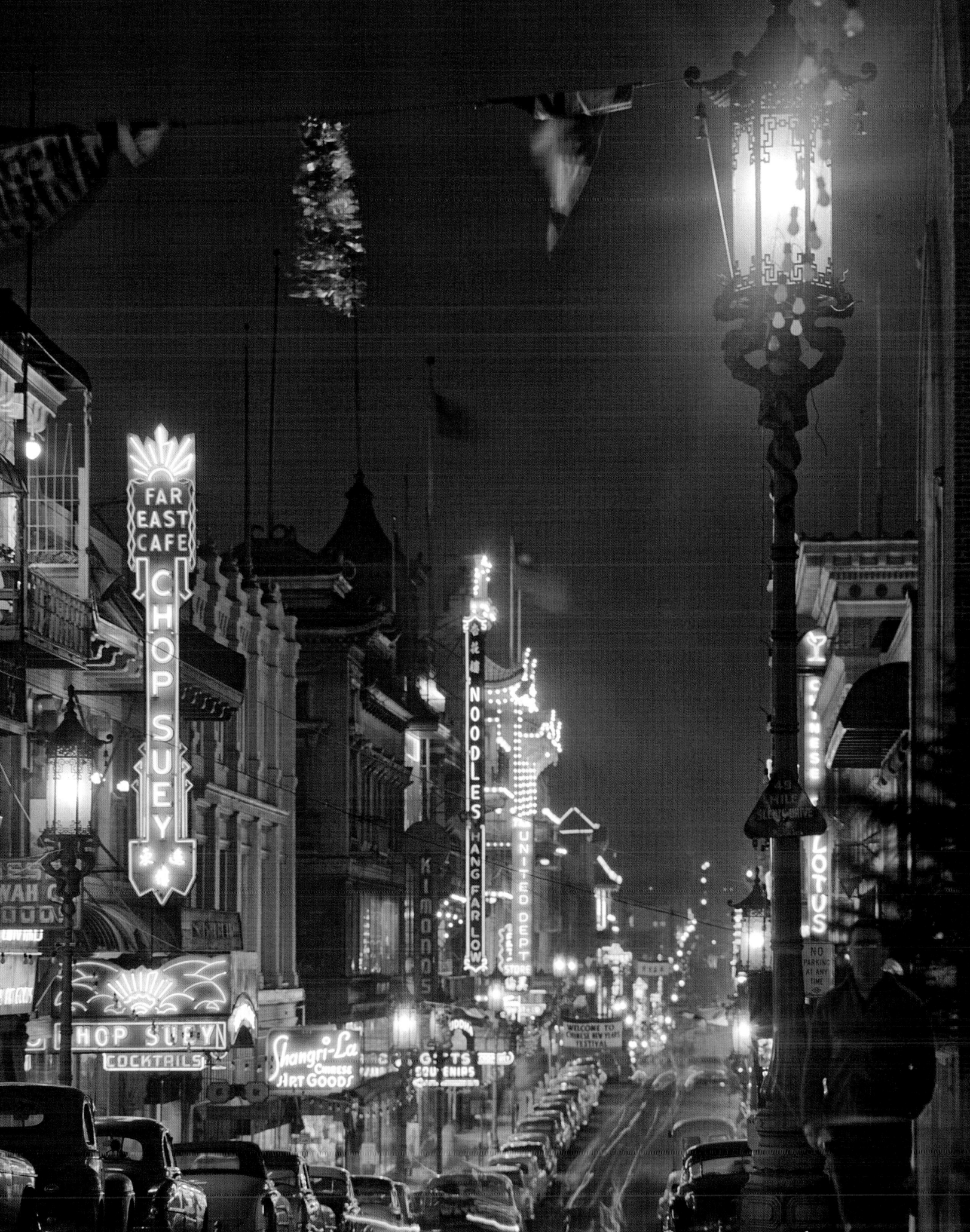

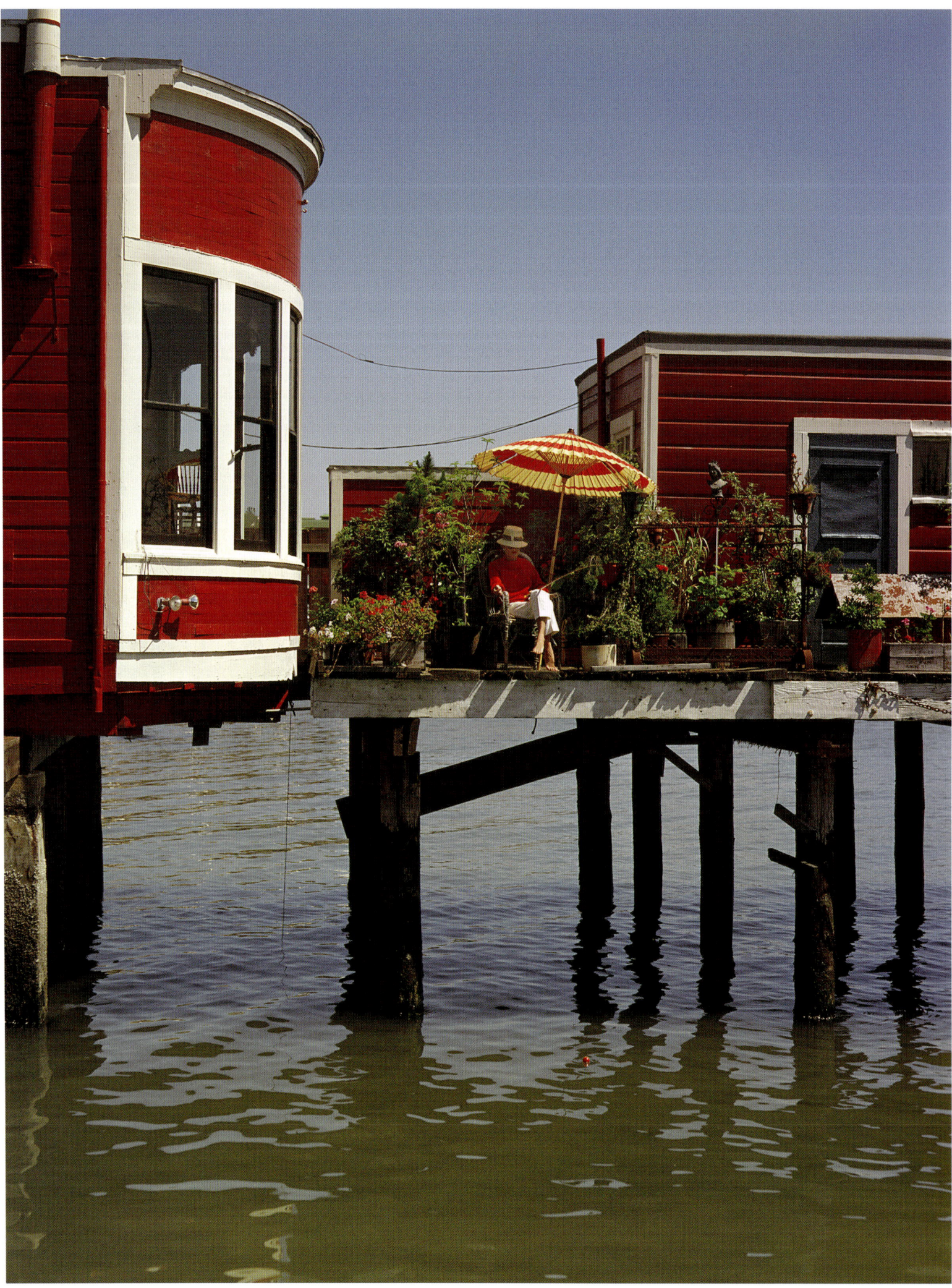

with Alexey Brodovitch, the art director at *Harper's Bazaar*. Zachary attracted star talent. When Lyon signed on with *Holiday*, he joined the ranks of other distinguished lensmen including Slim Aarons, Henri Cartier-Bresson, Ansel Adams, Robert Capa, Elliott Erwitt, and others who worked for the magazine. Zachary, describing what he looked for in a photograph for *Holiday*, said he wanted pictures to "create illusion rather than transcribe mere fact. In the words of the famous dictum, it is not the tiger we wish to portray; it is his tigerishness."[145]

Joining the magazine in 1951, Lyon gave *Holiday* readers the "tigerishness" of what he photographed. "*Holiday* was a marvelous little club," Lyon says. "I have no idea how I got swept into it, except Charles Rado probably thought I would be a good fit there and lobbied Zachary on my behalf."[146] The pages of *Holiday* and the design aesthetic of Frank Zachary were expansive enough to accommodate black and white or color, whichever served the vision of the photographer for the story. Lyon says, "At *Holiday*, we were anointed as part of this country club, a big sandbox that was happy. We were given lots of freedom to photograph how we wanted."[147]

Lyon was a natural choice for *Holiday* stories and profiles related to San Francisco or his and Anne's adopted hometown of Sausalito or Northern California wine country. A pal of Lyon's, the famed San Francisco newspaper columnist Herb Caen, could be counted on to give Lyon plugs for his upcoming *Holiday* spreads: "Sausalito looks so glamorous and faraway—via Fred Lyon's photos in the current *Holiday*—I can't wait to make a trip there someday."[148] The subjects of Lyon's stories for *House & Garden*, *Vogue*, and *Holiday* were thrilled to open their houses to him and the magazines.

Lyon's work increasingly put him and Anne in the company of interesting and accomplished people, some of whom became lifelong friends of the couple. One couple they befriended was Lucinda and Charles Crocker. Charles "Charlie" Crocker is the great-grandson of railroad magnate Charles Crocker, one of the "Big Four" founders of the Central Pacific Railroad, the first American transcontinental rail line. In 1971, Charlie and Lucinda bought a small vineyard of eleven acres in St. Helena to have a place to escape the city fog in the summer. They expanded their vineyard over time, buying adjacent properties when they became available and growing Cabernet Sauvignon and Cabernet Franc. Napa and especially the town of St. Helena were very different when the Crockers arrived. Crocker

OPPOSITE: The Glad Hand restaurant on a pier in Sausalito. Lyon's photograph appeared in the May 1958 issue of *Holiday* magazine.

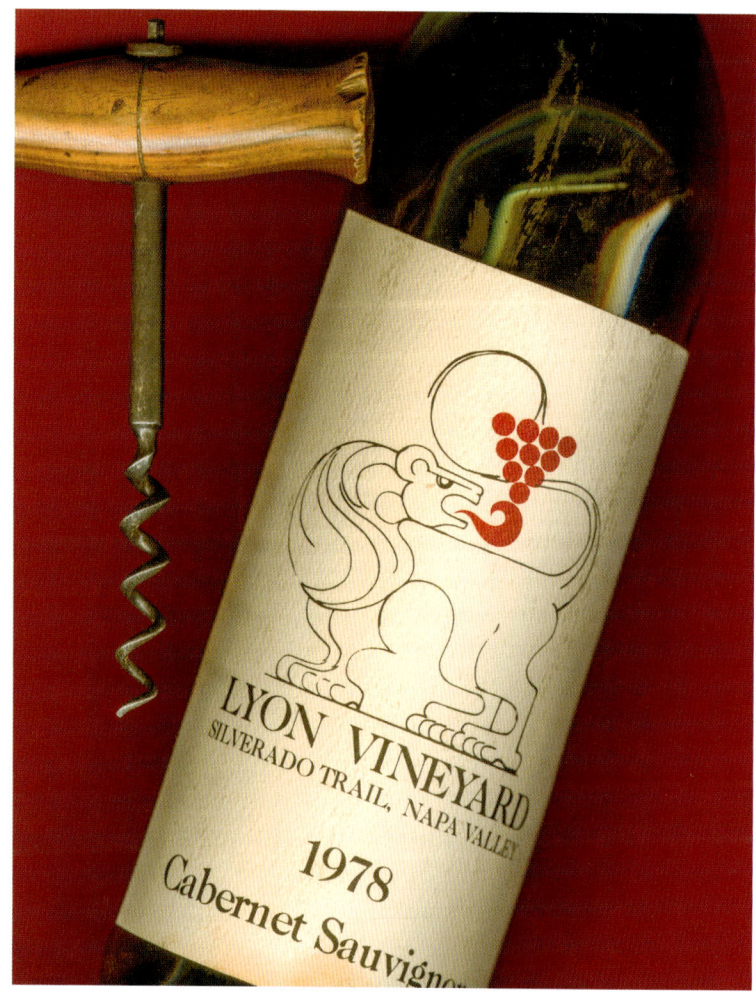

LEFT: Wine label for Lyon Vineyard, created as a gift for Fred Lyon by noted graphic designer Barbara Stauffacher Solomon, 1978.

says, "In St. Helena, you could buy tractor parts and blue jeans on Main Street. There was a bowling alley and maybe two or three restaurants in town. It was still a simple farming town then."[149] When the Crockers came to Napa, he adds, "there was a small but visible social group who went back and forth between Napa and the city. The group gradually increased."[150]

A constellation of other young socialites formed a moveable feast between San Francisco and Napa. At its center were John and Dede Traina. Dede Traina, later to become Dede Wilsey, would earn a role in society that eclipsed even Celia Clark. When Wilsey first met the Lyons, she was a twenty-year-old new-

lywed. Wilsey says, "I remember I thought Anne was so glamorous, grown up, and sophisticated. And Fred, of course, was divine."[151] The Trainas, the Crockers, and their friends had beautiful country houses surrounded by some of the best acreage in Napa. Fred and Anne joined them, buying a very small vineyard in Oakville. Lyon says, "We bought the land, but it did not have a house on it. The first piece was a little over three acres. Later we bought the adjacent parcel, which gave us seven acres. The land did not cost much back then."[152]

For a time, Lyon and Charlie Crocker joined forces in winemaking. The Lyons and the Crockers tended the vines, sweated bud breaks each spring, picked the grapes in the late summer heat, and ran the crush. "We had a destemmer-crusher that was hand operated," Crocker recalls, "Then Fred modified a washing machine to separate the juice from the grape must. Fred rigged the washing machine to spin and retain the must while the juice flowed into a pail."[153] This was very different from the day jobs these men had. Lyon, of course, was a working photographer. Crocker, in addition to his family's investment interests, was involved in technology and started several companies. "Fred and I stopped making wine for two reasons," Crocker says. "It was a lot of work because we and our families did everything; and the wine we made was okay, but not great. It was better for us to sell the grapes and buy the wine."[154] Lyon continued as a grape grower, doing the hard work in the vines and, of course, enjoying the Napa lifestyle. Charlie and Lucinda Crocker went on to acquire, over time, one hundred acres of prime St. Helena land and founded Crocker & Starr, a premier maker of Napa Valley wines.

When it came time to design a house for his property, Lyon considered his contacts from his work with *House & Garden* and interior decor photography. "I met the architects Charles Porter and John Robert Steinwedell when I was photographing a Gardner Dailey house," Lyon says. "They worked in Dailey's firm. Eventually, Dailey stopped doing residential work himself and turned over those commissions to the two architects. Charles and Robert set up their architecture practice in the early 1950s and did some remarkable houses. They were a couple and lived together in an apartment at the top of Julius' Castle, the restaurant atop Telegraph Hill. Right amid the parapets of that building. They would host wonderful brunches with lots of snappy people."[155] Porter was short and Steinwedell was tall and skinny, so opposites attracted for a time. When they designed the Lyon house, they had broken up their personal relationship but still worked together.

The design was the brainchild of Porter and Steinwedell, but the landscape was inspired by a post-dream stroll. Lyon says, "I was at Lake Como on an assignment. After a post-lunch nap, I awakened and walked down to the lake. There was a slight fog, and I stood amid the trees and watched a few boats glide by. That scene stuck in my mind, and I wanted to recreate the effect in Napa."[156] To do this, Fred and Anne planted two rows of eighteen fruitless mulberry trees along an infinity pool that seemed to stretch into the valley. Dede Wilsey remembers, "It was a wonderful house that reflected them. They always had great taste and style. Everything they did was just beautiful. On a sunny day, they had these lovely luncheons, and it was like a stage setting, only it was livable. It was a wonderful home."[157]

FRED LYON HOUSE
Oakville, 1997

My first wife, Anne, and our two boys loved spending time in the Napa Valley. Many of our friends had houses and vineyards there. In the early 1970s, I was able to buy a couple parcels of land in Oakville along the east side of the Silverado Trail. We had seven acres in total. There was nothing on the land except old Cabernet vines that produced wonderfully. To design our house, I tapped my friends Charles Porter and Bob Steinwedell. By this time, they were hot architects and much in demand, but they agreed to do the job as long as they would not have to supervise the construction. I did that myself.

We built something like a French farmhouse, but in concrete block with a hip roof. We couldn't afford to build it with stone, but concrete block is an honest material. The blocks are eight inches wide, which give a feeling of depth. At the windows, the blocks are turned sideways, giving the impression that the walls are sixteen inches thick. For window shutters, we used twelve-inch stair treads that we stained and joined

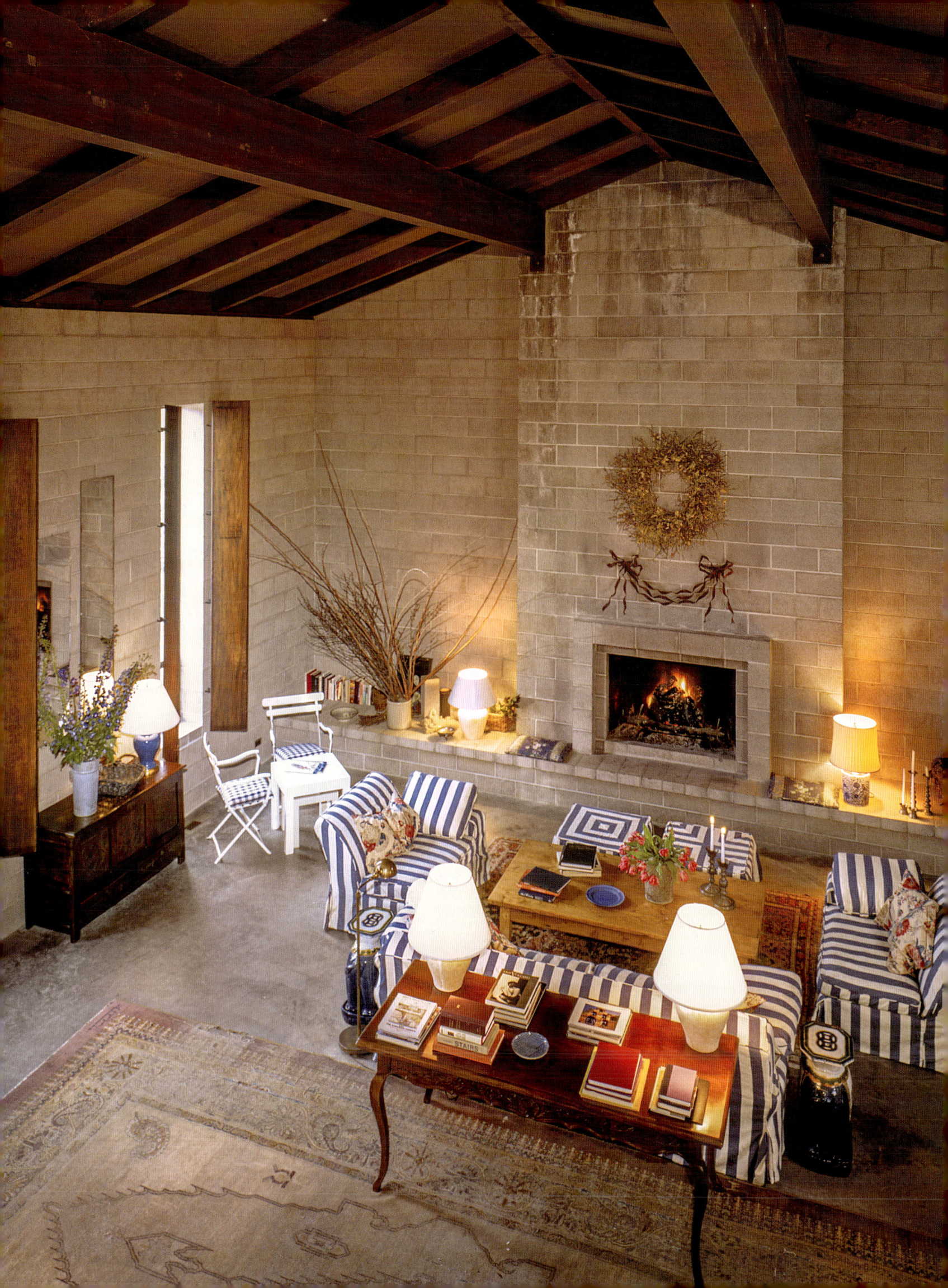

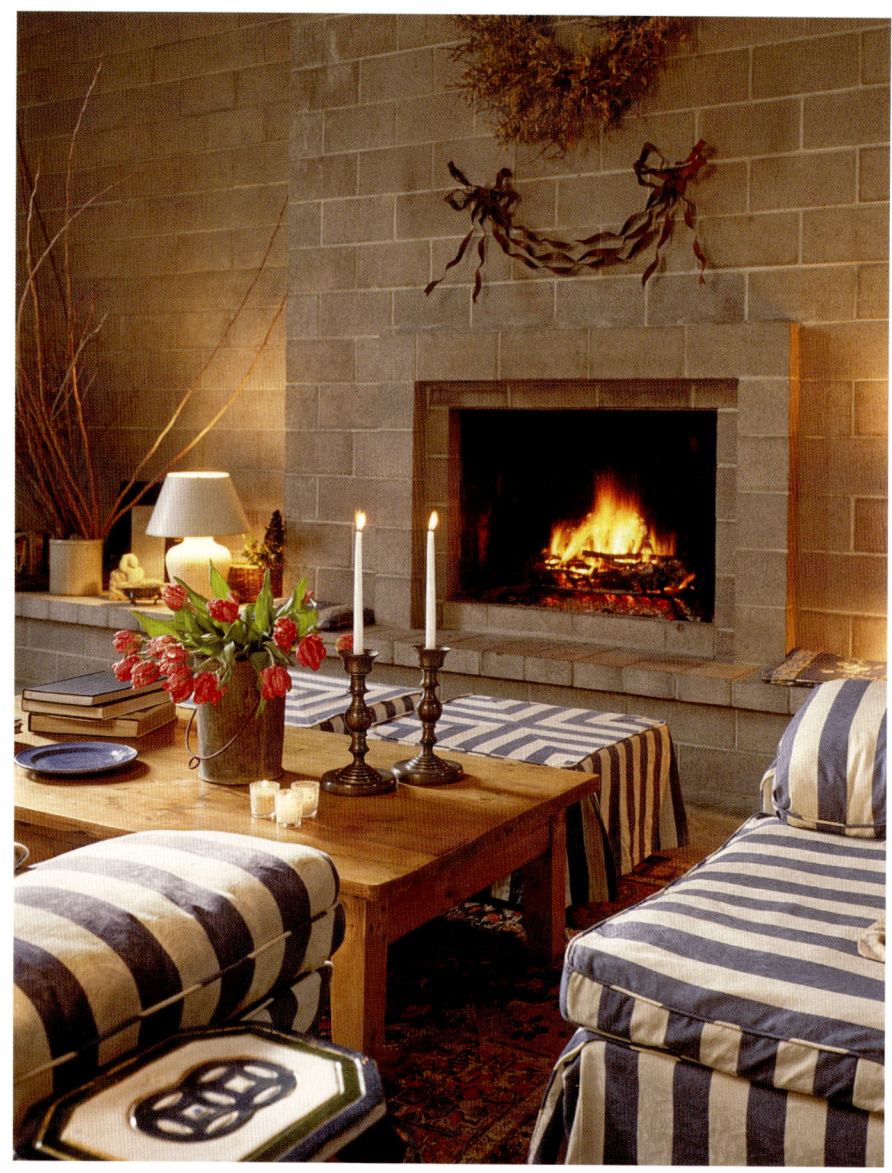

together. The house faces west to the valley. We put our swimming pool at a right angle to the house on the central axis.

Penny has since added a number of refinements to the decor of the place. One large improvement she made was the entry doors. For years, I had never been satisfied with them. Penny designed double doors with a herringbone pattern, thirty-six inches for one door and twelve inches for the other. We had our favorite cabinetmaker fabricate them using an up-and-down herringbone pattern on the left and up herringbone pattern on the right. It is a marvelous addition. —F.L.

PAGE 187: Living room, Fred Lyon house, designed by Porter and Steinwedell, Oakville, Napa Valley, 1997. Tall, narrow windows with heavy wood shutters face the tree park, pool, and vineyard. The floor is poured concrete. ABOVE: The seating area around the fireplace. OPPOSITE: Behind the freestanding wall is a staircase leading to the primary bedroom suite. The kitchen is visible through the door on the left.

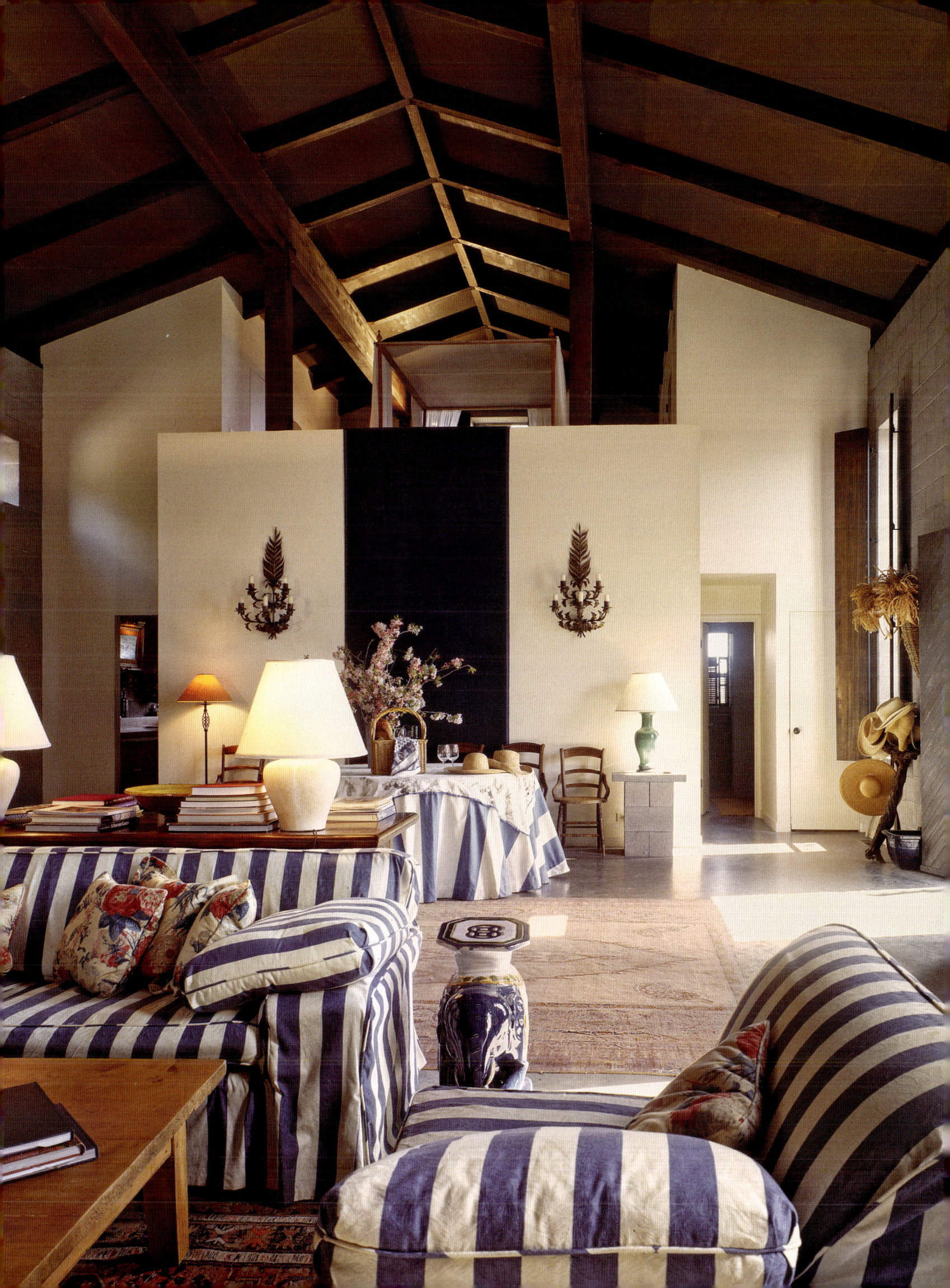

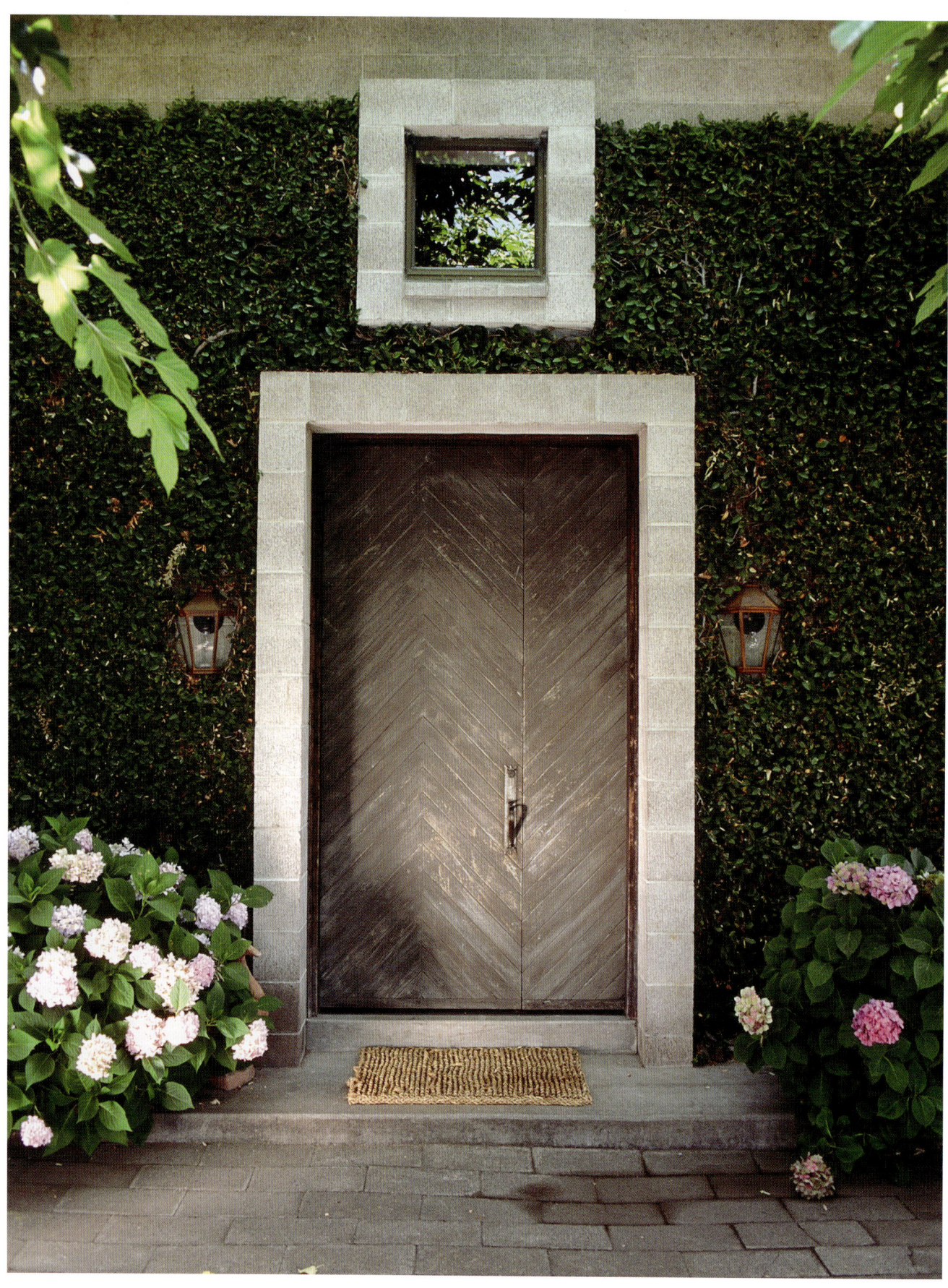

ABOVE: Manicured climbing fig covers the concrete-block construction around the herringbone door, which was designed by Penelope Rozis. OPPOSITE: View across the dining table through the front door. Beyond are the pool, tree park, lawn, and vineyards. In the distance is Mount Veeder, at the western border of Napa Valley.

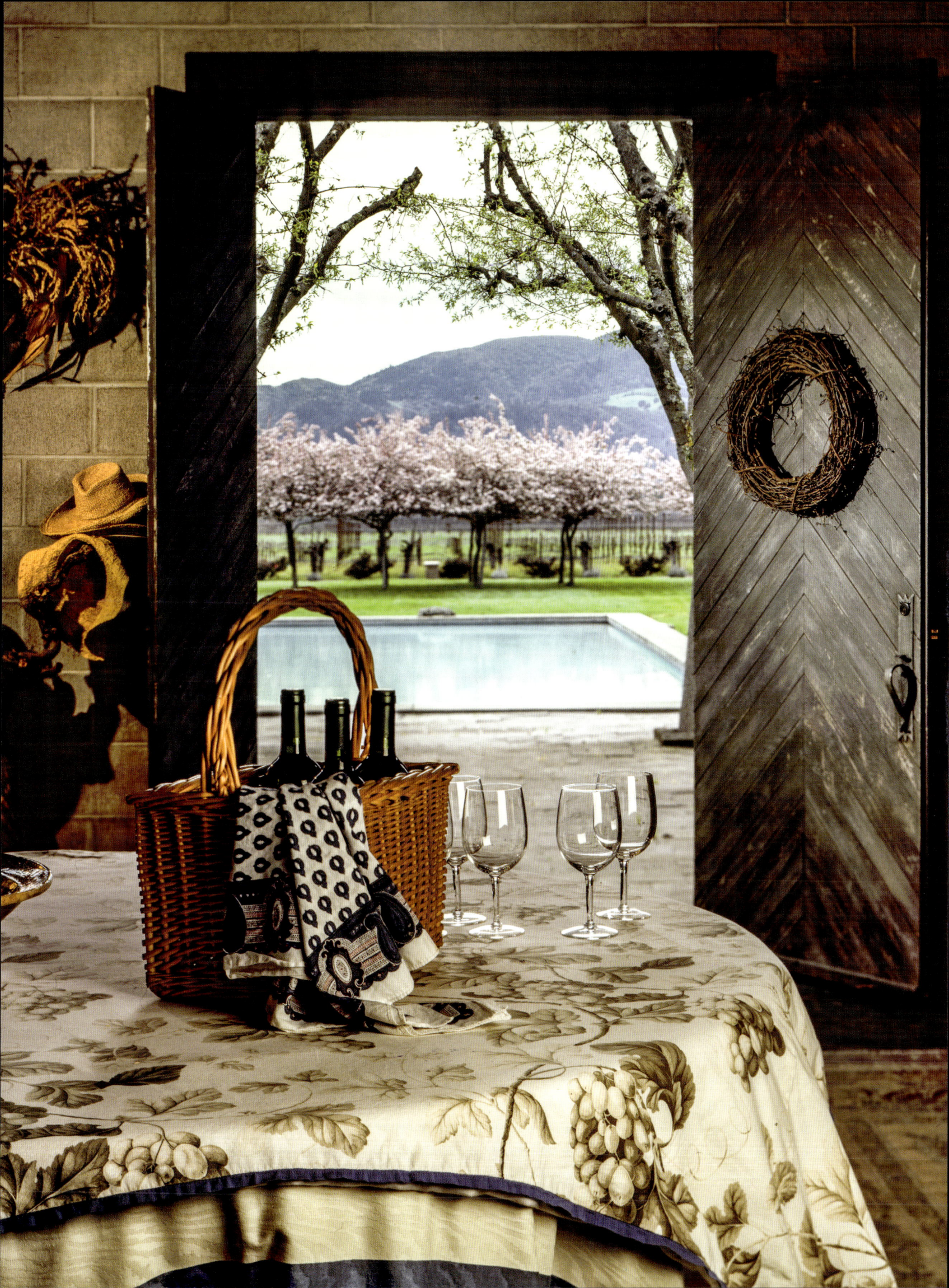

PENELOPE ROZIS HOUSE
Napa, 2010

This ranch house, built in 1950, is typical of its period. It was composed of small rooms, and most of the windows faced the street and not the back of the house, which looked out onto many acres of beautiful vineyards. Over time, Penny made several corrections to the original lackluster layout. A good example is the kitchen. Penny converted it from a series of three tiny rooms—the kitchen, the pantry, and the laundry room—into a larger (but not too big), approximately fifteen-by-twenty-foot space. I have a snapshot of Penny with a wrecking bar tearing out the old kitchen cabinets.

To expand the views from the interior, Penny added windows and an antique Victorian door. The panorama now includes a beautiful large swimming pool, wonderful landscaping, and neighboring vineyards beyond. In the kitchen under a large round window, Penny created a seating space. She often perches there reading new recipes for meals, for which I am the happy beneficiary.   —F.L.

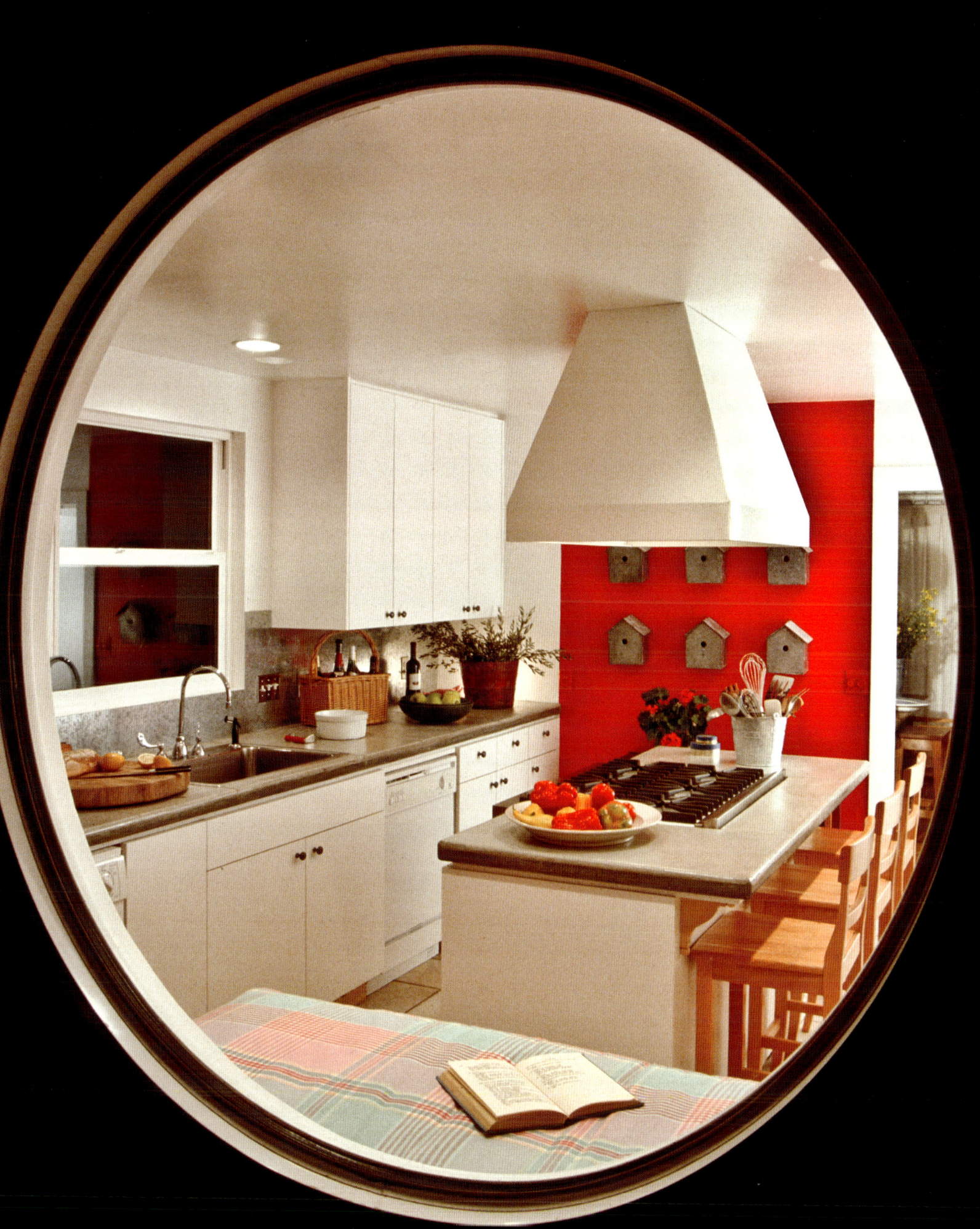

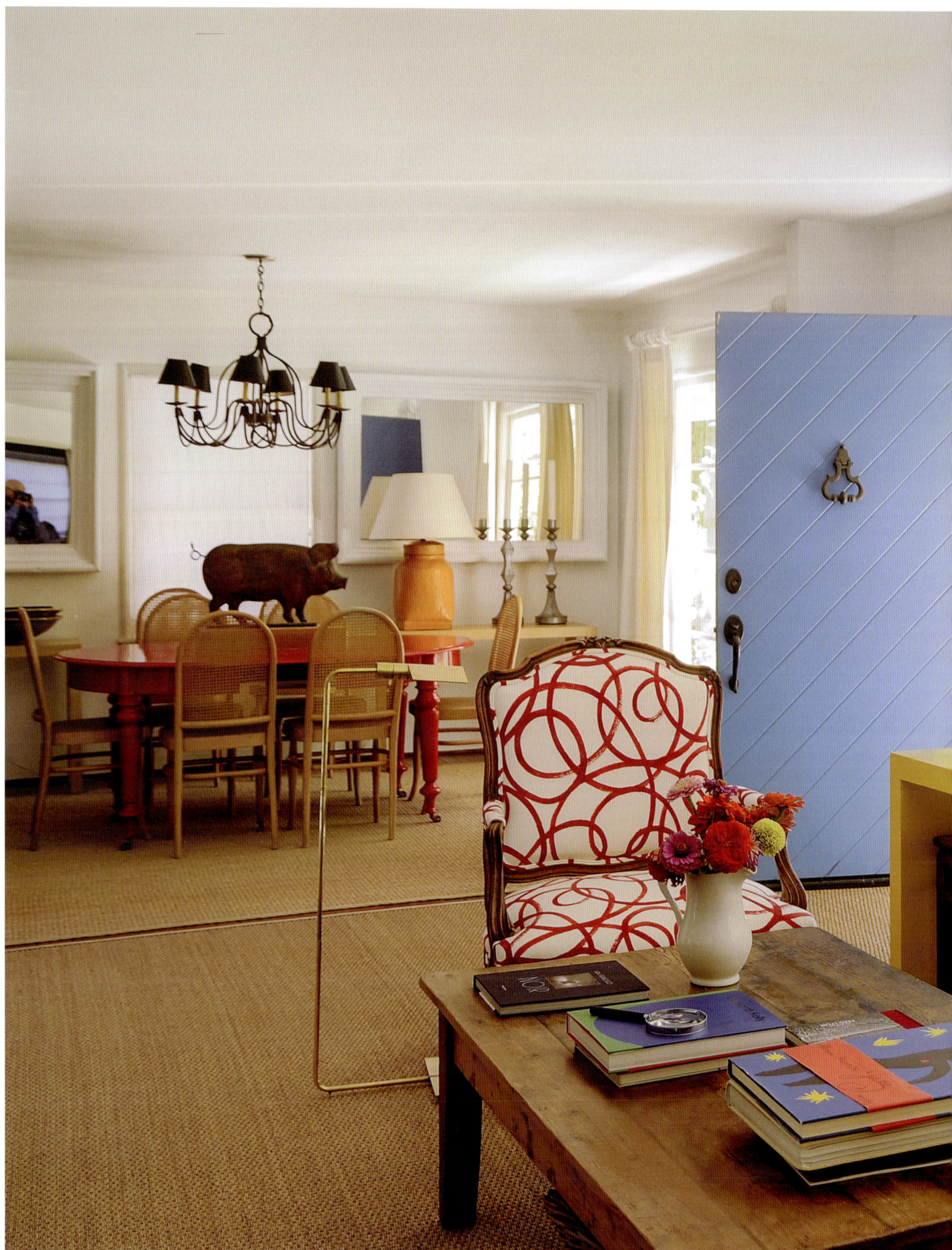

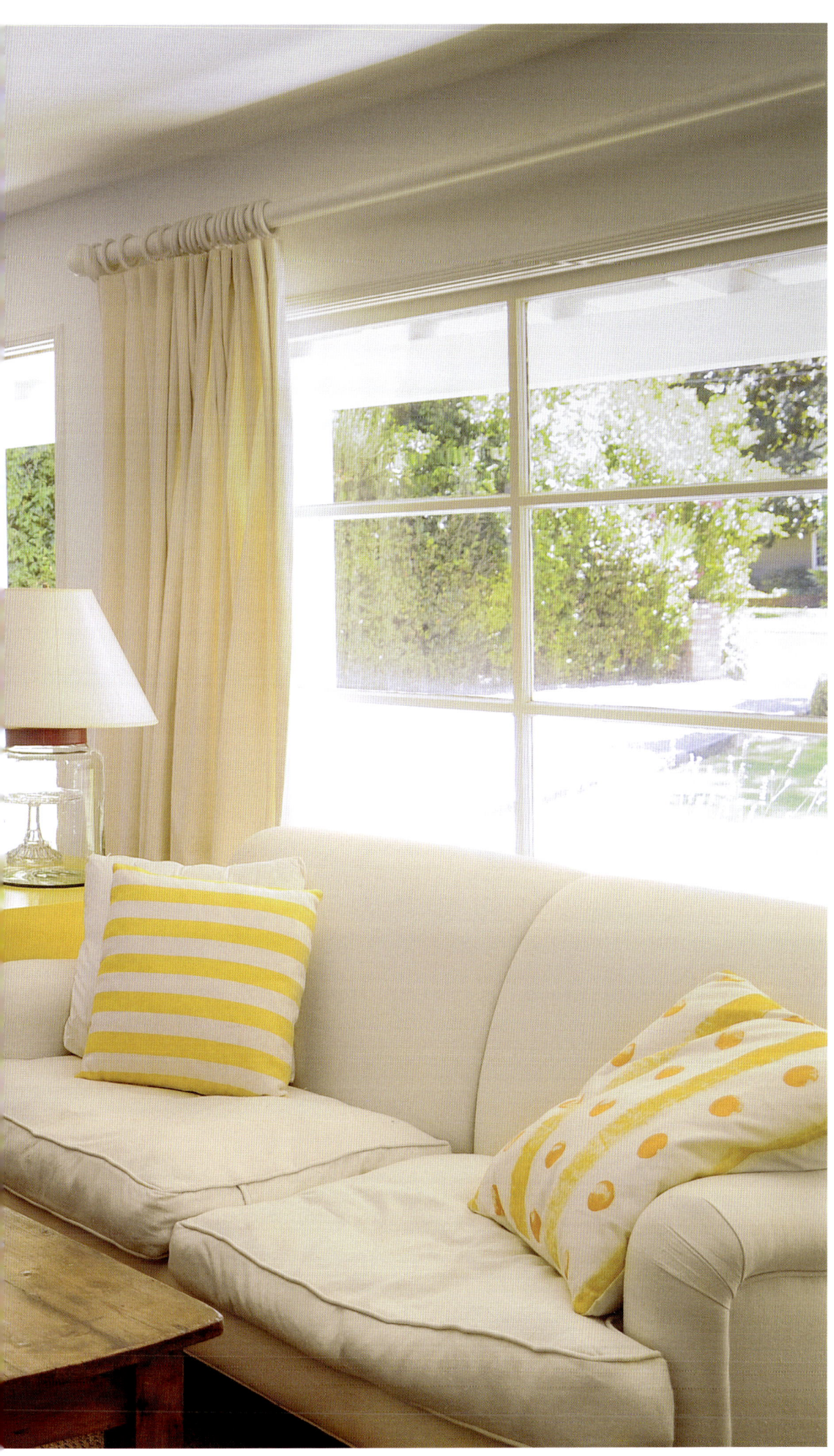

PAGE 193: View through the oeil-de-boeuf window into the kitchen, Penelope Rozis house, Napa, 2010.

LEFT: View from the living room toward the dining area. Three small rooms were combined to create a large, single space.

195

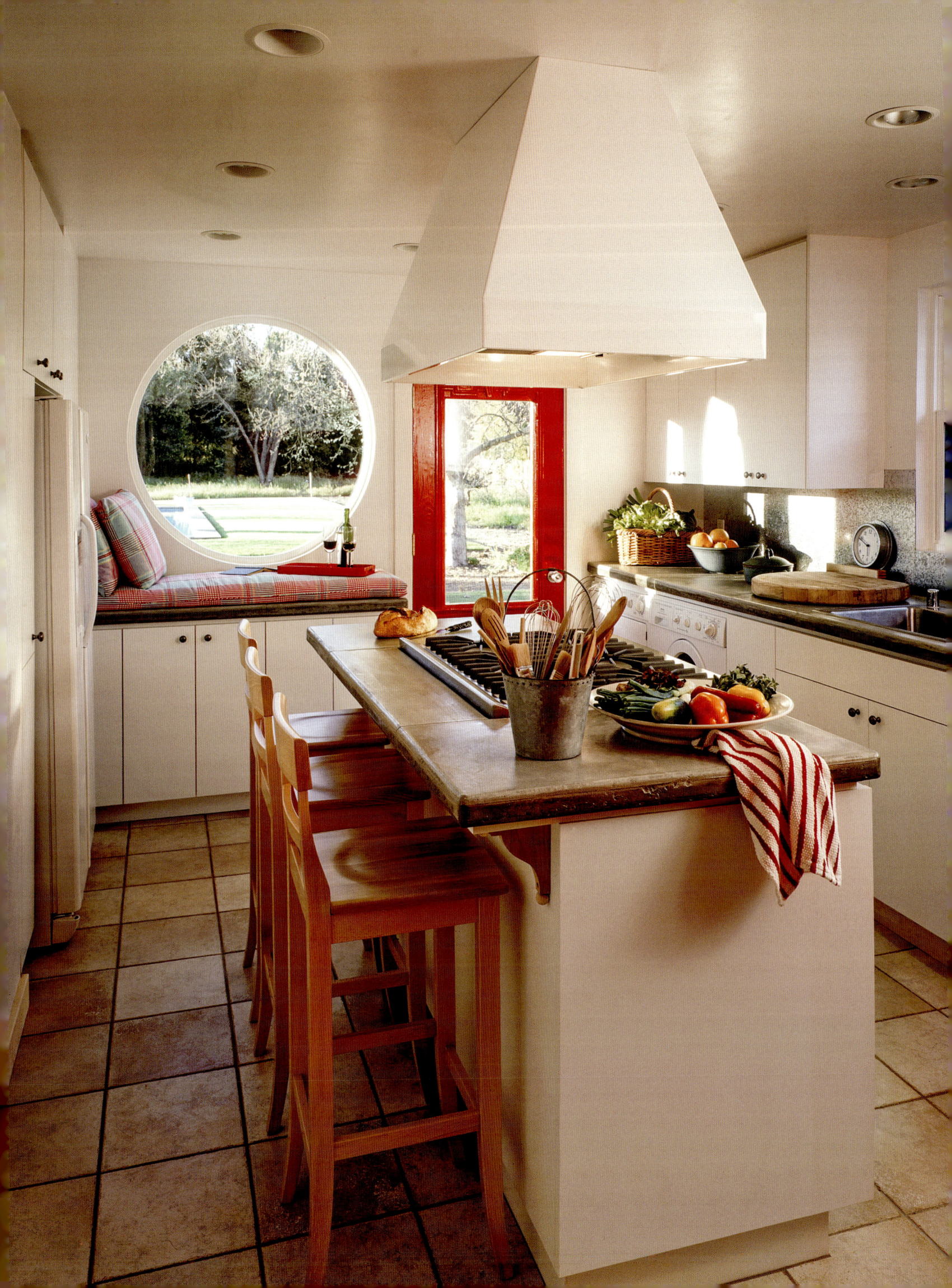

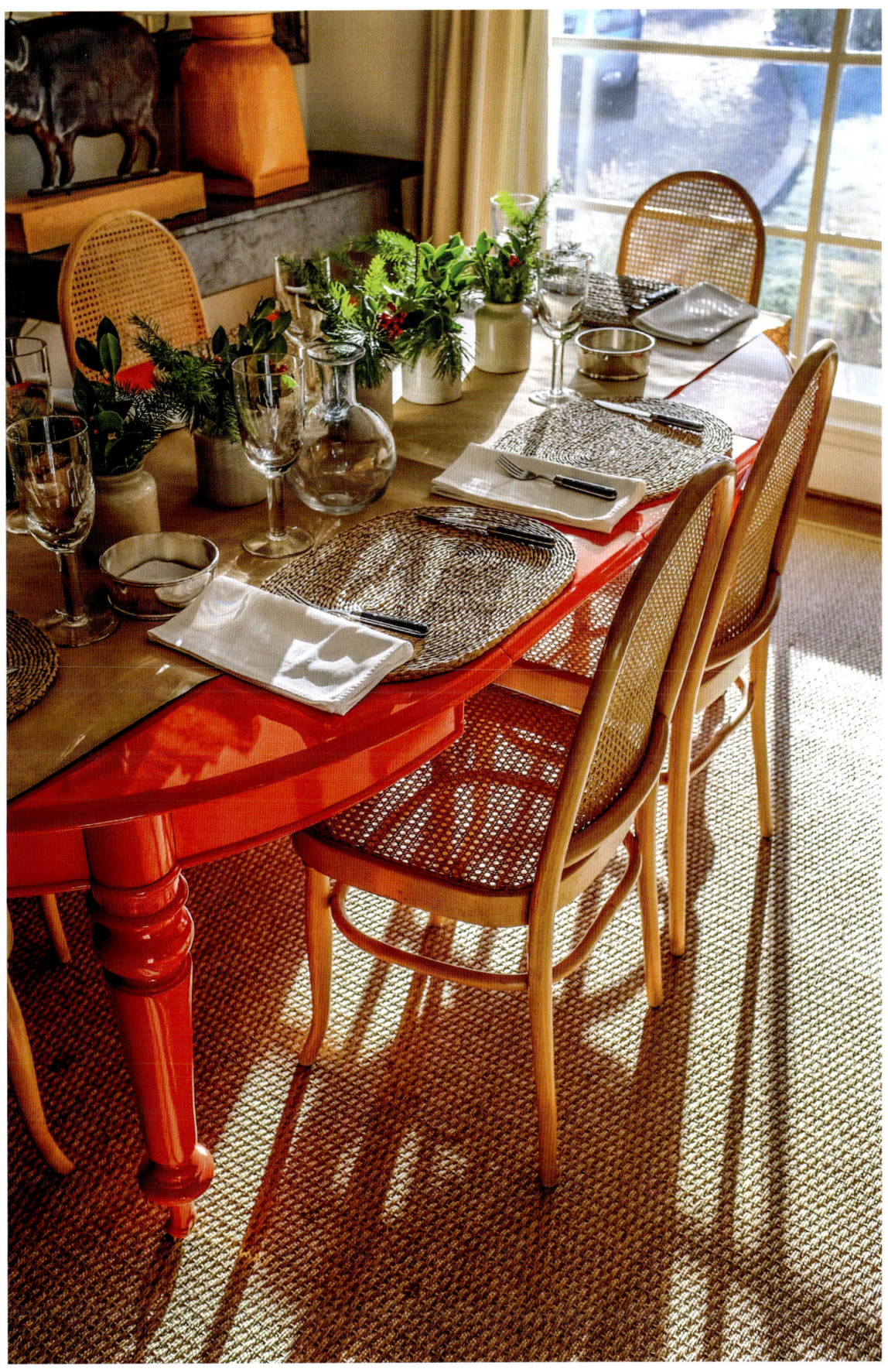

OPPOSITE: Rozis used humble materials in the kitchen—concrete counters, a galvanized-metal backsplash, and a Victorian farmhouse door. ABOVE: The sleek red-lacquered dining table provides a striking contrast to the natural tones of the 1960s Ward Bennett caned chairs and the sisal carpet. PAGES 198–199: View from the north end of garden to the main house.

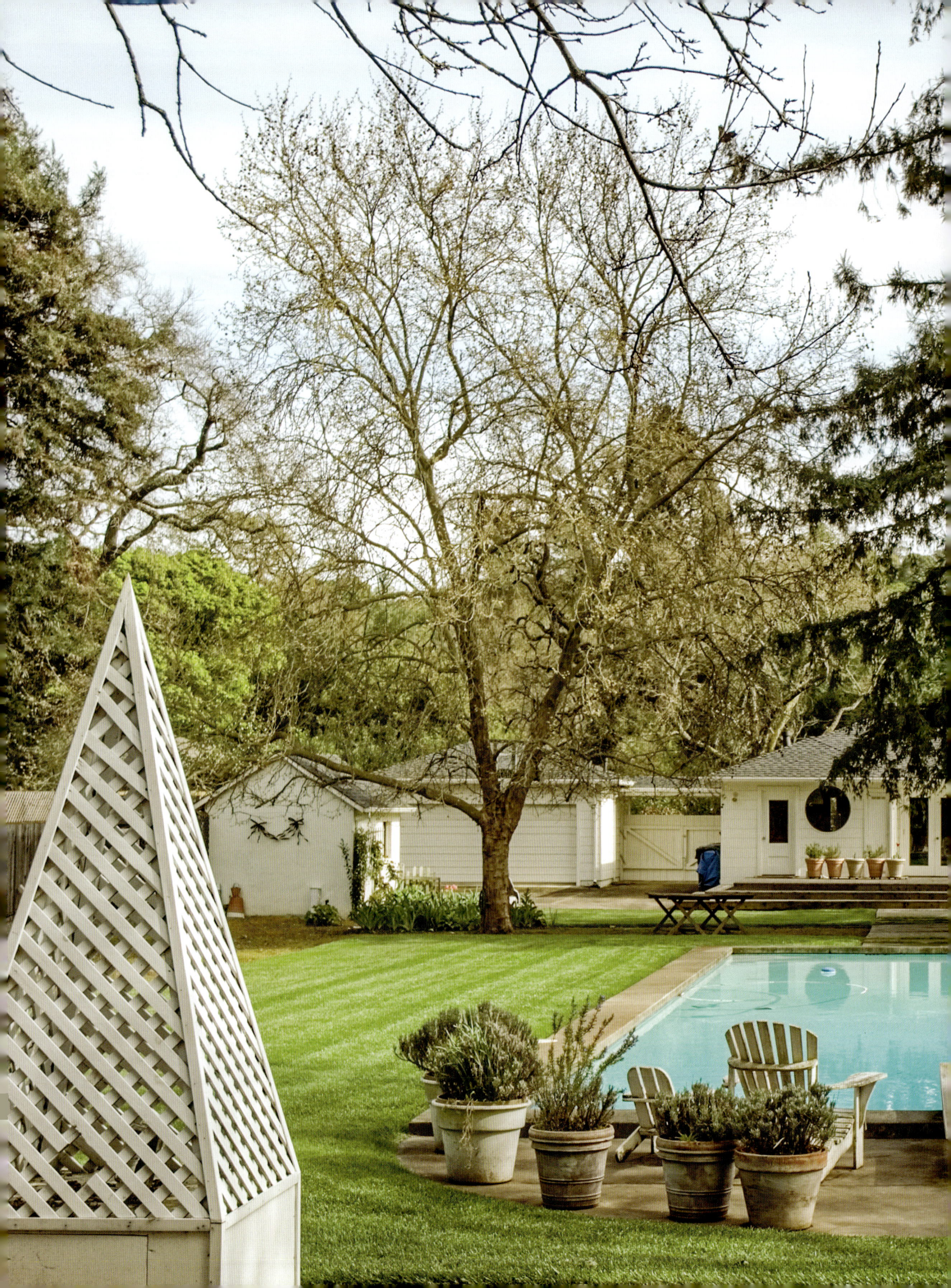

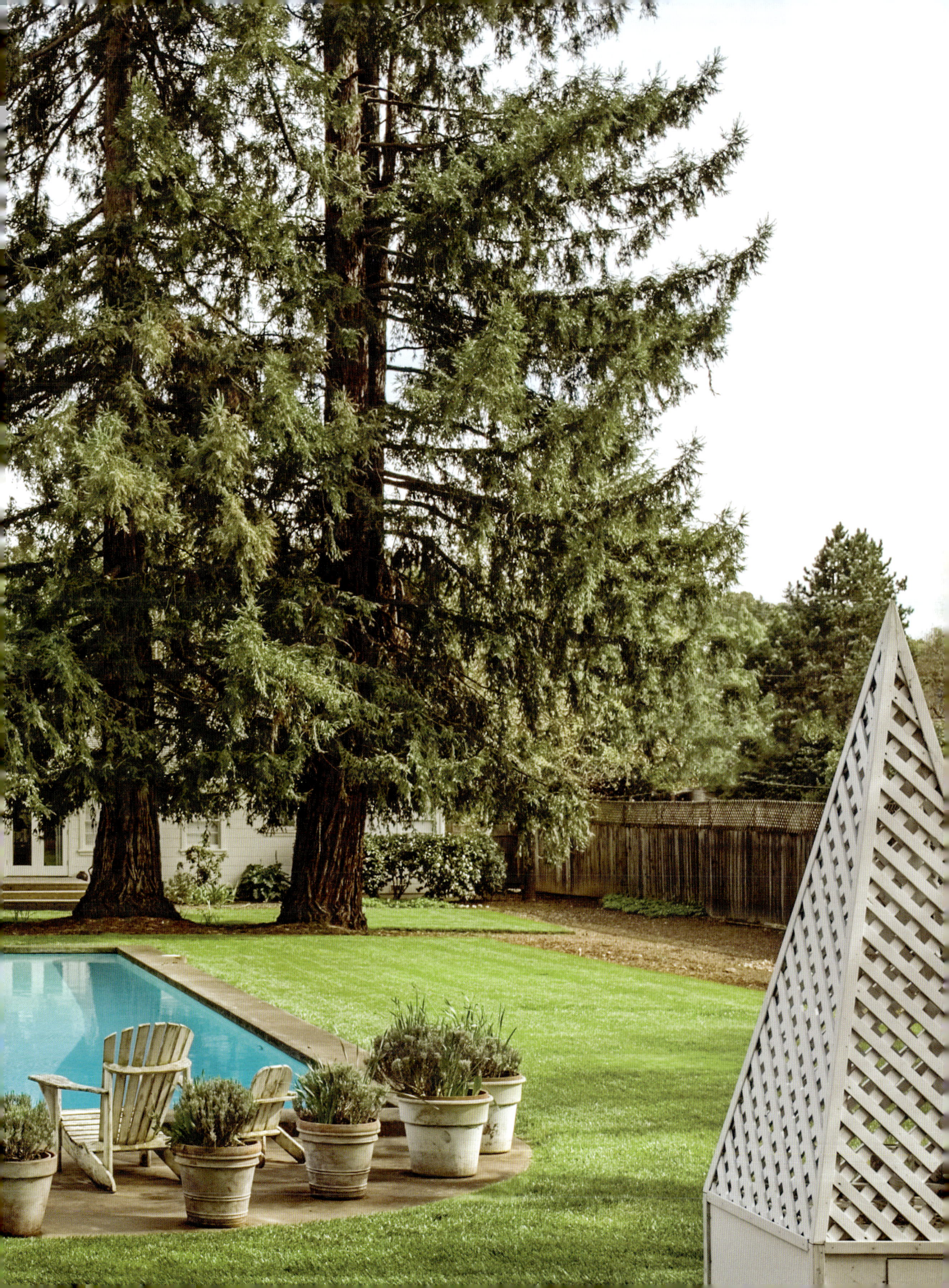

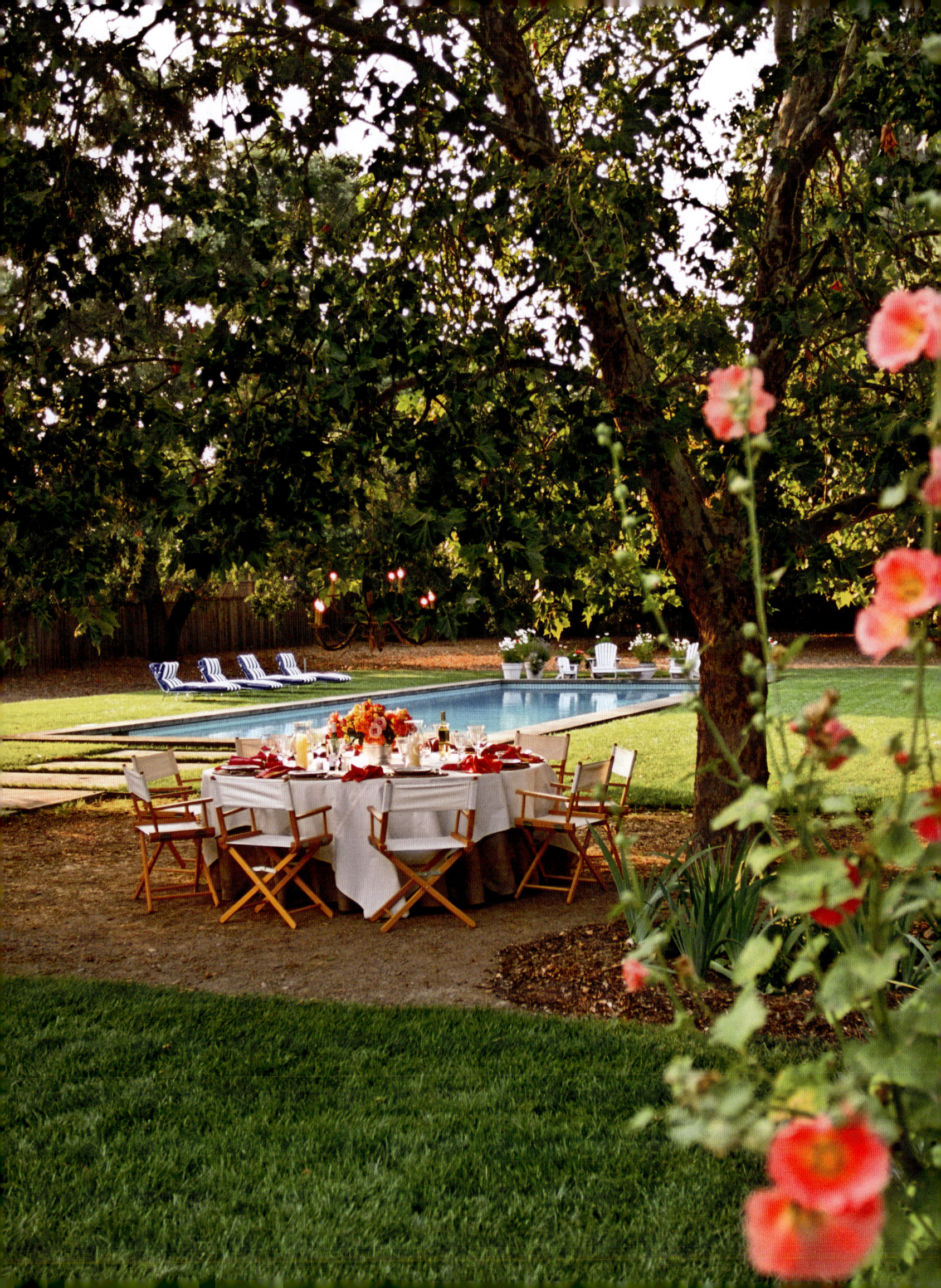

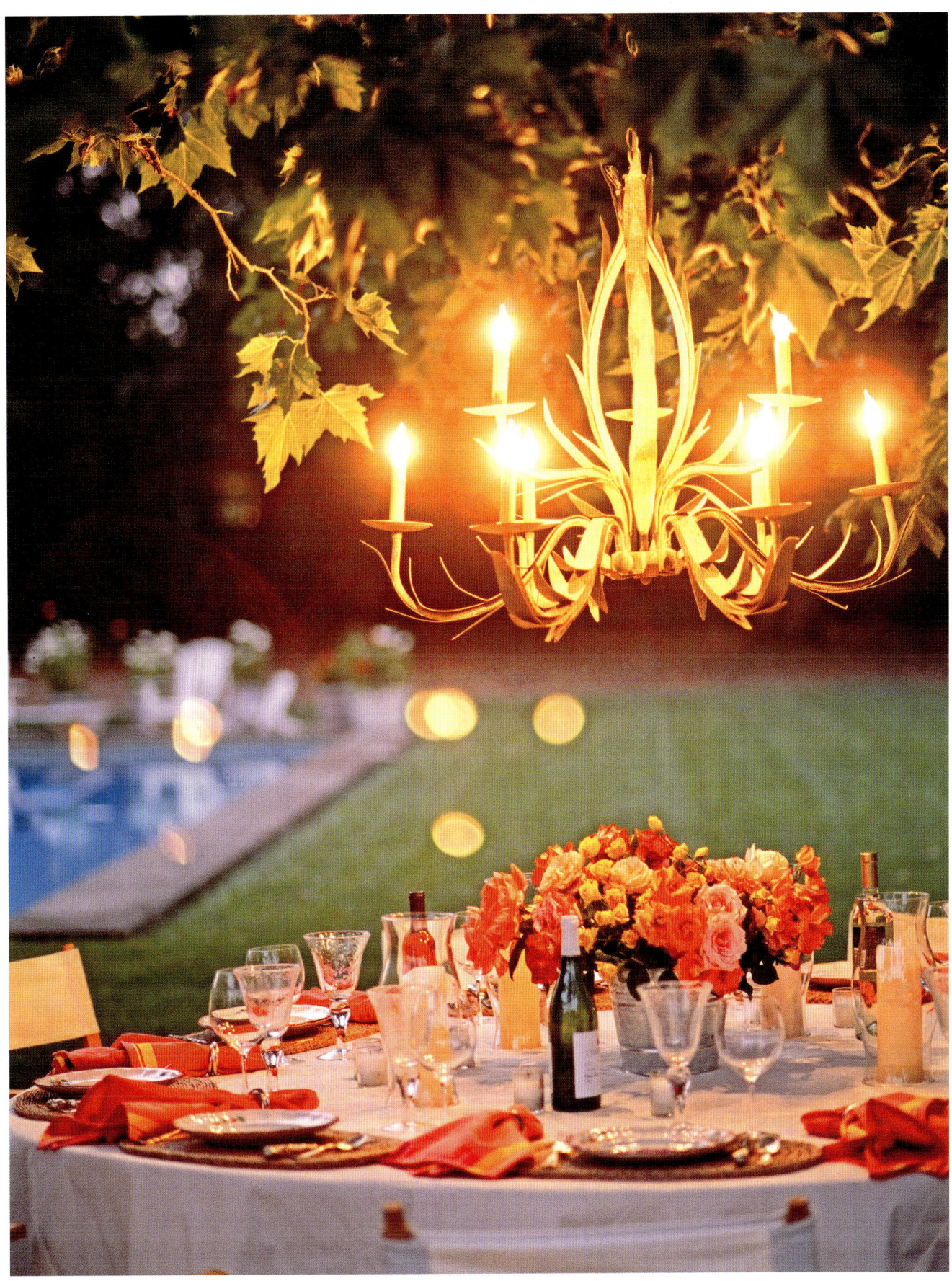

OPPOSITE: Alfresco dining by the pool. ABOVE: Detail of the table set
for a dinner party, with a chandelier hanging from a plane tree.

IX.
UNDIMINISHED BY TIME:
Looking Back at Design Luminaries

When Fred Lyon photographed interiors, it was usually to document recent projects, with the designer by his side making last-second tweaks to the decor. This was not the case in 1958 when *Holiday* magazine sent him to photograph Hearst Castle, whose owner, the storied William Randolph Hearst, and architect, the distinguished Julia Morgan, were already dead and the premises locked in a kind of amber as a state historical monument. *Holiday* was the premier lifestyle magazine at that time, and the newly formed foundation that ran the property gave Lyon freedom to roam "the enchanted hill" and take photographs for an article they hoped would entice the public to visit. These photographs were a portal to a lost time when they were taken, and they remain so today.

Lyon had long been busy photographing interiors for *House & Garden* and *Vogue*, as well as doing magnificent work for *Fortune*, *Life*, *Holiday*, and *Sports Illustrated*—each magazine requiring the best photography from their artists who usually specialized

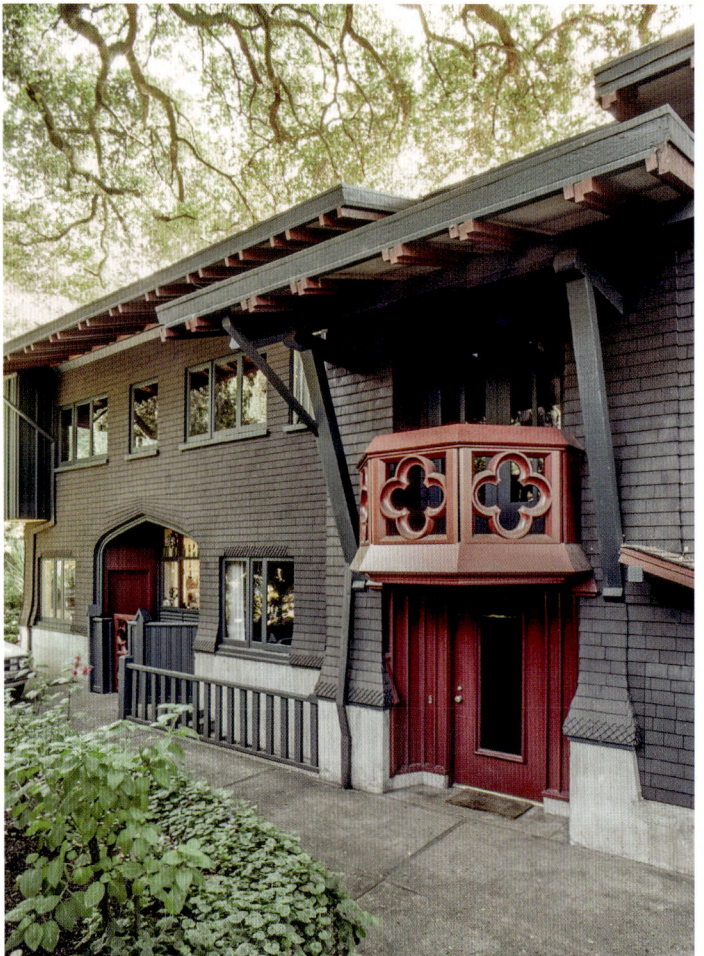

LEFT: Guy Hyde Chick house, Berkeley, designed by Bernard Maybeck, 1914. The house was owned by art dealer Foster Goldstrom when Lyon photographed it in 1983. OPPOSITE: Elizabeth Roos chats with author Barnaby "Barny" Conrad in front of the baronial hearth and fire screen Maybeck designed for the Elizabeth and Leon Roos House, Presidio Heights, San Francisco, 1909. Lyon took the photograph in 1974 for Conrad's book on Maybeck, which was never completed.

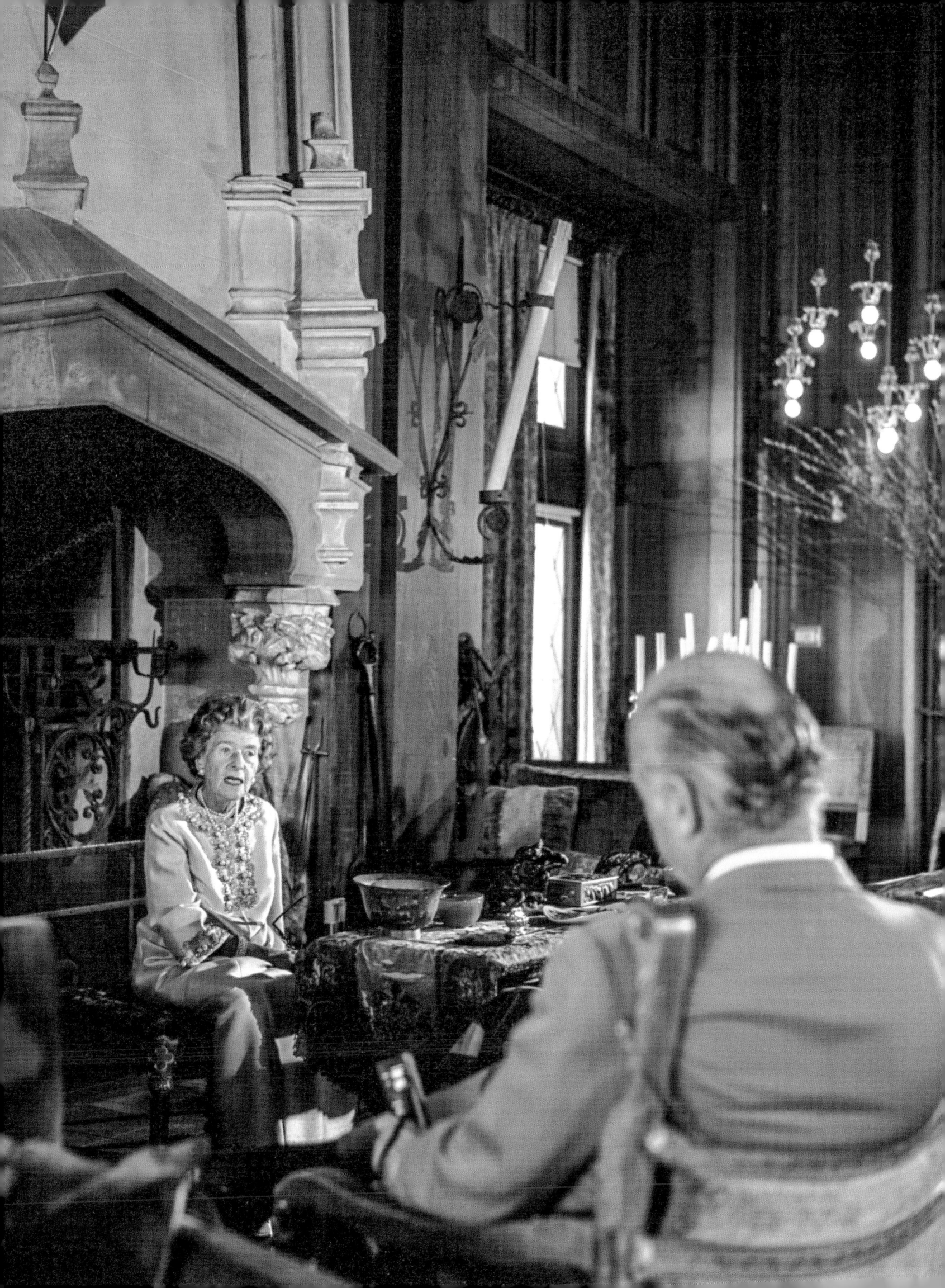

in that magazine's genre. By the 1960s, Lyon's work in interiors had given way to other opportunities. He went on far-flung assignments for travel and lifestyle magazines; developed a specialty in food photography, working on pioneering food and wine books for Time Life just as this country was discovering exciting cuisines and wines; worked regularly with N. W. Ayer, one of the most prominent advertising firms during the heyday of the *Mad Men* era; and was a father to two growing boys, a husband, and a grape grower and winemaker. From time to time, however, Lyon was enticed back to interiors with rare and special opportunities. In 1974, Lyon teamed with a friend, the ex-matador, bon vivant nightclub owner, and writer Barnaby "Barny" Conrad, to photograph significant Bernard Maybeck houses for a book Conrad was contracted to write about that great California architect and designer. The project was irresistible to Lyon because it gave him the chance to work with a good friend and get entrée to some of Maybeck's best work still extant in San Francisco and Berkeley. For Lyon, the highlight of this job was visiting the Roos House, designed by Maybeck in 1909. In 1974, the house was still presided over by its original owner, Elizabeth Roos. Conrad and Lyon interviewed Mrs. Roos, whom Lyon found to be "elegant and charming."[158] The house remained a triumph of craftsmanship. It was Lyon's favorite of Maybeck's work. Many of its rooms were surprisingly intimate, and Lyon says its ornamenta-

tion "was pure Maybeck."[159] Alas, Conrad never completed the book, and Lyon's images for this project remained unseen.

In 1983, Lyon was given another chance to revisit Maybeck's work when he was commissioned by the prestigious *Connoisseur* magazine to photograph some of the best remaining work of Maybeck and Frances Elkins for a series the magazine ran on those two icons of Northern California design. In this engagement, Lyon photographed the stunning E. C. Young House, a seminal Maybeck design in San Francisco. The interiors of this house, which was built in 1913, are a symphony in redwood.

As for Elkins, there could be no photographer better qualified to revisit her work. Thirty years after her death, this *Connoisseur* assignment had Lyon once again photographing the designs of the woman who helped launch his career in interior design photography. The most poignant days of this assignment were spent at Casa Amesti, Elkins's residence in Monterey for four decades. For this shoot, Lyon enlisted the help of Elkins's daughter, designer Katie Boyd. She worked with Lyon to carefully re-create rooms in Casa Amesti as Elkins had left them when she died.

Other significant houses decorated by Elkins that Lyon visited on this assignment also were still alive with her style. The Griffin House in Pebble Beach, done in 1926, was one of Elkins's first commissions. In 1983, it remained largely unchanged.

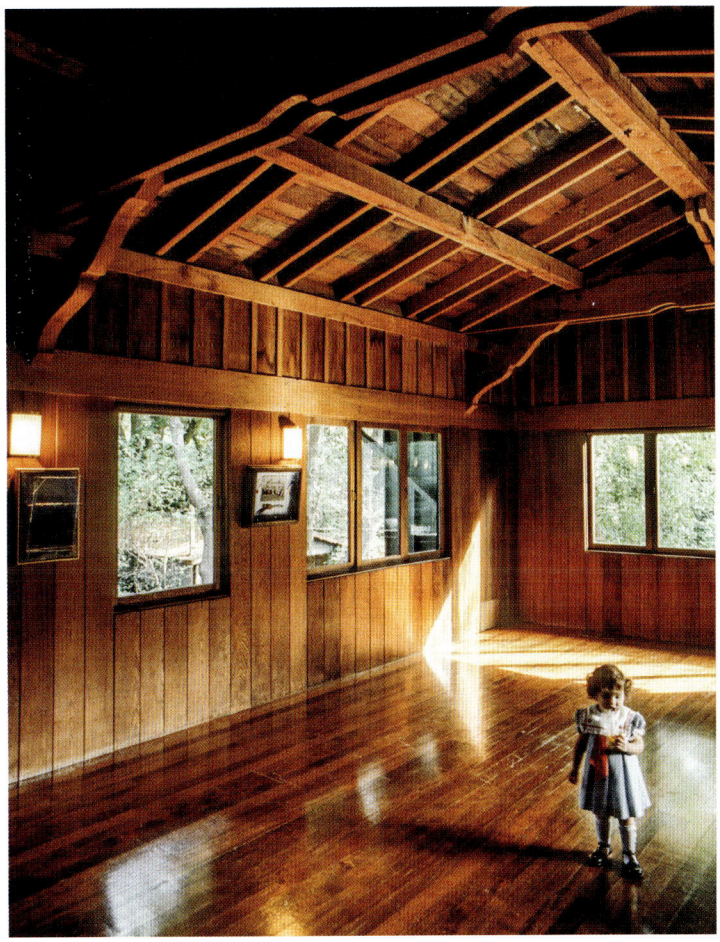

Lyon remembers, "Mrs. Griffin received me very kindly. She told me she was very pleased with Frances's work and saw no reason to change it."[160] Although it was a much smaller property, the Winslow House, also in Pebble Beach and decorated in 1948, remained largely unchanged for the same reason. This house was the last collaboration Elkins did with her brother, David Adler, before he died. Lyon says, "The decor was quintessential Frances Elkins, and the house also was notable because it expressed David Adler's love of symmetry."[161] The Zellerbach house in San Francisco shows the wide range of Elkins's design abilities. The Giacometti plasterwork and avant-garde furnishings, Lyon says, "struck me as being total Frances Elkins, and they spoke to her influ-

ences and sources."[162] The vitality of Elkins's decor for these projects remained undiminished over the decades since her death. Lyon recaptured it all.

In 1999, Lyon undertook a private commission to photograph a very special residence. Completed in 1930 and situated atop a bluff at Pebble Beach, this mansion was designed by acclaimed California architect Arthur Brown Jr. It is a rarefied place set among residences designed by the likes of Bernard Maybeck, Julia Morgan, Willis Polk, George Washington Smith, and other great architects. These images have never before been published and, like the other photographic homages by Lyon, represent some of the finest, and in some cases only, documentation of the work of Northern California design legends.

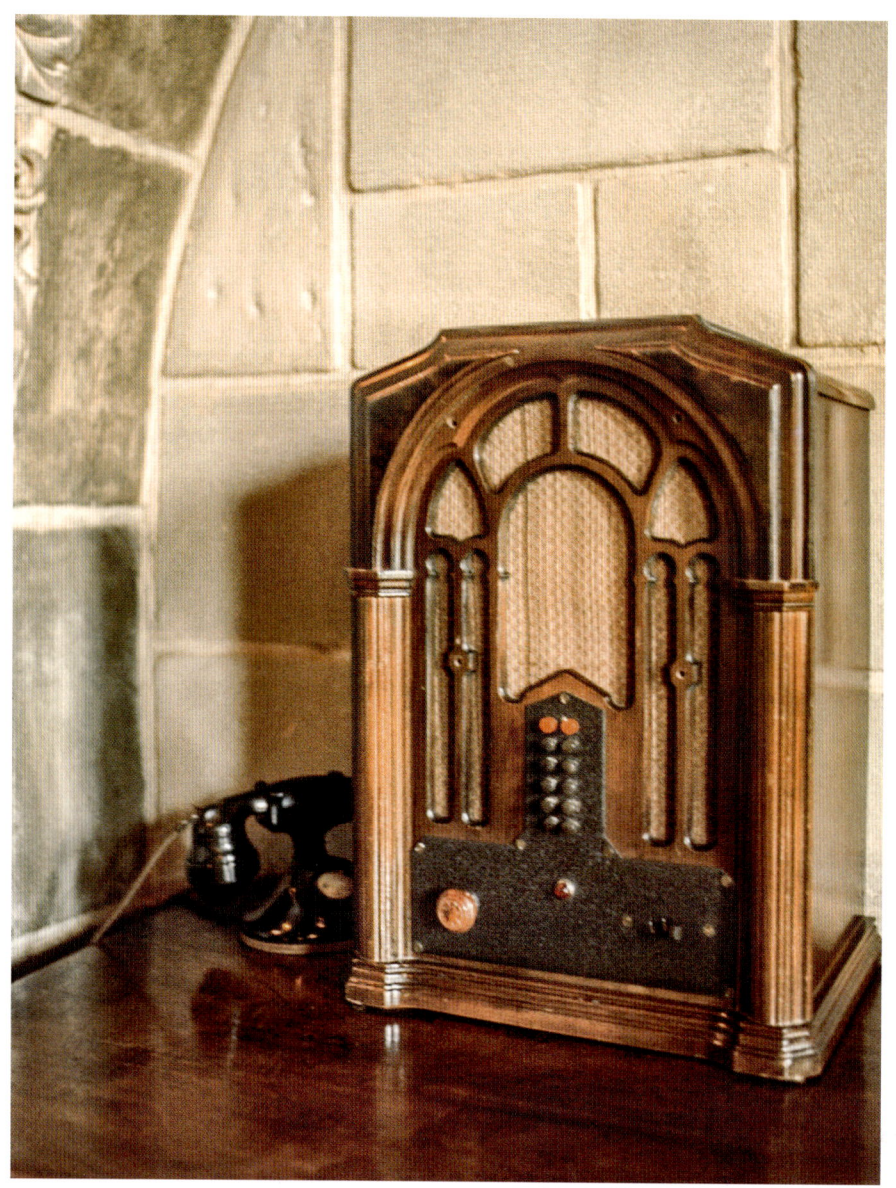

LA CUESTA ENCANTADA

San Simeon, 1958

Some of the rooms of the William Randolph Hearst residence, known as Hearst Castle, are decoration overkill. Many themes are expressed in the endless rooms. I don't blame architect Julia Morgan for the overabundance. Hearst used the Refectory to entertain his guests at meals—I'd always heard that he insisted on having bottles of ketchup at the ready. I like the tiny alcove off of the Refectory because it had a vintage telephone and radio, which seem to capture the time that Hearst lived there.

The aerial view of the residence was taken on assignment for an article on Monterey, which appeared in the December 1959 issue of *Holiday* magazine. I took the interior images while on a private tour.   —F.L.

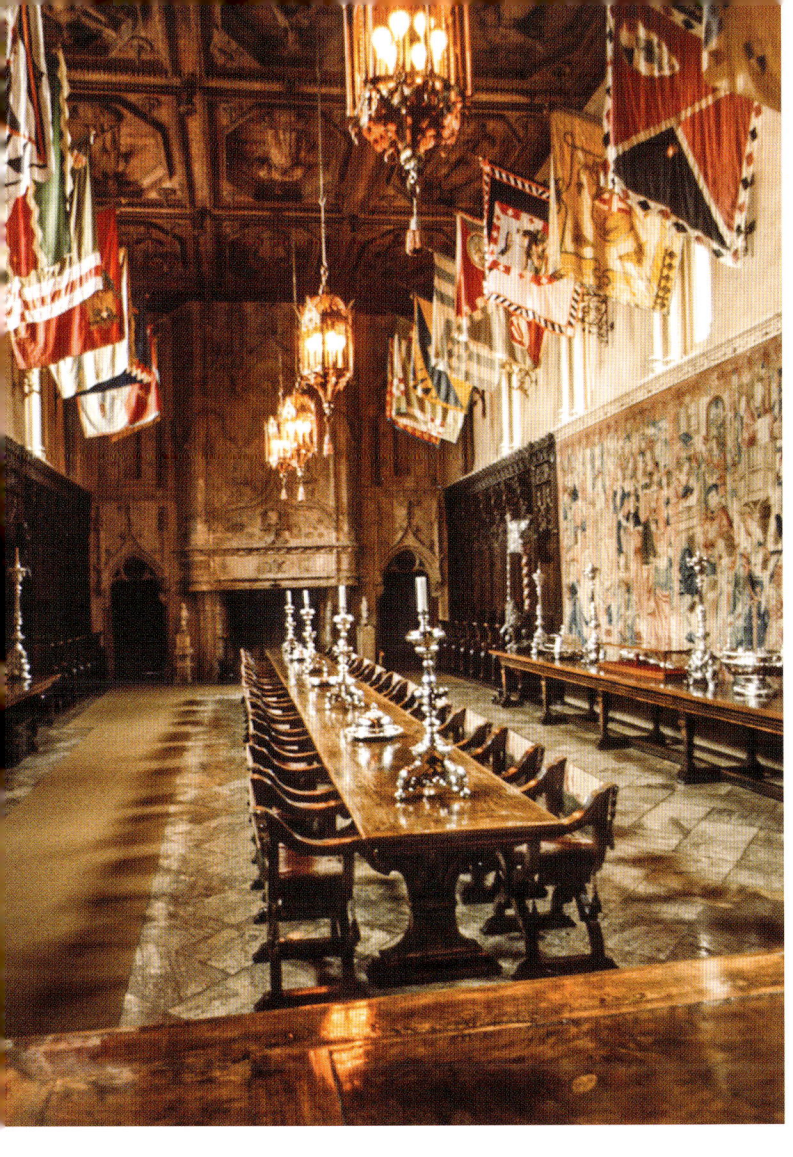

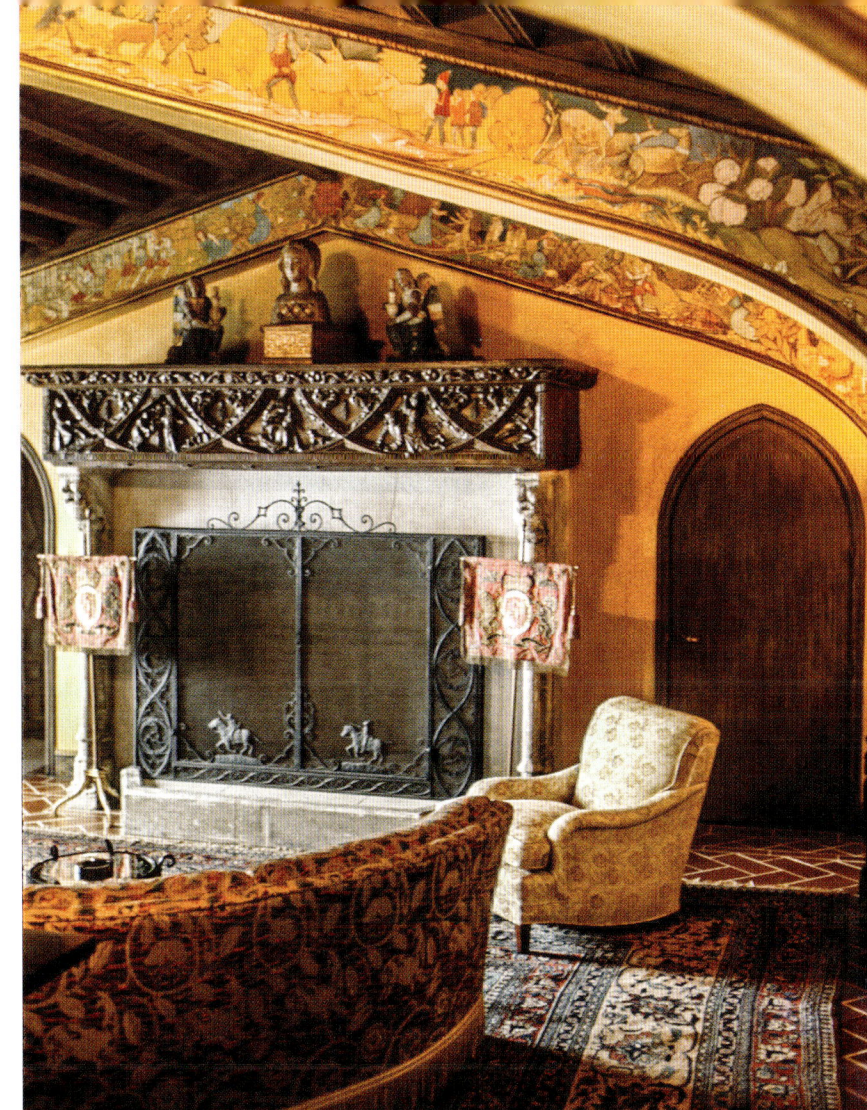

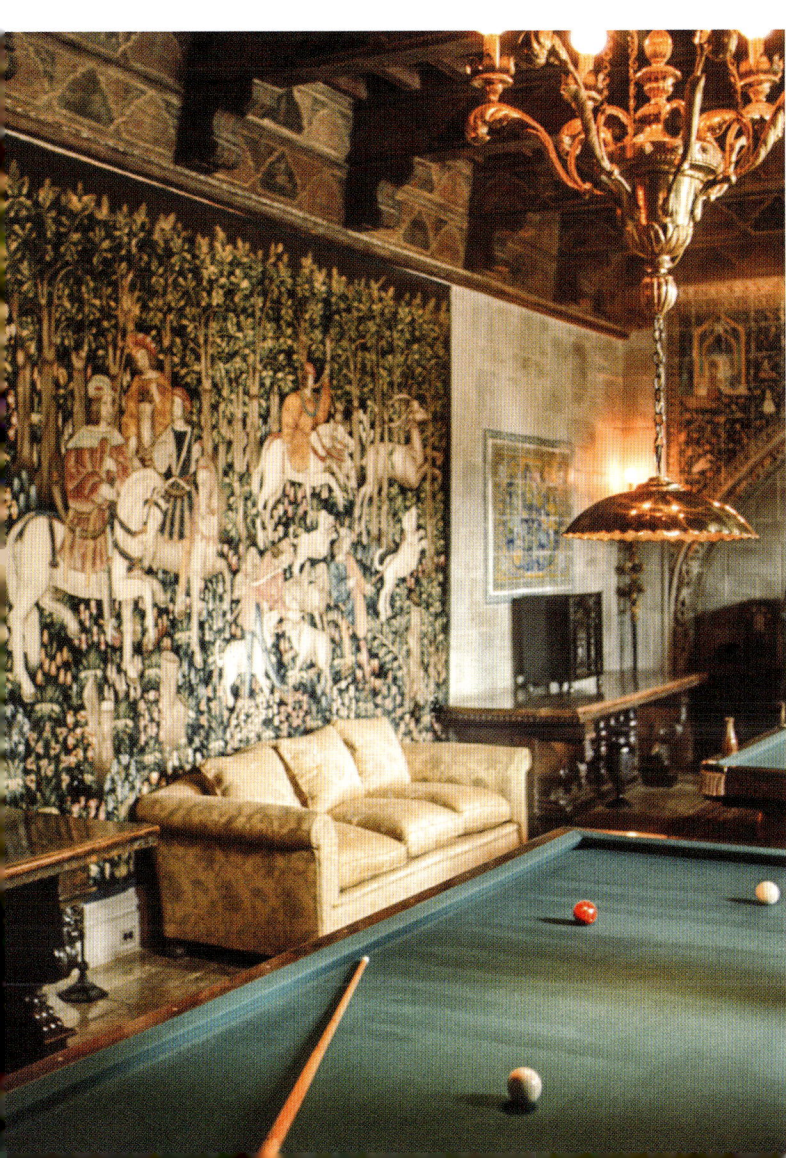

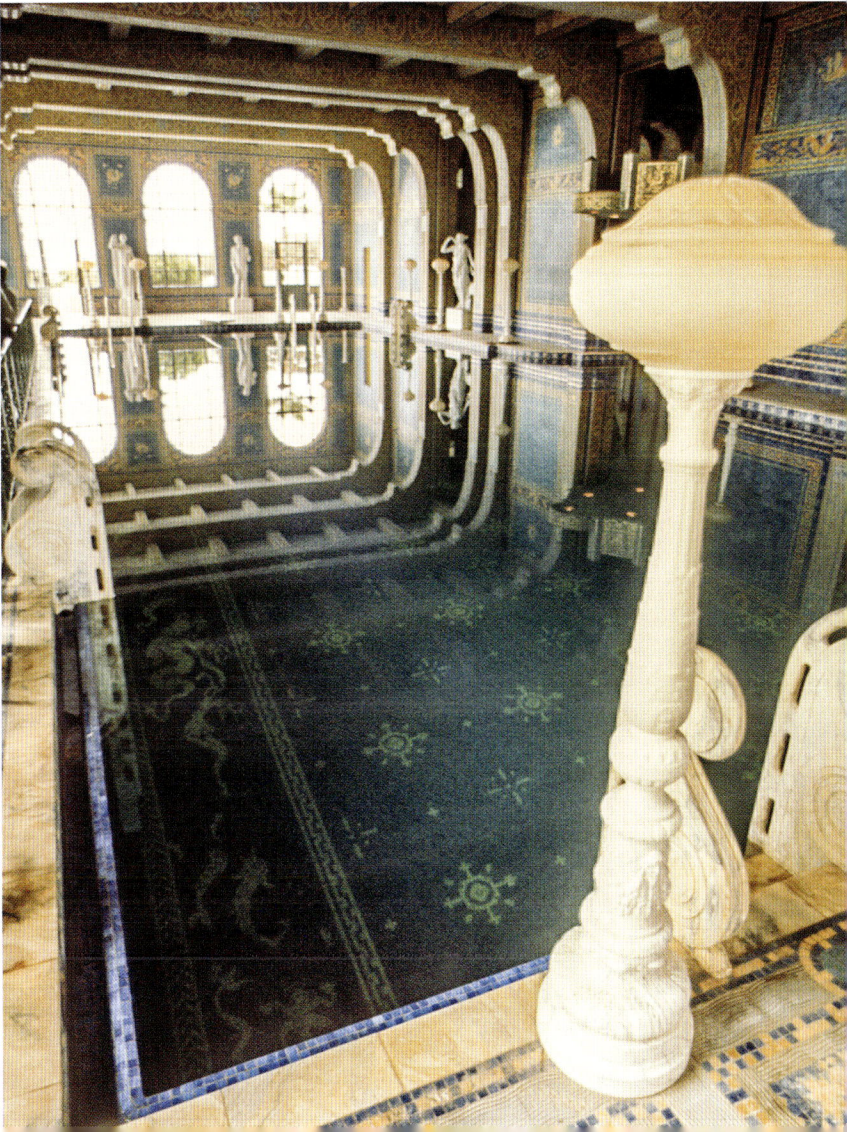

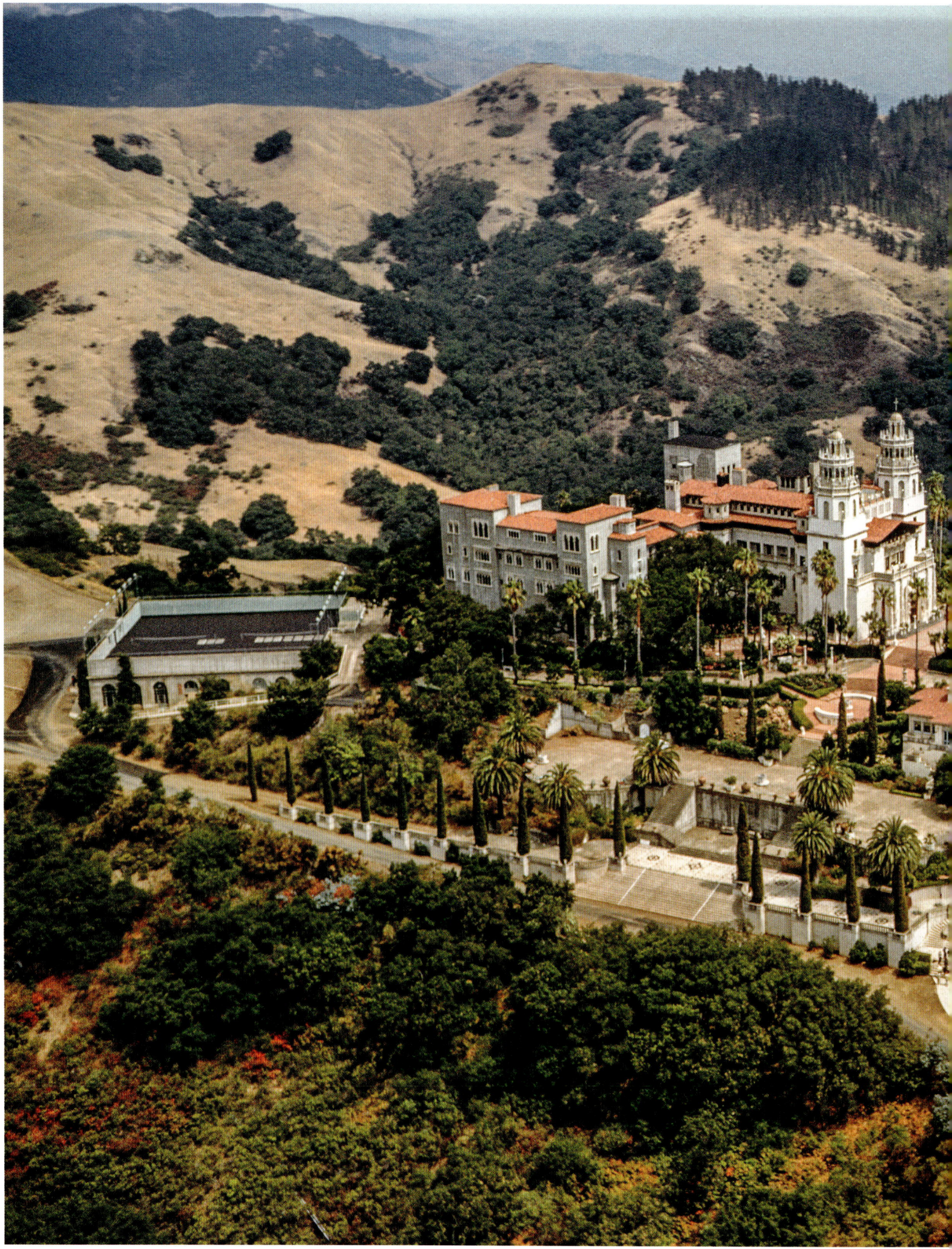

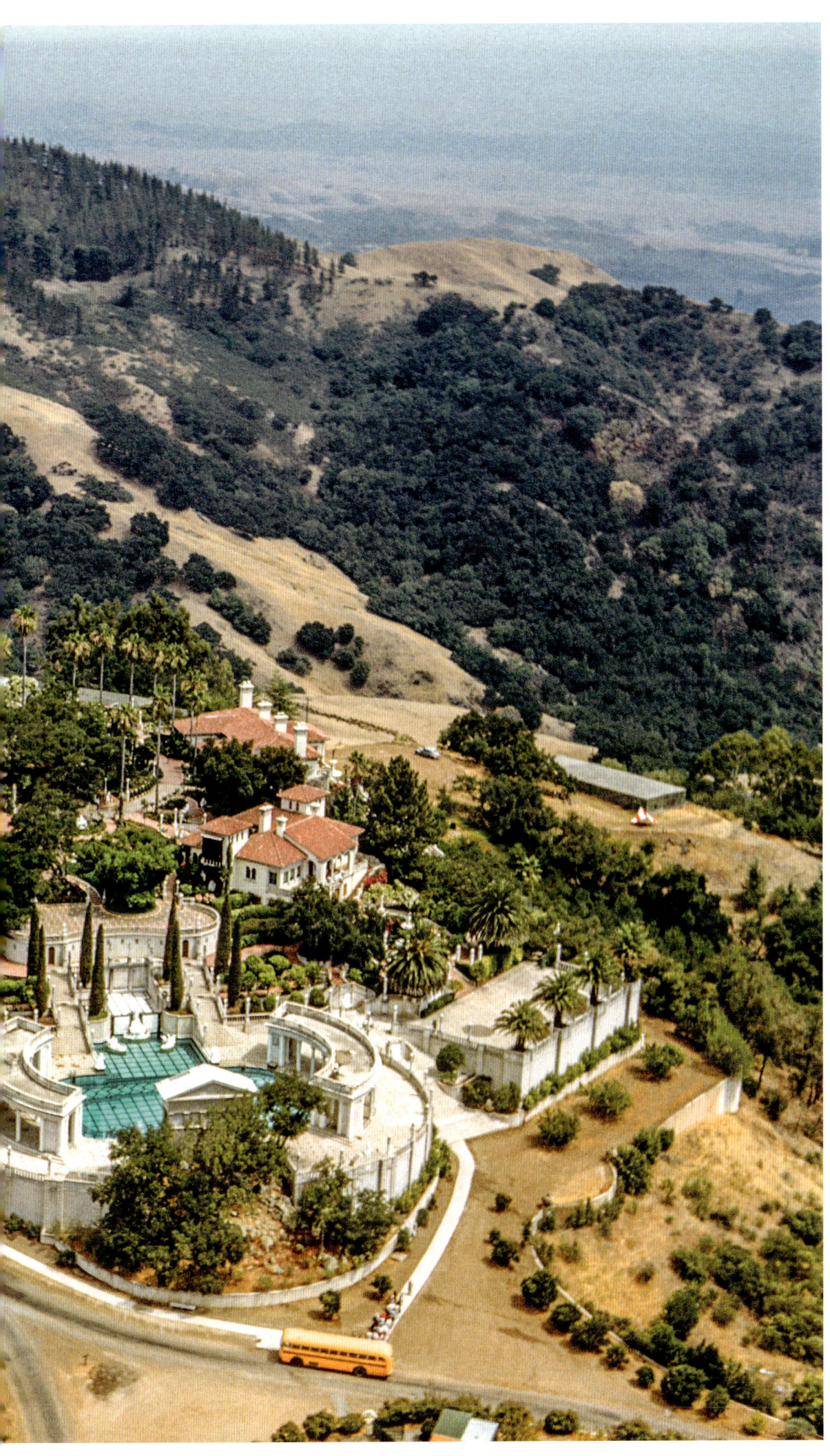

PAGE 206: Hearst Castle, San Simeon, designed for William Randolph Hearst by Julia Morgan, 1919. Photographed by Lyon in 1958. A period telephone and radio in the alcove off of the Refectory.
PAGE 207, CLOCKWISE FROM TOP LEFT: Refectory; sitting room in one of the guest bedroom suites; indoor swimming pool; billiards table. LEFT: An aerial photograph taken shortly after the estate became a state park. Published in *Holiday* magazine (December 1959).

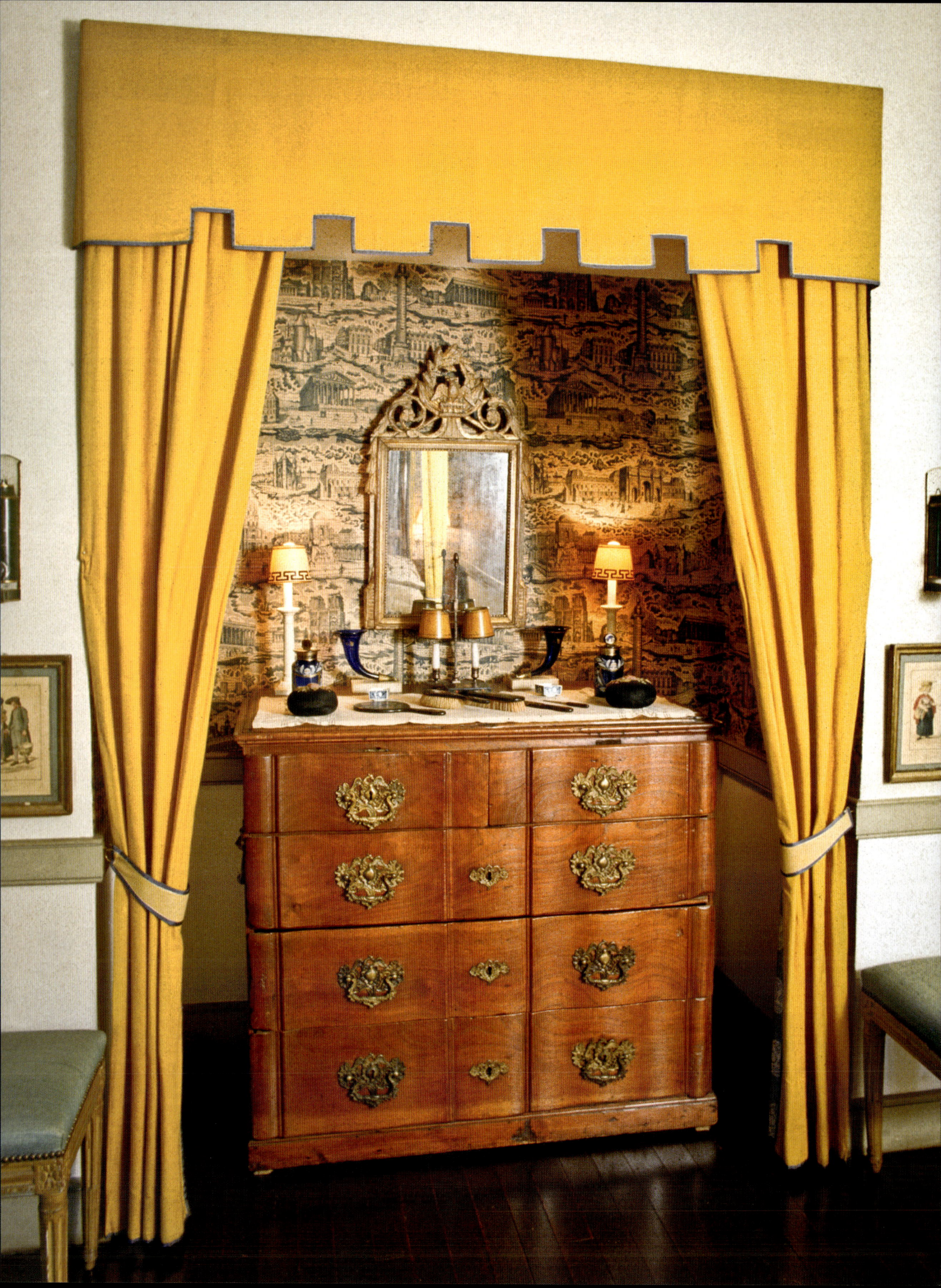

CASA AMESTI
Monterey, 1983

This two-story historic adobe, built in the 1830s, was in very bad condition when Frances Elkins and her husband, Felton, purchased it in 1918. Elkins collaborated with her brother, acclaimed architect David Adler, on the architecture and landscape. The work on her own interiors demonstrated Frances's talents and showcased unique design trademarks, including the use of vibrant colors and a penchant for combining modern pieces with antiques. Elkins's marriage to Felton was short-lived, but she remained at Casa Amesti for the rest of her life. After she died in 1953, the house was bequeathed to the National Trust for Historic Preservation. In 1955, the building was leased by the Old Capital Club, which maintained the house and garden during its occupancy.

I took these photographs of Casa Amesti, in addition to other extant projects of Frances Elkins, in 1983 for the January 1984 issue of *Connoisseur* magazine. Over a period of three days, I worked with the designer's daughter, Katie Boyd, and her husband, William, to decorate the spaces as Frances had lived in them. Katie, who is also a designer, was kind enough to bring a truckload of furniture and accessories that her mother had used in the house. She arranged the furniture in the way that she and I remembered the interior was when Frances lived there. It was an arduous shoot. We felt Frances's presence as we worked. Katie and I were both understandably intimidated. As I took the photographs, we looked over our shoulders and hoped we would not be hit by a disapproving bolt of lightning.   *—F.L.*

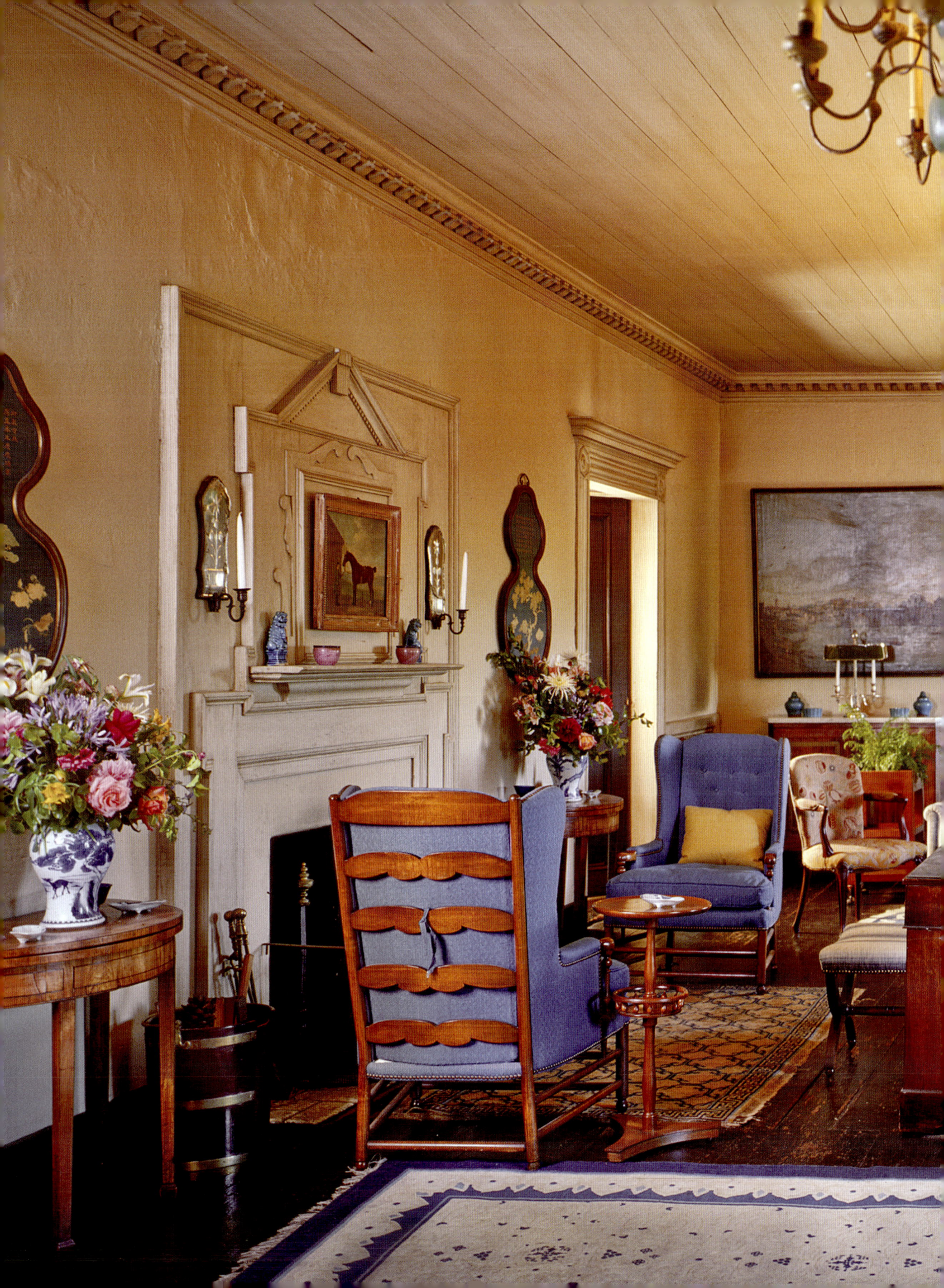

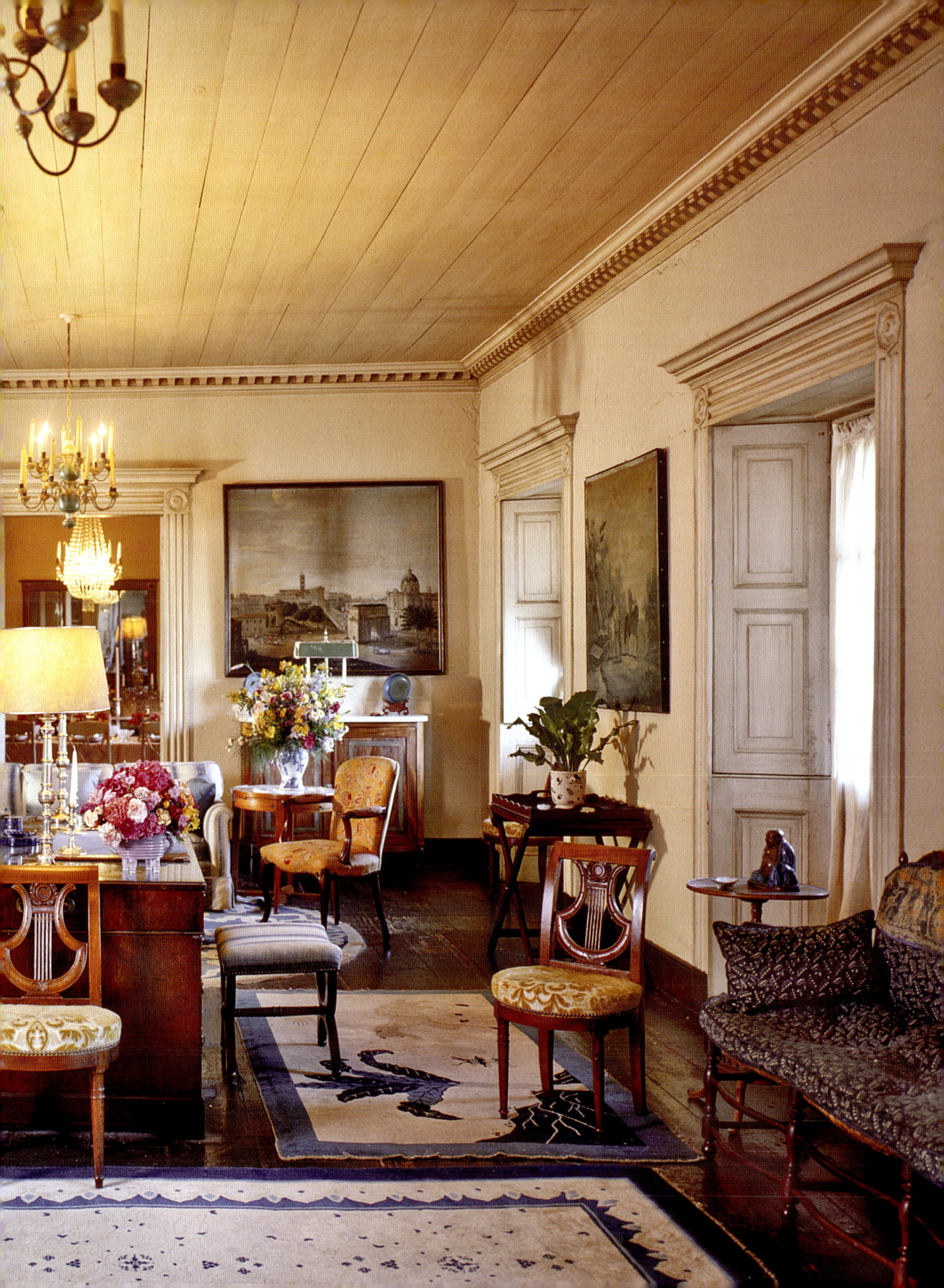

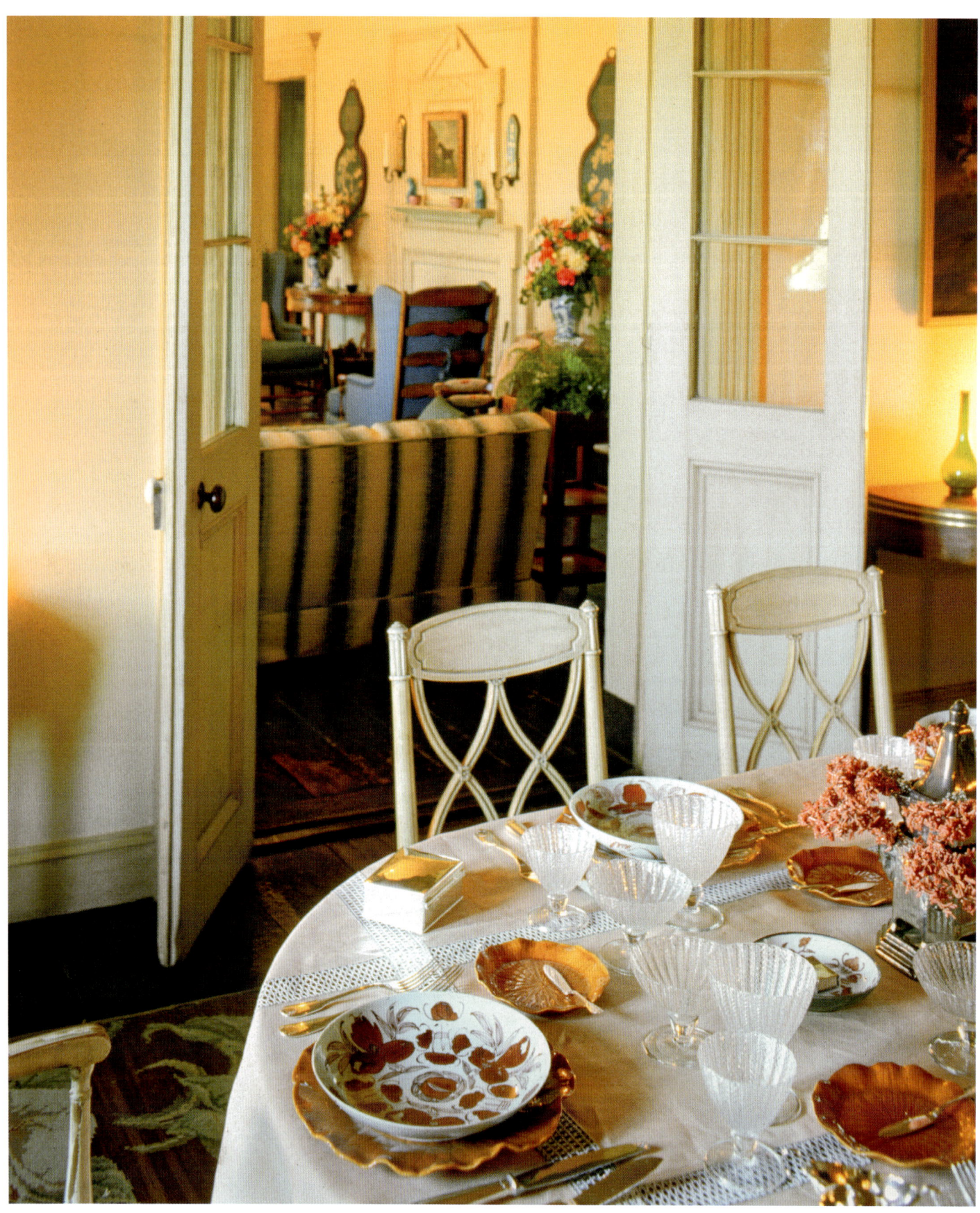

PAGE 210: Casa Amesti, Monterey, lived in by Frances Elkins between 1918 and 1953. Photographed by Lyon in 1983. Dressing niche in the room known to Elkins's daughter, decorator Katherine Elkins Boyd, as "Uncle David's bedroom," referring to Elkins's brother, David Adler. PAGES 212–213: The living room represents a collaboration between Elkins and her brother. Adler supplied the traditional framework, to which Elkins introduced an eclectic assortment of furnishings united by a blue-and-yellow palette. ABOVE AND OPPOSITE: The dining room with Elkins's original furniture, including a suite of George III ivory-painted chairs. Boyd provided the table settings for the shoot. The beaded coral centerpieces were made by Misia Sert.

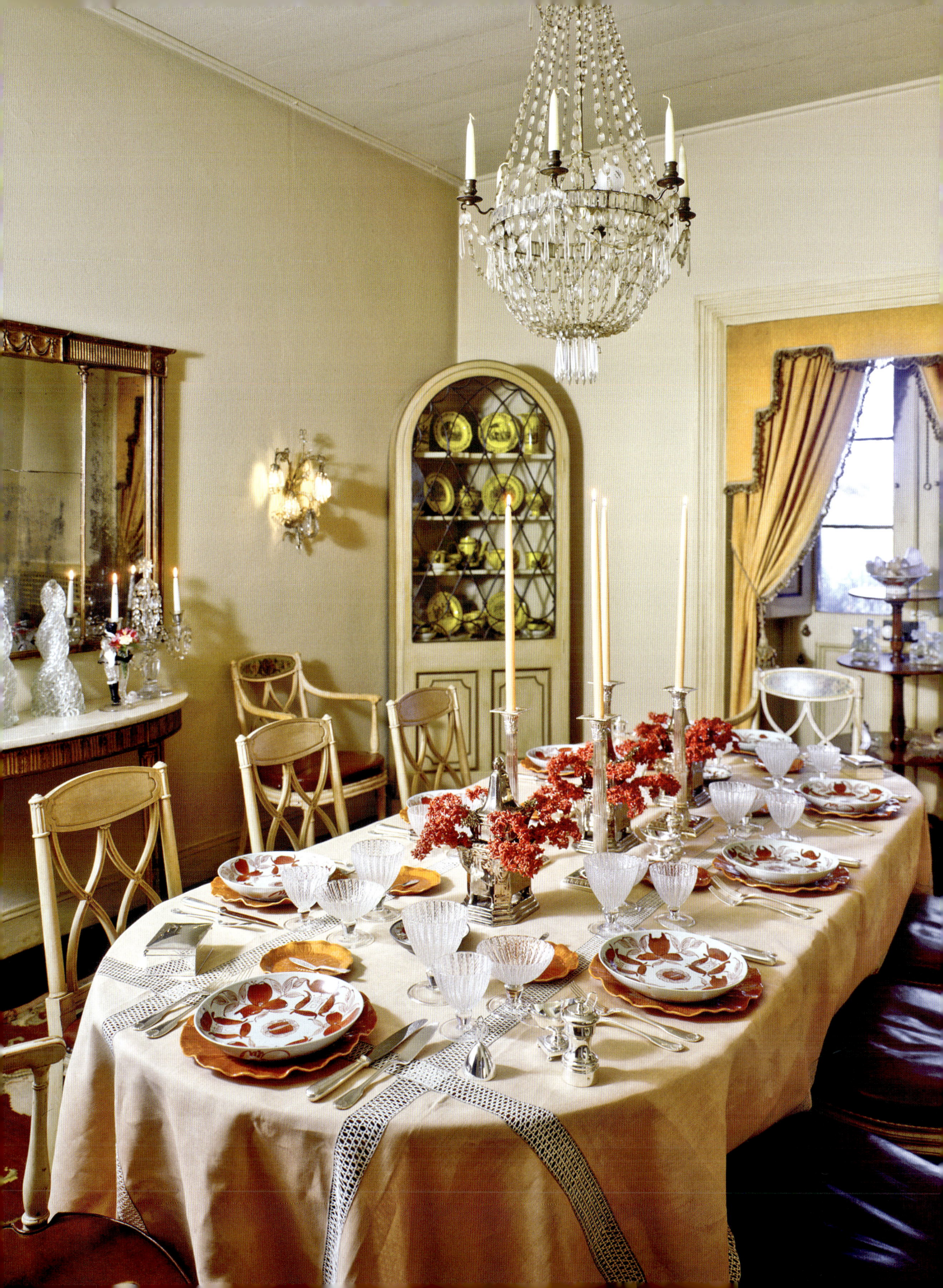

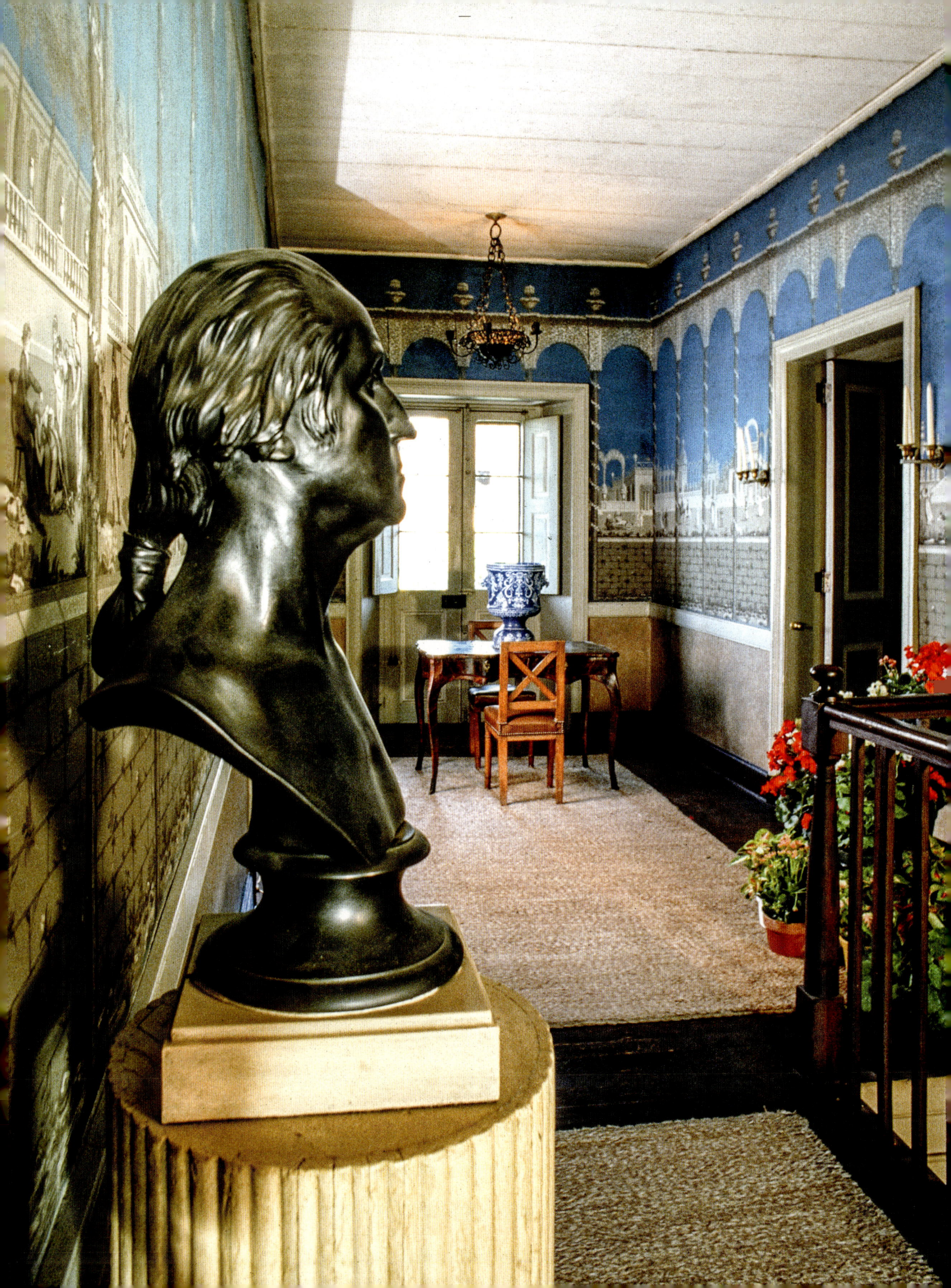

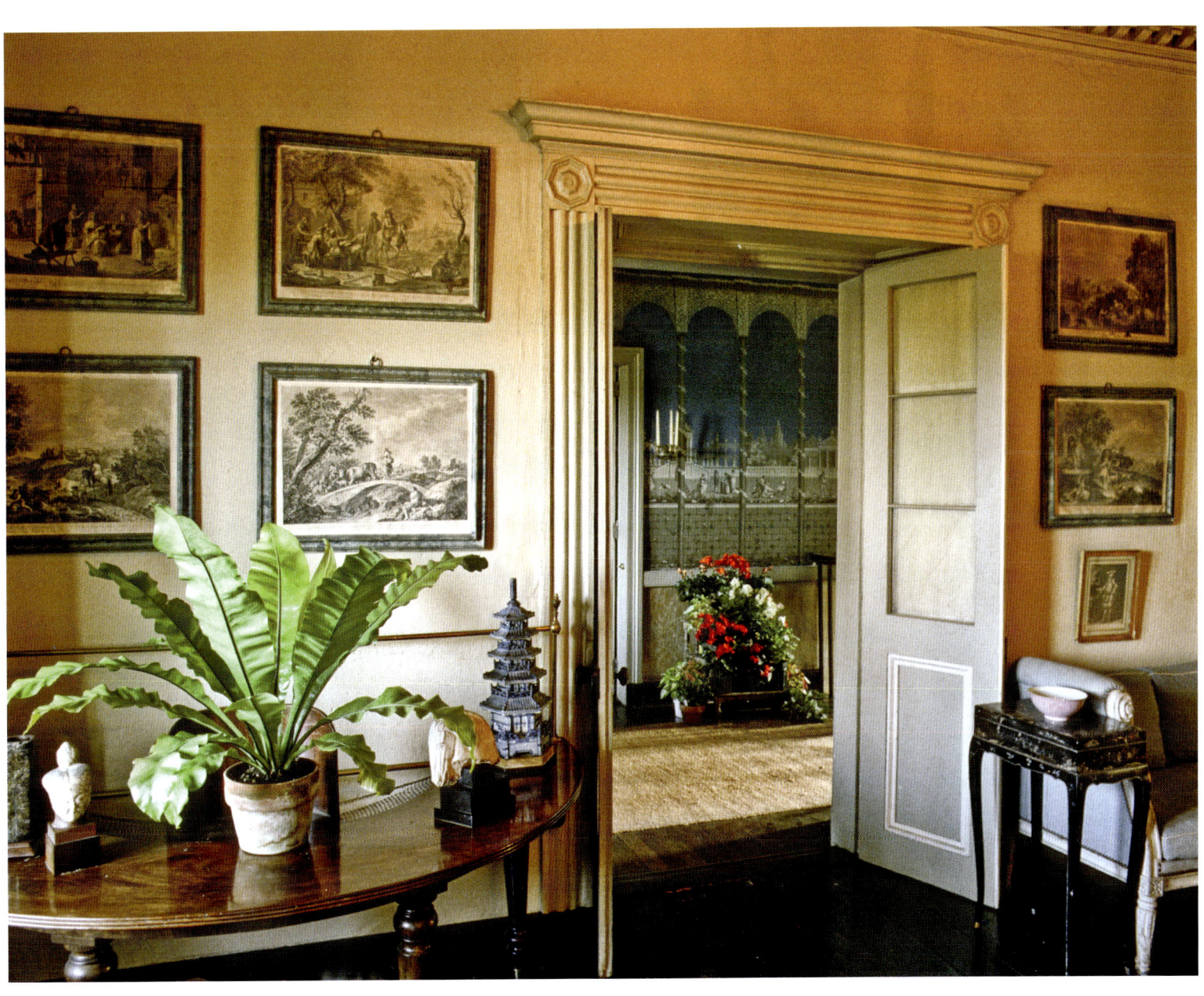

OPPOSITE: The second-floor hallway runs the length of the house. Elkins paired French scenic wallpaper ("Le Palais Royal") with a blue-and-white ceramic urn. Boyd arranged the pots of red and white flowers in the spirit of her mother. ABOVE: The view into the hall and staircase from the living room.

HESTER AND ALLEN GRIFFIN HOUSE

Pebble Beach, 1983

Frances Elkins decorated this house in 1926 for Hester and Arthur Hately. It was one of Elkins's first professional commissions. Almost six decades later, Mrs. Griffin (formerly Mrs. Arthur Hately) received me with kindness and charm. She was very pleased with Frances's work and was happy to share it. It was a large Spanish colonial revival house, and Mrs. Griffin hadn't changed the interiors much since Frances decorated it. I photographed the interiors for *Connoisseur* magazine.

The classical spaces, with architecture by George Washington Smith (1876–1930), received the designer's traditional, yet avant-garde, handling. This was the most intact Frances Elkins house I saw in the decades since her death. Everywhere I pointed the camera, I was happy.   —*F.L.*

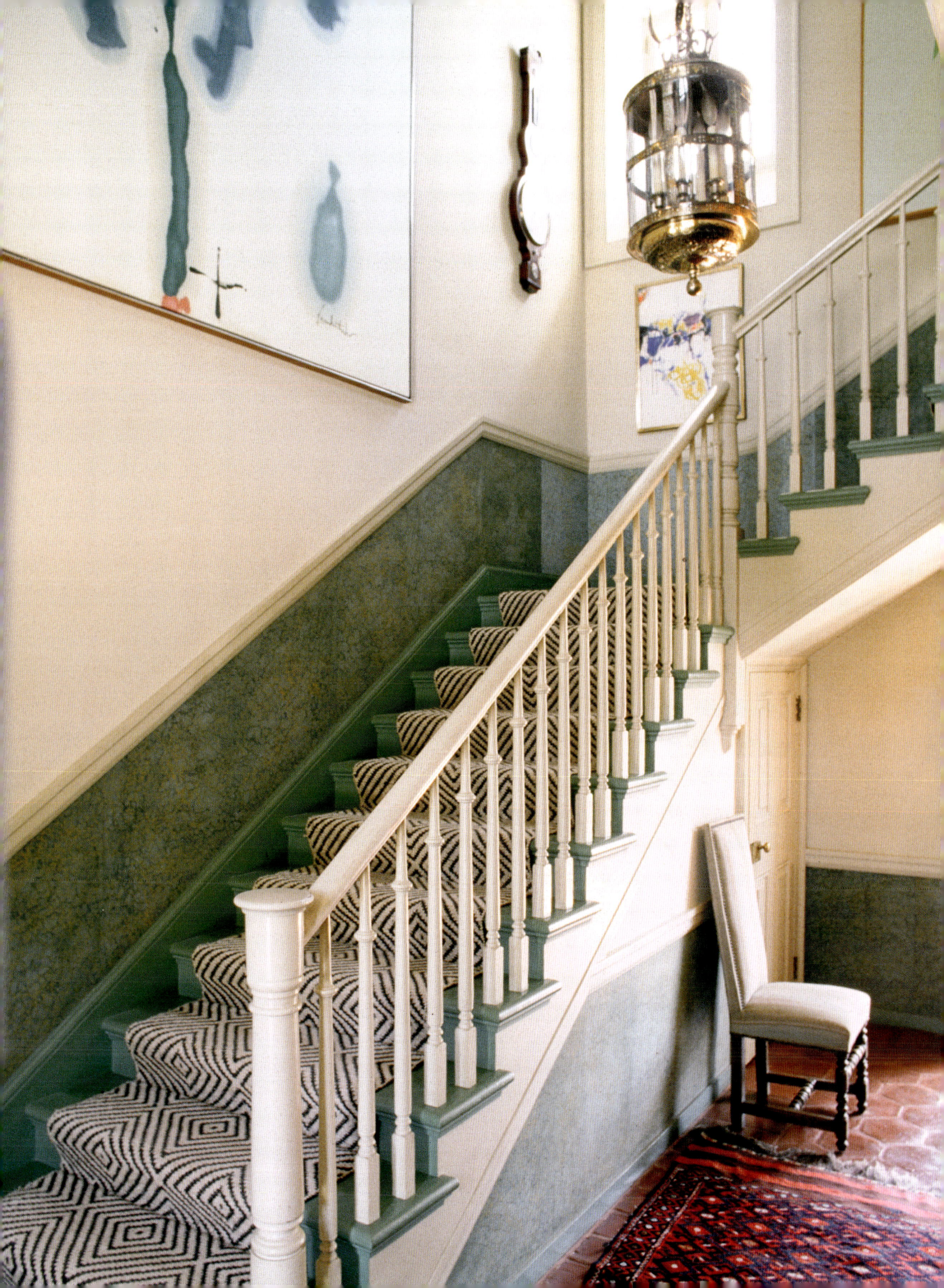

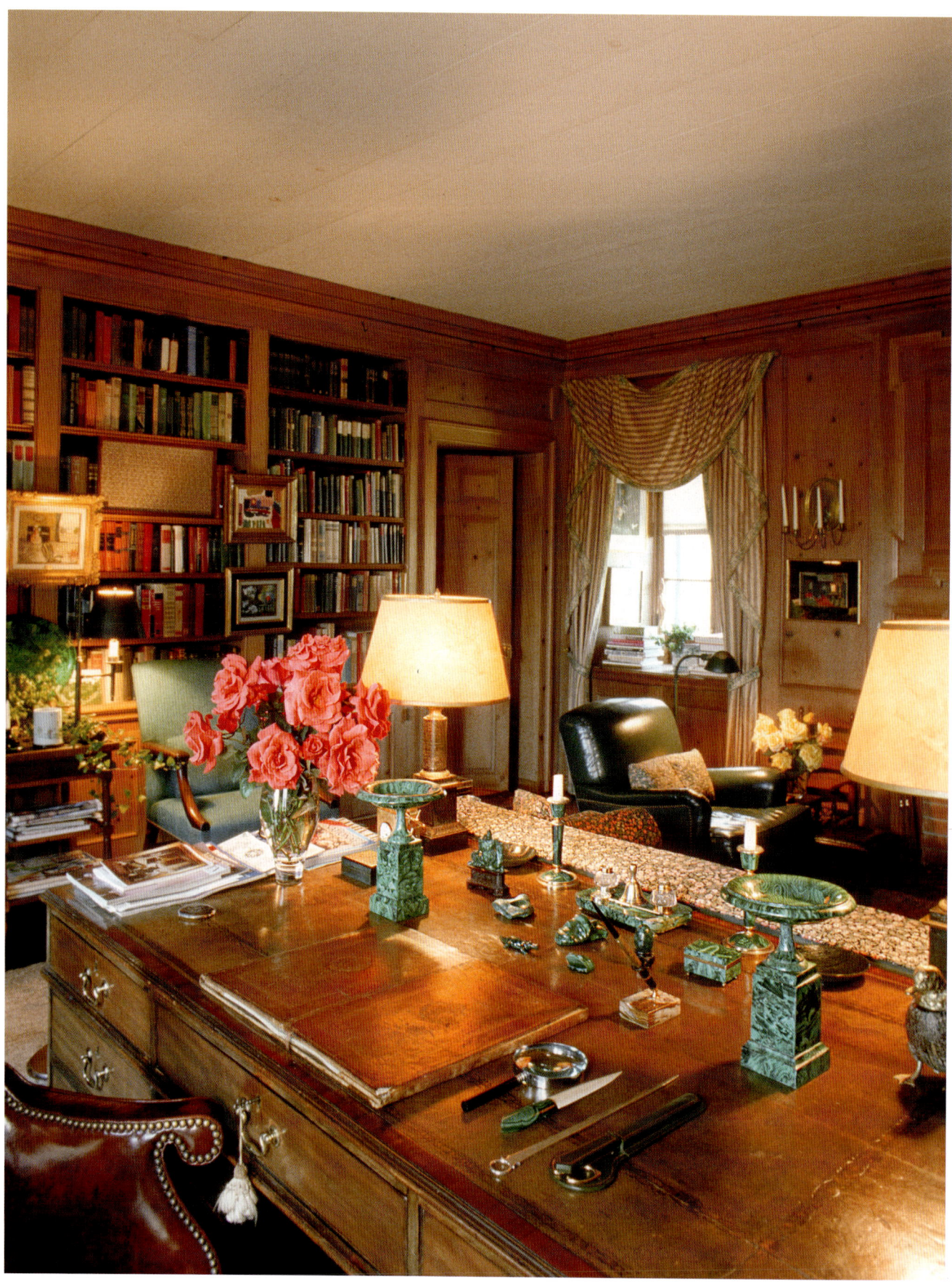

PAGE 219: Hester and Allen Griffin house, Pebble Beach, decorated by Frances Elkins, 1926. Photographed by Lyon in 1983. The black-and-white staircase runner and marbleized paper are forward-looking for their time; the Helen Frankenthaler painting, acquired later, does not look out of place in a space that had been designed decades before. ABOVE: The mahogany partner's desk in the library displays a collection of malachite objects. OPPOSITE: In the living room, Elkins juxtaposed a lacquer screen, pine chests, and a terrazzo-topped coffee table.

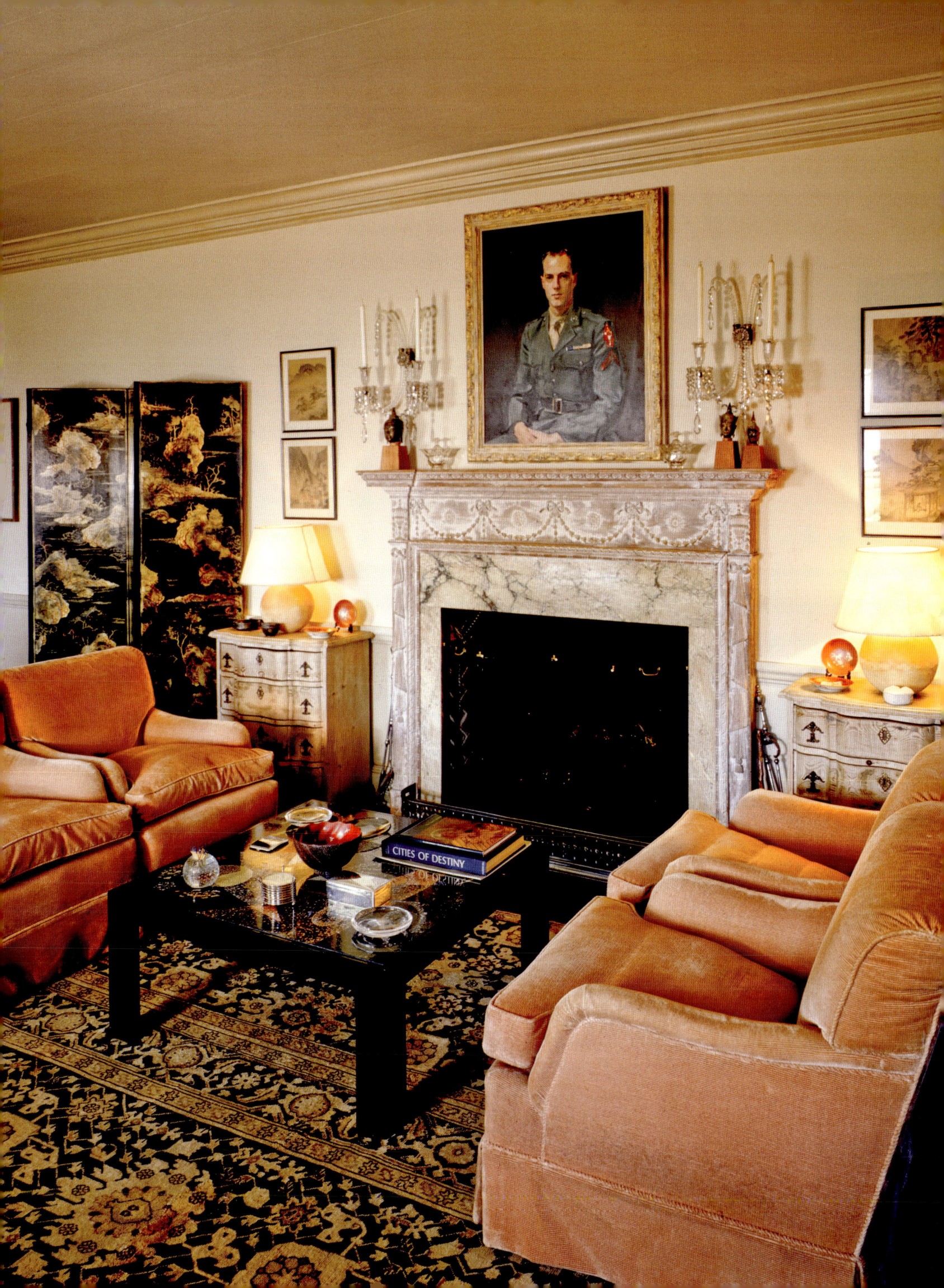

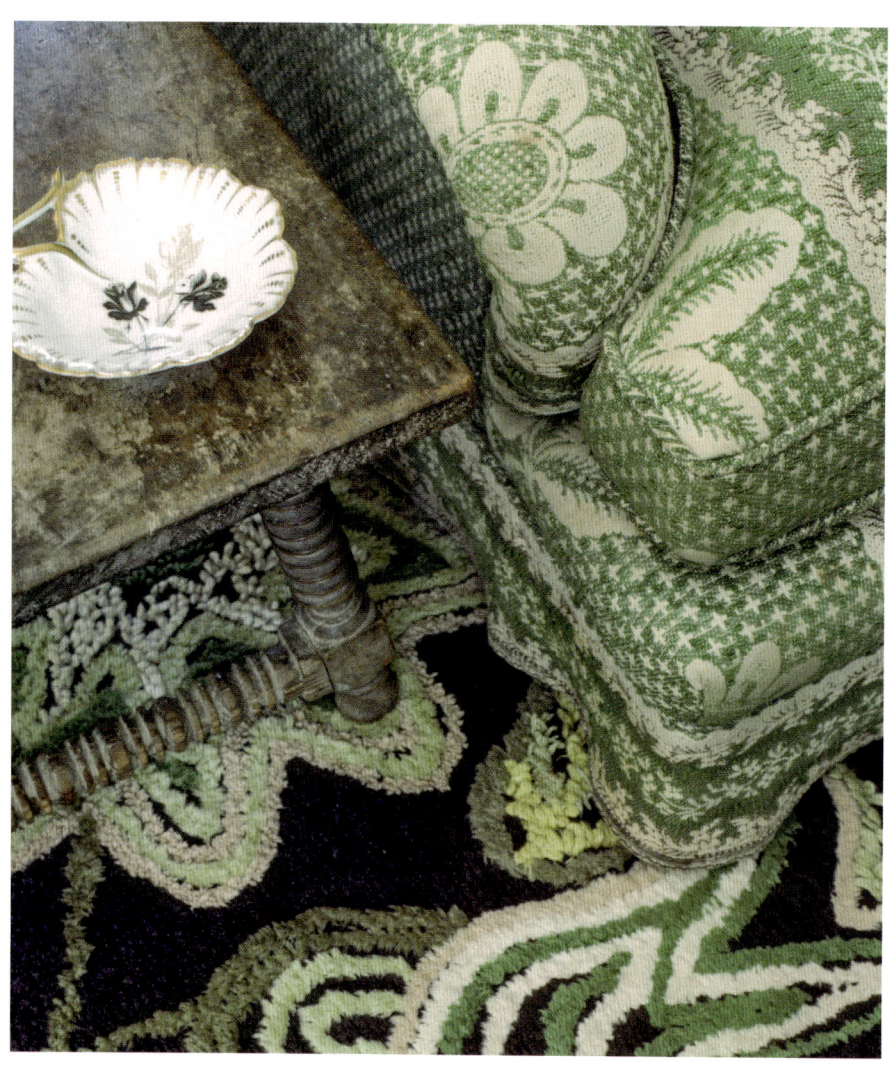

RUTH AND PAUL
WINSLOW HOUSE

Pebble Beach, 1983

This is a handsome house. It was the last project that Frances worked on with her brother, architect David Adler, in 1948. The structure showed Adler's love of symmetry, but it did not look like anything else I remember him doing. Mr. Winslow was no longer alive when I photographed the house in 1983 for *Connoisseur* magazine, but Mrs. Winslow was there. I remember her as a very compact, charming lady.

The house was situated above the Pebble Beach Golf Links and was surrounded by tall woods. Frances and David Adler made it a cheery, upbeat house. I loved that the dining room had red walls. You just knew people had fun here. It was an exuberant place.

—F.L.

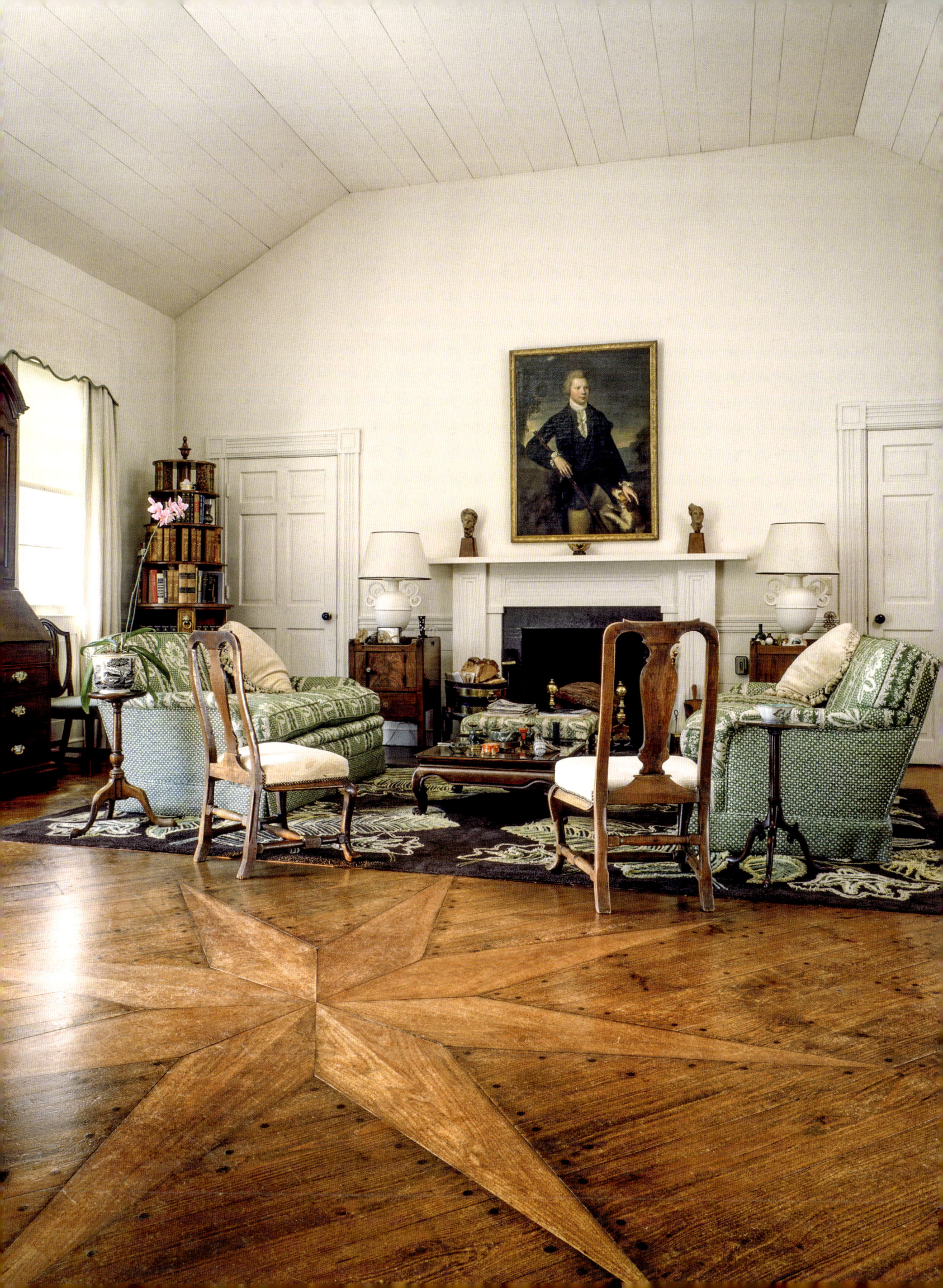

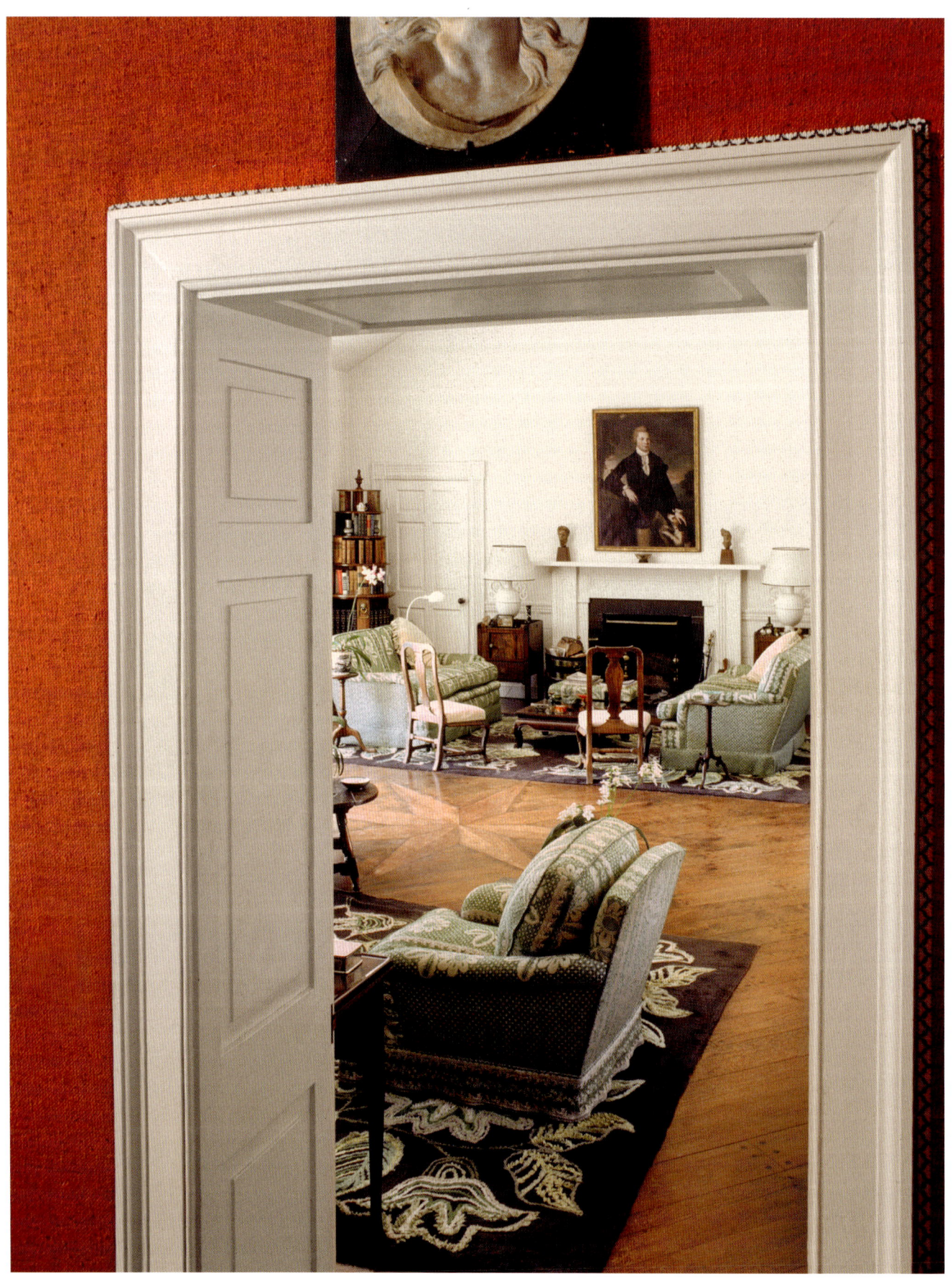

PAGES 222 AND 223: Ruth and Paul Winslow house, Pebble Beach, decorated by Frances Elkins, 1948. Photographed by Lyon in 1983. For the living room, Elkins employed a green-and-white palette. The room's floor features wide pine planks inlaid with a walnut star at its center. ABOVE: A view from the dining room into the living room. OPPOSITE: The dining room's walls were lined with bright red Mexican hopsacking and the curtains made to match. The seats of the English Regency dining chairs were covered in black horsehair.

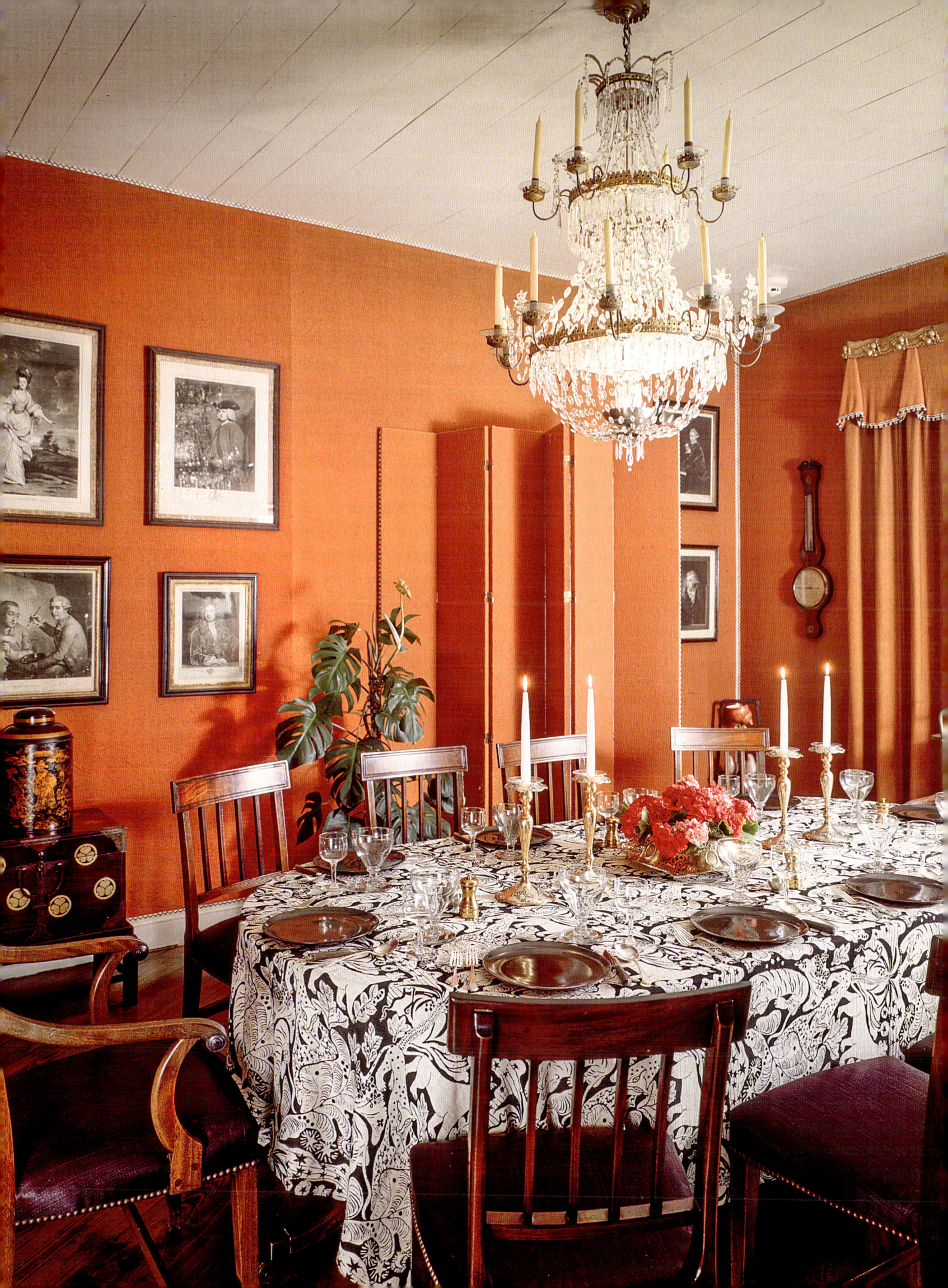

HANA AND JAMES ZELLERBACH HOUSE

San Francisco, 1983

Going to this house was like visiting a museum I had always wanted to see. The front hall was stunning. I recall that much of the plasterwork was by Alberto Giacometti. Even after Frances Elkins was gone, one could locate the casts of many of the plaster pieces she used at Western Art Stone in South San Francisco.

The barroom was a perfect companion to the adjacent card-room. In the bar's seating area was a Jean-Michel Frank water-fall coffee table. Frances used much whimsy in these small spaces—the jaunty silhouettes of the spider chairs and custom couch, the seashell sconces, and the elegant bar stools with hooved feet.

The front hall, barroom, and cardroom strike me as being the quintessence of Frances Elkins's style. I especially enjoy that some of her favorite artists, including Frank and Giacometti, are represented in these rooms. Frances was unafraid to mix and match. The rooms still look as fresh as when she created them in 1937.   —F.L.

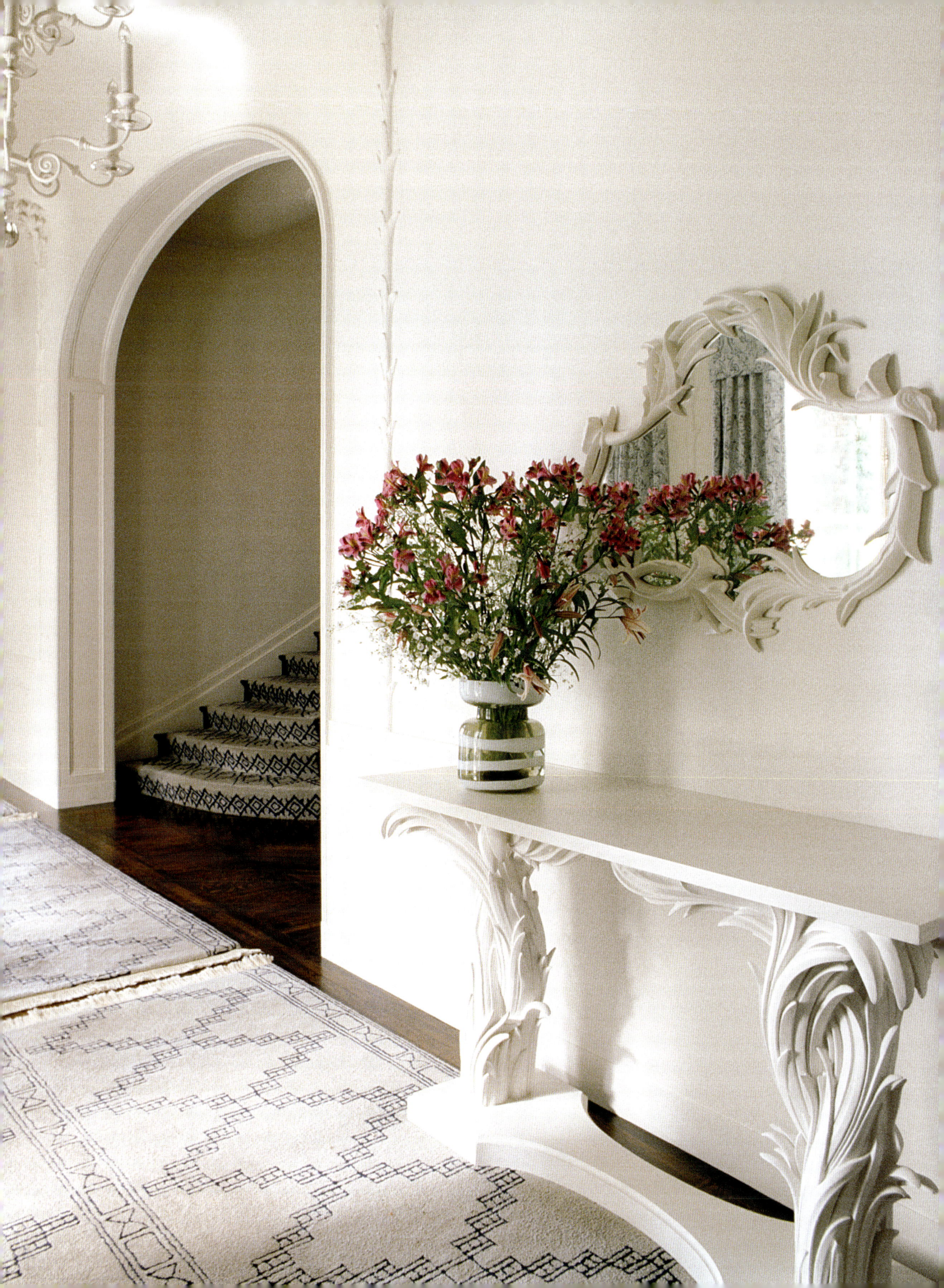

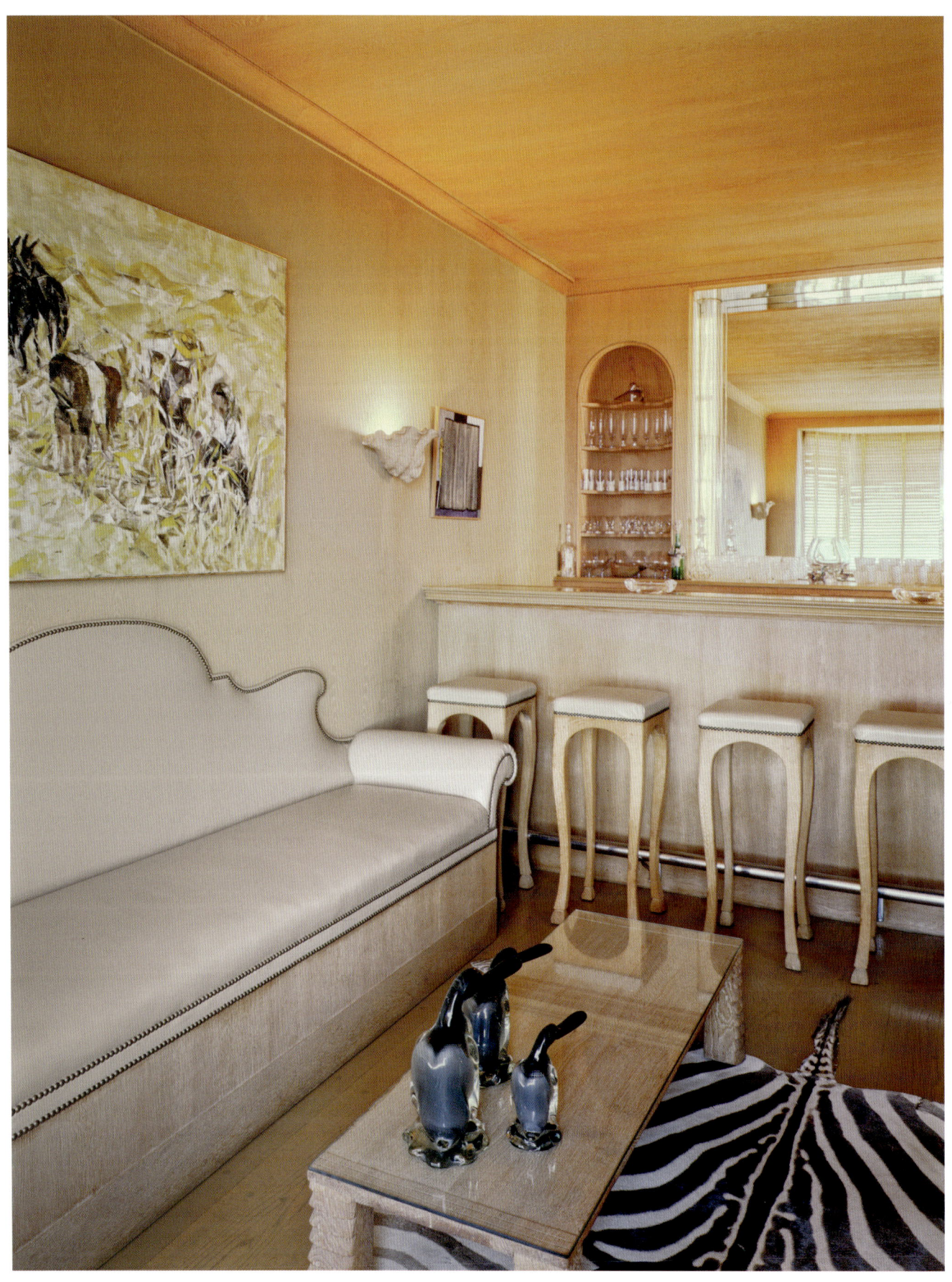

PAGE 227: Hana and James Zellerbach house, Pacific Heights, San Francisco, decorated by Frances Elkins, 1937. Photographed by Lyon in 1983. In the gallery, plaster palms flanking the archway were designed by David Adler; the plaster console and mirror were designed by Emilio Terry for Jean-Michel Frank's shop in Paris. The cotton carpets were Moroccan. ABOVE: The sofa in the bar was designed by Elkins to suggest the English Georgian style. The oak low table was designed by Jean-Michel Frank. OPPOSITE: The cardroom opens off the bar.

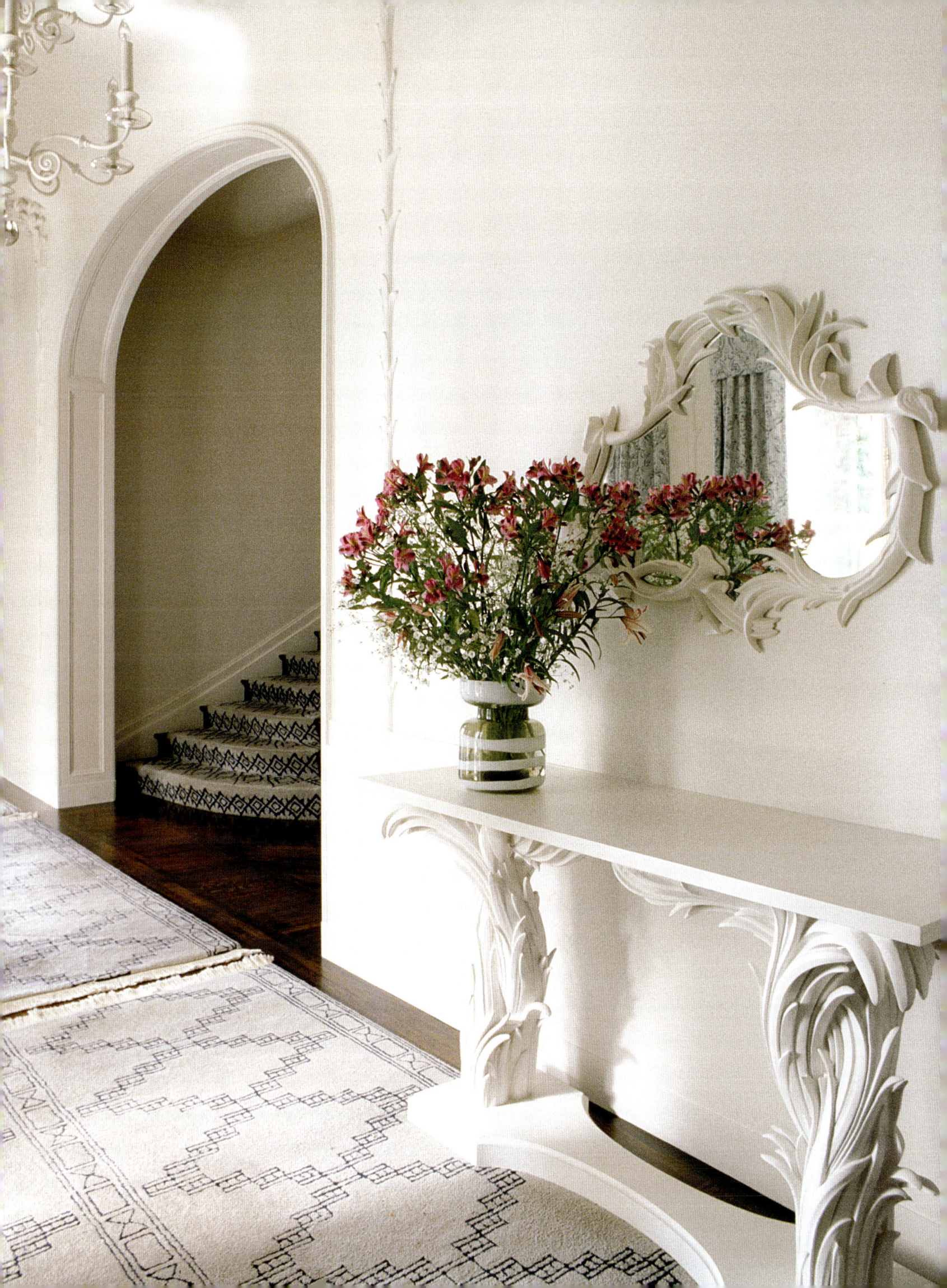

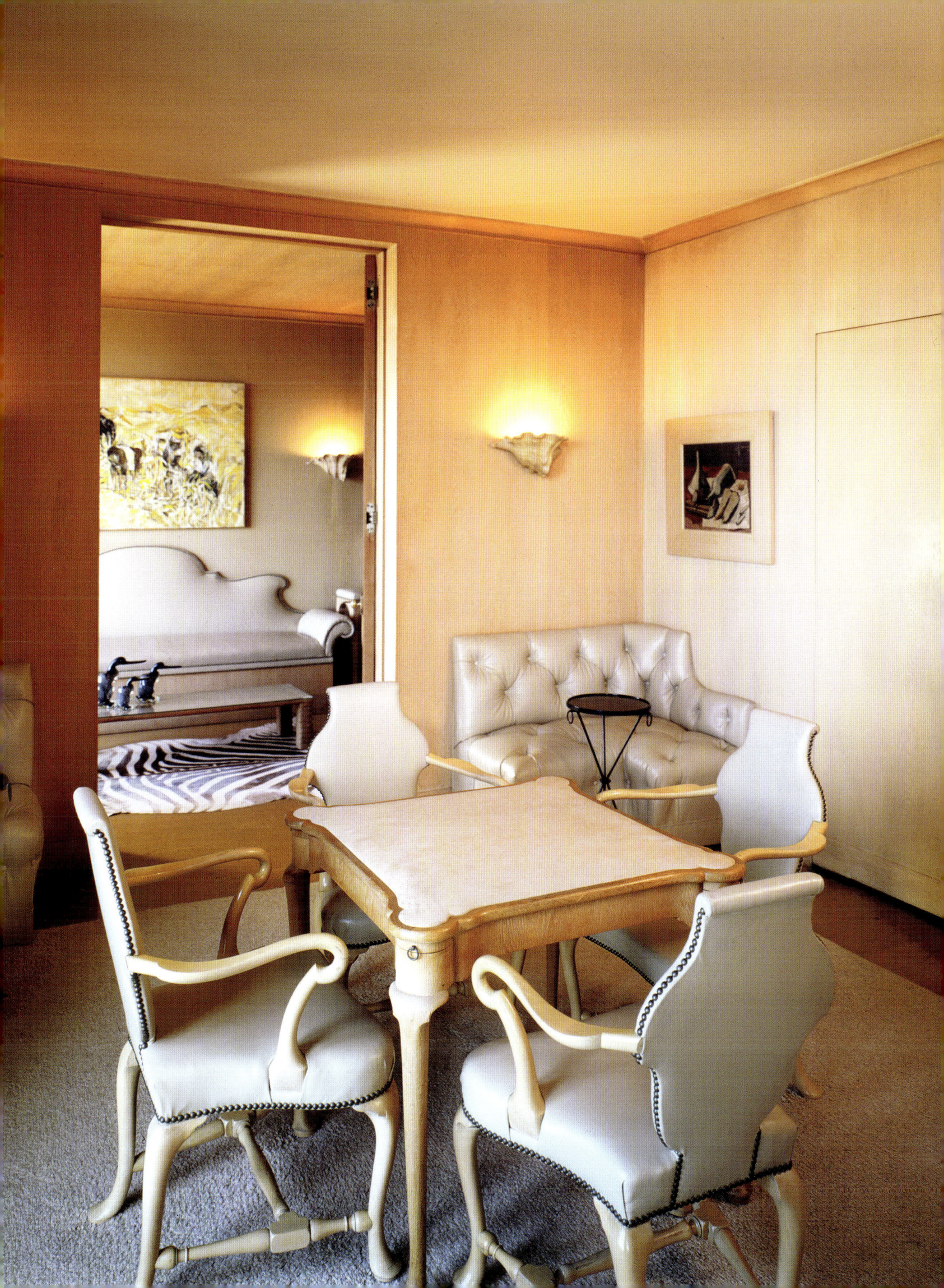

ELIZABETH AND LEON ROOS HOUSE

San Francisco, 1983

Bernard Maybeck designed this house for Elizabeth and Leon Roos in 1909. The three-story residence, located in Presidio Heights, is larger than it appears from the street. I photographed the house a couple of times. Barny Conrad and I were working on a book about the Arts and Crafts architect, but Barny never got around to finishing it. We interviewed Mrs. Roos, who was an elegant lady, in 1974. The photographs here, from 1983, were taken for *Connoisseur* magazine.

The house is a beautiful job of craftsmanship. It features three-to-four-feet-wide panels of redwood, which was a favorite material of the architect. The ornamentation is pure Maybeck, with many pieces of furniture designed by him. The dining room has a relatively low ceiling, to add a feeling of coziness associated with dining. I like this house best of Maybeck's work.   —F.L.

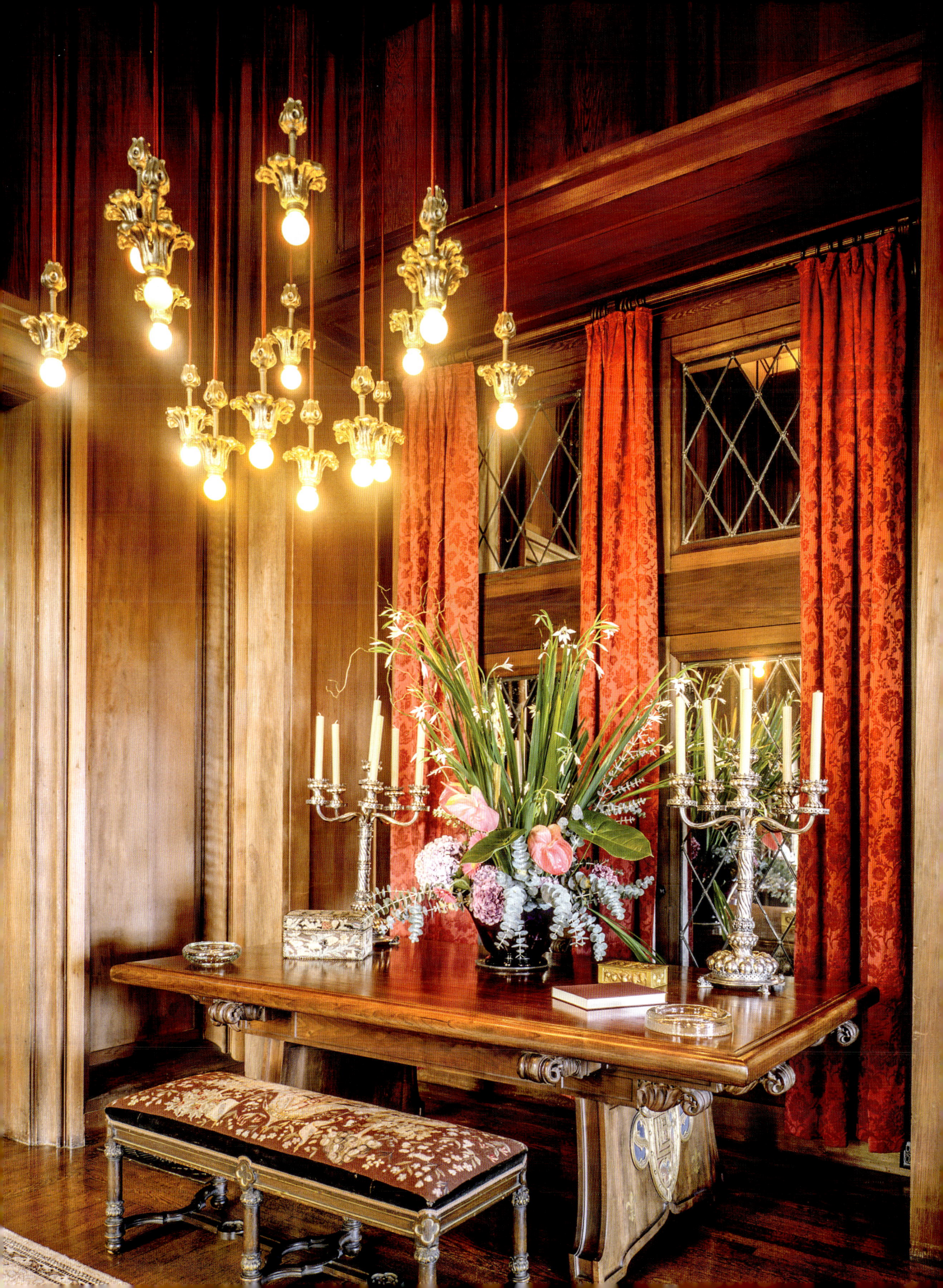

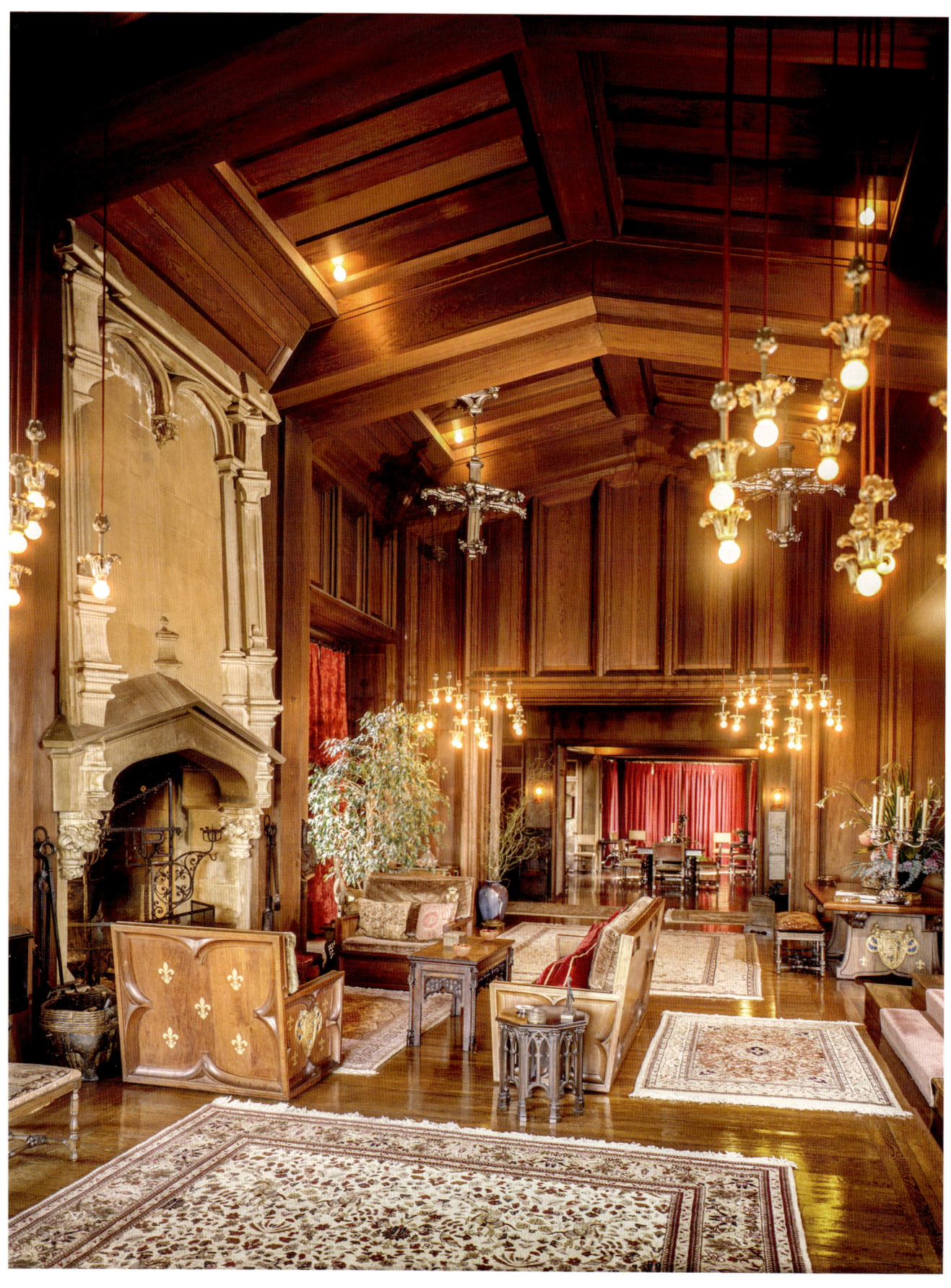

PAGE 231: Elizabeth and Leon Roos house, Presidio Heights, San Francisco, designed by Bernard Maybeck, 1909. Photographed by Lyon in 1983. A corner of the living room. ABOVE AND OPPOSITE: Many of the living room's furnishings—including the light fixtures and seating furniture—were designed by Maybeck.

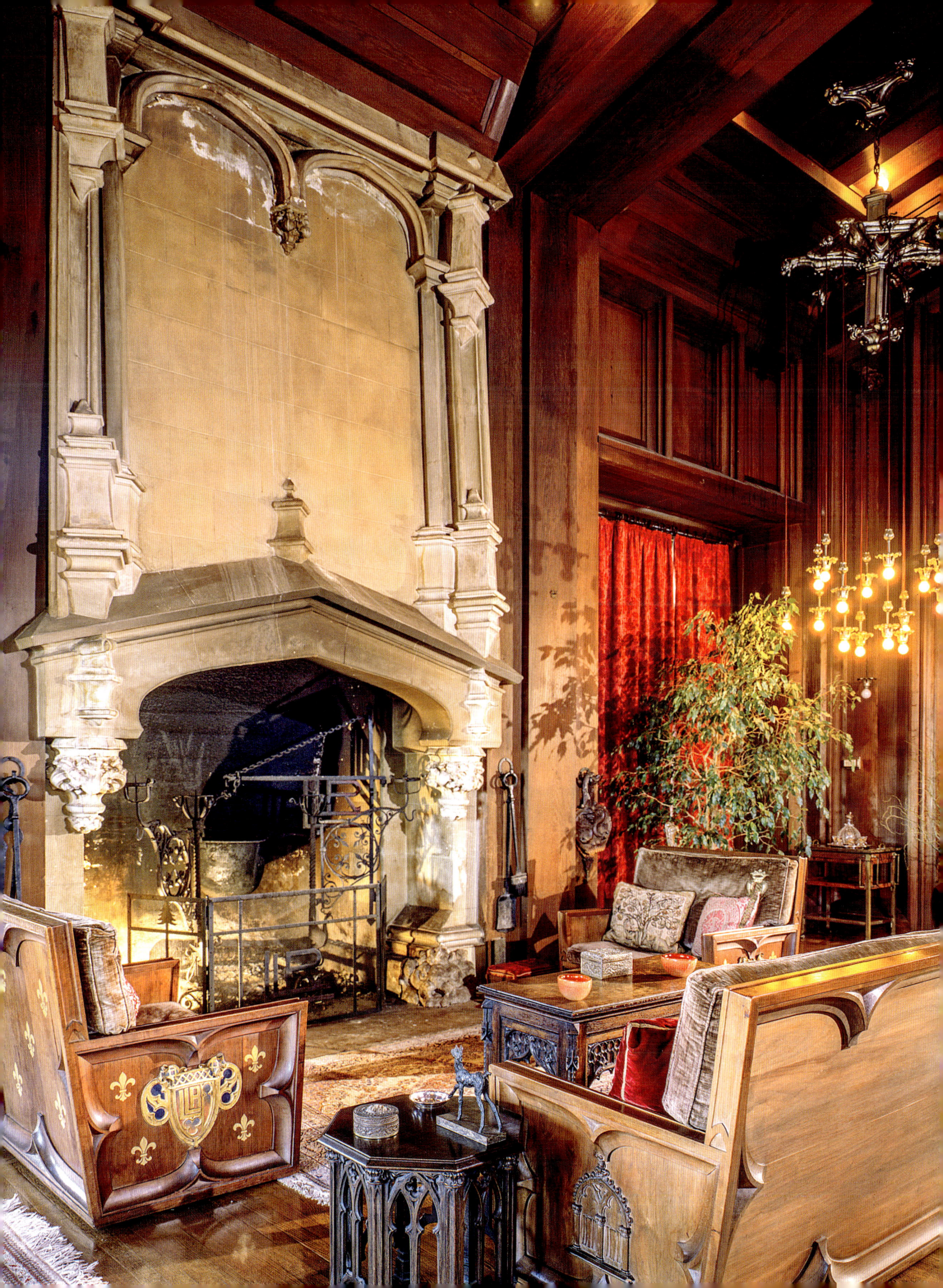

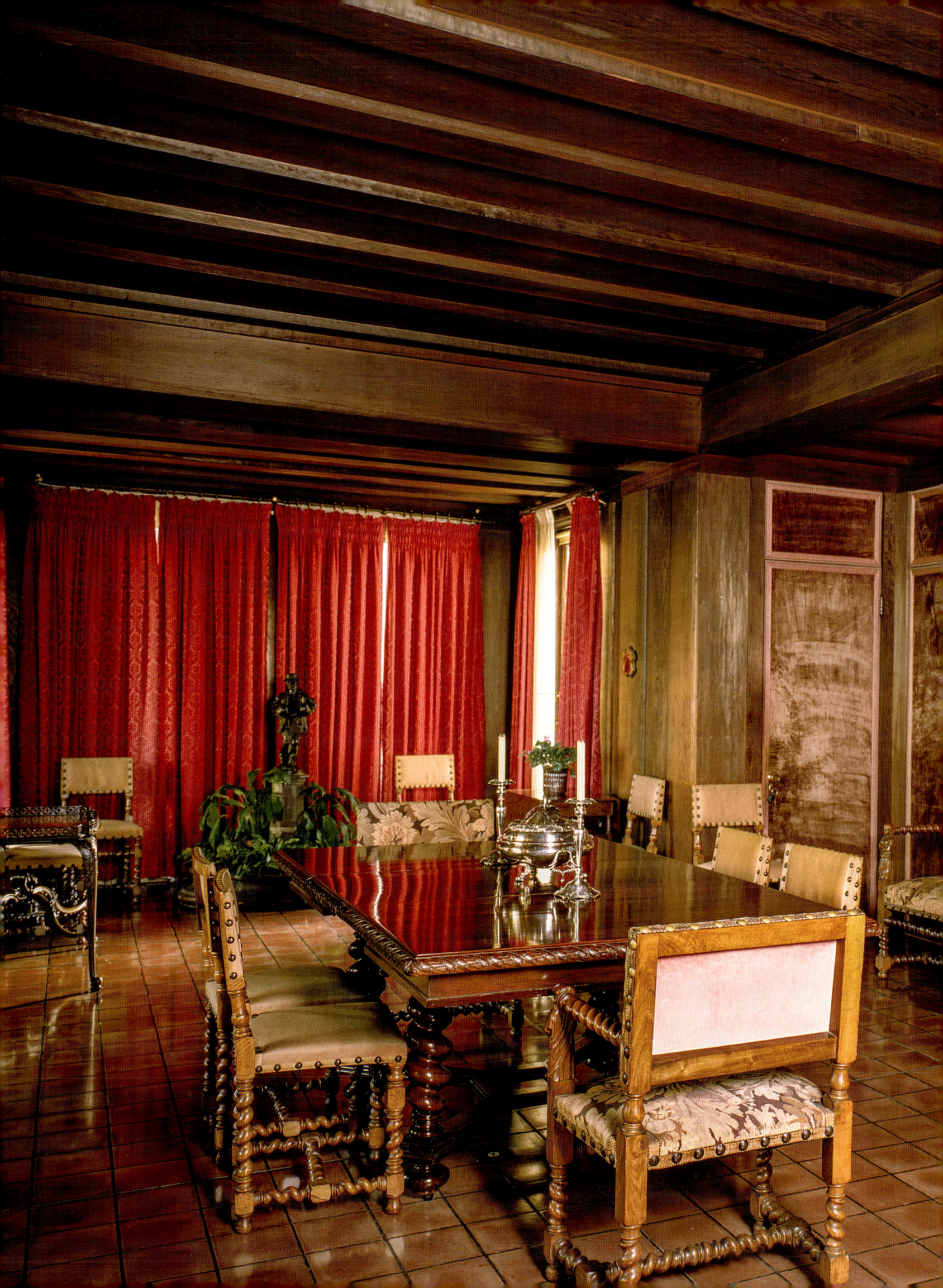

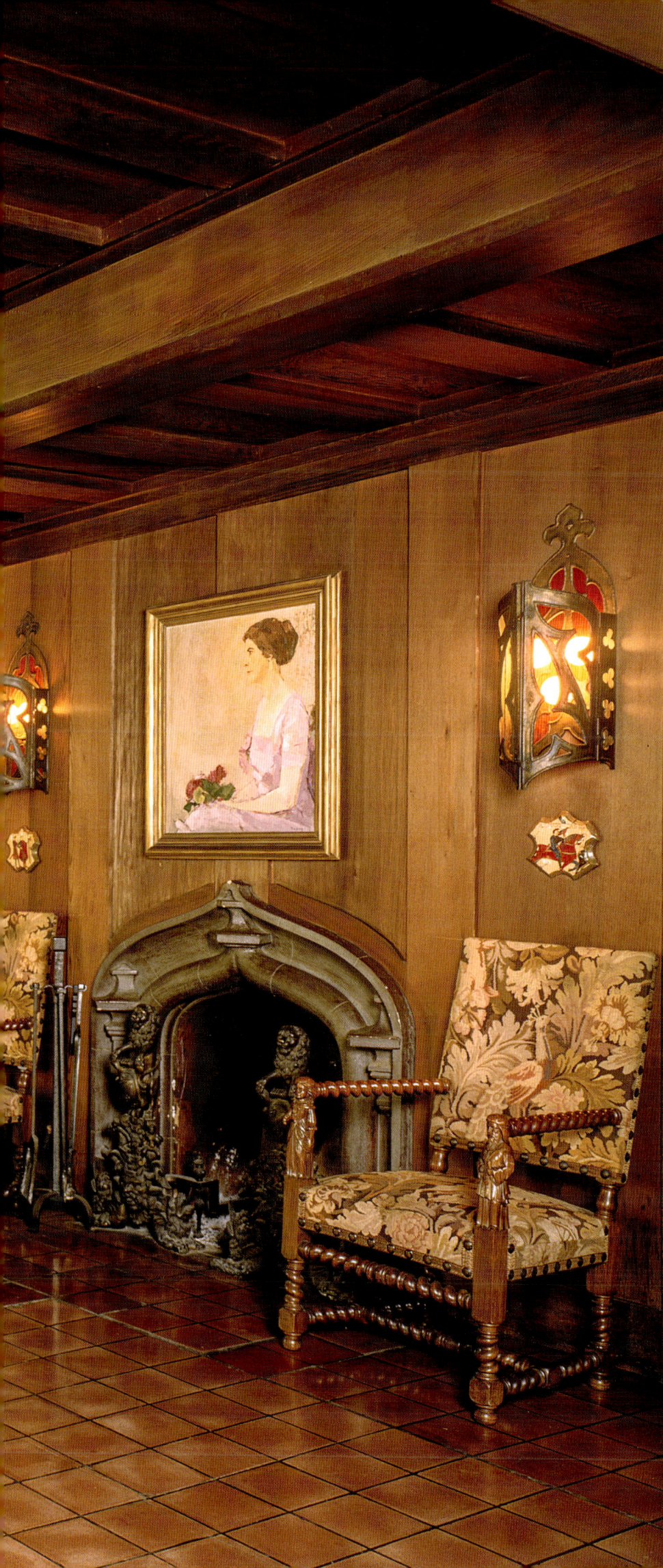

LEFT: View of the dining room.

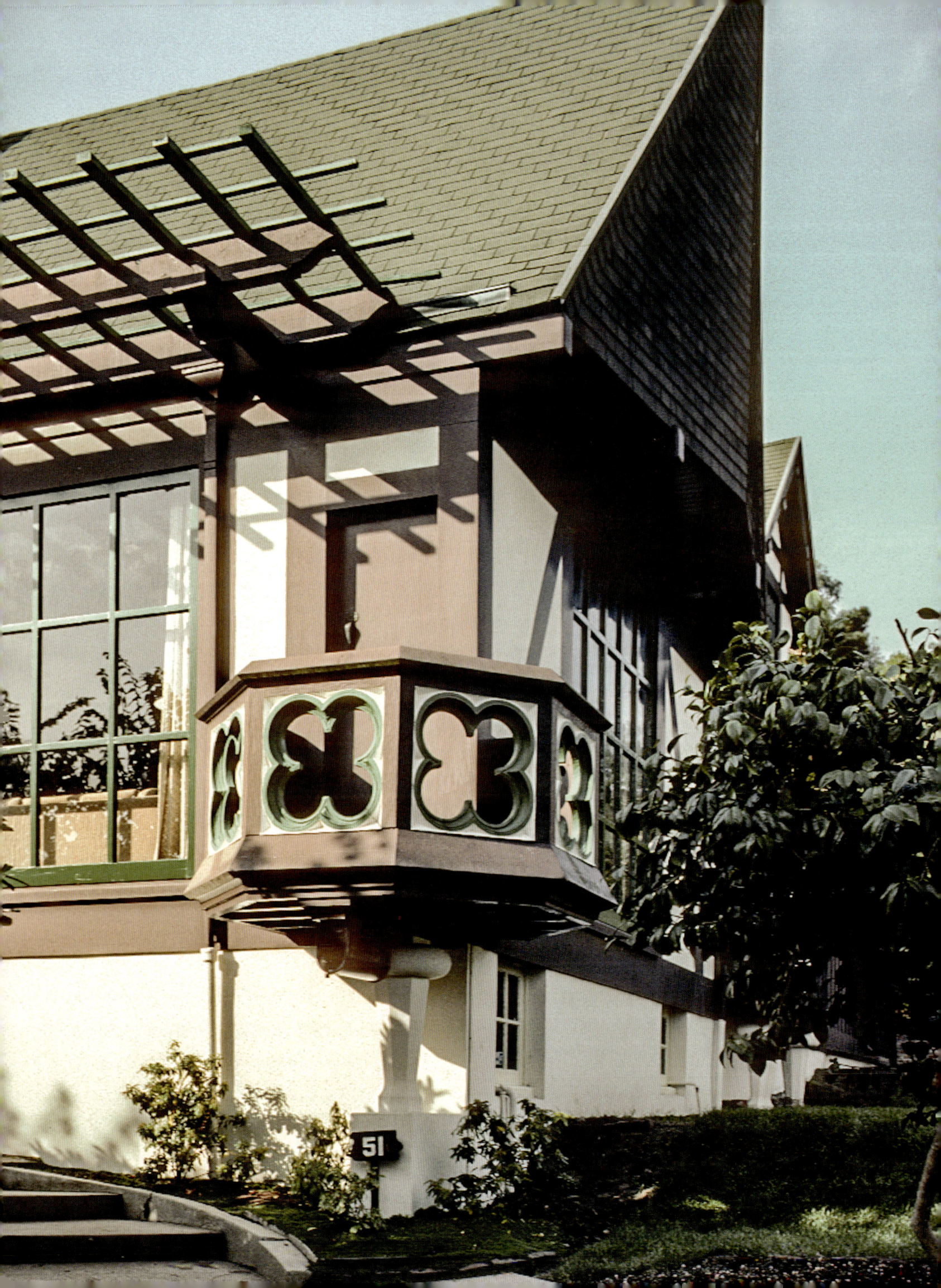

EDWIN C. YOUNG HOUSE
San Francisco, 1983

Bernard Maybeck designed this residence, on a hilltop in the Forest Hill area of San Francisco, in 1913. I photographed the house for a *Connoisseur* magazine story in 1983. The house was built on an east-west axis, which gave the main rooms on the ground floor a southern exposure. The latticework over the tiny exterior deck was a repeated motif in Maybeck's work. Like the Roos house, this structure looks deceptively small from the street.

The living room has a fanciful chandelier, which I think Maybeck designed. There are little oil boats hanging from the fixture's arms. At one time, the boats may have accommodated small candles. If so, they were wildly impractical. I like the ornamentation throughout this house, as well as the lovingly waxed redwood surfaces.   *—F.L.*

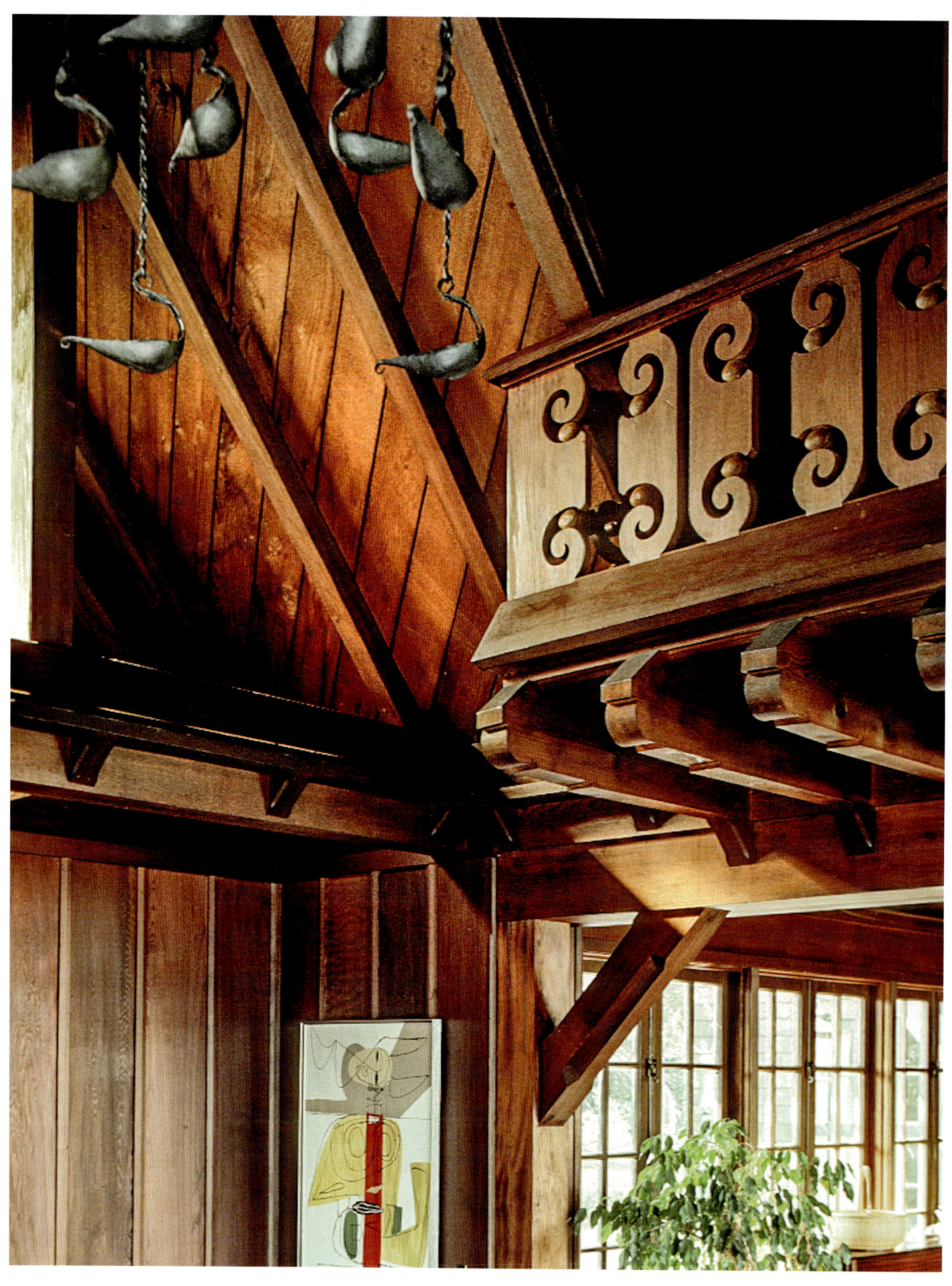

PAGE 236: Exterior of the Edwin C. Young House, Forest Hill, San Francisco, designed by Bernard Maybeck, 1913.
Photographed by Lyon in 1983. ABOVE: Detail of the living room and chandelier, designed by Maybeck.
OPPOSITE: The living room with its large fireplace. This room, like the entire house, is warm, light, and cozy.

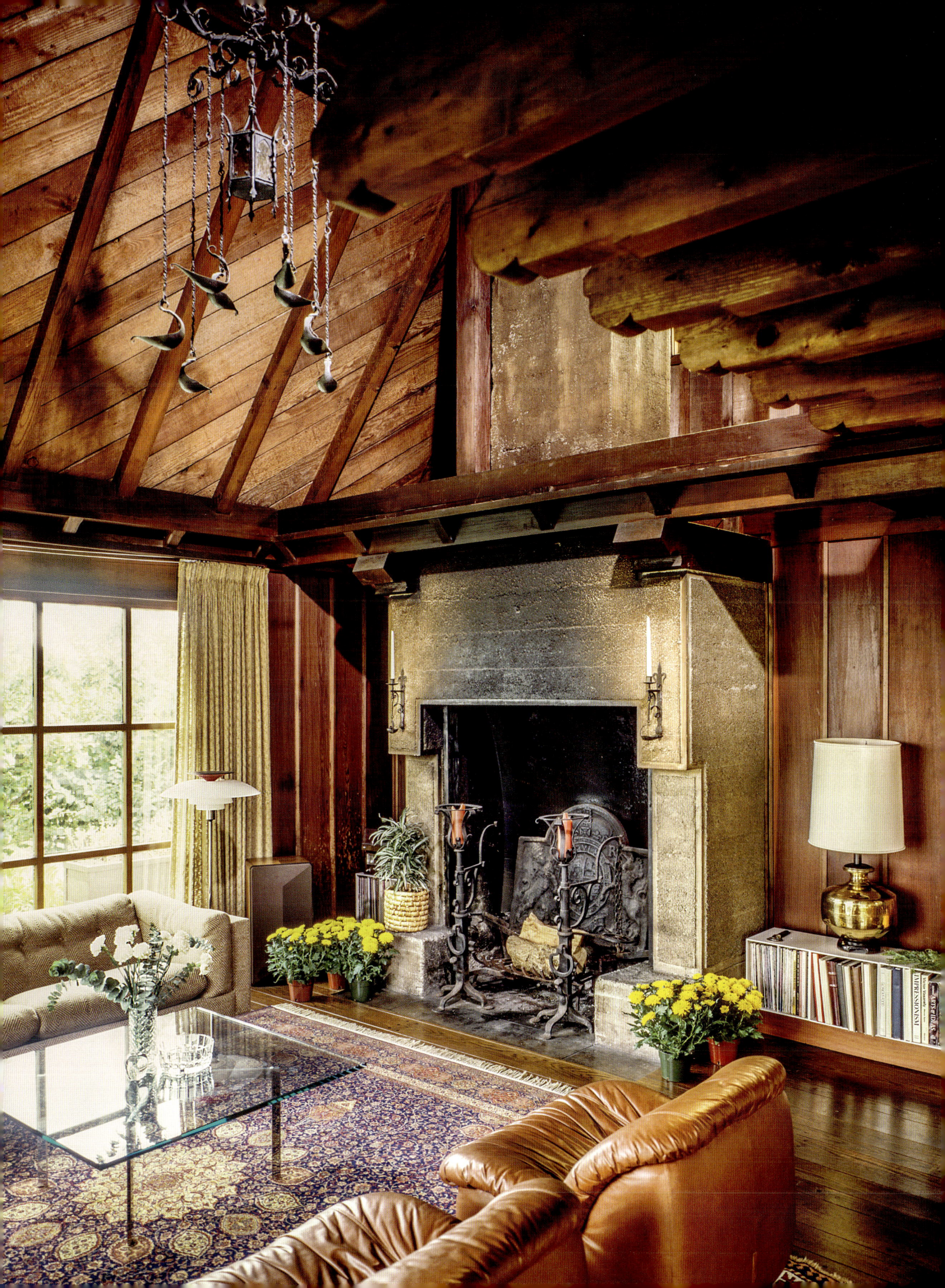

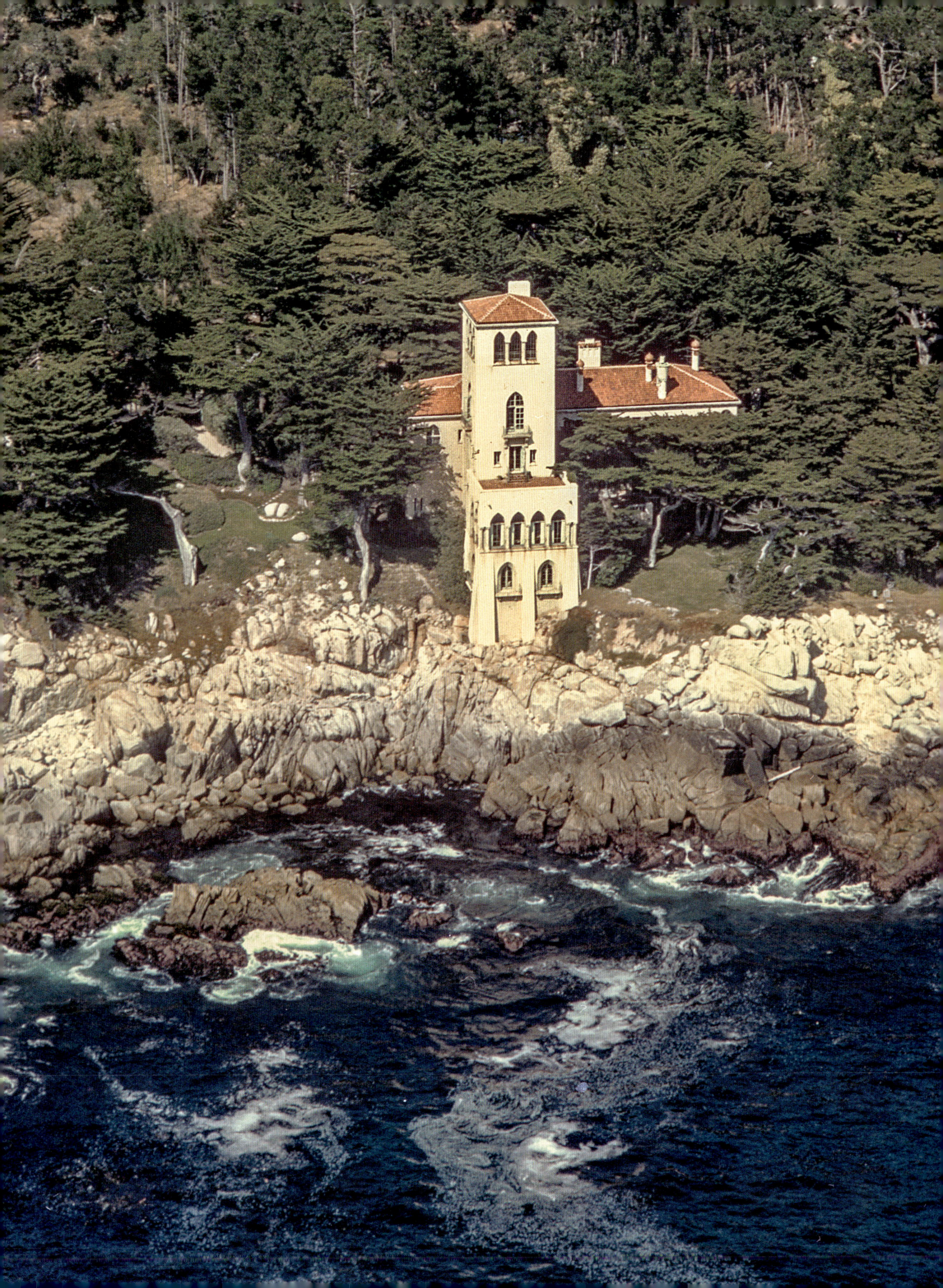

PRIVATE RESIDENCE
Pebble Beach, 1999

This house is located along the famed 17-Mile Drive, which runs between Pebble Beach and Pacific Grove on the Monterey Peninsula. The house was designed by architect Arthur Brown Jr., acclaimed for designing San Francisco City Hall, Coit Tower, and numerous other landmarks in Northern California. Construction began in 1928 and was completed in 1930. Elsie de Wolfe was its first decorator.

The property transports you back in time to an era only available in books now. Whenever I went there, I felt like I was returning to a bygone time that somehow had been left intact. On one visit, I ventured to the tower. Nobody ever went up there. The tower had been used as a gymnasium by the original owner—his old boxing gloves were hanging on the wall. Gymnastic rings still hung from the ceiling. The house has endless views of the Pacific Ocean.   —F.L.

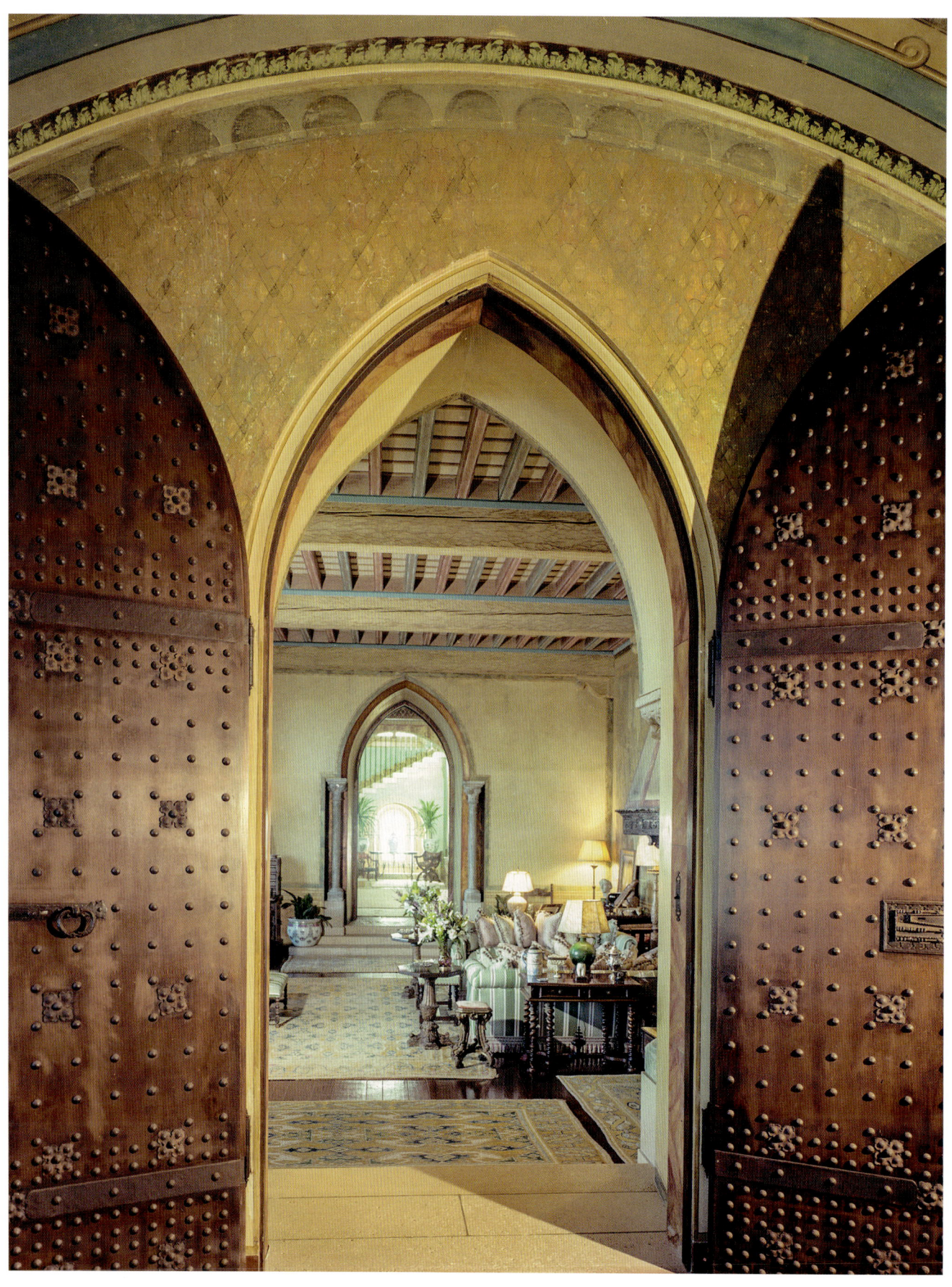

PAGE 240: Aerial view of a Mediterranean-style villa, Pebble Beach, designed by Arthur Brown Jr., 1930. Photographed by Lyon in 1999. ABOVE: View from the dining room through the large central living room, into the entrance hall. OPPOSITE: The living room retains its Gilded Age glamour.

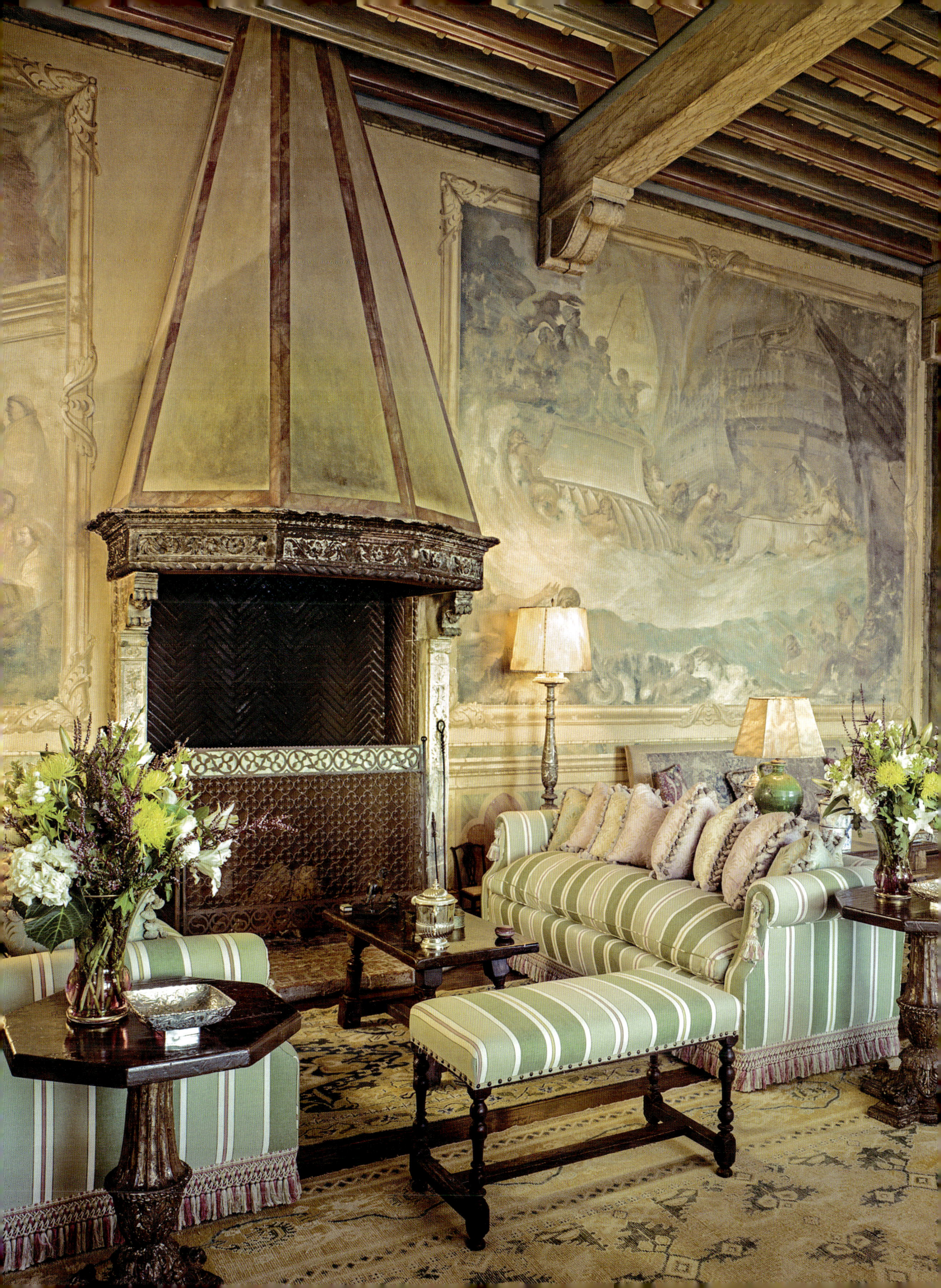

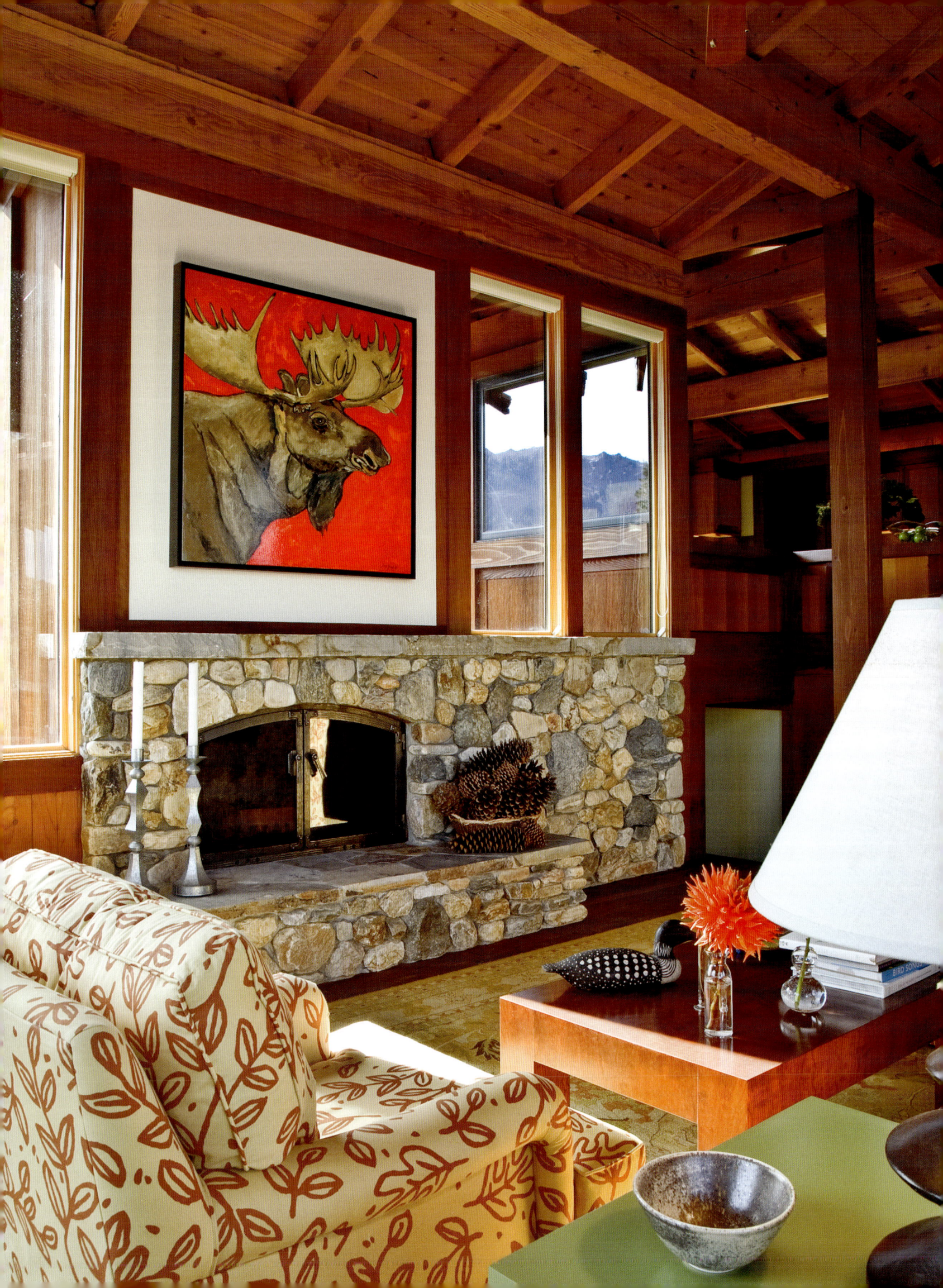

X.
CODA:
New Love and a Return to Interior Photography

n 1989, Anne Lyon suffered a brain hemorrhage at a Christmas party on Nob Hill and died. Columnist Herb Caen reported the news: "If Anne and Fred were there, you knew it was a good party. They were the best looking, the best dressed, the most amusing. . . . Their names were as one. Now there is only Fred."[163] Lyon says, "When Anne died, I was numb. For a while, I pretended to be alive. I went to our Napa house and entertained my sons and their friends and lost myself in the vineyards."[164] Lyon threw himself into his work. By this time, he had drifted away from interior design photography, putting more of his attention to food, wine, and vineyard photography.

In 1992, Lyon and Penny Rozis crossed paths at a memorial service for the partner of a mutual friend. In the twenty years since Lyon had worked with Penny Whelan photographing the Bank of America Building, she had risen through the ranks at SOM, married, and had two children. She joined her old boss at SOM, noted architect and designer Charles Pfister, in his firm. When Pfister died in 1990, Whelan, using her married surname of Rozis, launched her own design practice, taking

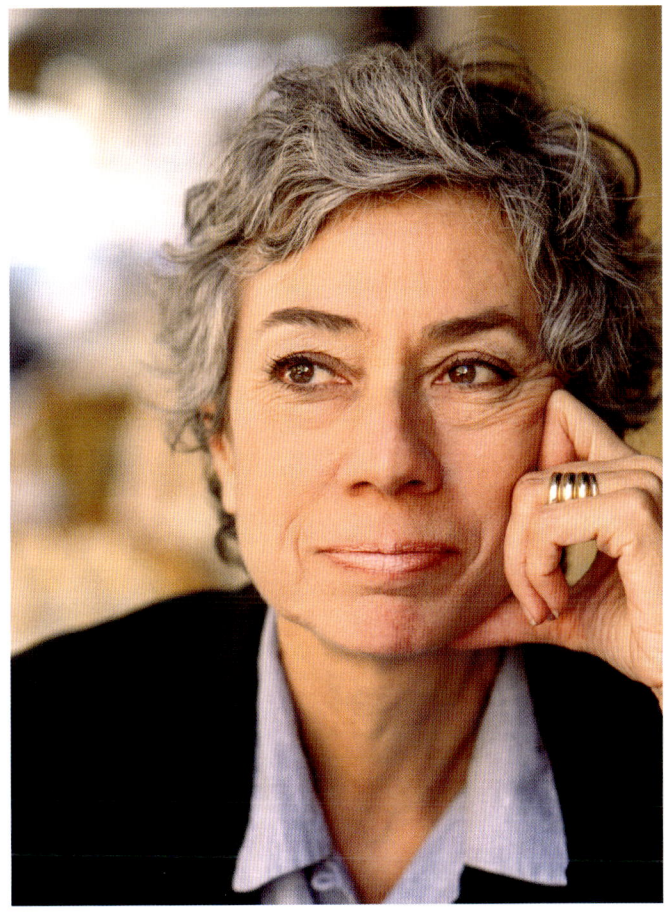

OPPOSITE: Living room of a ski house, Lake Tahoe, designed by Penelope Rozis, 2008. The painting was commissioned from artist Ira Yeager. RIGHT: Lyon's portrait of Rozis, 2000.

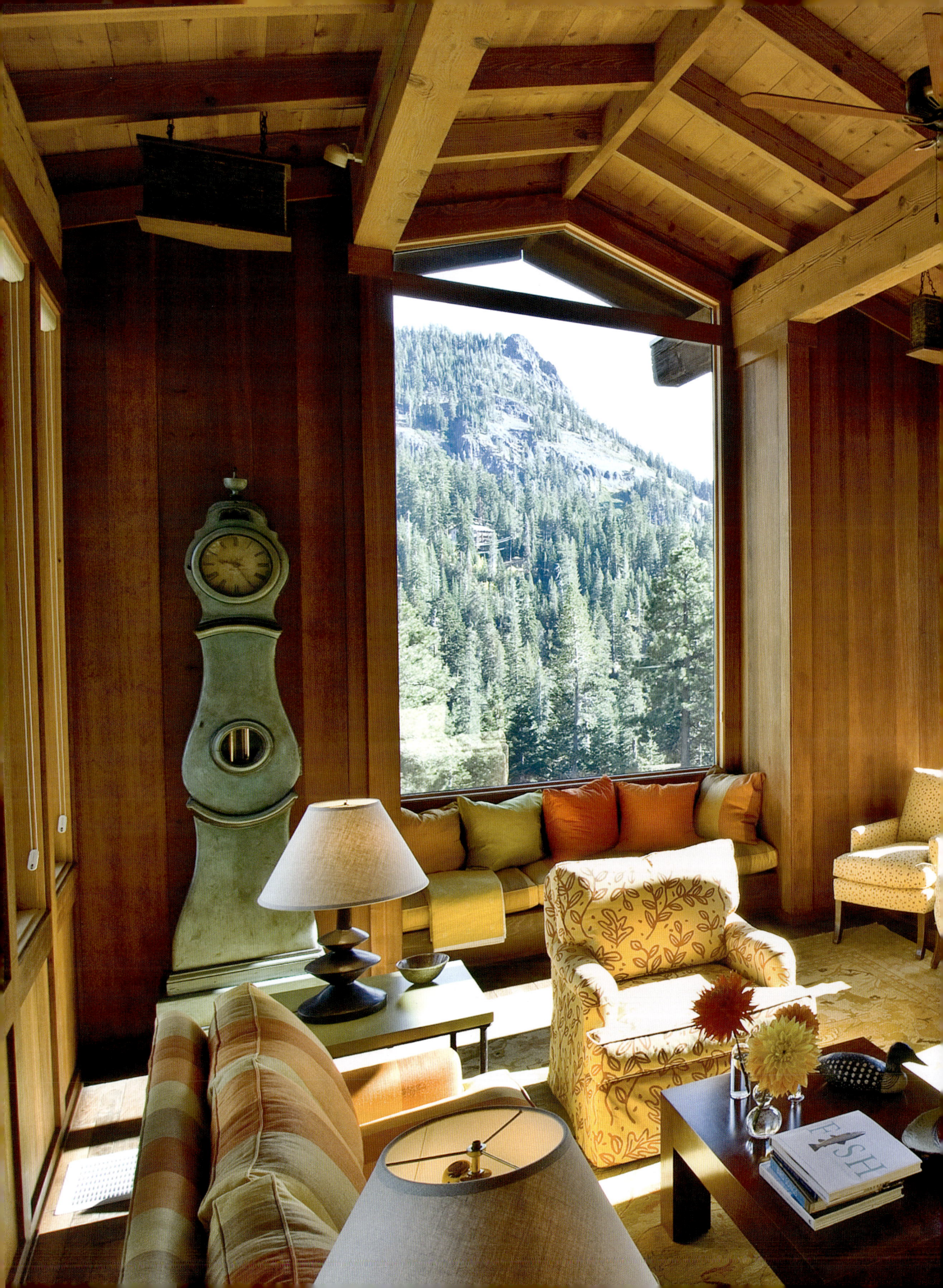

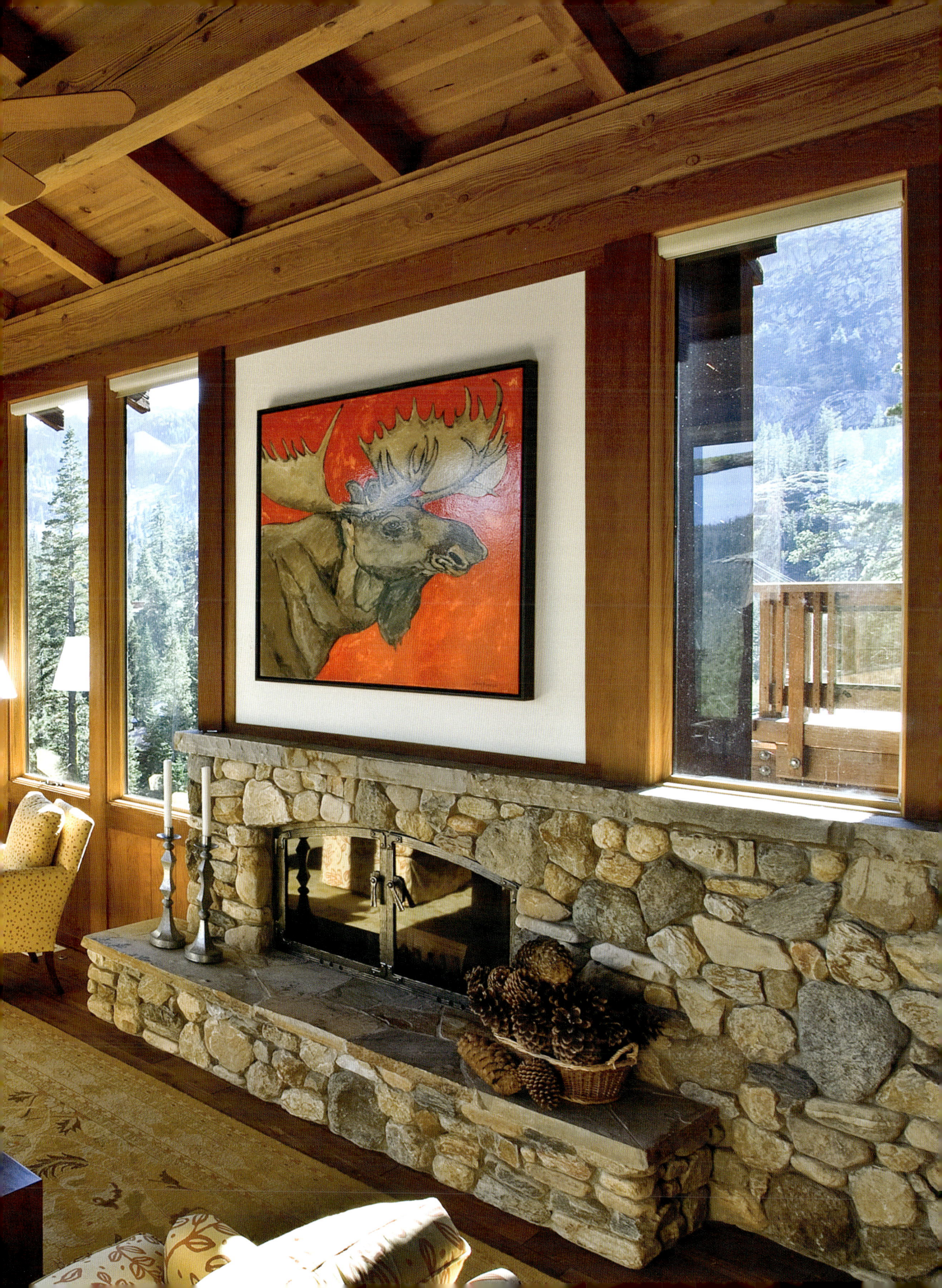

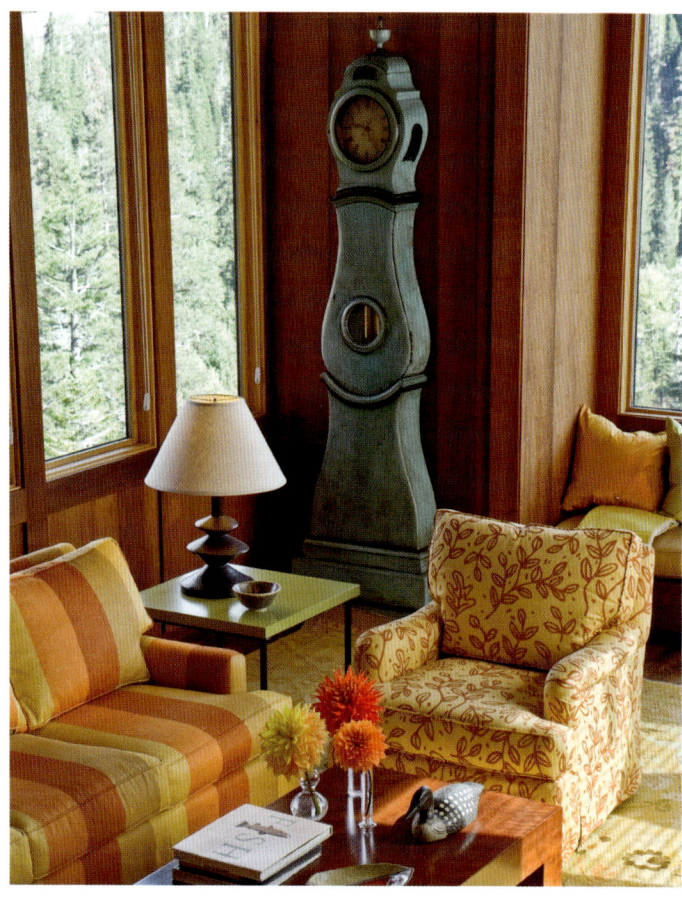

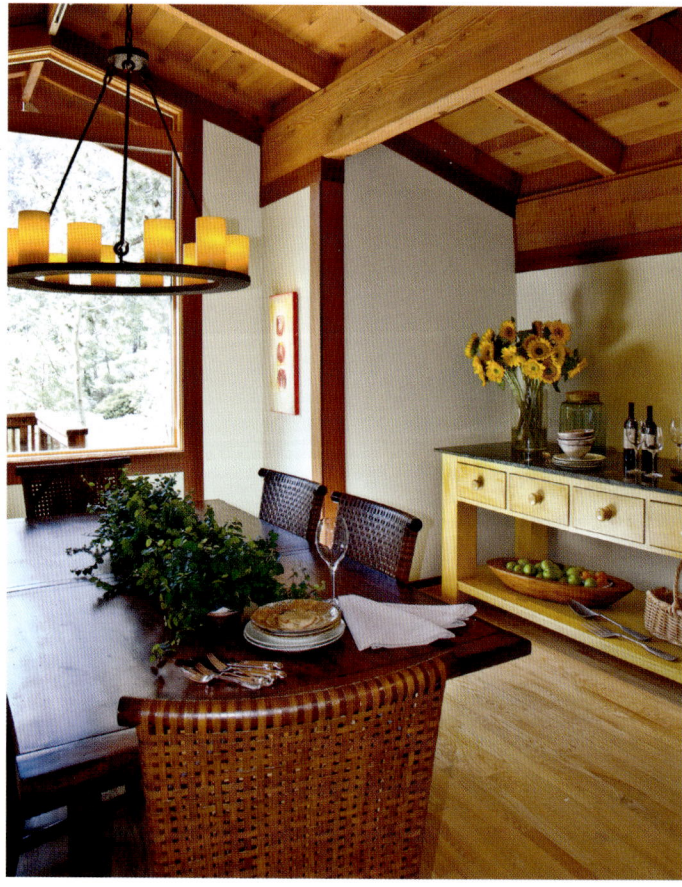

with her several of the clients she had worked with at the shuttered Pfister Partnership.

Their meeting was fortuitous; Rozis had a full roster of clients and needed a photographer. She had considered seeking out Lyon a few years earlier for an assignment, but Charlie Pfister told her he thought Fred was no longer doing interiors. Lyon says, "I got a little burned out on interiors. But after a long while I was getting back into a few. I told Penny to bring me her drawings and we'd discuss it."[165] The designs Rozis showed Lyon of her work looked promising to him, but he says, "It had been twenty years since I had worked in architectural photography, and I was wary about whether I could still do it well."[166] Lyon didn't take a de-

posit for the job. "If working with Penny turned out to be a disaster, at least it would be a contained disaster," Lyon recalls.[167] In part to keep down expenses for Rozis and in part because he did not know how the shoot would go, Lyon did not bring an assistant. The homeowner, Susan Maguire, who was present during the photo shoot, remembers, "Fred was calm, precise, exacting, and meticulous. Also, he was a lot of fun."[168] The job lasted one long day. There were no romantic sparks between Lyon and Rozis that day, but the precursor certainly was there. Lyon recalls, "I had to concentrate, think about the natural light, which is constantly moving, and how best to capture Penny's designs. Shooting a house is a team effort, and Penny was great

PAGES 246–247: The living room has sweeping mountain views. Rozis included Giacometti lamps and a Swedish tall case clock among the comfortable furnishings. ABOVE LEFT: Detail of the living room. ABOVE RIGHT: A farmhouse table dominates the dining room.

to work with. She had everything ready in this very large house. Lots of accessories, flowers—all these things are important in the photography. We were moving furniture to create the best photographs."[169]

Rozis was pleased with Lyon's work. Six months later, she hired him again. Lyon found Rozis to be fun and talented. He was smitten. "I've always been attracted to strong, beautiful women," he says.[170] A little while later, in 1994, Rozis invited Lyon to her fiftieth-birthday party, at the famed "21" Club in Manhattan. Lyon attended. In his late sixties, Lyon had been marking time, but the relationship that they began started to reawaken and inspire him. After Rozis and her husband divorced, she and Fred became a couple. Margo Grant Walsh says, "Penny infused Fred with another life."[171] After living together for several years, the couple eloped to Beverly Hills in 2003. Lyon is direct when speaking about Rozis. In addition to listing her considerable charms and talents, he flatly states, "I am alive today because of Penny. She sacrificed opportunities in order to help me in my career, and she has taken care of me when I needed it most."[172] There are almost twenty years separating the two, but little else. Walsh sees Fred and Penny's relationship as a symbiosis. She says, "Fred married Penny because she inspires him. She created new life in him, and he did the same for Penny. Theirs is the most loving and successful marriage I know."[173]

When Lyon was eighty, he began to revisit material he had shot for himself over the years, following advice he had received in his twenties from his agent Charles Rado. The work had retained and even gained power over the decades. Although he took these images to satisfy himself, Lyon was now ready to share them. He sought the advice of one of the nation's premier fine art photography educators and advisers, Mary Virginia Swanson. When she first encountered Lyon's work, Swanson says, "I was blown away by what I saw. When I came to understand the depth of his archive, and consistency of style and attention to craft, I felt confident that I knew the right fine print dealer to represent him. I called Peter Fetterman and made an introduction."[174] Fetterman, one of the foremost gallerists in the United States, specializes in the work of classic twentieth-century photographers such as Henri Cartier-Bresson, André Kertész, Bill Brandt, Lillian Bassman, and Ruth Bernhard. Swanson sent Fetterman some of Fred's images, and the gallerist was intrigued. Seeing Fred's work, Fetterman knew he was looking at something special. He describes Lyon's qualities as an artist: "Fred has great humanity, deep empathy, and a wonderful eye. When you mix together all of Fred's qualities, you get a cocktail of someone special. Other photographers maybe have one or two of those qualities. It is rare to find someone like Fred who has them all."[175]

It was this combination of taste, technical ability, and affability that made Fred Lyon an effective photographer for some of the best interior designers of Northern California, and that made him welcome in the magnificent rooms of that place and time.

AFTERWORD BY FRED LYON
The Craft beneath the Art

As I scrabbled about, trying to launch a career with a camera, I never aspired to have the title Architectural Photographer. Indeed, my effort was a craftsman's concern for storytelling with attractive images. That's what the magazines were striving for, and I desperately longed for success in those pages. My obsession with beautiful photography dictated my approach to every assignment.

Photographing interiors, I quickly realized the difference in this subject matter from other areas I pursued, such as fashion or sports photography. Unlike all the other subjects, animate and inanimate, that attracted my camera, interiors are the product of an architect, an interior designer, a property owner, a landscape architect, and an array of building tradespeople. Here, my job was to show the architect's or decorator's work to people who would not be able to walk through the rooms and see the work for themselves, so I have always felt strongly that it would be ethically and aesthetically inappropriate for me, or any photographer, to impose a personal style.

My process was not complicated. Large cameras, 4 x 5 and 8 x 10, had been the tradition, but I added roll film, 2 ¼ x 2 ¼ and 35 mm, from my work in fashion and sports. Happily, my early experience with color film and artificial lighting gave me a competitive advantage at that crucial moment. I discovered that moving the camera to the optimum viewpoint is the key to composition. Learning to work quickly allowed opportunities for my favorite "what if?" variations and experiments. I liked to work fast and in natural light if I could, but I was not afraid to use my own lighting if the subject needed it.

For anyone dreaming of pursuing this field, be prepared for long hours of hard work. Try to bring an innocent and receptive eye. A sense of humor couldn't hurt. And wear comfortable shoes.

OPPOSITE: Chuck Ashley, photograph of Fred Lyon in action with his Hasselblad camera, 1957. Ashley was one of Lyon's assistants.

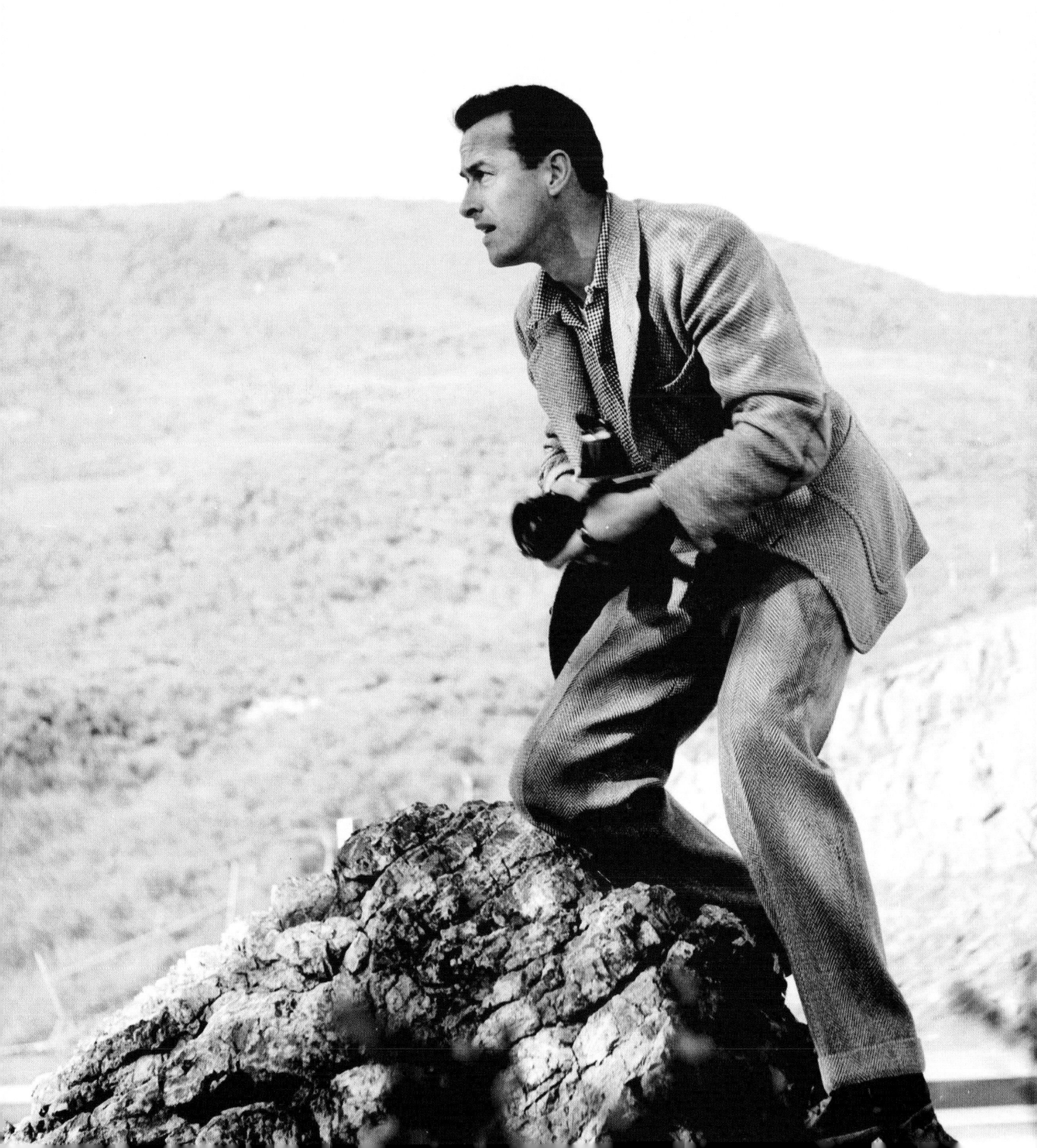

ACKNOWLEDGMENTS

This book started from a chance encounter I had with a Fred Lyon image about ten years ago. One day I stumbled across a photograph, *Man Walking on Pine Street* (1954); see page 256. The photo was credited to Fred Lyon. I had not heard of him. The angle of the street is so steep that the adjacent sidewalk is a concrete staircase, the midcentury cars parked perpendicular to the curb and atilt from gravity, and the confident yet relaxed stride of the man at the bottom of the frame with his porkpie hat set at a subtly jaunty angle capture so much of what I love about San Francisco. This was my gateway photo into Fred Lyon's work.

To learn more about his photography, my wife, Marjorie Qualey, and I read Fred's previous books and attended his shows and talks at the Harvey Milk Photo Center and the Leica Gallery in San Francisco. Later, we got to know personally Fred and his wife and muse, the interior designer Penelope Rozis. They are a talented and charming couple who work and play together like newlyweds. Spending time with Fred and Penny is like participating in a master class in living well.

Many people helped me write this book. I am grateful to Stephen M. Salny, an authority on the work of the designers Frances Elkins, Michael Taylor, and others, and on interior design in general, who was unstinting in helping me learn about his areas of expertise and sharing his enthusiasm for Fred's work. Also, Steve introduced me to Scott Powell, a design historian who, like Steve, was generous sharing his knowledge with me. Another expert who was instrumental in

helping with this project is the design author Diane Dorrans Saeks. Diane has written numerous books on interior design, architecture, travel, and style. Diane personally knew some of the designers discussed in this book and of course knows Fred well.

In doing research for this book, I spoke to several people who worked with Fred. Some have been friends or clients or both of Fred's for decades. The appreciation each has for him as a person and for his work was palpable in my interviews with them. These are Ali Banks, who hired Fred for important wine and vineyard photography later in his career; entrepreneur Charles Crocker, Fred's longtime friend and co-winemaker for a time; Susan Maguire, a friend and client of Penny's and owner of the first houses Fred shot for Penny; magazine editor Ann Sonet, who worked with Fred and after a shoot went with him and his first wife, Anne, to see Janis Joplin at Fillmore West in 1967 (what a night that must have been); architect John "Sandy" Walker, who is a longtime friend of Fred's and Penny's and who worked with many of the artists discussed in this book; noted interior designer Margo Grant Walsh, who has been an influential leader in corporate interior design; and philanthropist Dede Wilsey, who has long known Fred, hired Michael Taylor, and has good stories about both.

As somebody who enjoys twentieth-century photography in particular, a bonus for me in researching this book has been getting to interview many knowledgeable figures in that world. I am grateful to them for sharing their thoughts about Fred's work and twentieth-century photography. These are Professor Nadya Bair and Professor Kim Biel, who are members of a new generation of scholars in photography and history; talented artist and writer Jonathan Blaustein; the influential gallerist Peter Fetterman; filmmaker Michael House (look for his wonderful movie about Fred titled *Fred Lyon: Living Through the Lens*); artist Alex Ramos and his colleagues at the Leica Gallery in San Francisco; educator and photography adviser Mary Virginia Swanson, who provided Fred and me with valuable guidance and who, along with her husband, Hal Strich, read and commented on an early draft; art director and stylist Sara Slavin; and photographer Laurel Thornton, who has worked with Fred for many years and was instrumental in preparing the photographs in this book.

Fred has published books about other aspects of his career. The team behind those books kindly shared with me their valuable insights into his work. These are book designer Ben English; editor Jennifer Thompson; and publisher and photography collector Nion McEvoy.

Fred's career began when he was quite young. Jean Moulin, a daughter-in-law of the late Gabriel Moulin, shared her memories of the Moulin Studios, where Fred worked as a teenager. Remarkably, the high school yearbook that contains some of Fred's earliest work is digitized and was provided to me by Burlingame High School principal Paul Belzer and teacher Michelle Riley. Art Center librarian Cathy Folgate shared with me important material from the college's archives.

Gordon Lyon, Fred's younger son, shared stories about Fred as a dad and travel companion (spoiler alert regarding both: he is fun). Interior designer Janet Bland, who studied under Rudolph Schaeffer, read and commented on an early version of this text. I had looked forward to presenting this book to my friend and decor enthusiast Constance Eleanor Hawkins, but alas cannot.

As with all of my books so far, I owe thanks to the wonderful San Francisco Public Library and especially the Marina Branch for the deep collection and friendly service there.

Any book is a collaboration between author, editor, publisher, and book designer. I have been lucky to work with an outstanding editor, Philip Reeser, and Rizzoli International Publications, a leader in art, design, photography, and fashion publishing. Their range of expertise and good taste mirrors Fred's. Book designers Doug Turshen and Steve Turner took my text and Fred's wonderful photographs and stories and made them dance as a book. Thanks also to art historian Jared Goss for his insightful foreword. Additional thanks to Cynthia Cathcart, Marianne Brown, and Cole Hill for support and research at Condé Nast and to Richard Slovak for copy editing.

I have been lucky to have a supportive and fun family: Edward, Grace, Robert, Sara, Robbie, Juliana, Marjorie, Caitlin, Kristen, and Scarlett. Most of all, thanks are due to my wife, Marjorie, not least because she is patient when I say "hang on a tick" while I stop to take some street picture. Fred and I dedicate this book to her and Penny.
                                                —*Philip E. Meza*

ENDNOTES

1   Email, Fred Lyon to Philip E. Meza, August 17, 2021.

2   See Philip E. Meza text in this volume, 36.

3   Suzanne Slesin, "A California Touch in New York," *New York Times*, March 20, 1980, C1. In his 1986 obituary in the *Los Angeles Times*, Taylor was given credit for his "innovative 'California Look.'" Burt A. Folkart, "Known for Innovative Style: 'California Look' Design Guru Dies." *Los Angeles Times*, June 6, 1986. Slesin's wording and definition were adopted for Taylor's obituary in the *New York Times*, although writer Carol Vogel called it the "California style" rather than the "California Look." Carol Vogel, "Michael Taylor Is Dead at 59; Innovative Interior Designer," *New York Times*, June 5, 1986, B16.

4   See Philip E. Meza text in this volume, 42.

5   Albert Hadley, foreword to *Frances Elkins: Interior Design*, by Stephen M. Salny (New York: W. W. Norton, 2005), 7.

6   Interview with Stephen M. Salny, November 28, 2020.

7   From the quatrain by John Collins Bossidy: "And this is good old Boston, / The home of the bean and the cod, / Where the Lowells talk to the Cabots, / And the Cabots talk only to God."

8   The Burlingame High School 1941 yearbook looks like a high school version of *Take Ivy*, the cult classic study of Ivy League campus fashion. Fred reports that he did all the photography and design for this yearbook and remains proud of it eighty years later.

9   Interview with Fred Lyon, February 5, 2020.

10   Kevin Starr, *The Dream Endures: California Enters the 1940s* (New York: Oxford University Press, 1997), 9.

11   https://www.moulinstudios.com/about/.

12   Ibid.

13   Starr, *Dream Endures*, 239.

14   See *104 Years of Experience*, Art Center School catalog (1931), unpaged, https://archives.artcenter.edu/uploads/r/art-center-college-of-design-archives-4/e/3/e3920bbdd893e01a2bf9c8aa8aa6d76c1cae0bfa9ef335518b17cb310a8ded9e/104YearsofExperience.pdf.

15   Interview with Fred Lyon, February 13, 2020.

16   *104 Years of Experience*.

17   *The Art Center School*, Art Center School catalog (1941), 45.

18   Interview with Fred Lyon, March 16, 2020.

19   "Ansel Adams: Conversations with Ansel Adams," interview by Ruth Teiser and Catherine Harroun in 1972, 1974, and 1975, Oral History Center, Bancroft Library, University of California, Berkeley, 1978, 370, https://digicoll.lib.berkeley.edu/record/217383?ln=en.

20   Interview with Fred Lyon, February 5, 2020.

21   Ibid.

22   "Ansel Adams," 219.

23   Interview with Fred Lyon, February 5, 2020.

24   Ansel Adams with Mary Street Alinder, *Ansel Adams: An Autobiography* (New York: New York Graphic Society, 1985), 9.

25   Interview with Fred Lyon, February 4, 2020.

26   Aviation Training Division, Office of the Chief of Naval Operations, *Introduction to Naval Aviation*, US Navy, January 1946, OPNAV 33-NY-85, 333.

27   "U.S. Navy Transfer Form," December 17, 1944.

28   Interview with Fred Lyon, February 11, 2020.

29   Ibid.

30   Ibid.

31   Betty Houchin Winfield, *FDR and the News Media* (New York: Columbia University Press, 1994), 114.

32   E. B. White, "Here Is New York," *Holiday*, April 1949, 41.

33   Interview with Fred Lyon, January 31, 2020.

34   Ibid.

35   Ibid.

36   Ibid.

37   https://www.sfmoma.org/exhibition/martin-munkacsi/.

38   Interview with Fred Lyon, January 31, 2020.

39   Interview with Fred Lyon, February 13, 2020.

40   Ibid.

41   Douglas Martin, "Dorian Leigh, Multifaceted Cover Girl of the '40s, Dies at 91," *New York Times*, July 9, 2008.

42   Ibid.

43   Interview with Fred Lyon, February 13, 2020.

44   Ibid.

45   Ibid.

46   Interview with Fred Lyon, January 31, 2020.

47   Interview with Fred Lyon, January 29, 2020.

48   Interview with Fred Lyon, January 31, 2020.

49   Ibid.

50   Deana Sidney, quoting a tribute to Naomi Barry from the Overseas Press Club, http://lostpastremembered.blogspot.com/2013/11/remembering-naomi-barry-with-alexandre.html.

51   Ruth Reichl, *Remembrance of Things Paris: Sixty Years of Writing from "Gourmet"* (New York: Modern Library, 2004), xii.

52   Interview with Fred Lyon, January 31, 2020.

53   Ibid.

54   Zahid Sardar and J. D. Peterson, *San Francisco Modern: Interiors, Architecture & Design* (San Francisco: Chronicle Books, 1998), 15.

55   Email, Fred Lyon to the author, December 11, 2020.

56   Interview with Fred Lyon, January 31, 2020.

57   https://www.nps.gov/people/whitney-warren.htm.

58   Cecil Beaton, *The Unexpurgated Beaton: The Cecil Beaton Diaries as He Wrote Them, 1970–1980* (New York: Alfred A. Knopf, 2007).

59   "Nine Americans Get the French War Cross," *New York Times*, February 9, 1917.

60   Sam Whiting, "Telegraph Hill Home's Pedigree Surprises Owner," *San Francisco Chronicle*, January 3, 2010.

61   Interview with Fred Lyon, January 31, 2020.

62   Ibid.

63   Mitchell Owens, "The Rebel Wore Pearls," *New York Times*, October 9, 2005.

64   "All architectural photography at that time was done using large and heavy cameras, which meant you needed a long exposure and much more light. We only had tungsten lighting at that time. The problem was compounded by the mixed light sources with interior photography, for example daylight bleeding into rooms, complicating the shot. Also, the films were desperately slow. I remember Kodachrome, which was the first stable color film, had an ASA or ISO of about 4 or 6. These limitations made interior photography difficult and unattractive for many photographers." Interview with Fred Lyon, October 5, 2020.

65   Interview with Fred Lyon, October 6, 2020.

66   See "Week End in Reverse," *House & Garden*, November 1948, 213.

67   Interview with Fred Lyon, January 31, 2020.

68   Ibid.

69   Interview with Fred Lyon, February 4, 2020.

70   Ibid.

71   Interview with Fred Lyon, January 31, 2020.

72   Stephen M. Salny, *The Country Houses of David Adler* (New York: W. W. Norton, 2001), 111.

73   https://mtprof.msun.edu/Spr2014/edger.html.

74   "Miss Celia Tobin Weds C. W. Clark, the Son of Montana Millionaire," *San Francisco Call*, August 5, 1904.

75   https://westegg.com/inflation/infl.cgi.

76   Interview with Fred Lyon, January 31, 2020.

77   Ibid.

78   Ibid.

79   Ibid.

80   Ibid.

81   Ibid.

82   Ibid.

83   Ibid.

84   Salny, *Country Houses of David Adler*, 114.

85   Interview with Fred Lyon, January 31, 2020.

86   Ibid.

87   Ibid.

88   "Dorothea Walker; SF Writer, Arbiter of Taste," *Los Angeles Times*, March 11, 2000.

89   "Dorothea Walker," *San Francisco Chronicle*, March 9, 2000.

90   "Dorothea Walker," *Los Angeles Times*.

91   "Dorothea Walker," *San Francisco Chronicle*.

92   Interview with Fred Lyon, February 4, 2020.

93   Interview with Fred Lyon, October 5, 2020.

94   Interview with Fred Lyon, January 31, 2020.

95   Enid Nemy, "Nan Kempner, 74, Hostess Devoted to Fashion and Art, Dies," *New York Times*, July 5, 2005.

96   Interview with Fred Lyon, January 31, 2020.

97   Ibid.

98   https://archives.ced.berkeley.edu/collections/church-thomas.

99   Thomas D. Church, Grace Hall, and Michael Laurie, *Gardens Are for People* (Berkeley: University of California Press, 1995), 29.

100   Interview with Fred Lyon, May 4, 2020.

101   "San Francisco House," *Vogue*, April 15, 1952, 95.

102   Ibid.

103   Interview with Fred Lyon, January 31, 2020.

104   Stephen M. Salny, *Michael Taylor: Interior Design* (New York: W. W. Norton, 2008), 8.

105   Ibid., 17.

106   Zahid Sardar, "Living History: An Incomplete But Not Indifferent Retelling of the Golden Age of San Francisco Interior Design," *San Francisco Chronicle*, January 19, 2005, https://www.sfgate.com/bayarea/article/LIVING-HISTORY-An-incomplete-but-not-2704350.php.

107   Salny, *Michael Taylor*, front cover flap.

108   L. Pierce Carson, "Hotel King Claude Rouas' Liaison with Lady Luck," *Napa Valley Register*, January 6, 2013.

109   Interview with John "Sandy" Walker, February 8, 2021.

110   Ibid.

111   Ibid.

112   Ibid.

113   Ibid.

114   Interview with John "Sandy" Walker, March 2, 2020.

115   Ibid.

116   Ibid.

117   Saeks, "Photographer I Love: Fred Lyon."

118   Christopher Petkanas, "Living Large," *New York Times*, September 25, 2008.

119   Interview with Fred Lyon, February 5, 2020.

120   Saeks, "Photographer I Love: Fred Lyon."

121   Interview with John "Sandy" Walker, March 2, 2020.

122   Christopher Hemphill, "Hail the Decorator's Decorator," *Town & Country*," May 1987.

123   Diane Dorrans Saeks, "An Uncommon Life: Fred Lyon," *Paper City*, August 2003.

124   Wendy Moonan, "Antiques: The Decorator as Auteur." *New York Times*, June 11, 2004, E40.

125   Ibid.

126   Hannah Martin, "Foot Fetish: How John Dickinson Transformed a Cheap Import into a Trophy of Chic," *Architectural Digest* 74, no. 11 (November 2017): 30–32.

127   "John Dickinson, 63, Designer," *New York Times*, March 6, 1982, 10.

128   "90 Miles of Furniture on Display," *New York Times*, October 18, 1965, 40.

129   Interview with Fred Lyon, May 4, 2020.

130   Ibid.

131   Ibid.

132   Zahid Sardar, "Living History / An Incomplete but Not Indifferent Retelling of the Golden Age of San Francisco Interior Design," *San Francisco Chronicle*, January 19, 2005.

133   Ibid.

134   Ibid.

135   Saeks, "An Uncommon Life: Fred Lyon."

136   https://www.knoll.com/designer/Charles-Pfister.

137   Weisman quotation in "Charles Pfister for the IIDA," International Interior Design Association (IIDA), video by Steve Burns, https://youtube.com/watch?v=rHwKZnlQy9g, 0:17.

138   "Charles Pfister, Interior Designer, 50," *New York Times*, October 4, 1990, 24.

139   Interview with Margo Grant Walsh, May 2, 2020.

140   Email, Margo Grant Walsh to the author, May 16, 2020.

141   Email, Penelope Rozis to the author, May 18, 2020.

142   Ibid.

143   Ibid.

144   Ibid.

145   Richard K. Popp, *The Holiday Makers: Magazines, Advertising, and Tourism in Postwar America* (Baton Rouge: Louisiana State University Press, 2012), 100.

146   Interview with Fred Lyon, January 29, 2020.

147   Ibid.

148   Herb Caen, *The San Francisco Chronicle*, May 5, 1958, 21.

149   Interview with Charles Crocker, February 25, 2020.

150   Ibid.

151   Interview with Dede Wilsey, March 24, 2020.

152   Interview with Fred Lyon, February 5, 2020.

153   Interview with Charles Crocker, February 25, 2020.

154   Ibid.

155   Interview with Fred Lyon, February 5, 2020.

156   Ibid.

157   Interview with Dede Wilsey, March 24, 2020.

158   Interview with Fred Lyon, March 9, 2021.

159   Ibid.

160   Ibid.

161   Ibid.

162   Ibid.

163   Herb Caen, *The San Francisco Chronicle*, December 12, 1989, 27.

164   Interview with Fred Lyon, February 26, 2020.

165   Interview with Fred Lyon, February 21, 2020.

166   Ibid.

167   Ibid.

168   Interview with Susan Maguire, May 12, 2020.

169   Interview with Fred Lyon, February 21, 2020.

170   Ibid.

171   Interview with Margo Grant Walsh, May 14, 2020.

172   Interview with Fred Lyon, May 4, 2020.

173   Interview with Margo Grant Walsh, May 14, 2020.

174   Interview with Mary Virginia Swanson, February 24, 2020.

175   Interview with Peter Fetterman, March 24, 2020.

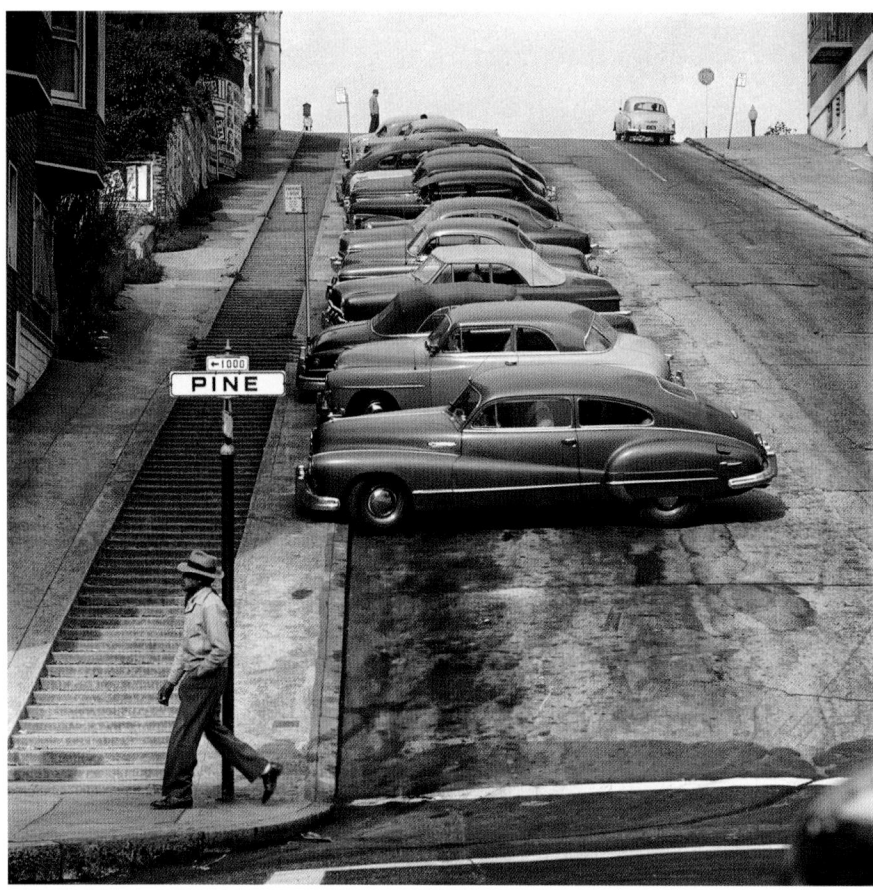

Fred Lyon
*Man Walking on
Pine Street,*
San Francisco, 1954.

First published in the United States of America in 2022 by
Rizzoli International Publications, Inc.
300 Park Avenue South
New York, New York 10010
www.rizzoliusa.com

Publisher: Charles Miers
Senior editor: Philip Reeser
Production manager: Alyn Evans
Design coordinator: Olivia Russin
Copy editor: Richard Slovak
Proofreader: Claudia Bauer
Managing editor: Lynn Scrabis

Designer: Doug Turshen with Steve Turner

Copyright © 2022 by Philip E. Meza
Foreword by Jared Goss

All images copyright © 2022 by Fred Lyon except for those
on the following pages:
8: © Travis Jensen
11 (upper left): © Ezra Stoller / Esto
11 (upper right): Horst P. Horst / *Vogue* © Condé Nast
11 (lower right): Courtesy of Historic New England
11 (lower left): © Simon Watson
14, 38, 39, 43, 46–49, 51–55, 73, 74, 76, 102–105, 107, 109–111,
135: Fred Lyon / *House & Garden* © Condé Nast
19: Photograph by Sonia
21, 28: Courtesy of Fred Lyon
31: Getty Images / Bettmann
35: Photograph by Richard Avedon for *Harper's Bazaar* © 2022
Hearst Communications Inc. All rights reserved.
77: Fred Lyon / *Vogue* © Condé Nast
180: Courtesy of Atelier Franck Durand
251: © Chuck Ashley

ISBN: 978-0-8478-7152-0
Library of Congress Control Number: 2021941204

2023 2024 2025 2026 / 10 9 8 7 6 5 4 3 2

Printed in Hong Kong

PAGE 2: Entrance hall, Diana Dollar Hickingbotham house, San Francisco,
designed by Michael Taylor, 1967. Photographed by Lyon in 1981.
PAGE 5: Pomeroy Galleries, San Francisco, with courtyard by landscape
designer Thomas Church, 1960. Photographed by Lyon in 1960.
PAGE 6: Outdoor table, Dorothy and Charles Fay house, Aptos Beach,
designed by Michael Taylor, 1967. Photographed by Lyon in 1967.